HAYWIRE

CRAIG BROWN

Haywire

The Best of Craig Brown

4th ESTATE • *London*

4th Estate
An imprint of HarperCollins*Publishers*
1 London Bridge Street
London SE1 9GF

www.4thestate.co.uk

HarperCollins*Publishers*
1st Floor, Watermarque Building, Ringsend Road
Dublin 4, Ireland

First published in Great Britain in 2022 by 4th Estate

1

A catalogue record for this book is
available from the British Library

ISBN 978-0-00-855744-7 (hardback)
ISBN 978-0-00-855745-4 (trade paperback)

Extract from *The Complete Poems* by Philip Larkin used with permission of Faber and Faber Ltd

Paraphrased lyrics from Carly Simon's 'You're So Vain' page 496–8 © Carly Simon

Photo credits: Les Dawson p. 68 Radio Times/Getty Images; Sigmund Freud p. 68 IanDagnall Computing/
Alamy; Kenneth Williams p. 73 Allstar Picture Library Ltd/Alamy; Henry 'Chips' Channon p. 89 Bettmann/
Getty Images; Vivienne Westwood p. 124 jeremy sutton-hibbert/Alamy; Mr. Carson p. 169 Jaap Buitendijk/
Focus/Kobal/Shutterstock; Princess Margaret p. 244 Lichfield/Getty Images; What's My Line? p. 255
© BBC Archive; Simon Dee p. 260 Pictorial Press Ltd/Alamy; Paddington p. 263 Lifestyle pictures/Alamy;
Claudia Winkleman p. 267 Karwai Tang/Getty Images; Alan Yentob with Tracey Emin p. 285 David M. Benett/
Getty Images; Blofeld and Baxter p. 298 Jeff J Mitchell/Staff/Getty Images; Poirot p. 318 Pictorial Press Ltd/
Alamy; Jacob Rees-Mogg, p. 323 Simon James/Getty Images; Reagan p. 351 UniversalImagesGroup/
Getty Images; Frankie Howerd p. 358 Popperfoto/Getty Images; Donald Trump p. 358 PA Images/
Alamy; Brian Epstein p. 390 Heritage Image Partnership Ltd/Alamy; Piers Morgan p. 417 Hollie Adams/
Stringer/Getty Images; Kim Jong-Un p. 417 WENN Rights Ltd/Alamy; Dale Carnegie p. 476 Underwood
Archives/Getty Images; Carly Simon p. 496 Archive PL/Alamy; Joan Collins p. 514 Silver Screen
Collection/Getty Images; Zebedee p. 545 Sipa/Shutterstock.

Set in Minion Pro
Printed and bound in the UK using 100%
renewable electricity at CPI Group (UK) Ltd

MIX
Paper | Supporting
responsible forestry
FSC™ C007454
www.fsc.org

For Ian Hislop and Francis Wheen
and
in memory of Robin Summers

CONTENTS

THE GREAT AND THE GOOD

THE BIG QUESTIONS

PANICS

FASHION

HISTORY

CELEBRITY

BORES

POLITICS

POP

BAD HATS

ROYALTY

SELF-HELP

MEMORY LANE

INTRODUCTION

What is James Bond's middle name? While I was compiling a Christmas quiz, I hit upon the idea of a section devoted to the first names of famous characters in fiction. What, for instance, was Jeeves's first name? And what was Captain Hook's?

My thoughts strayed towards middle names. Did James Bond have a middle name? Like Captain Hook, he was an Old Etonian (precociously so: both were expelled). Etonians tend to have fancy middle names. Boris Johnson's is de Pfeffel; Ian Fleming's was Lancaster. It seemed likely that Fleming had come up with something similarly off-centre for Bond.

So I did what all researchers do these days: I typed 'James Bond middle name' into Google. This gave me 2,020,000 results. The first directed me to a website called Quora, which confidently informed me: 'James Bond's middle name is Herbert. He is James Herbert Bond.'

Ever the martyr to accuracy, I thought I'd better double-check, so I clicked on the next site, which was Yahoo Answers. Here, to the question 'What is James Bond's Middle Name?', came the answer: 'Bond's middle name was Herbert (*On Her Majesty's Secret Service*).'

By now, I was feeling pretty confident that I could offer 'Herbert' as the answer to my Christmas quiz question. But just to make absolutely sure, I clicked on another site, called Theory of Names, which boasts of having been set up with the laudable aim of 'giving parents inspiration and options when making the most important (and happiest) decisions of their adult lives'.

'We asked ourselves does the most famous name in British Spy history have a middle name?' they announced, before going on to confirm the seemingly universal opinion that, yes, Bond's middle name was, indeed, Herbert. Readers were then directed to the original source of the information, so I clicked on the link, just to be sure. To my surprise, the source was given as 'Craig Brown'.

I have a terrible memory, not least for my own writing, so I couldn't remember ever having stated that James Bond's middle name was Herbert. But here it was, reprinted in full, from an article I had written ten years before, called 'Thirteen Things You Didn't Know About James Bond'.

Number one was: 'James Bond's middle name is revealed only once in the entire canon. In *On Her Majesty's Secret Service* (1963), Bond is being held in a raffia-work cage suspended over a pool of piranha fish while the villain, Dr Peevish, taunts him by saying, "Herbert, Herbert, Herbert" over and over again. Finally, Bond can bear it no longer. "Go on – kill me, kill me, PLEASE!" he screams. But at that very moment he spots Dr Peevish's Christian name on the laundry mark attached to the raffia-work cage and shouts, "Do your worst – Dibdin!" While Peevish is blocking his ears in anguish, Bond makes good his escape.'

I double-checked all the other sites and, sure enough, the Herbert trail always led back to me. Somewhere along the way, a joke had been transformed into a fact, and now, like the prankster who balances a bucket of water on the top of a door and then forgets it is there, I had stepped into a trap of my own making.

I still find it hard to believe that anyone who read my original article could have taken it seriously, particularly as all the other claims I made about Bond were equally preposterous. One read: 'For the past forty years, James Bond's older brother, Basildon, has been a leading figure in the stationery business.' And another was: 'James Bond's sister, Jennie, was the BBC Royal Correspondent from 1989 to 2003, and later proved her family mettle on *I'm a Celebrity ... Get Me Out of Here!* (2004). The first full-length Jennie Bond movie, scheduled for release in early 2007, is rumoured to be less stridently manly than the usual Bond films, and features the all-action heroine grappling with the Earl and Countess of Wessex in a six-inch-deep pool of ornamental goldfish.'

In the glare of the internet, the border has been blurred between true and false, authentic and concocted, nutcase and expert. Ignorance is now an accepted form of omniscience. On social media anyone can rule the world, free to say what's what, unshackled by the constraints of knowledge or expertise. Of course, this makes my job all the easier. A world gone haywire has long been the satirist's guiding star, hence the mix of scorn and delight with which Thomas Middleton titled his 1605 comedy *A Mad World, My Masters*. If Donald Trump can be President and Boris Johnson can be Prime Minister, then why shouldn't James Bond's middle name be Herbert?

FUN AND GAMES

It Doesn't Add Up

The story so far: Suave Detective Inspector Jim Oldman is called to an empty room. Neighbours have reported nothing amiss. There's not even a corpse. It's fifteen minutes into the episode, and they're growing increasingly concerned.

'There's something about this room that tells me it's empty,' says Oldman. There's no reply. He takes this as confirmation, and puts a call through for back-up.

'Apple Banana Celery, can you read me?' he says to his walkie-talkie. He's a smoothie. 'We're three episodes in, Sarge, and the plot's gone missing! We're in danger of losing 'em!'

The Armed Response Unit arrives. Six armed officers rush up the staircase, in visors, turning around 360 degrees on each stair. When they get to the top they feel dizzy, and take a few minutes to get their bearings. Presently, the leader of the Armed Response Unit, Inspector Gary Youngman, kicks down the door of the empty room.

'ARU!' he screams.

'Very well, thanks,' replies DI Oldman. 'And ARU?'

'Could be worse. But I thought you said this room was empty!'

'Well, it was before I got here! At least I think it was. There was no one around to ask.'

'So how do you account for all these people in black, then?' says Inspector Youngman, aggressively.

'We're the other members of your unit, sir.'

'So you are! You look so different with those visors on! As you were!'

Meanwhile, over in the picture-postcard village of Much Askew, Detective Sergeant Cliff Hanger has been called to the corner shop run by kindly old Ted Sinister. He sniffs around, and then blows his nose. He scans the shelves. Rice Krispies … Corn Flakes … Coco Pops. And then a gap. Call it experience, call it sixth sense, but he knows something's not quite right.

'There's a cereal filler on the loose,' he says.

Back in the once-empty room, DI Oldman puts an urgent call through to HQ.

'Hilary Quinn, how can I help you?' she replies.

'Xylophone Yesteryear Zygodactyl,' he says. He's at the end of his tether. 'Someone's made off with the plot. I've reason to believe a corrupt officer has infiltrated the anti-corruption unit.'

'We'll get the anti-anti-corruption unit on to it,' barks Hilary.

'But there's something I don't quite trust about the anti-anti-corruption unit,' says DI Oldman. 'This looks like a job for the anti-anti-anti –'

'I'll have to interrupt you there, boss. There's an ad break on the way, and there's nothing any of us can do to stop it.'

Three minutes and seventy-three cut-price sofas later, PC Gonemad is faced with a simple question. 'If Helen overheard what Kevin said to Jack, then why the hell didn't Tony tell Mike that Jill thought that Maureen already knew that Mike had told Tony what Jack said to Kevin?'

And then another simple question occurs to him.

'If what Jack said to Kevin was true, then why didn't Ian tell Crystal that Katie claimed that Fred thought he saw kindly old Ted Sinister spying on Detective Sergeant Hanger in the deserted hut behind the rubbish tip in front of the multi-storey car park?'

Suddenly, there's a screech of brakes and another simple question leaps out of the car.

PC Gonemad is left with no alternative but to call Sergeant Charlie Roger of the POU, or Plot Overload Unit.

'Things are kicking off big-time, Sarge!' he yells. 'There are hundreds of plots coming at us from all sides, and I don't have enough men to keep up with them!'

As Sergeant Roger hangs up the phone, an unknown assailant

shoots him dead. Seconds later, the unknown assailant is shot dead by an unknown assailant. But was the first unknown assailant the same as the second? If so, it could be suicide by a person or persons unknown.

An urgent call comes through to DI Oldman.

Shocking news: a man has been spotted on CCTV footage – and he wasn't wearing a balaclava. 'Refusal to wear a balaclava on CCTV in a prime-time police procedural? We've got our man,' he concludes. Only then does he spot a crumpled scrap of paper in the empty room. It reads '2 + 2 = 5.'

Is it a clue? If so, it just doesn't add up.

My Lockdown Diary

March 2020

- I thought I spotted Imelda Staunton hovering over the ready-mixed salads in Sainsbury's. It turned out to be someone who looked a bit like her. Or do I mean Celia Imrie? Anyway, it wasn't either of them.

April

- I bought a pair of brown slip-on shoes online. They turned out to be a bit too big. I couldn't be bothered to send them back, so I wore them for a few days to try to get used to them. Then I put them in a drawer, along with a blue V-neck sweater I ordered two weeks earlier, which had turned out to be too small.
- I looked out of the window and noticed my neighbour three doors along had a visitor when the Covid rules clearly stated she wasn't meant to. Three days later, I let someone into our house, but that's different, because he was a close friend.
- We started watching more news. We wanted to know all about the virus.
- We stopped watching so much news. It just went on and on about the virus.

May

- My neighbour three doors along was sitting in her garden, talking to someone I didn't recognise. Neither of them was wearing a mask. I was furious. It's so irresponsible!

- We organised a family quiz on Zoom. They're all the rage. One of the questions was about the length of the Forth Road Bridge, and another was about John Wayne's real name, which was something unexpected like Sharon. Someone said Boris Johnson's middle name is Shirley. I wonder if that's true.
- I enjoyed chatting with a friend in the garden. We didn't bother to wear masks as we knew each other.
- I thought of taking up birdwatching and tried it for a bit, but they wouldn't sit still.

June
- I watched *Steph's Packed Lunch* on Channel 4. Steph was joined by former Chancellor of the Exchequer Nigel Lawson and Baby Spice Emma Bunton. They didn't seem to have much to say to one another. A chef demonstrated an easy way to cook flapjacks, and let them both try one.

July
- We thought of buying new tiles for the kitchen, but decided against.
- I read somewhere that the Duchess of Cambridge's favourite colour is navy blue.
- We suggested another family quiz, but there wasn't much take-up, so we watched an old *Morse* instead.
- I thought of taking up knitting, but decided against.

August
- In the supermarket, I spotted a woman whose mask had slipped below her nose. She wasn't doing anything about it. I was furious, but I didn't want to cause a scene, so said nothing.
- I sorted through the kitchen drawer. I found half a dozen drawing pins, two pairs of nail clippers, an unworn paper hat from a Christmas cracker, three old keys we never use, a broken cassette tape of The Bee Gees' greatest hits, a key ring, three supermarket receipts, a marble, a jigsaw piece and thirteen rubber bands. I

didn't know what to do with them, so I put them back in the drawer, thinking they might come in handy some day.

- In the supermarket, my mask was making me feel fugged up, so I slipped it off my nose for a while. I saw a woman glaring at me, though she didn't say a word. Some people take offence at the slightest thing!
- We spent most of the month catching up on the first four and a half seasons of *Line of Duty*, but couldn't work out what on earth was going on, so we gave up.
- I received an Amazon delivery of a cardboard box to put things in. It came in a cardboard box.

September

- I spotted my neighbour three doors down having a long chat with the man from Amazon. She seems to be having a delivery every day, none of it necessary. Some people are completely addicted to shopping!
- I watched *Steph's Packed Lunch* on Channel 4. Vince Cable was on. The chef was cooking scones. He let Vince Cable try one. Vince Cable said it was delicious, but he didn't look as if he meant it. Politicians will do anything for a vote.
- Amazon delivery – two new T-shirts, a mug with Matt Lucas's face on it, a book of household tips, e.g. how to get a milk stain out of a velvet pincushion using a mixture of red wine and vinegar and a novelty drinking-straw. I don't know how I'd survive without Amazon.

October

- I see from the newspaper that the Beckhams are holidaying in the Bahamas. She seems to have lost a little weight. She's almost too thin. You never see her smiling. And is that another tattoo on his neck?
- I overheard my neighbour talking on the phone in her garden to someone and telling them they must come and stay. I felt so furious. Haven't they heard there's a pandemic on?

November

- A friend called, and was thinking of coming to stay. He doesn't know whether it's in the rules or not. I said, well, as long as we are reasonably careful, I'm sure no one would have any objection. Mind you, there are some nosey parkers who would probably object to anything!
- I was going to read Booker Prize-winning *Shuggie Bain* but I read Anton Du Beke's autobiography instead. I forget what it's called. He's had quite a life!

December

- Out on a walk, I spotted someone not cleaning up after their dog. I thought of saying something, but decided against.
- I heard a joke and thought: 'That's good. I must write that one down.' But I couldn't find a pen, and now I can't remember what it was.
- Ordered five new ballpoint pens off Amazon.
- Regretted ordering the ballpoint pens off Amazon. Spent ten minutes trying to find out how to cancel the order, then gave up. They should arrive tomorrow.

January 2021

- We were forty-five minutes into watching *Location, Location, Location* before we realised it was a repeat from 2019. But having watched so much of it already we thought we may as well watch to the end, so we did. At the end, they told Kirsty they had decided to stick with the house they already owned and enlarge the kitchen. She was clearly disappointed, after spending so much time trying to find a new house for them.

February

- I was walking in a strong wind when my hat flew off. But it didn't go far, so thankfully I was able to pick it up and put it back on.
- In the newsagent's, a woman was looking at a photo on the front page of a paper. I heard her saying to her friend: 'You'd have

thought Boris could afford a decent haircut with all that money. I mean!' Her friend replied: 'Well, he must have a lot on his mind, what with one thing and another.'

March
- At lunchtime, I watched *Steph's Packed Lunch* on Channel 4. Alan 'Chatty Man' Carr and Ann Widdecombe were on. They both tasted the vegetarian lasagne the chef had made, and seemed to like it. Apart from that, they didn't seem to have a lot in common.
- I answered the phone. It was someone offering me a huge amount of free money at a very reasonable price. But then something made me think it might be a hoax. I didn't say anything, but just kept chatting to him, as I had nothing better to do, and he seemed perfectly friendly.

April
- I bought a bag of twelve 'easy-peel' satsumas on special offer at the supermarket. They had no taste to them. I stared at a cloud in the sky this morning. After a while, it began to look a bit like Superintendent Ted Hastings in *Line of Duty*. I was going to take a photograph of it, but by the time I'd found the camera the cloud had changed shape.

The Betting Book

What do we do when we have nothing to do? At the beginning of the summer holidays, this is perhaps the most important question facing us all. Personally, I like to dragoon my companions into a round or two of the Vegetable Game. The rules are simple. Each player picks the name of a different vegetable and announces that choice. The first player then has to repeat the name of any other player's vegetable three times as fast as possible – e.g., 'Broad bean, broad bean, broad bean' – before that other player manages to say it once. If the first player fails to say the vegetable three times without interruption, he has to try again with either the same or another player's vegetable. If he succeeds, then the other player takes over; if not, he carries on.

The Vegetable Game may sound unsophisticated, perhaps even a mite imbecilic. I doubt you would catch Lord Rees-Mogg, say, or Lady Warnock playing it with any great gusto on a rainy afternoon. But – perhaps because names of vegetables are, for some reason, intrinsically comical – it is a game that has provided me and my family with hours of entertainment down the years.

I was reminded of it after chancing on an obscure, privately published and long out-of-print work called *The Betting Book of the 2nd Battalion (78th) Seaforth Highlanders, 1822–1908*. It is simply a list of all the wagers taken by the members of this battalion over an eighty-six-year period. It turns out to be one of the funniest books I have ever read – and one of the most moving, too.

Historians and biographers deal only in exceptional lives and events. Sociologists and anthropologists may sometimes touch on ordinary, uncelebrated lives, but they are only really interested in large groups of nameless people, all doing the same gloomy things (foraging, rioting, attending football matches, dying) at the same time. There are a few books about individual professions – what it was like to be a basket-weaver in the nineteenth century and so forth – but it is hard to think of another non-fiction work that captures so exactly that vast expanse of life beyond achievement, work and incident, a book that answers that vital question we so often end up asking ourselves: 'What do we do when we have nothing to do?'

On the first page, we discover that, garrisoned in Kilkenny, on 19 November 1822, 'Lieut Mitchell bets he shoots 12 larks in one day. Lieut Hemmans bets he will not. One bottle of port.' In the 'Lost by' column on the right-hand side of the page, Lieutenant Mitchell is declared the loser. On the final page, in Aldershot on 27 November 1907, 'Lieut K. B. Mackenzie bets 2nd Lieut Allenby that he will not break an egg in an empty sack. Lieutenant Allenby knows that this bet has often been lost before. The bet is for one bottle best port.' Oddly enough, Second Lieutenant Allenby fails to break the egg.

Between these two entries, there are bets on anything, everything and virtually nothing: who will win the Eton–Harrow match; whether 'God Save the Queen' was written by a foreigner; if Southwark should be pronounced 'suthark'; and if 'ajar' is an adjective or not. Most of the bets are not only rewarded with alcohol but, I suspect, fuelled by it, too. On 25 December 1824, for instance, 'Mr Cooper bets Mr Wilson one bottle of port that he drinks with a spoon a bottle of beer while Mr W is eating a penny roll. Mr W. is not to take anything with the bread and is to whistle afterwards to show that his mouth is empty.'

Breaking an egg in a sack is one of the perennial bets that excites the battalion down the years. Stationed in Armagh in 1836, 'Mr McIntyre bets Mr Pattison one bottle of Champagne that he (Mr P.) will not break an egg in an empty dirty clothes bag, provided Mr Pattison does not use an iron sledge hammer of greater weight than 15lbs.' Once again, the bet is lost by the egg-basher. Quite why an egg should prove so resilient is anybody's guess. Fifty years later, Lieutenant Lumsden fares no better. 'Lt and Adjt C. J. Mackenzie bets Lt G. M. Lumsden that he will not break an egg in an empty sack. The sack may be beaten against the wall or floor but may not be trodden on or hammered with a hammer. The egg may be provided by Lt Lumsden, provided it is a hen's egg and intact. Lt Lumsden is aware that this bet has been made and lost in this book before. Lt Lumsden is allowed six hours to accomplish this feat. The bet is for one bottle of Champagne.'

A few of the bets require some degree of general knowledge, precursors to today's pub quizzes. Stationed in Bareilly, on 2 April 1886 Lieutenant Mackintosh bets Lieutenant and Adjutant Mackenzie a bottle of champagne that fuschia is spelt 'fuchsia'. The bet is lost by Mackenzie. In Fermoy, on 25 November 1825 Major Douglas bets Captain Lardy a bottle of wine that it was in the reign of Henry VIII that Columbus discovered America. In Belfast, on 4 February 1872 Captain Lecky bets Maitland Kirwan that the word 'magnitude' is not mentioned in the definitions of Euclid, and loses.

Yet it is not all so highfalutin. At Stirling Castle, on 15 April 1833: 'Mr Menzies bets Captain Vassall one bottle of wine that urine is used in some parts of the process of the illicit distillation of Scotch whisky.' Happily, Mr Menzies is the loser.

Those who worry that civilisation has been going downhill since its Victorian heyday may be reassured by the entry for 1 April 1871: 'Ensign McDougall bets Captain C. Mackenzie that a porpoise is a hedgehog.' Poor old Ensign McDougall was, we can only suppose, thinking of a porcupine, not a porpoise; his error cost him a bottle of champagne.

More often than not, the bets revolve around brawn rather than brains, breaking things rather than remembering them. Even odder than the egg-breaking craze is the recurrent gamble on whether or not a bottle will break if thrown on the floor. In 1823, Ensign Price bets Captain Lardy that he can break a bottle by throwing it on the floor of the mess room. Captain Lardy loses. Eighty years later, stationed in Dublin in 1903, they are still at it: 'Captain Holland bets Major Arbuthnot one bottle of port wine that he will break a soda water bottle by throwing it on the floor.' The bet, it emerges, is 'Lost by Capt Holland (who broke a lamp but not the bottle)'.

Other sporting wagers are more energetic: stationed in Kilkenny, in December 1822 Lieutenant Cooper bets Ensign Gore a bottle of port wine that he can walk on a pair of stilts from the mess room door to the officers' door on the other side of the square, and Cooper wins. In Halifax, in December 1870 Lieutenant Waugh bets Lieutenant Fordyce that he will not shoot a moose while he is out in the woods; Fordyce fails to bag his beast, and Waugh wins a bottle of champagne.

Many of the bets are reminiscent of a Beckett play. They have a similar sense of characters trapped in a room, desperately waiting for something to happen, all the while groping around for things to tickle their minds. In Edinburgh on 16 April 1829, the *Betting Book* notes that 'Mr Smith bets Captain Vassall one bottle of wine that the shadow inside the fender is not caused by the lamp on the table.' In the 'Lost by' column on the right-hand side of the page, Mr Smith is declared the loser. On 25 April 1836 in Kandy, 'Mr Haliburton bets Mr Lamert two bottles of French claret that the number of links in the chain suspending the centre lamp are nearer 45 than 60.' In addition, 'Major Douglas bets Captain Vassall one bottle of claret that from the top of the table to the door is 30 ft.' Finally, 'Mr McNeil bets Mr Collins one bottle of claret that from the head of the table to the wall is 20 ft.'

Garrisoned in Stirling Castle in April 1824, members of the battalion are so bored that they take to betting on the relative breadth of each other's noses. First, 'Mr Menzies bets Captain Armstrong that his, Mr Menzies', nose is broader than Captain Armstrong's,' then 'Captain Vassall bets Mr McNeill that Mr McNeill's nose is the least in breadth of the party.' After many more nasally based bets, Mr Menzies decides to ring the changes: 'Mr Menzies bets Mr McNeill that Captain Vassall's mouth is the largest in the room.' Finally, having run out of anything else to bet on, 'Mr McNeill bets Captain Armstrong that he, Captain A., has not lost as many bets as the rest of the party this evening' – a bet lost, alas, by Mr McNeill.

With nothing else to bet on, they bet on bets. Five years later, in Edinburgh in April 1829, 'Mr Fisher bets Major Mill that he has not lost twice as many bets as those he has won. The bet is one bottle of wine.' Mr Fisher loses. But at other times inspiration literally flies into the room: garrisoned in Perth on 30 May 1831, 'Mr McNeill bets Mr Browne that the beasty in the window is a waspy.' Again, this is a bet that McNeill loses.

Often the entries have an almost Chekhovian feel to them, the shortest of short stories still hinting at an intricate world beyond. In Perth on 2 April 1831, 'Mr Fisher bets Mr Montgomery one bottle of wine that the girl in Cameron's shop that served us out the tooth brushes has not got red hair.' More bizarrely, in Glasgow on 16 March 1839, 'Mr H. Hamilton bets Captain Vassall that Miss Finlay of Eastree Hill married within the last few months a man without thumbs.'

There is something strangely moving about reading of the mess-room squabbles conducted by a group of men 170 years ago. That such energy could be so devoutly expended on such trifles! 'Mr Montgomery bets Major Mill 8 bottles of port that the History of Scotland written by Sir Walter Scott is styled Tales of 'a' not Tales of 'my' Grandfather,' reads one of the entries for 19 January 1829. The size of the wager – most involve just one bottle – suggests that both men were treating this daftest of quibbles with the utmost gravity. And others in the room obviously felt the same: 'Major Mill bets 4 bottles more with Mr Smith on the same bet,' continues the entry, 'and Mr Montgomery bets 2 bottles more with Mr Burns.' The bet is then lost by Major Mill and Mr Burns.

I don't know if battalions still keep betting books and, if so, whether they still bet on such a diverse range of subjects. Presumably, the bets on general knowledge have been cut short by the internet.

It is perhaps surprising how little the world beyond impinges on the thoughts of the Seaforth Highlanders, though sometimes they bet on the Derby or the Eton–Harrow match, and just occasionally on the likelihood of this war or that. In Poona on 27 July 1877, 'Captain Smith bets Sir A Mackenzie a dinner, present company included, that England is at war with Russia before the end of the present year 1877. If in Edinburgh, at the New Club.' Captain Smith loses.

But what really makes *The Betting Book of the 2nd Battalion (78th) Seaforth Highlanders* more than just an eccentric catalogue of wasted time is its lightning strikes of mortality, each suddenly illuminating the surrounding frivolity in all its mad urgency. Stationed at Fort George on 30 April 1899, Lieutenant Chamley bets Lieutenant Blair a bottle of port that he will outdrive him on the golf course during the month of May. Alongside the bet, in the 'Lost by' column is the stark inscription: '(Bet off: Captain Blair killed S. Africa).' Further down the same page, two more bets are cancelled when Lieutenant Cowie and Captain Clark also meet their deaths in South Africa. Small wonder that soldiers grow addicted to bets when even the words 'To be or not to be' are no longer a matter of choice, but of chance.

The Thrill Has Gone

We thought we'd watch a thriller, so I turned to Amazon Prime and found one called *Fear*. The description read: 'Mark Wahlberg, Reese Witherspoon and Alyssa Milano star in this riveting suspense-thriller about a passionate romance that transforms into a nightmarish obsession.' This seemed to tick the right boxes, so I pressed the button to buy it.

The film opened at an attractive wooden house beside a lake. A man was running in some woods. As he arrived at the house, I experienced a strong sense of déjà vu. 'I think we might have seen this one before,' I said. And soon the whole plot had come back to me: against her parents' advice, Reese Witherspoon falls for a young man who turns out to be a psycho, the dog gets killed, then the dad gets killed, and it all ends in a bloodbath. Why hadn't I remembered seeing it before? I told myself that *Fear* was an oddly forgettable title which could be applied to any thriller.

An hour in, we thought we'd cut our losses, or rather double our losses, but cut our boredom, by ordering another thriller instead. So we clicked on 'Customers Also Watched ...', and up came a list of other thrillers on offer.

First was *Guilty as Sin* with Rebecca De Mornay. 'A hot-shot criminal defence attorney is caught in a web of manipulation by her smooth-talking playboy client accused of murder,' read the description. Had we already watched this one too? I certainly didn't want to be caught out again. So we clicked on the next. Up came *Final Analysis* with Richard Gere and Kim Basinger. 'Psychological thriller about a psychiatrist who becomes a murder suspect after allowing himself to become more than professionally involved with two wacky sisters.'

Had we seen this one? We had certainly watched a number of thrillers with Richard Gere playing smooth, upmarket characters who either aren't suspected of what they have done or are suspected of what they haven't done. In fact, it's high time an ambitious director cast him as a man who is suspected of what he has done, or – even more radical – isn't suspected of what he hasn't done.

Worried we had seen *Final Analysis* before, I clicked on the next: *No Good Deed*. 'Terri is a devoted wife and mother of two, living an ideal suburban life in Atlanta when Colin, a charming but dangerous escaped convict, shows up at her door claiming car trouble.' This, too, sounded familiar. In thrillers, charming but dangerous escaped convicts are always showing up at ideal suburban doors, most of them claiming car trouble.

Next! *Trapped* with Kevin Bacon. 'When Will and Karen are held hostage and their daughter is abducted, a relentless twenty-four-hour plan is set in motion that will challenge everything they took for granted.' Next! *Deceived* with Goldie Hawn. 'A wife discovers evidence of her husband's murder.' Next! *Domestic Disturbance* with John Travolta. 'A divorced father discovers that his twelve-year-old son's new stepfather is not what he made himself out to be.' Next! *Guilty as Sin* with Rebecca De Mornay. 'A hot-shot criminal defence attorney is caught in a web of …'

This one certainly rang a bell. Ah, yes! I had been reading about it barely two minutes before. And so it went on. By now, I was beginning to suspect that I had already watched every thriller ever made, and a good proportion of those yet to be made. 'When a young doctor suspects she may not be alone in her new Brooklyn loft, she learns that her landlord has formed a frightening obsession with her,' reads the description for a film called *The Resident*. Who could honestly remember whether they had seen it or not?

By now, thrillers have run through every plot variation, countless times: the man who is not who he says he is, the charmer who turns out to be a crazy psycho, the woman who senses there's someone else in the house, the passionate romance that turns into a nightmarish obsession. And so on, and so on. Over time, the suspense thriller has lost its suspense and its thrills. Instead, it has become comforting in its predictability, like a cuddly toy, a digestive biscuit, or a game of Snakes and Ladders.

Sex Sessions in Tyne and Wear

Is it just me, or is Tyne and Wear the place where everything interesting happens?

Newcastle Crown Court has been home to one of the most enthralling cases in recent years. A judge and two magistrates have been listening to a ten-minute recording of what are these days termed 'sex sessions' between Mr and Mrs Steve Cartwright of Hall Road, Washington, Tyne and Wear.

It all began when Mr and Mrs Cartwright's neighbours complained that the couple's nightly sex sessions, which would start at midnight and last an impressive three hours, were so noisy that they were drowning out the sound from their televisions. Of course, in the early hours of the morning there is precious little on television apart from actors pretending to have sex, but I suppose if you specifically wanted to watch actors pretending to have sex then the sound of real people having sex might prove a distraction. Apparently complaints were also received from the local postman; that a postman should be delivering letters at three in the morning is yet another reason why we should all be moving to Tyne and Wear.

Mrs Cartwright is at present appealing against her conviction for breaching a noise abatement notice that banned the couple from 'shouting, screaming or vocalisation at such a level to be a statutory nuisance'. Apparently, 'specialist equipment' installed by the council in her neighbour's flat recorded noise levels of between thirty to forty decibels, with a high of forty-seven decibels.

Though this may sound very noisy, my researches suggest that it is in fact pretty hushed, even discreet. Thirty decibels is defined as being as loud as 'a very quiet library', while fifty is 'a quiet suburb or a conversation at home'. You would have to reach seventy decibels before you were as loud as a vacuum cleaner, eighty before you were as loud as the dial tone on a telephone, and ninety before you were as loud as a power drill.

If ever Mrs Cartwright began to blast off like a power drill, there might be cause for complaint, although somewhere between a very quiet library and a quiet suburb sounds to me extremely subdued, even lacklustre.

Two council officials – environmental health managers, no less – popped round to the houses on both sides of the Cartwrights, clipboards at the ready. One official, Marion Dixon, reported to the court: 'I heard a male voice howling loudly, which I felt was very unnerving.' Her colleague, the happily named Pamela Spark, found Mrs Cartwright even noisier than Mr Cartwright. She reported 'hysterical, almost continuous, screaming', adding: 'It sounded like she was being murdered.'

Well, either the libraries in Tyne and Wear are unusually noisy or Ms Dixon and Ms Spark have hypersensitive eardrums. On the other hand, there is something undeniably off-putting about overhearing the noises made by copulating couples, however attractive that couple may be, and Mr and Mrs Cartwright are, from the look of them, a far cry from Brad Pitt and Angelina Jolie.*

In fact, even if it were Brad Pitt and Angelina Jolie who were going at it like vacuum cleaners next door, I might still be tempted to call in the environmental health managers. It would be an interesting court case if Brad and Angelina were to argue that, at the time of my complaint about their undue noise drowning out my television, I had been watching a video of them in their steamy film *Mr & Mrs Smith*. They might then be able to argue that their live performance was a bonus in stereo or even Sensurround, and that I should be charged extra for their efforts.

Now, where was I? With a story like this, it is only too easy to get sidetracked. For this reason I have every sympathy with the judge and

---

* I wrote this piece back in 2009, when Mr Pitt and Ms Jolie were still going strong.

two magistrates at Newcastle Crown Court. It would have been fascinating to observe them as they furrowed their brows, sucked on their pencils and listened to their recording of the cacophonous Cartwrights.

Now would not be the time for the clerk of the court to pipe up: 'A penny for your thoughts!' But was ten minutes long enough? If each sex session lasted three hours, and there were five in all, then that makes fifteen hours: a ten-minute 'greatest hits' medley would surely not do them justice, however skilfully edited.

Alas, Mrs Cartwright maintains that the stress of the complaints made her turn first to drink and then to antidepressants – Wine and Tears in Tyne and Wear – but they have done little to lower her volume. 'After I got the noise abatement notice, I tried to control it. I even tried to use a pillow to try to lessen the noise. I wasn't enjoying it so I started to cry and my husband said: "If you want to make a noise, make a noise."'

So it's all go in Tyne and Wear. If I were the postman, I'd try whistling very loudly to block out the noise. But that still leaves the poor neighbours. Might some sort of cladding do the trick?

Four TV Chefs

Delia Smith
Became the subject of myth
Having caused quite a stir
Screaming, 'Cwam on! Let's be 'avin yer!'

Raymond Blanc
Never imports plonk;
His preferred cargo
Is Château Margaux.

Gordon Ramsay
Is like all those old hams; he
Behaves like a yob
But if you pinched him, he'd sob.

Fanny Cradock
Found haddock
Very handy
When flambéd in brandy.

The Lift to Outer Space

The number of different floors at the Grace Brothers' department store in *Are You Being Served?* has long been a matter for conjecture. A close study of the theme song, set in a lift and spoken over the clash and tinkle of a cash register, offers precious little help:

Ground floor perfumery,
Stationery and leather goods,
Wigs and haberdashery,
Kitchenware and food ... going up!
First floor telephones,
Gents' ready-made suits
Shirts, socks, ties, hats,
Underwear and shoes ... going up!
Second floor carpets,
Travel goods and bedding,
Material, soft furnishings,
Restaurants and teas ... going up!

Close textual analysis of these lyrics suggests there were at least three floors, not including the ground floor. And I have a vague recollection that the spacious wood-panelled office of the Young Mr Grace was on the top floor. Presuming that the general customer would never have been permitted to get out at Young Mr Grace's floor, then it's most likely that the entire Grace Brothers' department store was four storeys high.

I thought of *Are You Being Served?* and its famous lift, from which Mrs Slocombe, Mr Rumbold, Captain Peacock and the others would emerge so jauntily, when I read a report that Japanese engineers are working on plans to build a lift into outer space.

Once the project is completed, thirty passengers at a time will be able to travel in a lift for 22,000 miles at 120 mph. The entire journey will take a week. When the doors finally open, they will step out into some sort of space station, from where they will be able to enjoy magnificent aerial views of Earth and its surroundings.

Will it all be worth it? In my experience, even the most spectacular view takes only five minutes before you get used to it. So if you allow a further two minutes for buying postcards, this gives you just seven minutes before everyone begins to grow fidgety. It's unclear what the space tourists will do then. Let's hope there will be a restaurant, as there was in Grace Brothers'.

If so, it should be possible to kill at least an hour by enjoying the view, shopping for postcards and then lingering over a chicken salad. After that, there will be nothing for it but to join the queue for the lift back down. I would guess that the trip down will also take about a week, or perhaps a little bit less, allowing for gravity. All very well, but I wonder if Dr Obayashi, the mastermind behind the proposed space elevator, has really thought it all through? After all, a week may be a long time in politics but it is infinitely longer in a lift, particularly if the ride comes without the welcome interruption of the doors opening and closing every few seconds, with familiar faces leaving and new ones coming in.

The atmosphere during even the briefest trip in a lift can be dreadfully awkward, at one and the same time both dull and tense, with everyone trying to avoid exchanging glances and any conversation grinding to a halt under the weight of self-consciousness.

After a few seconds, most passengers simply stand in complete silence, staring intently at the strip of numbers that indicates the floor you are approaching. Sadly this little distraction will not be available on the space elevator, as it will only have a ground floor and a first floor, with 22,000 miles between the two.

Music may be another problem. These days, music in lifts is less fashionable than it once was. Until about twenty years ago, whenever you travelled in a lift you could be sure of hearing, or almost-hearing, the silky strings of Bert Kaempfert or James Last and their respective orchestras as they glided their way through a medley of easy-listening classics. To soothe the nerves of the first-timer, this tradition will have to be revived, though after a week of listening to 'Can't Take My Eyes Off You' for the umpteenth time even the most hardened space-traveller may be forced to swallow an extra dose of sedatives.

Other pitfalls will emerge with time. Getting planning permission for a structure 22,000 miles high could prove a problem, particularly in the Home Counties, and who on earth are you going to get to do the repair works to the lift shaft? If the space elevator is operated by Virgin, passengers must expect severe delays; then it will grind to a halt after the first few hundred miles, at which point they will be transferred to a coach.

Many people find that lifts induce claustrophobia and prefer to use the stairs, but Dr Obayashi has made no provision for an adjacent staircase. Personally, I would prefer an escalator, though you would need to hold on tight if it was going at 120 mph, and that last little leap on to terra firma would be even more nerve-racking than usual.

A Cricket Critic with an Erratic Racket

Like many men who play tennis, when I hit a ball into the net I always look daggers at my racket, reproaching it for playing so badly when I myself have been trying so hard. The other day, I threw a further insult in its direction. 'An erratic racket!' I said. I tried to repeat it. 'An erracit rattik!' And again. 'An erracit rattik!' At that moment, it dawned on me that I had just invented a brand-new tongue-twister.

After the game was over, I bet each of the three other players £5 that they could not say 'An erratic racket' very fast five times in a row. Two of them went wrong on the second erratic racket, and the third went wrong on the fourth. My money was safe, and a classic new tongue-twister was born, every bit as tricky as 'Red lorry, yellow lorry', and rather more classy.

One of my fellow players pointed out that 'An erratic racket' was itself a variation on 'cricket critic', so I suggested combining the two to create 'A cricket critic with an erratic racket', and entering this great new tongue-twister into the World Tongue-Twisting Championship, which no doubt takes place in Aberystwyth, or perhaps, in a particularly tough year, in Llanfairpwllgwyngyllgogerychwyrndrobwllllantysiliogogogoch.

I think the first tongue-twister I ever learnt was 'Peter Piper picked a peck of pickled pepper', followed closely by the wittier 'How much wood would a woodchuck chuck if a woodchuck could chuck wood?', which comes with the non-committal answer: 'A woodchuck would chuck all the wood he could chuck, if a woodchuck could chuck wood.' Needless to say, an American pedant once worked out an accurate answer to the great woodchuck question, calculating that, if a woodchuck could chuck wood, then a woodchuck could chuck about 700 pounds of wood, if it was chucking very hard. So now you know.

With an erracit rattik still ringing in my ears, I tried it out on a couple of children, with equal success. I had half-imagined that, in these days of computer games, the tongue-twisting tradition might have died out among the younger generation, but not a bit of it: both of them tried plenty of their own tongue-twisters on me, some old, some new.

I found 'A proper cup of coffee from a proper copper coffee pot' particularly troublesome. I sailed through the first section – 'A proper cup of coffee from a …' with ease, but fell over head-first on the second – 'a popper cropper poffee cot'.

A new favourite among children seems to be 'Ken Dodd's dad's dog's dead', which presumably also has the merit, after all these years, of being true. (Incidentally, I know a second joke, this one not a tongue-twister, concerning Ken Dodd, though it requires a certain amount of knowledge about his act. When you meet someone in a public place, you should say, 'Ken Dodd came here yesterday', to which they invariably reply, 'Did he?', and to which you then exclaim: 'No – Doddy!')

Some tongue-twisters contain additional booby traps, so that the old words re-emerge as proper new words, giving the original sentence an entirely new meaning. My favourite of these is 'One smart feller, he felt smart.' I won't repeat here what happens to it once it has been tongue-twisted, but I can guarantee the new sentence will produce howls of uncontrolled laughter, particularly if you happen to be a little boy under the age of seven.

One of the many joys of tongue-twisters is that they serve no purpose beyond fun. So when you say, or at least try to say, 'She sells sea shells on the sea shore' or 'Of all the felt I ever felt, I never felt a piece of felt which felt the same as that felt felt, when I first felt the felt of that felt hat', there is something pleasing in its non-utilitarianism – itself a modest one-word tongue-twister.

It is only if you happen to be a newscaster that the tongue-twister spells peril. American newscasters are said to dread having to get through the phrase 'Former New York City Mayor Rudi Giuliani', while here in Britain, our very own James Naughtie lived up to his surname when he stumbled over those fatal words 'Culture Secretary Jeremy Hunt'.

The only tongue-twister that has ever served any real purpose is 'The Leith police dismisseth us', which is said to be the phrase police ask suspects to repeat so as to prove they are not drunk. In the P. G. Wodehouse novel *Jeeves and the Feudal Spirit*, Bertie Wooster gets Jeeves to repeat 'Theodore Oswaldthistle, the thistle sifter, sifting a sack of thistles thrust three thorns through the thick of his thumb' for the same reason. Needless to say, Jeeves passes the test with flying colours, and with 'an intonation as clear as a bell, if not clearer'. But, for all his polish, would even Jeeves fare quite so well with 'A cricket critic with an erratic racket'?

Three Magicians

Uri Geller
Is a single-minded feller:
He's been around for many moons
Yet he persists in bending spoons.

Harry Houdini
Was a little bit mean, he
Would sigh, 'Drat! I can't unlock it!'
When asked to dip into his pocket.

David Blaine
Is at it again:
But I'm not sure he oughter
Dive blindfold in a straitjacket head-first from 300 feet into a
    teacup full of water.

Lockdown Dreams

YOU WANT to explain every aspect of Covid while everyone listens in respectful silence.

YOU'D SETTLE FOR knowing what 'R' means.

YOU GET into a heated argument with a twelve-year-old about whether or not you washed your hands for the full twenty seconds.

YOU WANT to do the shopping for all your most vulnerable neighbours.

YOU'D SETTLE FOR keeping an eye on the elderly couple next door.

YOU GET annoyed by the sound of the elderly couple next door enjoying their online exercise classes and pop a note through their door asking them to kindly pipe down.

YOU WANT to nip up North without too much kerfuffle.

YOU'D SETTLE FOR being spotted by a friendly neighbour and exchanging knowing smiles.

YOU GET top slot on *News at Ten*, with sixty photographers outside your front door and protesters chanting 'Hypocrite! Hypocrite!' as you try to get to your car in your least flattering T-shirt and tracksuit bottoms, while MPs and commentators demand your resignation.

YOU WANT a civilised game of Scrabble.

YOU'D SETTLE FOR a game of Scrabble that doesn't end in tears.

YOU GET out the dictionary and say, 'As I thought! There's no such word as "EW"', whereupon your daughter stomps out of the room saying, 'That's so unfair!' and your son says, 'Well if she's not playing, nor am I' and your wife says, 'Why do you have to ruin everything?'

YOU WANT to perform fifty press-ups in a row, followed by a bracing cold shower.
YOU'D SETTLE FOR practising online PE with Joe Wicks.
YOU GET waylaid into watching a video on YouTube of a goldfish that looks like Alan Sugar.

YOU WANT to Zoom six close friends, sharing your hopes and fears and achieving a rare degree of intimacy.
YOU'D SETTLE FOR zooming two acquaintances and after twenty-five minutes all agreeing that it must be so much worse for large families stuck in high-rise blocks.
YOU GET baffled by which buttons to press and end up failing to hear what anyone's saying because you can't work out how to unmute them.

YOU WANT to be serene.
YOU'D SETTLE FOR being pleasant.
YOU GET increasingly irritated by the way your mother-in-law keeps offering magisterial pronouncements on the spread of Covid-19 ('You get it from household pets, I blame the Swedes') and end up flouncing out of the room with your hands over your ears screaming 'I can't take much more!'

YOU WANT to lose a stone.
YOU'D SETTLE FOR losing a pound.
YOU GET a thick-crust pizza, six cans of Heineken, two family bars of Galaxy and a twelve-pack of Walkers crisps.

YOU WANT to recite a long poem every day from memory.
YOU'D SETTLE FOR reciting a short poem every week from memory.

YOU GET out your old copy of *The Oxford Book of English Verse*, find all the poems a bit too heavy-going, and end up watching a repeat of Alan 'Chatty Man' Carr interviewing Sporty Spice, Alan Titchmarsh and Richard 'The Hamster' Hammond.

YOU WANT to grow sweet peas, petunias and six varieties of rose, courgettes, runner beans, tomatoes, carrots, potatoes and lettuces.
YOU'D SETTLE FOR mowing the lawn.
YOU GET a sunlounger.

YOU WANT to keep calm and carry on.
YOU'D SETTLE FOR keeping relatively calm and just about carrying on.
YOU GET worried that the slight tickle in your throat is an early sign of Covid and start to fret about whether cremation is better than burial.

YOU WANT to look cool in a facemask.
YOU'D SETTLE FOR looking happy in a facemask.
YOU GET a sweaty forehead and your glasses all steamed up so you can't read the sell-by date on the salad in Tesco.

YOU WANT to write a novel.
YOU'D SETTLE FOR writing a short story.
YOU GET down to writing 'Chapter' and 'One' at the top of a sheet of paper and then put it off until tomorrow.

YOU WANT to keep abreast of the Covid news, hour by hour.
YOU'D SETTLE FOR one Covid bulletin an evening.
YOU GET caught up in the first three minutes of *Channel 4 News* before switching over to a repeat of *Celebrity Antiques Road Trip*, with Diddy David Hamilton and a lady who used to be on *Emmerdale*.

YOU WANT Aneurin Bevan.
YOU'D SETTLE FOR Jeremy Hunt.
YOU GET Matt Hancock.

YOU WANT to teach your husband and children to play Bridge, so
 you can all enjoy it together.
YOU'D SETTLE FOR teaching your husband and children to play
 Cribbage, so you can all enjoy it together.
YOU GET a round of Snap before your son says, 'This is SO
 BORING!' and goes back to playing Robot Candy Smash on his
 mobile.

YOU WANT to read Henry James.
YOU'D SETTLE FOR reading P. D. James.
YOU END UP reading E. L. James.

YOU WANT to perform ten push-ups, ten jumping jacks and ten
 jump squats in quick succession.
YOU'D SETTLE FOR performing five push-ups, five jumping jacks
 and five jump squats in slow succession.
YOU GET out of your chair with a groan, walk to the kitchen, pick up
 a KitKat and return to your chair, sighing 'Oof!' as you sit down.

YOU WANT to revive the long-lost art of conversation.
YOU'D SETTLE FOR a few minutes' chat about last night's telly.
YOU GET into a heated row about whose turn it is to do the dishes.

YOU WANT all your neighbours to put their heads out of their
 windows and join you in a rousing chorus from *La Traviata*.
YOU'D SETTLE FOR all your neighbours putting their heads out of
 their windows and joining you in a patchy rendition of 'God Save
 the Queen'.
YOU GET the neighbour next-door-but-one singing 'My Way'
 off-key and the neighbour three down screaming back 'shut it!
 Some of us are trying to get some sleep!'

COMEDIANS

A Whole Lotta Relephants

A pun is a word that doesn't mean what it says, or, rather, it means what it says but also means something else. It is a signpost bearing one destination, but pointing in two directions.

The longest pun-free period in *Duck Soup* is at the beginning, after the unsettling opening shot of ducks paddling in a cauldron over a hot fire. We are in the majestic council chamber of the government of Freedonia. A meeting is in session. Zander, the President, is asking the wealthy Mrs Gloria Teasdale, widow of the late Chester V. Teasdale, for a further $20 million, so that he can announce an immediate reduction in taxes. Mrs Teasdale, played by the redoubtable Margaret Dumont, complains that she has already donated half her fortune, and will only lend more money if a new leader is put in place.

It is already a minute in, and there is still no pun in sight. Instead, the language of negotiation fills the air: this could be any political film, at any time, dealing with the usual problems of borrowing, taxing and spending. You almost feel that, if you looked very hard, you could spot George Osborne or Vince Cable in the background, beavering away.

'In a crisis like this, I feel Freedonia needs a new leader,' declares Mrs Teasdale. 'A progressive, fearless fighter, a man like ... Rufus T. Firefly!'

Firefly is, of course, Groucho Marx, but we have still not had a glimpse of him. Instead, the scene switches to an absurdly lavish ballroom, its vast staircase flanked by overly plumed guards and trumpeters with exceedingly long trumpets. It is the reception for His Excellency Rufus T. Firefly, who has yet to arrive. After various formal introductions, a troupe of ballerinas enters, scattering flowers along his projected walkway. Everyone choruses:

His Excellency is due
To take his station,
Beginning his new administration
He'll make his appearance when
The clock on the wall strikes ten!
We'll give him a rousing cheer
To show him we're glad he's here!
Hail, hail Freedonia!
Land of the brave and free!

In 1933, when *Duck Soup* was first released, this deadbeat song with its patriotic lyrics would have brought to mind the forced jubilations of Stalin's Soviet Union or Hitler's Germany; even today, it remains the prototypical song for countries such as Azerbaijan and North Korea, speaking of order and shared purpose, of a population pointing in the same direction. And still no sign of a pun.

The minutes tick by, and the ceremony keeps on stopping and starting as His Excellency fails to appear. All eyes are on the entrance when Groucho Marx finally lollops in from the side, unseen. Finally, he is greeted – 'I welcome you with open arms' – by a clearly besotted Mrs Teasdale. The moment he enters, the puns come thick and punishingly fast, with no let-up. The more Mrs Teasdale coos, the more he undermines her with his crazed wordplay. 'You can leave in a taxi. If you can't leave in a taxi you can leave in a huff. If that's too soon, you can leave in a minute and a huff.' These quick-fire speeches have a topsy-turvy logic all their own, each word changing its meaning the moment it is uttered.

Everything about Groucho was a pun. His father was called Simon, not Sam, and Marrix, not Marx; his mother's real name was Miene Schönberg, but her stage name was Minnie Palmer. Groucho was born Julius; he only transformed into Groucho in a break between shows, when a fellow comedian allotted nicknames to each of the Marx Brothers: Milton wore rubber boots, hence Gummo; Leonard chased women, or 'chicks', hence Chico, and Adolph played the harp, hence Harpo. And as for Julius, he carried a small drawstring bag known as a 'grouch'.

Groucho's most visible characteristic is itself a sort of pun. It is both a moustache and not a moustache. Instead, it is a painting of a moustache – *ceci n'est pas une moustache* – that he first daubed on his face with greasepaint in 1921, having arrived late for a performance, with no time to glue on his artificial whiskers. Before long, his eyebrows followed suit. Between them, they were to become the great symbol of the Marx Brothers, loved by lowbrows and highbrows alike.

The world of Freedonia is a world built on order. Everything is where it should be and does what it is meant to, before the Marx Brothers send it all haywire. After their arrival, nothing is allowed to remain in its rightful place, or to be what it is meant to be. Everything is transformed into something else. The world has become a pun.

Amid much bugling, successive guards announce 'His Excellency's car!' But even the car is not a car: following another fanfare, Harpo appears on a motorcycle. 'I'm in a hurry,' cries Groucho, stepping into the sidecar. 'To the House of Representatives! Ride like fury. If you run out of gas, get ethyl. If Ethyl runs out, get Mabel. Now, step on it!' And with that, Harpo accelerates off, leaving the sidecar firmly in place. 'Well, it certainly feels good to be back again,' says Groucho, having got nowhere.

When Harpo next appears, he is with Chico. They arrive at the ambassador's door as his appointed spies, both wearing bearded masks and hats, with Harpo's eyes whirling around on springs. But the mask itself is then unmasked: Chico turns Harpo round; his real face is on the other side of his head. The pair are double agents, or human puns.

And so it goes on, order overturned, conformity unravelling, idiocy at the gates. Later – I was about to say much later, but the whole film lasts barely an hour and ten minutes – we are in a courtroom, with the two spies on trial for selling Freedonia's secret war code and plans. 'Sure. I sold a code and two pair of plans,' chips in Chico. Under the pressure of the courtroom, the puns bubble over, particularly when Chico turns turtle on the prosecutor:

CHICO: Now, I ask you one. What is it has a trunk, but no key, weight 2,000 pounds and lives in a circus?

PROSECUTOR: That's irrelevant.

CHICO: A relevant! Hey, that's the answer. There's a whole lotta relephants in a circus.

JUDGE: That sort of testimony we can eliminate.

CHICO: 'At's-a fine. I'll take some.

JUDGE: You'll take what?

CHICO: Eliminate. A nice cold glass eliminate.

FIREFLY: Gentlemen, Chicolini here may talk like an idiot, and look like an idiot, but don't let that fool you. He really is an idiot.

One pun leads to another: they bounce with the speed and precision of a polished stone skimmed across a lake.

MINISTER OF FINANCE: Something must be done! War would mean a prohibitive increase in our taxes!

CHICO: Hey, I got an uncle lives in Taxes.

MINISTER OF FINANCE: No. I'm talking about taxes – money, dollars.

CHICO: Dollas! That's where my uncle lives. Dollas, Taxes.

It is the rat-a-tat-tat speed of their delivery that distinguishes the Marx Brothers from their contemporaries and stops them growing old. Other comedies from that era now seem sluggish and laborious: *Duck Soup* is alive and kicking.

Harpo, was, of course, the silent one, but the scenes in which he appears are generally far louder, and more perilous, than any of the others. He is a bundle of anarchic energy, targeting the pompous and the self-regarding, like all the vengeful characters in *Struwwelpeter* rolled into one. Always taking out his scissors and going snip-snip-snip, he snips off the ends of Chico's frankfurter and Firefly's quill pen, he snips off the peanut vendor's apron, the ambassador's tailcoat and the soldiers' fancy plumes. Instead of speaking, Harpo grins like a madman and honks his horn. Having broken into a house, he tries to open the safe, but he twists the volume dial of a radio by mistake. It starts to blare, so he has to smash it. Whenever he is on screen, even the most inanimate of objects cannot be trusted to stay quiet. At one point, he shows Groucho a tattoo on his stomach of a house. As Groucho takes a closer look at the tattoo, a dog pops out of it; when Groucho says 'Miaow!' the dog starts barking.

The most celebrated scene, and the most sublime, revolves around another visual pun: a mirror that is not a mirror, a reflection that is not a reflection. Harpo, disguised as Groucho, tries to fool Groucho into believing that he is looking at himself in a mirror. Groucho, suspicious, executes a random series of increasingly ludicrous movements in the hope of catching him out. But whatever movement he makes, however daft, Harpo anticipates him and does just the same. Even when Groucho walks into what should be the mirror, and out the other side, Harpo does the same, but in reverse. Eighty years on, that visual gag is still going strong: in an episode of the gloriously perverse American cartoon series *Family Guy*, the baby-man antihero Stewie is transported back to 1930s Berlin, where he disguises himself as Adolf Hitler. Then Hitler himself comes into the room, and Stewie has to convince him that he is looking into a mirror.

The world in 1933 was becoming increasingly overpopulated with tin-pot dictators. Is *Duck Soup* a political satire? Many intellectuals and academics have argued as much, though they tend to belong to the school of criticism that likes to stamp all the jokes out of comedy so that they can praise its high seriousness without fear of contradiction. A *New Yorker* cartoon once showed a professor of semiotics saying: 'The tautology of their symbolism thus begins to achieve mythic proportions in *A Day at the Races*, *Duck Soup* and *A Night at the Opera*.' As is so often the case with *New Yorker* cartoons, it veers from reality only by a couple of degrees.

Over the years, *Duck Soup* has been praised for its understanding of paranoia in international diplomacy and of the economics of warfare. It is full of gags about the futility of war and its financial advantages. At one point, Groucho is told of a peace plan and replies, 'It's too late, I've already paid a month's rent on the battlefield.' At another, Groucho puts his hand on Harpo's shoulder and tells him, in ringing tones, 'You're a brave man. Go and break through the lines. And remember, while you're out there risking life and limb, through shot and shell, we'll be in here thinking what a sucker you are.'

This joke was echoed, thirty years later, in *Beyond the Fringe* ('I want you to lay down your life, Perkins. We need a futile gesture at this stage.'), but, taken as a whole, *Duck Soup* is too explosively nonsensical to let itself succumb to the discipline of satire, which might loosely be described as comedy with an agenda. (Nonsense is not an alternative version of sense, but rather its negation.)

On 14 November 1933, three days before the release of *Duck Soup*, Harpo took a ship to the USSR via Hamburg. He was to be the first American artist to perform in Moscow since the USA, under President Roosevelt, had recognised the Soviet Union. Without realising it, he was about to enter a real-life looking-glass world, where draconian decisions are taken for all the wrong reasons.

In his otherwise delightfully breezy autobiography *Harpo Speaks*, he says that in Hamburg he saw 'the most frightening, most depressing sight I had ever seen – a row of stores with Stars of David and the word "Jude" painted on them, and inside, behind half-empty counters, people in a daze, cringing like they didn't know what hit them and didn't know where the next blow would come from'.

On the train out of Warsaw he bumps into a fellow American, who tells him he'll have to pay for excess baggage at the Russian border and kindly lends him a hundred roubles, saying it will be cheaper to pay in roubles than dollars. But when Harpo offers roubles to the inspector, mayhem ensues. 'Bells rang. Buzzers sounded. Boots clomped all over the place as guards came running.'

Harpo is hauled off to a shed, where he is cross-questioned. 'Where did I get the roubles? A guy on the train lent them to me. What was his name? I didn't know his name. I was lousy at remembering names. I was lying, the Russian colonel said. Tell the truth now: where did I get the roubles? I gave him the same answer.

'A squad of guards lugged my trunk and harp into the shed. "Open the trunk, please," said the officer. I unlocked it and the Russians began unloading it. When at first they only found a raincoat and an assortment of pants, shirts and ties, they were obviously disappointed.

'Then they hit the jackpot. From the trunk they removed 400 knives, two revolvers, three stilettos, half a dozen bottles marked POISON, and a collection of red wigs and false beards, moustaches and hands. More bells rang. More buzzers sounded. Whistles blew. More officials and more guards came clomping into the shed.'

Harpo is grilled. 'Would I please explain why I was transporting weapons and disguises? I told them they were all props for my act. Act? What act? I said I had come to Russia to put on a show. Americans do not entertain in Russia, they said. I had better tell the truth.'

They ask what is in his harp case. A harp, he tells them. They order him to play something. 'This would have been my salvation any other time, any other place, but in an open shed when it was thirty below zero. I was so stiff from the cold that I couldn't get my gloves off. All I could do was run my gloved hands up the strings a couple of times and pray that somebody there would recognise the professional touch.'

But no: a guard gets the same noise out of the harp. The officials shake their heads and smirk. Harpo fears imprisonment, or worse, and begins to yell about his rights, but all to no avail. It is only when his fellow American pops up on the scene, and they accept his explanation, that Harpo is allowed to board the Moscow express. 'The train was unbelievably crowded, ten and twelve people to each six-passenger compartment, and it stank of disinfectant, but I thanked God I was lucky enough to be on it.'

His show is a terrific hit with the Russians, who love clowns, but on the way back to America Harpo can't shake off the awful feeling that for the past eight weeks he has been watched wherever he goes, 'by eyes I couldn't see. I never, not for a minute, felt I was really alone. I was a stranger who had stumbled into a deadly conspiracy, who had to be kept from finding out what the plot was all about.'

But one thing above all strikes Harpo about the USSR. 'I never saw anybody do anything just for the hell of it. I never saw anybody pull a spontaneous gag.' Rationality, he feels, is the only acceptable justification for everything in Stalin's USSR: something can only be funny if it has a reason to be funny. And this is why *Duck Soup* is so funny: because it has no reason to be funny.

Just Like That

Back in 1984, I went to the funniest auction – in fact, the only funny auction – I have ever attended.

'One string of sausages,' the auctioneer would announce, in his solemn tones, followed by 'One wooden duck (blindfolded)'.

It was the sale of Tommy Cooper's magical and stage properties at Christie's in South Kensington, and so, in a sense, the very last show of that wonderful comedian. For myself, I came away with two ropy old suitcases packed full of brightly coloured feather flowers, a real bargain for £100, especially considering some of them can, with the flick of a wrist, be made to bloom, and others made to wilt. I don't think I've ever spent £100 quite so wisely: the moment I produce the flowers and mention the name of Tommy Cooper, everyone starts to smile.

Cooper's whole life could be measured out in comical props. As a young boy of six or seven, he would startle onlookers by bicycling down the street with a newspaper in front of his eyes: little did they know that he had previously cut two small peepholes in it. His school-days were spent with his pockets filled with sneezing powder, plastic ink blots, giant springing snakes, and throughout his adult life he would design an array of objects especially doctored to produce laughs: a teacup with one straight side, so he could offer you 'just half a cup' of tea; a pack of cards with a small harmonica concealed ('they're playing cards'); a three-cornered hat that revolved round and round, while Cooper looked increasingly giddy; a 'genuine milking stool' which could be made to squirt milk from one of its legs.

Bob Monkhouse once saw him in his dressing room dangling a bath tap on a piece of elastic and asked him what he was doing. He said that it was a gag: he was going to come on, dangle it up and down and then say to the audience, 'Tap dance!' Monkhouse thought it the worst joke he had ever heard and begged him not to do it, as it was bound to fall flat. But he went ahead with it, and, needless to say, it brought the house down.

He would always take seventeen bags of daft magic on tour with him, and even they were not enough to keep him amused: he always wanted more. His fellow comedian Jimmy Jewel once recalled the time he offered Cooper a lift home from Blackpool. Jewel had had an accident onstage that week, and had been forced to wear a neck brace. 'Tommy was the type of man who had to try everything – if you had a sandwich, he'd want a bite – and he said, "Can I try your neck brace?" I said, "Don't be daft. I need it."' But Jewel eventually gave it, and the for the rest of the journey Cooper sat there smiling in the neck brace while Jewel drove on in agony.

He was, in a sense, in thrall to laughter, both its master and its slave. When he left the stage, his jokes followed him and wouldn't leave him alone. A friend went with him into a tailor's shop on Shaftesbury Avenue. Cooper tried on the suit he had ordered, then turned to the tailor and said, 'Do you mind if I take it for a walk round the block?' Permission granted, he removed a small block of wood from his pocket, placed it on the floor, and walked round it. In a public library, he asked for a pair of scissors and snipped the bottom off one of his trouser legs. He then went up to the librarian and gave it to her, saying, 'There's a turn-up for the books!'

Cooper was a perpetual child, his many friends and admirers seem to agree, and with the ruthlessness and attention-seeking of a child. As others pursue fame or wealth, so he pursued laughter. 'All day yesterday I heard a ringing in my ears,' he once wrote in a letter. 'Then I picked up the phone and it stopped.' The odd thing about this letter – jammed full of gags, and nothing else – was that he wrote it in his forties, to his ageing mother. Right up to the end, he was always putting plastic beetles in his wife's bath, or severed hands in her laundry basket. After she discovered a wind-up spider in her make-up bag, 'he laughed and laughed and laughed, lying on the bed with his feet in the air'.

He regarded everyone as a potential stooge, even the Queen. In the line-up after the Royal Variety Show in 1964, he was disconcerted that she hadn't paid him enough attention, so, just as she was moving on, he called her back. 'I say, Your Majesty – may I ask you a personal question?'

'As personal as I'll allow,' replied the Queen.

'Do you like football?'

'Not particularly.'

'Well, could I have your tickets for the Cup Final?'

He came from a suitably comical family: whenever they went to the beach, his father liked to perform a comical routine with a recalcitrant deckchair. His Uncle Jimmy used to borrow a watch, then pretend to swallow it – mysteriously, it could be heard ticking in his tummy. Even Cooper's hard-working mother, a haberdasher, would thread some of young Tommy's invisible string through all her stock, and thus catch shoplifters unawares.

Tommy was obsessed with magic. Leaving school at fourteen, he went to work for a boat company. The management asked him to perform at their Christmas party, but he was overcome by nerves and his tricks went horribly wrong, an upturned bottle of milk pouring over the stage rather than staying in place. 'The more I panicked and made a mess of everything, the more they laughed. I came off and cried, but five minutes later I could still hear the sound of the laughter in my ears, and was thinking maybe there's a living there.'

It was to be the defining moment of his life. In the magic trick that goes pear-shaped, he had stumbled on a universal truth – comic or tragic, depending on the angle you look at it – about the bright-eyed hopelessness of human endeavour. Six foot three, with size-thirteen feet and hands the size of hams, his vast nose, mouth and jaw forming a cavern out of which poked his bewildered eyes, Tommy Cooper looked like God on an off day.

His jokes were to do with dreadful mistakes and misunderstandings, recounted with the cheerful innocence of a child: 'Man came up to me, said, "I haven't had a bite in three days. So I bit him."'

'It's strange, isn't it? You stand in the middle of a library and go

"Aaagh!" and everyone just stares at you. But you do the same thing on an aeroplane and everyone joins in.'

'My dog took a lump out of my knee the other day. A friend of mine said, "Did you put anything on it?" I said, "No. He liked it as it was."'

Again like a child, he could cry to order. One of his gags involved arriving onstage with a stuffed budgerigar stuck to the top of his fez. He would then hunt everywhere around the stage, wailing 'I've lost my budgie!' and bursting into tears. Barry Cryer noticed that he was able to produce these tears naturally.

There was, inevitably, a dark side to this sun. He was unbelievably tight-fisted, never buying anyone a drink, and sneakily intent on short-changing his scriptwriters. Tipping taxi drivers, he would always shove something into their top pocket, saying 'Have a drink on me'; only after he had gone would they find it was a teabag. He blamed his parsimony on an impoverishing lifetime contract he had signed with his agent, but his biographer, John Fisher,* diligently reveals this as a lie.

The champagne that came with success (and what success – £7,000 a week by 1976) soon mired him in alcohol. It caused him to be snappy and even violent. 'He was a child with an infant's rage,' explained Monkhouse, of this greatest of all the surrealists.

---

* *Tommy Cooper: Always Leave Them Laughing* by John Fisher (2006).

Becoming Mainwaring

Has there ever been an actor who looked and behaved so unlike an actor? Certainly, nothing in Arthur Lowe's past or in his physiognomy suggested he would ever take to the stage. Even at the age of seven he looked like a middle-aged clerk, 'an unnerving miniature replica of the future Captain Mainwaring', in the words of his biographer, Graham Lord.*

Aged twenty, 5 feet 4 and already thin on top, he passed for a man twice his age. His background was as far from showbiz as you could possibly get. He was born in 1915, in a terraced house in a Derbyshire village, the son of a railway clerk. He left school aged fifteen, determined to enter the Merchant Navy, only to be rejected on account of his poor eyesight. His first job was as a barrow boy for a Manchester motor-accessory firm. He was then promoted to a clerk's desk in the company's bicycle department.

'He was a bit pompous even then ... even in those days he was already Captain Mainwaring,' recalls a fellow clerk called Ethel Hulme. And this is the osmotic refrain that runs through his biography like a linking thread: how Arthur Lowe became Captain Mainwaring, and how Captain Mainwaring became Arthur Lowe. 'He was Mainwaring and Mainwaring was him,' his son Stephen was to say after his death. 'If people asked me was Dad like Mainwaring at home, I would look at them as if to say "Bugger off!" But maybe I was like that because he was, and I didn't want it to be that way. He was fixated with unimportant detail, had an inflated sense of his own importance, tripped over

---

* *Arthur Lowe: A Life That Led to Mainwaring* by Graham Lord (2002).

things and banged his head. But he was brave, too, and I saw him once put his fists up to a man twice his height.'

Appropriately enough, it was the coming of the Second World War that turned Arthur Lowe into an actor. Had he not become a soldier and been posted way behind the lines in the Middle East, he would never have tried to relieve his boredom by dabbling in amateur theatrics. You might almost say that had Mr Hitler become a successful painter, then Arthur Lowe would never have become a successful actor.

Lowe was a diligent engineer, and was soon promoted to corporal, then sergeant. 'He was very pompous,' recalls a contemporary. 'He took himself seriously and strutted about. He was just like Captain Mainwaring.' But, of course, the job of acting is not nearly as simple as that: you only have to see how hard people find it to be themselves when a video camera is pointed at them to realise that playing oneself requires as much skill, and perhaps rather more subtlety, as playing any other character.

John Cleese once observed that every comic actor has one role, and that role is based on the character that as a young man he most dreads becoming. Thus the comic character is formed through the conscious exaggeration of the actor's own worst failings. The comic actor then finds that fame and prestige accrue to the character he hoped never to become, and his relationship with his alter ego grows more complicated than ever. In later life, Arthur Lowe would grow furious when he was confused with Captain Mainwaring and refuse to sign autographs. 'The public are so stupid,' he once told Lynda Lee-Potter.

Arthur Lowe walked straight out of the army on to the professional stage, without a day's training in between. After successfully auditioning at the Hulme Hippodrome, he was booked to play the part – surprise, surprise – of a pompous old man. He was still only thirty years of age. He was soon doing the rounds of the repertory theatres – he acted in forty-two different plays in one year alone – and was to remain in constant employment for the rest of his life.

Probably because he came to acting late, after serving in the army throughout the war, he always remained rather separate from other actors; some thought him aloof and stand-offish. And, unlike the others, he was a man of increasingly fixed habits and pernickety routines, always keeping a pair of nail clippers and a key for bleeding hotel radiators in his pockets, always demanding Mr Kipling cakes served just so, with exactly the right amount of tea in the teapot.

Like many who live by routine and go out of their way to enforce bourgeois standards (he had it written into his *Dad's Army* contract that he would never have to appear on screen without his trousers) he was, not far beneath the surface, a true eccentric. Most of his money, for instance, went into preserving a vast 53-ton wooden steam yacht, 104 feet long. He was never happier than when standing at its wheel, dressed in captain's hat and navy blazer, issuing orders to the only crewman, his son Stephen.

His marriage seems to have been a mixture of public respectability and private angst. He remained devoted to his wife Joan, but the two of them drank a great deal, even spreading their love of alcohol into their choice of food: port and melon for starters, followed by steak Diane, with sherry trifle to follow.

Joan was an alcoholic, often collapsing and having to be put to bed by Arthur, who would then sit on the edge of the bed, according to his son, with his head in his hands. But Graham Lord offers glimpses too of mutual happiness and devotion, the pair of them dependent on one another's company.

'To me it was a great love story,' says Frank Williams, who played the vicar in *Dad's Army*. Joan was not much of an actress, but towards the end of his life Arthur insisted she be included in the cast of any play he took on. Others have seen this as a sorry end to a glorious career, but one might just as well view it as a sign that love conquers all, even bad acting. Graham Lord does his best to redress Stephen Lowe's grim portrait of his parents' marriage, but sometimes his efforts appear almost too valiant. For example, the caption to a photograph of the two in old age reads: 'In love to the very end: Arthur's fond glance at Joan says it all.' Yet to me his glance looks rather less fond than downtrodden, or perhaps even fearful.

The chapter relating to *Dad's Army* is, perhaps inevitably, the most interesting. Personally, I can't read enough about the ins and outs of this most lovable of all series, with its remarkable cast, two of whom – John Laurie, who played the gloomy Scot, Frazer, and Arnold Ridley, who played the doddery Godfrey – were veterans of the Somme.

It becomes clear from the reminiscences of the cast and writers that though Arthur Lowe was very much like Mainwaring – ever more so, as the writers would feed Lowe's characteristics into the part of Mainwaring as the series progressed – he was also able to hover humorously above his creation, feeding subtle comic lines and facial expressions into this most po-faced of characters, gently sending up his alter ego. 'I treat every comic part as a straight part,' he once explained, adding, 'the man who slips on a banana skin doesn't do it on purpose.'

Every biography ends sadly, because every biography ends in death. Lowe's death, just before curtain up in a provincial theatre, had an additionally creepy quality, as his wife insisted that the show should go on, and went on with her hammy acting as though nothing had happened. She was even absent from his funeral, insisting to a friend that it was what he would have wanted.

It is right, then, that Graham Lord should end his biography of Lowe with paeans of praise for his acting. Gielgud, Richardson, Olivier and Scofield all rated him very highly, but for me their superlatives, though fully justified, never quite catch what made him unique. There was an unequalled lack of theatricality about him: however hard you looked, you simply could not see him *acting*. He was also the most natural, unaffected stage actor I ever saw, able to give the impression of mumbling and bumbling while still being heard from the back of the upper circle. The creation of such intimacy between an actor and his character and their audience demands an incredible skill – the sort of skill that allowed Captain Mainwaring to remain blissfully unaware that he was being played by someone else.

Tickled Pink

If ever you were to come across the psychological files on the key post-war British comedians – Frankie Howerd, Peter Sellers, Kenneth Williams, Spike Milligan, Tony Hancock, Max Wall – you would never guess that their job was to make people laugh. Looking at their strange fears and phobias, their weird compulsions and creeping misanthropy, you would take them for social outcasts, possibly fellow inmates in some day-release asylum for the severely depressed.

Even comics who aren't all that funny – Michael Barrymore, say, or Freddie Starr, or Dick Emery, or Charles Hawtrey – possess driven personalities, forever fleeing in fear from childhood ghosts, the beam of the spotlight their only sanctuary. For this reason, biographies of comedians are invariably more fascinating than the grander biographies of novelists or politicians or members of the Royal Family.

If Sigmund Freud were alive to turn his mind to Benny Hill, he would be gurgling with pleasure, his every theory made flesh in the person of this leering, gurning, hopelessly yearning TV comic.

Benny Hill was born Alfie Hill in Southampton in 1924. His father, an aggressive, overbearing character known as The Captain, worked for a company with the comical name of Stanley and Co., the larger part of its income deriving from the sale of condoms, with a thriving sideline in semi-pornographic sex manuals with titles such as *What Every Wife Should Know*.

'Alf-ie's dad sells French-ies' the other children in the playground would chant; in self-defence, Hill would impersonate all the different customers who emerged in furtive excitement from the shop. As a boy – Dr Freud, please note – Hill was caught by his headmistress, Mrs

Vane, trying to impress an older girl called Molly by writing his name in pee. Mrs Vane punished him with a caning.

In his early teens, he began to develop a passionate and lifelong interest in unattainable women. Decades later, on *Desert Island Discs*, he chose a song called 'With Every Breath I Take' by Bing Crosby, and told of how, aged fourteen, he had caught sight of a girl on a merry-go-round and fallen in love with her. Every day he would walk six miles there and six miles back, just to see this girl go in and out of a shop at lunchtime. 'I don't think I could ever love anybody the way I loved this girl,' he told Roy Plomley. Yet the girl remained entirely unaware of him, and he never even knew her name.

At the same time, he sat goggle-eyed watching the young ladies in their stockings in saucy variety shows – *Ooh La La L'Amour, Naughty But Nice, Toujours Les Femmes* – which would come on tour to Southampton, punctuated by unlikely stand-up comics such as Jack Joyce, The World-Famous One-Legged Dancing Comedian.

By the age of sixteen, he had wheedled his way into a semi-professional local variety troupe, often appearing in the role of a vicar. 'I am sorry to have to report that this year very few ladies have become young mothers,' he would intone, with a twinkle in his eye, 'despite the strenuous efforts of the bishop and myself.'

He worked as a clerk and a trainee manager at Woolworth's before finding a job he enjoyed, becoming a milkman, driving his horse and cart around the Hampshire countryside, all the while pretending to himself that he was riding a stagecoach through Dodge City. Thirty years later, he was to reproduce the experience in his number-one song 'Ernie – The Fastest Milkman in the West'.

He was still only sixteen when, without any qualifications, he sold his guitar and drum kit for £15 and left home for London, with less than £20 in his pocket. Stepping off the train, he walked straight to a café in the Strand, where he read through the advertisements in *The Stage* newspaper.

Sleeping in air-raid shelters, he managed to find a dogsbody job as an assistant stage manager. An initial break came when the straight man for a comedian called Hal Bryan went missing: at the very last moment, Hill stepped in and pulled it off. 'You're going to be a trouper, son!' said Bryan.

But despite his determination and extraordinary industry – even in those early years, he never watched an act without a notebook in his hand, ready to pinch jokes – he was never any good as a stand-up comedian. 'Passable material, but he has a quite unfunny personality and so just doesn't come over,' was a typical audience reaction.

As the unfunny member of a double act – first with Reg Varney, then with Alfred Marks – he enjoyed some success, but when he was allowed his own slot he was a disaster, always riddled with nerves. 'You've got a bloody rotten act, haven't you?' barked one theatre manager as Hill vomited into a sink, having been slow-handclapped offstage.

The new medium of television was his saviour. He loved TV, and TV loved him. Most comedians who had thrived onstage found it impossible to make the switch, but Benny (by now he had changed his name in tribute to Jack Benny) took to it like a duck to water, immediately realising it would allow him to play a tremendous range of comic characters without ever having to be himself. He was also well equipped to satisfy its voracious appetite for new material: he had built up a huge stock of comic ideas from far and wide, not only stealing from America, but also – uniquely – from the Continent. One secretary recalls how he was able to dictate an entire series from out of his head.

His success came in two waves: from the age of twenty-seven, he was the most famous comedian on British television, then suddenly, aged sixty, he became the most famous comedian on the planet, his Thames series screened all over the world, including China and Russia. Night-duty policemen in Alabama would greet each other with the Fred Scuttle salute. By 1985, he was earning £1,552, 863 from overseas sales alone, and his Halifax account was £4 million in credit.

How to account for his staggering popularity? Benny Hill wasn't, to my mind, the funniest of comedians, but he had somehow tapped into the hobgoblins of his own psyche – the leering buffoon, the stunted fantasist, the cowardly lecher, the self-deluding onanist – and found that they rang a universal bell.

He lived alone, surviving on fish fingers eaten off paper plates ('saves on the washing up'), but Bob Monkhouse, whose comments throughout this book are always sympathetic and astute, insists that this does not mean he was lonely. 'He had a kind of peaceful self-sufficiency … He was actually very contented.'

Benny Hill preferred his love unrequited, only proposing to women he knew would turn him down. His biographer reckons that he never had full sexual intercourse with a woman after 1954, after he had rejected the one woman who wanted to marry him. From then on, his sexual instincts ('Be nice to Uncle Benny') were passive, impersonal and Clintonian, his only real delight coming from being seen by others surrounded by dolly birds, without the need for any follow-through.

His biographer, Mark Lewisohn,* reveals that he was admired as a comedian by people as diverse as Charlie Chaplin, Michael Jackson and Anthony Burgess. In 1990, I was present at a private dinner party when Benny Hill met Anthony Burgess for the first and only time. Hill arrived first, tickled pink that his taxi driver had been a woman ('I told her, ooh, my love, you can drive me ANYWHERE!'). Burgess then tried to impress Hill with his photographic memory of every sketch Hill had ever performed, while Hill tried to boost his intellectual rating by rattling off all his favourite jokes in Shakespeare and Molière. He did not strike me then as an unhappy man, but I do remember thinking that he might have come straight out of one of his own sketches.

He died two years later, all by himself, with the television on, too ill to get to his parents' old semi in Southampton. At his funeral, his former showgirls wore stockings and suspenders in tribute. Alone in his coffin, Benny Hill found himself pursued in slow motion by a gaggle of admirers for one last time.

---

* *Funny, Peculiar: The True Story of Benny Hill* by Mark Lewisohn (2002).

Tragically I Was an Only Twin

Everyone who knew Peter Cook likes to boast about it. It was, I suppose, a bit like knowing God, though the God of Cook's imagination always suffered from an eternal hangover. 'When He wakes up and surveys the mess, He resolves to straighten it out at once. The trouble is that He always has a "little nip" to steady Himself, and the chaos continues,' he once explained.

But here goes my boast: like a lot of people, I used to receive telephone calls from Peter Cook at unlikely times of the day and night. One of his running jokes was to keep me up to date with the ever more successful career of the other Craig Brown, the Scottish football manager who shares my name.

Peter Cook had suffered a similar fate. Over lunch in an Australian restaurant, he once told me that at sometime in the early 1980s, when his career was at its lowest ebb, his press agency had sent him the largest packet of newspaper cuttings he had ever received. Imagining there must have been a sudden explosion in his popularity, he eagerly opened the package, only to find that all the cuttings referred to the Cambridge Rapist, who also happened to be called Peter Cook. Other celebrities would have been mortified to find their careers overtaken by a serial rapist; but Peter was thrilled to bits. He was a man who started haemorrhaging ambition in his mid-twenties and never stopped.

A good many of his sketches involve the random splicing-together of just such disparate elements as the comedian and the Cambridge Rapist. I was reminded of these pairings while reading this new compilation*

---

* *Tragically I Was an Only Twin: The Complete Peter Cook* edited by William Cook (2002).

– not nearly as 'complete' as the title boasts, but wide-ranging nonetheless – of Peter Cook's scripts and other writings. The man fed up with having to remove lobsters from Jayne Mansfield's backside, the one-legged actor auditioning for the role of Tarzan, the cowboy builders contracted to construct the pleasure dome at Xanadu: they all revolve around the clash of the mundane with the fantastic.

And they all have a touch of the macabre. A brilliant Pete and Dud sketch from the early 1970s involves a pompous passenger listening in horror as a cab driver takes increasingly macabre instructions from his radio ('Roger, Four Five. Pick up torso and drop on Wimbledon Common.' 'Is that cash or account?'). It is, of course, the question 'Is that cash or account?' that takes the joke on to a higher level. Lesser comics might have come up with the basic idea and let it rip, but Cook's particular genius was to ground everything, however bizarre, in a hopelessly humdrum reality. Thus he approaches the task of retrieving the lobsters from Jayne Mansfield's backside in a spirit of grudging tedium ('the worst job I ever had') and the builders of Xanadu ('we'll just budget for a regular pleasure dome, and see if we can pick up some stately trimmings down the market') remain resolutely unimpressed by their commission.

Laziness and its bedmate, boredom, were dominant genes in Peter Cook's make-up, but they also provided him with his material. By lounging around for the last twenty-odd years of his life, he was only practising what he preached. He was, you might say, the High Priest of Boredom, the Town Crier for Laziness.

Most of his characters were based on a butler at his public school called Arthur Boylett, a man of almost transcendental banality who liked to look hard at stones and twigs before pronouncing 'I thought I saw it move.' One of the characters Cook kept running throughout his career was the incredibly boring man who regales everyone with Interesting Facts, often about fish. ('The codfish relies almost solely for protection on blending with the natural seaweeds amongst which it lives.')

If only his jokes had been less funny, Peter Cook might have been rated the equal of Pinter and Beckett, perhaps even their superior. His vision is informed by their sense of hopelessness and restlessness, yet to my mind it is somehow less forced, less solemn.

'I've learnt from my mistakes,' says his character Sir Arthur Streeb-Greebling, 'And I'm sure I can repeat them.' Had Samuel Beckett produced this line in *Waiting for Godot*, it would now be in all the dictionaries of quotations, to be reverentially genned up by A-Level students. So would another Cook line, on God: 'I often wish he'd manifest himself a bit more ... He limits himself to once in a million years if we're lucky.'

Like Pinter's Caretaker, Cook's grotty characters are always placing the blame for their lives on the most unlikely things. 'I often think I might have done better if I'd kept off the milk,' says a man in a sketch he wrote aged twenty-two. He then changes his mind, thinking that if only he'd had the necessary flesh he could have been the Fattest Man in the World. 'Fate was against you,' agrees his companion.

Reading the sketches in *Tragically I Was an Only Twin* makes the extraordinary extent of Cook's comic influence clear. Monty Python and every show since have paraded versions of the mad shop assistant, but here is Peter Cook doing it in the late 1950s with, among others, the honest tailor. ('You must understand there is a perfectly good reason for the wretched quality of our product – we employ a lot of very old men in the factory.')

Mel Smith and Griff Rhys-Jones's head-to-heads – one stupid, knowing he's stupid, the other stupid, thinking he's clever – were clearly inspired by the dialogues of Dud and Pete; Harry Enfield's Self-Righteous Brothers came straight from *Not Only ... But Also* (1965): 'Bloody Greta Garbo, stark naked, save for a short nightie, hanging on to the window sill, and I could see her knuckles all white, saying, "Peter, Peter". You know how those bloody Swedes go on. I said, "Get out of it".'

It is hard to separate Peter Cook the writer from Peter Cook the performer, not least because his energy tended to come from off-the-cuff improvisation. One of the reasons he was no good as an actor of other people's scripts was that he never seemed fully engaged: his genius was propelled by instant invention; pre-packaged scripts, even his own, made him uncomfortable.

His stage persona was deadpan, unblinking and with a faint air of threat, making him entirely different from the jolly-jape comics who preceded him. This po-faced oddity can still be seen today in performers like The League of Gentlemen.

Reading the scripts reproduced in *Tragically I Was an Only Twin*, even those I had never seen before, I found Cook's voice echoing off the page. But is this book more than a souvenir, there to jog our memories and help call to mind the original performances?

The book's editor, William Cook (no relation), loyally suggests that the writing is of a uniform quality, as sharp towards the end of his career as it was at the beginning. 'An entertainer at the top of his game,' he says of Cook's spoof interviews with Clive Anderson. 'One of the best things he ever did,' he says of his Radio 3 programmes with Chris Morris. 'The gags are as good as ever,' he says of his LBC phone-ins as the lonely Norwegian Sven. But the truth is that he wasn't nearly as funny as he had once been: his scripts, once so tight and forceful, became long-winded and faltering, and where once he had been able to entirely inhabit his characters, he now approached them with an unprecedented diffidence, hesitant and unsure of himself, as though slightly embarrassed by it all.

I suspect Peter knew he lacked the demonic comic drive of his youth. 'I may have done some other things as good but I am sure none better,' he wrote of his early success in *Beyond the Fringe*. 'I haven't matured, progressed, grown, become deeper, wiser, or funnier. But then I never thought I would.' And in a way this was the bleak moral underlying his comic world view: that the longer we live, the less we know, and the more we strive, the dafter we grow.

Going Too Far:
The Jokes of Auberon Waugh

Auberon Waugh's opinions were not everybody's cup of tea. He liked what others disliked. 'I have never understood why horsemeat is not eaten in Britain,' he wrote. 'It is just as good as beef and rather healthier.' And he disliked what others liked: 'We are at least doing our bit to clear the world of these tropical rainforests,' he enthused.

Even his keenest readers would find themselves falling at the hurdle of at least one of his opinions. It is hard to imagine anyone who shared his dislike for Proust ('pages and pages and pages of self-indulgent drivel') also sharing his love of opium ('one had the feeling of being very drunk except that one's brain was remarkably clear and one felt an overwhelming benignity towards the entire human race').

He disapproved of old people, particularly on trains. 'In every compartment they can be seen flashing their false teeth from behind their Senior Citizen's Railcard, exerting their special brand of dumb appeal to make one carry their suitcases and budgerigar cages for hundreds of yards to where their sullen relatives are waiting to collect them.' But, then again, he distrusted youngsters too. One of the pieces in this collection* is titled 'Why Young People Wish to Murder Us'.

Even if you happened to share his love of horsemeat and opium and his dislike of rainforests, Proust, old people and young people, you might still feel a soft spot for birds, and in particular the dawn chorus, which he found hugely irritating, decrying it as 'the hideous cacophony of these warbling cretins' and stating that 'six or seven hundred of

---

* *Kiss Me, Chudleigh: The World According to Auberon Waugh* edited by William Cook (2010).

them, yelling and shrieking their silly heads off at five o'clock in the morning, are more than anyone can be expected to endure'. Personally, I love the dawn chorus, and, deep down, find myself disagreeing with at least half of his other opinions too. Yes, he goes too far, but so what? Auberon Waugh is always brilliantly and hilariously funny. Only those who are too cowardly or conceited to have their ideas of the world challenged by jokes – in short, only those without a sense of humour – could fail to see that this was the whole point of him.

As he lay dying, Auberon Waugh was asked about the purpose of his life. 'Well, I suppose I have made a few intelligent people laugh,' he replied. It was a neat summary of his entire mission as a writer. If he entertained opinions, it was only for the sake of the jokes that accompanied them. Most of his opinions were really just excuses for jokes about the absurdity of having opinions.

He saw comedy as something sublime, as the be-all and end-all. This meant he was able, quite literally, to laugh in the face of death. As a young man on National Service in Cyprus, he was examining a faulty machine gun, 'and having nothing else to do, resolved to investigate it. Seizing hold of the end with quiet efficiency, I was wiggling it up and down when I noticed it had started firing. Six bullets later I was alarmed to observe that it was firing through my chest, and got out of the way pretty sharpish … My first reaction to shooting myself in this way was not one of sorrow or despair so much as mild exhilaration … The incident deprived me of a lung and a spleen, several ribs and a finger but nothing else.'

It is those little asides – 'with quiet efficiency', 'pretty sharpish', 'but nothing else' – that transform horror into laughter and send self-pity packing. When Waugh thought he was dying, he said to a tough corporal called Chudleigh, 'Kiss me, Chudleigh', a humorous echo of Nelson's last words, 'Kiss me, Hardy'. But, as luck would have it, 'Chudleigh did not spot the historical reference, and treated me with caution thereafter.' This selfless pursuit of comedy is the reason Waugh esteemed P. G. Wodehouse above all other writers, praising him as 'the supreme exponent of the English attitude that whatever others hold seriously should immediately be seen as ridiculous to the civilised man'.

In one of his most heartfelt pieces, reviewing the grudging obituaries of his late father, Evelyn Waugh, he derided those who thought his father too snobbish or too Catholic, saying that 'the main point about my father ... is simply that he was the funniest man of his generation. He scarcely opened his mouth but to say something extremely funny, his house and life revolved around jokes. Wit is something indefinable and absolute. Can one ever hope to explain this to the mean and humourless prairie dogs who prowl around our literary desert? Is it even worth the effort?'

However cynical Waugh may sometimes have seemed, he was never, ever a killjoy. In fact, he reserves his most vituperative flourishes for those who want to stop other people enjoying themselves, such as the anti-smoking and -drinking lobbies, and most, perhaps all, politicians. 'The urge to power is a personality disorder in its own right, like the urge to sexual congress with children or the taste for rubber underwear,' he writes.

He has a horror of the self-righteous, and prevents his own opinions from ever sinking into self-righteousness by stretching them as far as they can possibly go, so that they become their own caricatures. One of the funniest pieces in the book is about the serial killer Dennis Nilsen, who happened to be a branch organiser of the Civil Service Union. With characteristic diablerie, Waugh offers Nilsen as 'a paradigm for the relationship between personal inadequacies, left-wing views and bureaucratic sadism'. He adds: 'Nilsen kept his corpses under the floorboards, retrieving them from time to time to sit them in an armchair and harangue them with his boring left-wing opinions, his grudges and grievances and the catalogue of his self-pity. Then, when the natural processes of decomposition made the corpses unacceptable company, even by his own undemanding standards, he boiled their heads, put them down the lavatory and started looking around for a new companion.' The phrase in this passage which made me laugh out loud was 'even by his own undemanding standards': magically, it turns horror into hilarity.

Waugh wrote in a comic persona based on a playful version of himself. It was the distorting lens through which he viewed the world.

He liked to tease himself as much as his readers. Attacking him for being 'effete, snobbish, sneering, racist and sexist' as the dreary *Guardian* columnist Polly Toynbee did is as daft as attacking Richmal Crompton, creator of the *Just William* stories, for lacking responsibility, or, if you will, Henrik Ibsen for looking on the dark side of life. Yet for all his comical exaggeration, Waugh managed to hit more nails on the head than any more ponderously 'serious' – i.e. humourless – commentator. He had an extraordinary instinct for humbug, and for the fallibility of received opinion.

'I stake my journalistic reputation as a leading British cynic on my conclusion that they are fake,' he said of the *Hitler Diaries*, the minute he heard of their existence. He also predicted the death of Princess Diana, the rise of mad cow disease, the unmasking of Jeremy Thorpe and the downward spiral of television. 'Today it is full of comedians with incomprehensible accents imitating other comedians I have never heard of,' he observed thirty-five years ago. He was the funniest prophet who ever set pen to paper; the world is a grimmer, less intelligible place without him.

Sigmund and Les in Blackpool

Jonathan Routh once painted a lovely series of pictures showing the sweet little figure of Queen Victoria, in solemn funeral weeds, enjoying a solo holiday in Jamaica. In successive paintings she is seen surfing, enjoying a beachside barbecue, tightrope-walking with an umbrella across a waterfall, and so on.

A new exhibition in London features a similarly incongruous coupling of tourist with holiday destination: Sigmund Freud in Blackpool. But while Queen Victoria's Jamaican jaunt was a figment of Routh's imagination, Dr Freud really did holiday in Blackpool. Furthermore, he liked it so much that he went back. 'I enjoy it much better here than anywhere else,' he wrote to his family from nearby Lytham St Anne's on 5 September 1908. 'Yesterday we spent almost the whole day apart from meals at Lytham and Blackpool … there is more pleasure in human contact here than elsewhere.'

For some reason, we have come to regard Queen Victoria and Sigmund Freud as the two great killjoys of recent centuries. It is almost as though we yearned for their disapproval. Yet in reality both were quite capable of getting the giggles. Queen Victoria's grandson William remembered his grandmother talking about the sinking of the *Eurydice* with the elderly Admiral Foley, who was hard of hearing. Struggling to change the subject to something more cheerful, Queen Victoria asked after Admiral Foley's sister. Still pursuing his train of thought over the *Eurydice*, the admiral replied, 'Ma'am, I am going to have her turned over and take a good look at her bottom and have it well scraped.' A horrified silence fell upon the room, but the effect on Queen Victoria was instantaneous: 'My grandmother put down her knife and fork, hid her face in her handkerchief and shook and heaved with laughter till the tears rolled down her face.'

In fact, Victoria always had a strong leaning towards *Carry On* humour: she howled with laughter when she heard of a poster outside the Duke's Arms pub in Dunkeld advertising a coach called the Duchess of Atholl. 'The Duchess of Atholl leaves the Duke's Arms every morning at six o'clock,' it read.

Sigmund Freud was also full of fun. His students found him a natural raconteur who would often tell jokes, finding them comparable to dreams in their logical absurdity. When his friend Wilhelm Fliess complained that the examples he gave in *The Interpretation of Dreams* were too funny, Freud countered that 'all dreamers are intolerably witty, and they are so because they are under pressure: the straight path is barred to them'.

In his lectures to students, Freud would often tell jokes to illustrate his more serious points. For instance, when he was trying to teach aspirant psychiatrists about the need to retain self-control during sessions with patients, he told them a joke about an insurance agent on his deathbed.

This insurance agent is a fierce atheist, but his family call in the pastor in the hope that he can make his peace with God before he dies. They wait anxiously outside the door, and the talk between the atheist insurance agent and the pastor goes on for such a long time that they begin to take heart. 'At last the door of the sickroom opens,' Freud concluded. 'The unbeliever has not been converted – but the pastor goes away fully insured.' Boom! Boom! Small wonder, then, that Freud made two trips to Blackpool, the centre of the knockabout joke, first as a nineteen-year-old medical student in 1875, the year the aquarium and menagerie opened to the public, and again in 1908, by which time the Pleasure Beach and the Tower were up and running.

His older half-brothers had emigrated to England when Freud was four, and he was often tempted to follow their example. 'I would sooner live there than here, rain, fog, drunkenness and conservatism notwithstanding,' he wrote upon his return to Vienna.

Les Dawson (another naturally funny man who favoured a po-faced persona) moved to Lytham St Anne's soon after he became famous. 'It's so posh in Lytham St Anne's,' he used to say, 'that when we eat cod and chips we wear a yachting cap.' I like to think of Les Dawson walking the same streets as Sigmund Freud. The two men would have looked for much the same raw material in them. Freud once drew attention to the 'fantastically ugly nannies' he spotted in England. Might they have been sisters or cousins or aunts of Les Dawson's notorious mother-in-law? 'I took my mother-in-law to the Chamber of Horrors, and one of the attendants said, "Keep her moving, sir – we're stocktaking."' Illness, neurosis, egotism, inhibition and awkward relations are at the heart of the visions of both Dawson and Freud.

'I went to my doctor and asked for something for persistent wind. He gave me a kite,' Les Dawson once observed. Freud was particularly fond of a joke that demonstrated the selfishness of the ego. 'If one of us dies,' an apparently devoted husband says to his wife, 'then I shall move to Paris.'

Comedy and psychoanalysis both operate in the gap between words and intentions. Freud defined his life's purpose as 'solving great riddles,' and he was always very precise in his use of language. Many of his cases involve visions of the same thing transplanted from childhood into adulthood, but with any conscious link severed: they are, if you will, double entendres, by which I mean, in Freudian terms, when you say one thing and mean a mother.

It is perfectly easy to imagine Les Dawson on a couch in Vienna in 1920, recounting this traumatic memory to Dr Freud: 'The wife's mother said, "When you're dead, I'll dance on your grave." I said: "Good, I'm being buried at sea."' But which of the two men would have been the last to keep a straight face?

Ken Dodd – another Blackpool regular – once famously complained that Freud's trouble was that he never played the Glasgow Empire on a Saturday night, but his library in Knotty Ash was home to a substantial number of Freud's works. Nor would he have denied that one of Freud's best jokes was cracked before an audience far harsher than the Glasgow Empire's. Before the German authorities allowed Freud to emigrate in 1938, they insisted he sign a statement saying that he had not been ill-treated. Freud signed it, but then added, 'Ich kann die Gestapo jedermann auf das beste empfehlen' – 'I can most highly recommend the Gestapo to everyone.'

Put It Away:
The Peculiar Life of Kenneth Williams

One day in 1986, Kenneth Williams was being driven by a friend on a country excursion to see Peterborough Cathedral when he spotted a sign to St Neots and demanded to go there.

In the middle of St Neots he bought a local map, and navigated the car to a run-down house on an estate. He then took out a notebook and jotted down lots of details about the house – peeling paint on the windows, overgrown garden, filthy curtains, etc. Without offering any explanation, he then asked his friend to drive on.

A few days later, he offered his friend an explanation. The man who lived in the house at St Neots – a total stranger – had written Williams a loony letter, of the type regularly received by celebrities, telling him that the Lord would strike him down for his homosexuality.

Instead of ignoring it, Williams had plotted his revenge. After driving to his correspondent's house and jotting down all the details, he had written back to him saying, 'Your mind is as filthy as your house. The front door wants painting, the windows are filthy, the curtain in the right window is ripped – on receipt of this letter I hope you have the most terrible illness, with excruciating agony for days, and eventually die a terrible death.'

On receipt of the letter, his correspondent realised he had been visited by Williams. Clearly terrified, he sent Williams back a letter of abject apology. But Williams was not one to let bygones be bygones. 'I'm amazed you're not dead yet,' he wrote back. 'And I still hope you will roll around in deepest agony and be afflicted with the worst possible suppurating boils.'

The venom behind this bizarre incident will come as no surprise to anyone who has read Kenneth Williams's brilliant, anguished, self-loathing, vengeful diaries. His comically grotesque public persona concealed something much less comical but infinitely more grotesque. 'Two personalities seemed to live within him like guests in a boarding-house who only ever passed on the stairs,' writes his biographer, Christopher Stephens.

Angst is the hidden engine of British comedy. Peter Sellers, Spike Milligan, Tony Hancock, Benny Hill, Frankie Howerd, John Cleese: they have all transformed their private fears, phobias and compulsions into the more palatable stuff of comedy.

Few were more desolate than Kenneth Williams, and in none of them was the distance between the public and the private so vast and unbridgeable. At home – a tiny flat with a single bed, its few cupboards filled only with pills – he lived like a neurotic monk. He hated being touched, was revolted by the idea of sex, and was so fastidious that he refused to let guests use his loo, instead directing them along the road to the gents at Baker Street Underground.

But whenever he entered the spotlight something would come over him. His face and voice would go wild and he would be transformed, as if by a caricaturist's pen, into a whirling dervish of lewd comedy, propelled by the force of his own self-loathing. On the *Carry On* sets he was an inveterate flasher. 'O! Kenny! Not that again! – put it away!' his fellow cast members would shriek as he lifted his toga on the set of *Carry On Cleo*. In a typically sharp observation, Russell Davies, the editor of his *Diaries* and *Letters*, writes: 'There is a paradox in the way he set about dismantling the whole idea of "English reserve" – affronting marchionesses and polluting restaurants with egotistical noise – while replacing it privately with something even more stultifying.'

At sedate dinner parties, he would be overcome by the vulgarity he privately deplored. 'He would change characters in the middle of a sentence,' recalled Derek Nimmo. 'He might start as one character and finish up as some total anarchic figure at the end of the sentence. It was very strange.'

There is an episode of *Just a Minute* from 1979 which kicks off with Nicholas Parsons asking Kenneth Williams to speak on the subject of 'My Other Self'.

'Kenneth, can you tell us about My Other Self in sixty seconds starting from now.'

'It is the side of me few people ever see,' begins Williams. 'I closely guard this private person because all of us do cherish some secret feeling which we feel if it were to be betrayed –'

At this point Barry Took presses his buzzer, on the grounds of deviation. 'I thought he was going on alarmingly. I mean, there was "feel" and "feeling". He was getting all emotional about himself.'

Parsons disallows the objection, and tells Kenneth Williams to continue.

'It was Emerson, I believe, who said we have as many personalities as we have friends. Mine consequently are varied and extraordinary. Many times, people say, "Well, we saw a side of you we didn't know existed! How WON-derful it was to have the curtain or the veil, as it were, lifted on your Pro-CLIV-ities!" [*audience laughter*]. We do like to see this sort of thing. And of course it is true that when we do see something which we didn't –'

Now it is Peter Cook who presses the buzzer. 'There's a constant stream of we-we's,' he says, to much laughter from the audience. And so Kenneth Williams's fifty-one seconds of self-revelation are brought to an end.

It's the fate of most TV and radio personalities to disappear into the ether. Even though we may have spent years of our lives in their company, once they are dead we struggle to remember who they were. But, thirty-four years after his sudden death in 1988, Kenneth Williams remains a vivid character, like something out of a fairy tale, with his richly enunciated and fabulously extended vowels, his monstrously flared nostrils and his contrary combination of the prim and the lewd, with nothing in between. However gregarious he is, however much the entertainer, he always remains a solitary presence, and strangely menacing. Rarely has comedy been so clearly fuelled by neurosis.

Kenneth Williams was born in a slum area off the Caledonian Road, just north of King's Cross, in 1926. His father, Charlie, was a God-fearing hairdresser who possessed a particular hatred of homosexuals. Kenneth remembered a man once coming into his father's barber shop in Marchmont Street and asking for a blow wave. 'You'll get no blow waves from me!' he thundered. Charlie Williams then accused his would-be customer of being a queer, and kicked him out of the shop.

Charlie – described by Kenneth's sister Pat as 'a real old-fashioned Victorian bully' – paired his hatred of homosexuals with a hatred of actors. Years later, Kenneth imitated his cockney rants on the Russell Harty chat show. 'I've had them in the shop with their la-di-da voices … they haven't got two ha'pennies to rub together.'

Within a few years, Kenneth Williams was to be famous as the possessor of the most la-di-da voice in the land. 'The impeccable diction, nasal resonance, flared nostril, upturned chin and the whinnying laugh like a horse played slow' was how the playwright Peter Nichols described his gargoyle persona. He had become just the sort of person his father would have refused to serve.

It was never going to be easy between the two of them, particularly once the nine-year-old Kenneth had taken to the boards as Princess Angelica in his school production of *The Rose and the Ring*. His father may have disapproved ('the stage is for nancies'), but the critic from the *St Pancras Gazette* had nothing but praise. 'Kenneth Williams with his mincing step and comical demeanour, as Princess Angelica, was a firm favourite with the audience, to whom his snobbishness and pert vivacity made great appeal.'

During the war, the teenage Kenneth was evacuated to Bicester, where he was put up by a retired vet in a large, glamorous house, complete with four-poster beds and an enormous library. It was, he recalled, 'a magical abode': he liked to copy the posh vowels of his host, who would recite poems by Byron and Shelley, and to sing old ballads in a very loud voice.

Kenneth returned to London with a new voice and a refreshed spirit of rebellion. 'My father was a cockney: he didn't talk like me at all. He hated my kind of talking. He said, "What d'you go round with a plum in your mouth for? Putting it on, giving yourself airs."' His sister remembered Kenneth's uncompromising approach. 'Ken used to look at our father with utter contempt.'

The civil war that he conducted with himself was, it seems, the internalisation of the war he had earlier conducted with his bullying father. 'My father and I didn't get on,' he once said. 'He liked to go to the pub for a pint of bitter. When I asked for a sweet sherry, he would be shocked. He would say, "You namby-pamby sod."'

His half-sister Pat remembered Kenneth showing merciless resolution against his father. 'Dad would say, "I wanna know how you're gettin' on at school, mate." "I fail to see why you're interested in me. I'm not in the least interested in you."'

His father once gave the young Kenneth a pair of boxing gloves for Christmas. 'What am I meant to do with these?' 'Put 'em on yer bleedin' fists and have a fight!' 'No, thank you.' The boy dropped them on his father's lap and walked out of the room. 'And the old man would go mad,' recalled Pat.

It would be hard to underestimate the courage that it took Kenneth

Williams to be himself, or the damage it caused him. Later in their lives, the boot would be on the other foot. The comic actress Betty Marsden remembered Kenneth coming into the *Round the Horne* studio on a Boxing Day, steaming with fury at his father's behaviour the day before. Kenneth – now a big comedy star – had given his father a beautiful sheepskin coat for Christmas. 'I don't want that!' his father had responded. 'That's a poof's coat, that is! That's a poof's coat. Give it to a poof!'

Charlie Williams committed suicide in 1962, downing a bottle of a poison called Thawpit from a cough mixture bottle. 'Show went OK. Audience good,' reads the entry in Kenneth's diary for that day. At the end of the year, he concluded, 'It was a good year really. Charlie's death released Louie from that rat trap of a marriage, and now she's happy.'

Up to the time of Kenneth's death – he predeceased her – his beloved mother, Louie, would always sit somewhere in the front two rows for his appearances on chat shows, quiz programmes and comedy shows. 'All his most salacious lines would be directed straight at his mother,' recalled Hugh Paddick, who played Julian to Kenneth Williams's equally outrageous Sandy on *Round the Horne*. 'She just lapped it up.' She would howl with laughter at every fresh shock, so he would try to shock her more.

In his entry for 5 July 1967, Joe Orton goes to Kenneth Williams's flat. Louie arrives a little later and has a sherry. 'She said she'd had a letter from Kenneth's sister. "She's touring," Mrs Williams said. "Getting all those big Greek sailors," Kenneth said. Mrs Williams gave a squawk. "I bet you wish you were there, don't you, Lou?" Kenneth said to his mother. "No, I don't!" Mrs Williams said. "She'll be getting the dick,"' Kenneth said. Even Orton was taken aback by the lewdness of their dialogue. 'I was a little surprised', he writes, 'to hear someone talk so freely in front of their mother.'

'Sexually, he really is a horrible mess,' observed Orton in his diary after being in Kenneth's company. 'He mentions "guilt" a lot in conversation. His only outlet is exhibiting his extremely funny personality in front of an audience and when he isn't doing this he's a very sad man indeed.'

At one radio recording, on 23 November 1958, the scriptwriter Alan Simpson thought to himself that Williams was the happiest man he'd ever seen, both adored by the audience, and the life and soul of the party after the show. But when Williams's diaries were published thirty-five years later, they contained a quite different impression. 'Did the Hancock show from the Piccadilly. It was a general disaster. Really terrible. The team is so dreary to me now ... this crowd are so listless and disinterested and their conversation is real pleb stuff. I don't care for any of them at all.'

Simpson read this entry with amazement. 'I've never been so astounded in my life.' This was Kenneth's Other Self, the self so briefly alluded to in that *Just a Minute* speech, 'the side of me few people ever see'. When the diaries were published, a few years after his death, Williams's friends were shocked at the depth of his contempt for them. Simpson's writing partner, Ray Galton said: 'It came as a complete revelation. I didn't know he was like that.' They both remembered him as wonderful company, laughing at all Sid James's stories. The diaries revealed that he would go home and record what a boring man Sid James was, and what an awful actor.

His view of himself was just as tart, often more so. On the photographs of redundant passports he would write caustic comments about his own appearance: 1955 ('V. Nasty'); 1965 ('I must look as I usually look and that is NOT smiling'); 1975 ('the lips are thin and pursed the ungenerous nature showing thro' them').

When he was sixteen, he was given a *Collins Emerald Diary* for Christmas. Over his lifetime he was to write over four million words in his diaries, making them nearly seven times the length of *War and Peace*. He had studied lithography at college, and had been apprenticed to Stanford's, the map emporium, so his handwriting in these diaries can be beautiful, but it is peculiar in its range and diversity: sometimes, he switches to and fro between half a dozen different scripts – now calligraphic copperplate, now spiky italic, now cursive, now florid, now neat, now condensed and joined up, now slack and separate. Bizarrely, these styles don't seem to reflect his mood or the subject matter. But what he wrote could be extremely revealing. In his notes for an autobiography he includes these thoughts on Tony Hancock – 'The idea of the comic as tragic figure – tragedy meaning man overstepping certain natural limits – a refusal to obey – to recognise a certain LIMIT and the awful consequences that proceed from it.'

The limits he placed upon himself – his refusal of intimacy, his puritanical disapproval of his own lewd comic talent – were so severe that they ended up creating the very tragedy they were designed to prevent. In some ways, he was not so much a comedian as a man trapped by comedy, like a bird in a cage.

He craved laughter but despised himself for craving it, often worrying that an audience were laughing at him rather than with him. And he was in two minds about fame, finding it at one and the same time alluring and revolting. One friend recalls walking with him in Regent's Park. He would make his voice louder and louder until eventually someone would recognise him, and then he would say, 'God, isn't it dreadful! One can't go anywhere!'

Onstage, he was ferocious in his need to steal other people's thunder, and would ruthlessly plot against any actor who was getting bigger laughs. At the age of nine, he had a hissy fit in his Princess Angelica role. 'After the dress rehearsal, I withdrew from the production because someone was rude to me,' he recalled, explaining, 'I knew I was an enormous asset and should be deferred to.'

Yet he was also claustrophobically fearful, once staying out of doors, shivering in the streets, rather than return to his block of flats, where the noise of the overhead fan in the bathrooms was driving him mad.

His diary entries tend to start with a list of his current ailments, plus the weather, room temperature, and the exact time of his last bowel movement. His terror of being alone was equalled only by his terror of having anyone sharing his life.

He was homosexual, but believed that 'homosexuality is a cul-de-sac and should be resisted'. He proposed marriage to both Barbara Windsor and Joan Sims, but only very half-heartedly. 'You don't have to worry, there won't be any hanky-panky, none of that saucy stuff,' he told Joan Sims. 'But Ken,' she replied, 'I rather like the saucy stuff.'

Watching his chat show appearances today, it is notable how often his confessions of loneliness and alienation are greeted with uproarious laughter. 'How is your love life?' asks Joan Rivers. 'I'm asexual,' he replies. 'I should regard any type of relationship as deeply intrusive. Privacy is the most important thing in my life. Everything which invaded it would be a threat … so consequently I live a life of celibacy. I'm not interested in the other.' These might be words from the casebook of a patient suffering from clinical depression, but the audience hoots with laughter, and so does Joan Rivers.

His delivery was at odds with his message. Whatever he said, people would howl with laughter, regardless of its content. One scriptwriter on *Beyond Our Ken* remembered feeling peeved when Kenneth Horne gave an interview saying that the cast were so brilliant that they could make a telephone directory sound funny.

'Now, I did take a bit of umbrage at this, because there I was, turning out a pretty good script every week, so I thought, Right, I'll get my own back.' The next week he wanted to make his point, so he told the producer to hand out telephone directories to the cast. 'There was a bit of a stunned silence and then Williams picked up one of the books and went, "The Pneumatic Drill and Tyre Company …" and made it hysterically funny.'

There was something innately comical about Kenneth Williams; perhaps this was his tragedy. The last words in his diary are: 'Oh, what's the bloody point?' If he had spoken them to an audience, no doubt they would have howled with laughter. Soon afterwards, he took an overdose, had a heart attack, and died.

Born Brilliant: The Life of Kenneth Williams by Christopher Stephens (2010); *Kenneth Williams Unseen: The Private Notes, Scripts and Photographs* by Wes Butters and Russell Davies (2008); *Kenneth Williams's Handwriting* by Nicolas Barker (2013); *The Kenneth Williams Diaries*, edited by Russell Davies (1993); *The Kenneth Williams Letters*, edited by Russell Davies (1994).

THE GREAT AND
THE GOOD

Chips with Everything

1

Most of the grander twentieth-century diarists had a sniffy air about them, looking down their noses at everyone, particularly each other. Henry 'Chips' Channon, so snippety in his own diaries, was sniped at in others'. James Lees-Milne thought him 'a flibbertigibbet'; to Nancy Mitford he was 'vain and spiteful and silly'. Kenneth Rose confided to his diary that Channon was 'a rather stupid man'. When the bowdlerised Channon diaries were first published in 1967, edited by Robert Rhodes James, Rose could not disguise his thrill at how badly they had gone down in his own smart set. At a 'luncheon party given by Raine Dartmouth at her pretty house in Hill Street … we talk a great deal about the Chips Channon diaries, and all agree how ghastly they are'. The next day, Rose chats to Channon's old boss, Rab Butler: 'He says he is disgusted by the Chips Channon diaries.' Two years later, Rose is still at it: 'Lord David Cecil, I hear, very much objected to Chips Channon's diaries, calling him a "traitorous bugger".'

Rose and the other diarists are no longer with us, which means they are spared the need to read this big, fat, spankingly unexpurgated volume.* In his introduction, Simon Heffer explains that many of Channon's victims were still going strong in 1967, so might have sued the publishers for libel, among them 'that scheming woman' Diana Boothby, who 'smells so strongly that I once nearly fainted when sitting next to her'. Channon's partner and executor, Peter Coats, expunged

---

* *Henry 'Chips' Channon: The Diaries 1918–38* edited by Simon Heffer (2021).

'page after page', including Channon's pre-war admiration for the Nazis, his dislike of Churchill, and his multifarious sexual exploits.

Channon's former wife, Lady Honor, also made merry with the blue pencil, striking out uncharitable references to herself and to the Queen Mother ('at heart snobbish and insincere') and King George VI ('he is completely uninteresting, undistinguished and a godawful bore!'). She also safeguarded their son Paul's political career by removing Channon's many snooty remarks ('I despise them really, and their silly standards') about the people of Southend, which, since 1918, had been the hand-me-down parliamentary constituency of her father, her mother, her husband and now her son.

Upwards of two million words were thus whittled down to 250,000. It says something for the resilience of Channon's indiscretion that, even after such a fierce whittling, so many readers were delighted and/ or offended. Now that everyone involved is safely dead and buried, Heffer has been charged with unwhittling them. He has done his job with scholarly aplomb, providing footnotes galore. This volume runs to 1,000 pages, and there are another two to come.

In his introduction, Heffer declares that Channon 'never minces his words'. Yet, in a funny way, the words mince by themselves, occasionally executing Firbankian pirouettes: 'The Queen of Romania looked ridiculous in a green sea-foam crêpe-de-chine saut-de-lit spotted with goldfish she had painted on herself. Her double chins were kept in place by strands of pearls attached to an exotic headdress.'

Even in its dull moments, of which there are quite a few, generally involving interminable lists of forgotten bigwigs attending showy parties, it remains a work of high camp. Might Alan 'Chatty Man' Carr be prevailed upon to narrate the audiobook?

It kicks off in Paris on New Year's Day 1918 (the original edition didn't start until 1934). 'To be forever 20 in Paris in the springtime ... what could be more divine?' asks Chips. At this point, Sergeant Heffer chimes in with a disobliging footnote: 'Channon had the habit of lying even to himself about his age.' Chips was in fact already twenty-one.

He is consumed by a crush on a young man called Bobbie Pratt Barlow. They plan to live together in London later 'and weave other impossible dreams that will never come true'. Bobbie goes off to the war. Chips reports that in his first letter from the trenches, Barlow says 'he thinks only of me when he is going into battle, which is nice of him'. In one of many thousands of crisp, helpful footnotes, Heffer notes that Barlow, who lived until 1959, 'later attracted notoriety for owning a Sicilian mansion … staffed entirely by prepubescent boys'.

Chips motors to the front in a Rolls-Royce, just to take a quick peek. While there, he enjoys a game of fireside bridge with General Blackader: 'We were so snug, it might have been a London club.' Back in Paris, his schedule remains hectic: 'Even with a sore throat, I pull myself to luncheon with the Princesse d'Arenberg and to dine at the Duchesse de Brissac's.'

Throughout his life he had the knack – invaluable for a diarist with dreams of publication – of bumping into all the right people. Edith Wharton, Mrs Patrick Campbell, Evelyn Waugh, Elinor Glyn, John Buchan, Aldous Huxley, Emerald Cunard, Noël Coward, Earl Haig, Salvador Dalí, Somerset Maugham, Henri Bergson and the naked Tallulah Bankhead all pop up in these pages. The young Elizabeth Bowes-Lyon is 'more gentle, lovely and exquisite than any woman alive … I mustn't fall in love with her'.

Often, entries read like a drunken round of Consequences. During one air raid on Paris, Chips shares a cellar with Winston Churchill, Elsie de Wolfe, the Duchess of Sutherland and Prince Luis of Spain, who is wearing mauve silk pyjamas. Staying at Hackwood for Ascot, he plays Sardines: 'For an hour Ld Londonderry, Lady Curzon, Biddy Carlisle, Jean Norton and the Aga Khan lay under a very hot bed.' At a dinner in November 1918, he is placed between Jean Cocteau and Marcel Proust ('his bloodshot eyes shine feverishly'). Eight years later, he refers again to Proust, 'whom I knew more intimately than I have confided in this diary'.

There are strong hints of sexual encounters throughout, sometimes with female prostitutes ('I wreaked my lust on her, undisturbed by her Northumbrian accent'), but more often with male contemporaries. He talks of going on a 'long honeymoon' with Viscount Gage, and the two of them enjoying 'deep long quaffs of intimacy'. Occasionally he ends up in bed with a society lady, but his enjoyment seems limited: 'Lunched with Mary Baker and tried unsuccessfully to ravish her. I couldn't get it in. How very ugly are the sexual parts of a woman.' He drops in on Montague Summers in Richmond and willingly follows him upstairs: '"You must let down your trousers." I undid them and let them slip down to my feet. The old priest, who is of course one of the most charming and learned men in the world, removed one of his slippers (red heel and a large buckle) and smartly struck me on my naked buttocks.' It's all a far cry from the diaries of Harold Macmillan.

Born in Chicago, Chips came to hate his parents, not least because they were so unashamedly American. 'I loathe – loathe – loathe them and despise their so-called civilisation.' He condemned his 'dreary' father as thoughtless, particularly where money was concerned: 'He never refuses if I ask him for it. I wish he would think of it on his own sometimes.' His father had made his money in banking and shipping. Other than fiddling about with a novel, Chips himself didn't do a day's work until 1935, when, aged thirty-eight, he was first elected to Parliament.

It proved an eventful year. His wife, a Guinness, helped buy them a house ('not too grand') in Belgrave Square. Chips decorated it in a style pitched somewhere between Liberace and Donald Trump. Around this time, Emerald Cunard introduced him to Wallis Simpson, whom he initially described 'a nice, quiet mouse of a woman, with large startled eyes and a huge, huge mole'.

Channon has long been celebrated as the beady chronicler of the courtship of Edward and Mrs Simpson. As he manoeuvres his way into their circle, he grows increasingly devoted to Mrs S, 'a woman of infinite charm, gentleness, courage and loyalty'. He even has a dream about her in paradise, the Archangel Gabriel at her side. 'You see, Chips,' she explains, 'if I couldn't be Queen of England, I've got to be the next best thing, for I'm Queen of Heaven.'

In this new volume there is plenty of fascinating stuff about those two odd-bods which was absent from the first edition. I particularly liked the tale of Walter Moyne being 'driven dotty' by Edward holiday-ing on his yacht for three weeks in 1934: 'The Prince sat up until 3 a.m.

He would then play the bagpipes on deck, with the result that not even the crew could get a wink of sleep – and he would sleep all morning.'

Channon has a voracious eye for detail. Over dinner at Belgrave Square, the new king suddenly leaps to his feet, announcing: 'I want to pump shit.' Just imagine the huffing and puffing if one of today's screenwriters were to put those words in his mouth.* Chips delights in being privy to such royal intimacies: 'I led His Majesty to our loulou! He then proceeded to pass water without shutting the door, talking to me the while.' When the word 'loulou' appears, the ever-assiduous Heffer pipes up: 'Channon's term for lavatory'. He is, incidentally, a wonderfully diligent editor. As a monoglot, I particularly appreciate the way he has rendered all Chips's fancy foreign phrases into English, no matter what. So when Chips writes, 'I feel *congestionné*', a handy footnote explains: 'Congested.' Every now and then, Chips turns his unforgiving eye on himself, writing in 1935:

> sometimes I think I have the character of a very clever woman – able, but trivial with flair, intuition, great good taste and second-rate ambition. I am susceptible to flattery, and male good looks; I hate and am uninterested in all the things men like, such as sport, business, statistics, debates, speeches, war and the weather; but I am riveted by lust, *bibelots*, furniture and glamour, society and jewels.

Not a natural fit, then, for an Essex constituency. But his constituents – 'those frumps and snobs' – were not the only people Chips considered common. All socialists were common, as were Mary Pickford, Ernest Simpson and Grace Curzon. Sir Hugh Walpole was 'extremely

---

* Soon after the *Spectator* published this piece, the editor received a letter from Libby Purves pointing out that 'since the subsequent royal event, shared by the keen diarist through an open door, consisted only of passing water, we must surmise that either Chips or his editor were ignorant of the urinary expression "pump ship". It is still common among naval and yachting types.' Simon Heffer confessed that he hadn't heard the phrase, 'but apparently neither had Chips, because he wrote "pump shit" in the MS'. He promised to include a clarificatory footnote in any subsequent reprints.

common'. H. G. Wells was also common: 'As Emerald said, he betrays his servant origin. His mother was a most excellent lady's maid and H. G. began life in the housekeeper's room.' Marking the death of J. M. Barrie, Channon notes that he was 'hopelessly undistinguished. These common little litterateurs are all alike when they reach a certain eminence; they bask in aristocratic surroundings.'

The lucky few who are excused his snobbish strictures included all the top Nazis, among them the 'amiable' Adolf Hitler: 'One felt one was in the presence of some semi-divine creature: I was more thrilled than when I met Mussolini.' At a Berlin party thrown by Ribbentrop in 1936, Chips is impressed by how the 'famous, fantastic' Göring's 'merry eyes twinkled. He seems a lovably disarming man.' Giddy from the social whirl at the Berlin Olympics, Chips can't decide whose party was the most enjoyable. Goebbels's dinner dance for 2,000, with fire-works, was 'in a way the most impressive', but then again 'it lacked the elegance and chic of Ribbentrop's and the extravagance and good taste of Göring's'.

Heffer loyally insists that Channon was 'not a fascist' but rather 'a devout anti-communist'. This is pushing it. In 1934, after a VIP tour of a dolled-up German labour camp, Channon concludes: 'The camps looked tidy, even gay, and the boys, all about 18, looked like the ordi-nary German peasant boy, fair, healthy and sunburned ... England could learn many a lesson from Nazi Germany. I cannot understand the English dislike and suspicion of the Nazi regime.'

As late as February 1938, he writes: 'I am always surprised when people here cannot understand the vigorous new civilisation of the Nazis.' In May, he complains: 'We produce nothing new, whereas Germany and Italy are seething with vigour and life; we have only choruses of cranks! Democracy is absurd.' In September, he hails Hitler as 'always right, always the greatest diplomat of modern times'.

In May 1955, Rose recalled in his diary that Channon had once complained to James Stuart, the Chief Whip: 'Why are you always so rude to me? I never miss a division or cause trouble.' To which Stuart replied: 'My dislike of you is purely personal.' Though Heffer asserts that Channon was both 'intensely loyal' and 'immensely civilised', the character that emerges from these diaries is, by turns, nosy, touchy, needy ('the PM called me "Chips"'), conceited, snobbish, disloyal, wrong-headed ('so like God himself', he writes of Mussolini), voyeuristic, sycophantic and shifty – all of them qualities most helpful to a great diarist.

2

Chips must rate as one of the most incongruous nicknames ever. Henry 'Chips' Channon probably never ate a chip in his life, unless he forced one down while winning over the voters of Southend, the constituency for which he served as Conservative MP from 1935 until his death in 1958. 'Simple food always gives one indigestion' is one of the *bons mots* in this, the second volume of his diaries.* Others include: 'Royalty is a heady wine' and 'Are all women mad? I suspect so.'

---

* *Henry 'Chips' Channon: The Diaries 1938–43* edited by Simon Heffer (2021).

Even as London is being bombed, he swans around town, shopping for bejewelled cufflinks, tucking into rich meals at the Savoy or Claridge's, throwing dinner parties for twenty-four at his home in Belgravia, or relaxing in a Turkish bath. A phrase that regularly pops up in the diaries is 'Had my bottom cleansed today', or words to that effect.

A convinced appeaser, as late as May 1939, we find him saying that 'all my sympathies' are with Hitler, and that the press has been unfair to the poor man. 'It is hopeless in England: give a dog a bad name and he can never recover.' On 24 August 1939, he asserts that 'The whole House expects war: only I … do not.'

Just ten days later, on 3 September, war is declared. On that day, Channon notes that this is proof of the Foreign Office's 'long hatred' of the Germans, 'and Jewry the world over triumphs'. On 5 July 1940, he notes that 'people are beginning to say that Hitler will never attack this country'. By the end of August, the attacks had begun.

And so it goes on, his uncanny instinct for faulty prediction. 'If Hitler does attack Russia, it will be the cleverest act of his whole career,' he writes in June 1941. 'His position would then seem impregnable.' Simon Heffer sets him right. 'A serious misjudgement by Channon: it was the attack on Russia that lost Hitler the war.'

Channon hero-worships Neville Chamberlain – 'the greatest man of all time' – and detests 'fat, wicked old Winston', labelling him 'the man who has never been right'. When Churchill finally becomes Prime Minister, he bursts into tears, exasperated that 'England in her darkest hour had surrendered her destiny to the greatest opportunist and political adventurer alive.' His only hope is that 'Winston, with too much rope, is certain to crash one day.'

His abuse of Churchill – 'a bully, an irritating tyrant, unfair, unkind, wrong' – continues, come what may. 'Winston is losing the war if he has not lost it,' he writes in June 1942. 'He is the most dangerous man in England.'

Like many a marginalised backbencher, Channon was convinced of his own centrality, believing that, with a quiet word in the right ear, he could shape world events. Consequently, he devoted an inordinate amount of time to fruitless plotting. 'The really only startling thing about my intrigues is that they always come off,' he confided to his diary. But he was talking nonsense: the only thing his intrigues always came off was the rails. In November 1942, having just been sacked from his lowly job of Parliamentary Private Secretary to an Under-Secretary of State, he sets his sights on the House of Lords. 'I want to be a peer: there are many ways of becoming one. The quickest would be Leslie Hore-Belisha to become Prime Minister. To do that he would first have to be a Conservative – so I had a confidential chat with him.'

One of the remarkable aspects of this volume is how little the war impinges on his social life. Bombs may fall, even on his own house, but he never lets them get in the way of a good party. Sadly, most of the grandees with whom he mixes are now forgotten figures. It may be fun to hear that Queen Marie of Yugoslavia was 'wicked, obese, obscene, evil-speaking and smelling', but it would be a lot more fun if we knew who she was. Simon Heffer does his best to revive these obscure royals and aristocrats by applying lengthy defibrillating footnotes to them – 'Gilbert James Heathcote-Drummond-Willoughby … succeeded his father as 3rd Earl of Ancaster' and so forth – but they remain determinedly lifeless.

Chips Channon reached his peak as a social diarist in the first volume, when he was still a member of Edward and Mrs Simpson's circle. But by 1938 they were in exile, and he had lost touch with them. Without their presence, his diaries become an endless succession of the same old names and titles, few of any significance beyond their power to irritate. He drops hundreds of names, but only the most snobbish and/or elderly of readers will be bothered to catch any of them.

Though the original volume of his diaries was heavily abridged, with many of the juiciest bits removed, it was about the right length. In these extended volumes there are nuggets to be found, but they lie buried beneath a suffocating morass of social and political hobnobbery. It's all too much. In April 1939, he writes: 'the Under-Secretaryship has been given to Osbert Peake, a popular, but not very great appointment. I should have preferred Ralph Assheton or Victor Raikes.' To which the most honest response is 'Who? Who? Who?'

But Chips carries on, regardless. 'I lead London society, my house is the loveliest – indeed the last and only stronghold remaining of the aristocracy and *ancien regime* – in society I am unrivalled,' he boasts on page 893. But by now, with the world in peril, he has clearly become too silly and marginal a figure for anyone of any real stature to bother cultivating. Churchill cold-shoulders him, and he barely ever meets the King George V1 and Queen Elizabeth, who fail to include him among their 800 guests at a ball at Buckingham Palace. 'I shall not forget this slight,' he rages, adding that the Queen is not only 'fundamentally treacherous' but 'remarkably snobbish'.

In 1941, no longer even a PPS, he sets his sights on becoming Governor of Bermuda, but fails. As a consolation prize, his old boss, Rab Butler, suggests making him Deputy Lord Lieutenant of Essex, but that never happens either.

This volume includes frequent tussles with his rich and flighty wife Honor, who, after affairs with, among others, a Hungarian count and a ski instructor, sets her sights on divorcing him and marrying a horse dealer. 'I think she is a nymphomaniac … she has a horrible character,' grumbles Chips. He worries that the scandal of divorce will mean the end 'of a peerage, of my political aspirations, of vast wealth, and great names and position'. He entertains doubts, not only about Honor but about all women. 'They are untrustworthy, usually, too emotional, and not very pleasant or constructive characters. I shouldn't mind if I never saw one again.'

Small wonder, then, that he starts plotting his own future with a dashing young lover, Peter Coats, 'a pierrot of charm and Aryan good looks', to whom he writes up to seven letters a day. No doubt their romance will be continuing at length in Volume Three, which is to be published early next year, but, after 2,000 pages, I seem to have lost my appetite.

No *Countdown* on Saturday:
Tony Blair's Diary

MONDAY: The truth is, these days I'm more 'in demand' than ever! I'm, quite literally, rushed off my feet!

I grab breakfast at home, and quickly scan Twitter for reaction to my major keynote speech on the Need for Global Interdependence. I'm frankly relieved to see that President Trump hasn't tweeted about it! Nor, incidentally, have my good friends Emmanuel Macron or Angela Merkel, though that's possibly explained by the time difference.

Overall reaction has been very encouraging. 'Excellent speech by Tony Blair on Global Interdependence, worth reading if you have the time,' tweets Alastair Campbell, and I'm delighted to say this one's been retweeted by independent assessors at the Tony Blair Institute for Global Change. And *BBC Wales Today* have also retweeted it, which is great. I've said it before, but it's worth saying again: we ignore Wales at our peril.

Spent the rest of the day at the Institute sifting through requests for personal appearances at world forums. Demand remains high. A pro-Europe group on the Surrey/Sussex border want me to address them in early September. They say they can guarantee an audience of anything up to 100. Terrific that so many people want to hear what I have to say – not just the so-called 'metropolitan elite'!

TUESDAY: Shocked by recent events in Syria, I put an urgent call through to my old buddy President Barack Obama.

'Yo, Barack! Tony here! How's it going? Just keen to touch base over Syria!'

The response is immediate.

'This is the office of President Barack Obama. Please leave your name and the purpose of your call and we will get back to you as soon as possible.'

Busy guy, Barack! I only hope I haven't added to his workload through all those media organisations wishing to get his response to my latest interventions in the Middle East.

I make a note to self to keep the lines open: he's bound to ring back the moment he hears who's called.

WEDNESDAY: Find I have a few hours free between a solo working breakfast and perhaps grabbing a bite to eat in the evening, so I go and get a breath of fresh air in the park. You'll never guess who I see walking towards me but my old Cabinet colleagues Peter Mandelson, Harriet Harman and David Blunkett!

I know they're every bit as proud of our achievements in office as I am, so I was frankly thrilled at the opportunity for a bit of a 'get-together'! But they clearly hadn't seen me, because as I waved and quickened my step, both Peter and Harriet seemed to dart away. But at least I could give David a nice surprise!

'David! It's Tony!' I said, clapping him on the back.

David seemed genuinely delighted. 'Tony!' he said. 'I'm genuinely delighted …'

'Brilliant to catch up with you, David. So how's things?'

David turned his wrist towards him. 'My goodness!' he said. 'Is that the time? Anyway, it was great to have had this little catch-up, Tony! Regards to Cherie!'

Fortunately, as David and his faithful guide dog were striding away – almost running, if I'm being honest! – I spotted Peter and Harriet emerging from behind a tree, so I was pleased to be able to collar them for a catch-up! 'I don't know if you've managed to read my speech to the Kazakhstan Board of Commerce yet,' I said.

'Very much in my in-box,' said Peter, and Harriet agreed.

'Know what? It feels just like the old days in Cabinet!' I said. 'Actually, I was going to get in touch with the two of you about Brexit and its consequences …'

'You'll have to forgive me, Tony. The plumber's due later this afternoon. Or tomorrow. Must rush,' said Harriet.

'Oh yes,' said Peter. 'The plumber! That reminds me! My tap's dripping! See you!' Respected colleagues, dear friends. Together, we changed things, before things changed.

Memo to self. Dry-cleaning ready for collection Friday a.m.

Barack Obama has still not phoned back. Hope nothing is wrong.

THURSDAY: I'm on great terms with my police protection guys. I like to exchange friendly banter with them as I go in and out of the house.

'Looks like being a nice sunny day!' I said this morning.

'Time to get our umbrellas out,' said one to the other. I guess they misheard what I said!

Still not a peep from Barack, incidentally. I hope I didn't miss the phone ringing while I was watching *Countdown*.

FRIDAY: I collected the dry-cleaning successfully. The Asian gentleman behind the counter seemed fascinated by what I had to say about the very real threat to democratic accountability from an over-hasty Brexit, but sadly had to break off our conversation when his phone rang.

No word yet from Barack. Cherie emails to let me know we've just bought an office block in Exeter, a luxury gated development in Costa Rica and a terrace house in Middlesbrough, plus 10,000 acres of prime agricultural land in Southern Romania. Our aim is to make globalisation work for the many, not the few.

On Twitter, there has been a very positive response to yesterday's important tweet from the Tony Blair Institute on the need to reshape national and international priorities. Alastair Campbell has retweeted it and so has the influential former head of RBS, Fred Goodwin. The guys at the Institute tell me there's been one helluva lot of media interest too. Looks like a busy weekend ahead!

SATURDAY: The guys at the Institute are falling behind! I ask if there's been any word from Andrew Marr or *The World at One* or *Newsnight* and they say they're working on it.

There's no *Countdown* on Saturday, so I put a call through to the influential Beverley Turner programme on LBC radio.

'It's Tony from Marylebone. I've got something important to tell Beverley about Syria. And something else about the creation of a new centre party.'

'Putting you through to Beverley now, Tony. Hang on, is that Tony Blair, by any chance?'

'Right first time!'

'Sorry, Tony – we've had a lot of callers today, but do try calling again soon, and thanks again for trying!'

Memo to self: try Jeremy Vine on Monday. Or could it be something for *You and Yours*?

As I leave the house, I tell the guys from my protection squad it's going to be a chilly day. A minute later, I glance back and notice they've removed their jackets.

Still no call from Barack.

Buzz Is What She Does:
The Hectic Life of Tina Brown

The finest diarists are able to view themselves with the detachment they apply to others. They become, in this sense, their own sharpest biographers, dividing themselves into both observer and observed, audience and performer, hovering eagle-eyed above themselves, ever curious to record, however unfavourably, their own imperfect ways. As Claire Tomalin puts it in her biography of Samuel Pepys: 'In writing it down, he detached himself from the self who acted out the scene.'

In her diaries of her years at *Vanity Fair*,* Tina Brown is certainly adept at noting, with her unforgiving eye, the flaws in others. Revulsion brings out the best in her. The Hollywood agent Swifty Lazar is 'tiny and bald and hairy in the wrong places. From the back his bald head and ancient baby's neck look like crinkled foreskin.' Nancy Reagan's walker Jerry Zipkin possesses a face 'like a huge inflated rubber dinghy, balanced on top of a short, Humpty-Dumpty body'. A social columnist at the *New York Times* is 'a bogus grandee ... a coiffed asparagus'. Jackie Onassis's face is 'always slightly out of whack with her expression, as if they are two separate entities at work. She has perfected a fascinated stare.'

Brown also has an ear finely tuned to the absurdities of the rich, the spoilt and the famous. She records them with relish. 'You know what?' Donald Trump shouts to her over dinner at Ann Getty's in 1987. 'Went to the opening of the Met last night. *Ring Cycle*. Plácido Domingo. Five hours. Dinner started at twelve. Beat that. I said to Ivana, what, are you

---

* *The Vanity Fair Diaries 1983–1992* by Tina Brown (2017).

crazy? Never again.' Minutes later, an unnamed Italian art dealer shares his misgivings about the American way of life:

> You know … it is easy in America to take a very tiny sum like five hundred thousand dollars and turn it into three hundred million! So easy! But you know what? I don't want to. Because eet means raping those poor fuckers the American public even more than they are already. You know what ees the difference between the European peasant and the American peasant? The American peasant eats sheet, wears sheet, watches sheet on TV, looks out of his window at sheet! How can we go on raping them and giving them more sheet to buy!

In moments like these, Tina Brown is the social diarist par excellence, skewering the pampered society grotesques of her time with a gleeful and merciless zest. 'To be a good diarist one must have a snouty, sneaky mind,' wrote Harold Nicolson in his 1947 diary, and Brown is clearly in possession of Nicolson's prerequisite. She snuffles around like a prize truffle hog, unearthing all the whiffiest gobbets of conversation. Her pocket-sized sketches have the cruel precision of caricatures by Gillray or Rowlandson and the comic verve of Edith Wharton. 'We had lunch with the preposterous Princess Michael of Kent,' she observes at one point,

> who looked about fifteen hands high in an orange silk wrap dress. She has developed a mad, false laugh and a new Lady Bracknell voice for dealing with inferiors. 'Row-eena,' she gushed at the cowed debutante she totes around as her 'lady-in-waiting', 'where is the Dom Perignon? It was sitting outside but those fooools have taken it away! Find it! [Mad false laugh.] Isn't the service quite diabolical? Do shut the kitchen door, Rowena. I hate to stare into a kitchen!'

Brown chronicles a world of fashion designers and film stars, perfumiers and politicians, each category barely distinguishable from the others. She particularly thrives on the fury caused by injured vanity: Oscar de la Renta is furious with Bob Colacello for suggesting that Geoffrey Beene's business is bigger than his. ('His business is not twenty times bigger than mine! Mine is twenty times bigger than his … When I see that cheap little nobody Bob Colacello he better get out of my path because I will knock him down.') The owner of Sotheby's is furious that 'the wife of a New York auction house chief' has been identified in *Vanity Fair* as a former Madame Claude girl. ('Are you aware how few auction house chiefs there are? … Do you think anyone thinks it's Mrs Alsop of Christie's?') Such contretemps suggest that little has changed since Dorothy Parker first observed, 'To see what God thinks of money, just look at all the people he gave it to.'

More often than not, though, Brown's jibes are too generalised, too hand-me-down, to draw blood. Take her anthropomorphisation of noses, for instance: at first, it's amusing to learn that Norman Podhoretz has a 'hard, pitiless nose' and that Stephen Spender has 'wonderfully malicious nostrils'. But she employs these preassembled constructions again and again, with diminishing returns. After Carl Icahn's 'big, humorless nose' and Warren Beatty's 'unserious nose' the joke wears thin, its meaninglessness exposed by repetition.

Brown spares herself the cynicism she accords others. In her babyishly boastful introduction, she excitedly tells the story of her own life as though she were narrating the trailer for her own biopic: 'I was swept off my feet in sophomore year by Martin Amis, then a twenty-three-year-old literary lothario.' An article she wrote for the Oxford student magazine apparently 'launched me as an enfant terrible of the British media', though this is the first the British media will have heard of it. Her gooey account of her first encounter with her husband, then *Sunday Times* editor Harold Evans, might have come straight out of *Fifty Shades of Grey*: 'The fact that the mighty Mr. E had read my insignificant jottings … and actually wanted to meet me was, to me, heart-stopping.' She is rarely backward in coming forward; even her humility carries a strong undercurrent of self-satisfaction, and she is deft at making breathless elisions between her own life and world events, as though the one were indistinguishable from the other. 'The same month I took over the editorship of *Tatler*, in June 1979,' she observes, 'a new Prime Minister took over 10 Downing Street.'

After a few years at *Tatler* she was dreaming of Manhattan, where she had spent a three-month 'sojourn' after graduating. 'I wanted to go back to Manhattan – and conquer it,' she writes, now firmly the star of her own movie. As luck would have it, in the spring of 1983 she received a call from Alexander Liberman, the editorial director of Condé Nast, and 'the strains of Gershwin's clarinet again began to rise in my head'. At this point his intentions were opaque, beyond a lunch meeting in Manhattan. But Brown already knew what she wanted. 'A tortured, perilous courtship for the editorship of *Vanity Fair* was about to begin' is the way she ends her introduction.

The diaries begin on 10 April 1983, with our modern-day Becky Sharp landing in New York City late at night, 'brimming with fear and insecurity'. As if by magic, both these emotions have disappeared by dawn. From then on, it's down to business. 'As soon as I woke up I rushed to the newsstand on the corner to look for the April issue of *Vanity Fair.*'

She does not like what she sees of the newly revived magazine, and judges that the 'incomprehensible' cover will 'surely tank on the newsstand'. Inside, there's a 'brainy but boring' essay by Helen Vendler, a poem by Amy Clampitt, and 'a gassy run of pages from V. S. Naipaul's autobiography'. As her diaries unfold, her weariness with the world of literature grows steadily more apparent. Of the handful of authors who merit a mention, Philip Roth is 'a bit of a disappointment', and Joan Didion and John Gregory Dunne are 'always a struggle'. Only Norman Mailer is really up to scratch, possibly because he represents yet another career opportunity: 'I feel I want to write down everything that comes out of his mouth. He needs a Boswell to follow him around.'

In her first diary entry, Brown has already set her sights on the target closest to hand. The question is, how long can Richard Locke survive as *Vanity Fair*'s editor? By the end of the month, Locke has been replaced, not by Brown – she feels she ducked the offer, though it remains unclear whether it actually came – but by Leo Lerman from *Vogue* ('Leo is about a hundred years old'). Brown has been made a consultant, secretly believing that 'there is no way Leo can do the *VF* job successfully'. The diary entry on her first day in her new advisory role includes what she calls a 'killer critique' of *Vanity Fair*, which she has diligently copied out of that month's *New Criterion*. 'Now I understand why they wanted me here so fast,' she concludes.

However crab-like her advance, it fails to pass unnoticed. Lerman 'looks at me with awful suspicion, like a manic, whiskery prawn, convinced I am Alex's spy'. Which, of course, she is. A month passes, during which Lerman rejects all her ideas. 'Doesn't he understand I could save his job?' she asks. But there's no time for an answer. Before the completion of that day's entry, she has buttonholed Condé Nast owner Si Newhouse – who scuttles in and out of these diaries like a goblin – and insisted to him that Lerman cannot provide leadership, and that she should be his replacement.

By the end of that year, her dream has come true. 'Bull's-eye! They were offering me the job!' Significant moments in her life may be measured out with exclamation marks. 'The first issue of my *VF* is on the newsstands at last! I love the way it looks, sexy and strong and clean!' (31 March 1984); 'A red-letter day! Si called me upstairs to give me a thirty-thousand-dollar raise!' (14 December 1987); '*Vanity Fair*'s fifth anniversary party! What a night!' (1 March 1988); 'Hooray! I love my job! I love *Vanity Fair*!' (5 January 1989).

Accordingly, her first entry for 1990 begins: 'A new decade!' After five years at *Vanity Fair*, her zeitgeist barometer has become super-sensitive, quivering uncontrollably at each fresh event, her favourite adjectives – epic, iconic, turbo-charged, hot – applied to everything, no matter how inconsiderable or underwhelming. 'It's amazing how fast the eighties recedes in the back mirror,' she observes, and it's still only 10 January. After all, '*Dynasty* finally bit the dust at the end of last year, and it now feels as antique as ancient Rome.' By the following September she has put Roseanne Barr on the cover because, apparently, 'proletarian chic is all the rage'.

She who lives by the zeitgeist must die by the zeitgeist. In its appetite for the new and modern, *The Vanity Fair Diaries* seems something of a period piece, full of trappings now almost as outdated as bustles, wing collars and horse-drawn carriages. In 1986, Brown is having a drink at the Ritz-Carlton with a flirtatious Warren Beatty ('so your husband's in Washington half the week? … How do we progress this now?') when a waiter brings a telephone to the table. Two years later, Brown is proud to have coined the term 'Acceleration Syndrome', because 'car phones and call waiting and home faxes are making everything so revved up'.

The pages are packed full with the relics of a bygone age – 'the mega-rich Reliance Insurance tycoon Saul Steinberg and his trophy wife, a slim brunette bombshell called Gayfryd', 'Paul Marciano, the marketing wiz behind the Guess Jeans ads', and so on, ad infinitum – mysteries to all but the most dedicated social antiquarian. At *Vanity Fair*'s fifth anniversary party, Brown ends the night conga-ing with Henry Kissinger, who would have been redolent of an earlier era even back then. The Kissingers were, as always, the first to arrive, along with Dennis Hopper and Jackie Collins. In Rupert Everett's witty memoir, *Vanished Years*, the actor recalled a similarly lavish, similarly random party thrown by Brown and the then still-greetable Harvey Weinstein in 1999 to launch the epic, iconic, turbo-charged, hot *Talk* magazine. Everett arrived with Madonna, to find Kissinger already there:

> Omygod, I think, this is the man who dragged Cambodia into the Vietnam War, but of course I say nothing, even when a waitress comes by to ask what we want to eat.
>
> 'What's on the menu?' asks Kissinger, and I can barely restrain myself from shrieking, 'What's on the *menu*, Henry? Would that be *Operation Menu*?'
>
> Instead I obsequiously offer to go and fetch some nibbles. With success comes compromise, and it's amazingly easy to forget two million massacred Cambodians as one is passing around the cheese straws.

There is nothing nearly as nimble in *The Vanity Fair Diaries*, nothing as ambivalent or funny or close to life. Instead, Brown makes the parties she throws and attends sound more like meat-processing plants, with herself as a senior foreman, present simply to deal with the assembled bodies, clipboard and bolt-pistol at the ready. A beady kind of joylessness abounds. 'This party is for a thousand careful Cinderellas,' wrote Everett, 'and even if their coaches don't turn to taxis at midnight, their serene fascinated faces revert to witches' grimaces if the evening's longevity exceeds by a minute the schedule prescribed by their publicist.'

Yet with her quiver of exclamation marks, Brown persists in portraying herself as the wide-eyed ingenue, even when she is taking an axe to her underlings. Perhaps the most chilling phrase in the diaries is 'Gotta clean house.' Soon after being appointed editor of *Vanity Fair*, Brown hears that a production editor has been complaining behind her back about rushed deadlines. She is furious. The production editor attempts to appease her with praise, but it is too little, too late. Within a few weeks she is out. 'Got back from Florida refreshed and fired Linda Rice,' Brown writes. And then she adds, breezily, 'Gotta clean house.' Little Orphan Annie has turned into Lizzie Borden, running amok with the axe: 'A few days away made me determined to remove negative elements from the office.' More casualties follow. In one particularly frosty passage – strangely reminiscent of Armando Iannucci's recent movie *The Death of Stalin* – Newhouse goads her by asking, 'Do you have a problem with firing people, Tina? I wouldn't have thought you did.'

> 'No,' I replied. 'And I feel I should start firing a few who are making problems.'
> 'All at once or one by one?' I felt he was teasing me now.
> 'I will let you know,' I said.
> I immediately went downstairs and kissed good-bye to Locke's golden girl Moira Hodgson. She writes well but her resentful politesse has been getting on my nerves.

A large part of the book is taken up with office politics, presumably more interesting to those involved and their immediate family and friends than to the rest of us. Might it be of use as a manual for aspiring editors? Brown offers little nuggets of advice, not least eternal vigilance, but it is doubtful that the set formula she has worked out by July 1984 – 'Celeb cover to move the newsstand, juicy news narrative like Vicki Morgan, A-list literary piece, visual escapism, revealing political profile, fashion. If we nail each of these per issue it's gonna work' – could be successfully transferred to any other magazine over thirty years later.

'Juicy news narrative' invariably involves the murder of and/or by someone extremely wealthy and/or glamorous. If there has been a shortage of well-heeled slaughter that month, then an untimely death must suffice. On 17 June 1986, Brown records the news that 'Olivia Channon, the Guinness heiress and Oxford undergraduate, overdosed on heroin and died.' Bingo! Her excitement is palpable, though she is careful to cloak it in sympathy. ('Who let her down?') Within a week, Brown has hotfooted it to Oxford, researcher and notebook at her side, busily attempting to 're-create her story' for *Vanity Fair*. As it happens, her article never appeared, a fact that passes unmentioned in the diaries, which are devoted to narratives of professional success, not personal failure.

Brown does not share Pepys's ability to detach the diarist from the self; there is an element of personal PR in almost everything she writes. In one entry, Harold Evans makes what Brown calls 'the cunning point' that 'people believe what they see in print even if it happens to be in your own publication'. Acting on this advice, she starts introducing excited reports of *Vanity Fair*'s epic, iconic, turbo-charged, hot success into her editor's letters. Any candour is largely restricted to people other than herself, many of them, like Leo Lerman, now safely dead and buried. But in one area of her own life she is remarkably frank.

By and large, the diary form follows the vicissitudes of life too closely for a shape or clear themes to emerge, but one way of reading *The Vanity Fair Diaries* is as the record of one woman's gradual realisation of her ever-increasing market value. In this, she is free with her facts and figures: when she takes over the editorship, she accepts a salary of $130,000. Within six months, her agent, Mort Janklow, tells her that she has been offered 'in the region of 250K' for a novel. She has never written one before, but that is not the reason she hesitates: 'The catch is, I have no time to write it.'

In under four years, her stock has risen high enough for Swifty Lazar to phone her with the question, 'How does two million dollars sound to you? ... that's what I can get for a novel by you.' Four months later, Newhouse raises her salary by a further $100,000. But this is peanuts: within a year she has hired a lawyer to up the stakes. 'Thanks to Mort, five years in I am now paid six hundred thousand a year on a three-year contract with a million-dollar bonus at the end, plus my parents taken care of and no debt on our apartment.' That debt, with Newhouse, mentioned almost as an afterthought, had been for $300,000.

The decisiveness she brings to her job is less evident in her life beyond it. Throughout the diaries she see-saws, to the point of tedium, between wanting to live in the USA and wanting to live in England. One moment she is mad about New York; the next, London, and then it's New York, and then it's back to London. 'My fascination with New York success is beginning to pall,' she writes on New Year's Eve, 1985. 'In fact, I realize more and more, I love New York City, period. London seems to get smaller and smaller to me,' she writes on 7 May 1986.

Her prose, too, whips restlessly back and forth across the Atlantic, often within the course of the same sentence. Rupert Everett neatly described it as 'the hilarious compromise an English speaker arrives at with the American dialect'. At times, she reminds me of an escaped prisoner in a hammy B-movie, desperately hoping to pass herself off as a native abroad, having memorised a dodgy phrasebook. 'Gotta get some movie-star covers and see what's popping on the West Coast after so long holed up in long-knived Manhattan,' she writes on a plane to Los Angeles.

Hyperbole acts on her diaries like a virus. At one point, she describes the launch party for her husband's book as being 'so high-powered the energy threatened to lift the lid off the restaurant'. Elsewhere, articles 'explode', glamour is 'drop-dead', and, come December, New York's pace 'hots up to a burning crescendo'. Meeting Michael Jackson, she judges him 'a Mozartian kind of genius', and does not stop there. 'His gift, like that of anyone world-class, is fostered by lonely discipline, obliterating obsession, and the desperate drive for the extinction of ego by the gift itself.'

A pivotal word in her diaries is 'buzz'. In July 1985, she rails against it: 'I'm sick of people writing about the "buzz" I "create" with *Vanity Fair* … They call it "buzz". I call it engagement. I feel a nagging sense this "buzz" bullshit would not keep being said about a male editor.' But before long she has forgotten her high-minded objections; as the diary progresses, she begins sprinkling the word approvingly. 'By week's end the buzz on the new *VF* was deafening,' she writes in February 1991. 'I expected some buzz, but not what is unfolding,' she observes the following July, after the naked and pregnant Demi Moore has appeared on the cover.

Buzz is what she does; the busy buzz of self-promotion – hers, her friends' and her enemies' – is the background noise throughout these diaries. In 1986, someone called the Countess of Romanones telephones Brown from Acapulco following the death of the Duchess of Windsor. It is the countess's duty to escort the Duchess's corpse to its final resting place in the shadow of Windsor Castle. She wants *Vanity Fair* to provide a free seat on the Concorde and to ask a top designer to supply her with a free funeral outfit. Brown relays this tale of avarice and insensitivity with her usual gusto. 'Is there anyone left who is not hustling?' she asks. Sensibly, she does not look to herself for an answer.

Get You, Maurice!
The Cloistered World of Maurice Bowra

Nowadays, Maurice Bowra is remembered, or almost remembered, for his waspish witticisms, or near-witticisms. In dictionaries of quotations, he tends to be represented only by his camp observation 'buggers can't be choosers', coined when he was facing marriage to a particularly plain young woman. His remark that he was 'more dined against than dining' sometimes manages to squeeze into books of humorous quotations, but, like so many such sayings, it doesn't improve with repetition.

Yet in his time (1898–1971), Bowra was a figure to be reckoned with; a worldly don who rubbed shoulders with Winston Churchill, W. B. Yeats, Charlie Chaplin and Evelyn Waugh. He was for thirty-two years the Warden of Wadham College, Oxford, and, as his Puffing-Billy of a biographer puts it in an ever-expanding balloon of hyperbole, 'one of the dominant Oxford figures of the 20th Century', 'without doubt the most famous or notorious Oxford don of his generation', and the subject of 'one of the most talked-about reigns in Oxford's history'.

He was one of those people around whom myths gather, even if most of those myths turn out to be just that. Lord Longford used to retell a rumour that, during his time as a soldier in the First World War, Bowra had shot an unpopular colonel during the heat of battle, but no one has come up with any proof that this ever happened.

Similarly, the story went around that, visiting Berlin in the 1930s, he had responded to the greeting 'Heil Hitler!' with the counter-greeting 'Heil Bowra!' In fact, Bowra was not present at the time: it was his friend Bob Boothby who had said, 'Heil Boothby!' and Bowra had liked the story so much that he asked Boothby if he could retell it of himself.

Like many academics, but more so, he was a keen hater, gathering around him a squad of like-minded sycophants and placemen, known locally as the Bowristas, who would assist him in his pursuit of lifelong vendettas against those who caused him offence, no matter how small. In one of a number of sentences in this book* that read like parodies of the small, vicious world of academe, we hear that Bowra once 'persuaded an American benefactress and the Duchess of Marlborough to establish a rose garden opposite Magdalen, knowing full well that the College's President, T. S. R. Boase, detested roses'. Ooh! Get you, Maurice!

He dismissed Virginia Woolf as 'a bore', W. H. Auden as a 'bad lecturer, bad scholar, bad man, drunk and dirty', Princess Margaret as 'a tremendous blood-sucker, and, like her sister, a bit of a sourpuss', Gore Vidal as 'unsavoury' and the po-faced critic F. R. Leavis as a 'ghastly' man, spouting 'meandering gabble'. He complained of his colleague Hugh Trevor-Roper that 'he shows off all the time, sucks up to me, boasts, is far from poor owing to his awful book, on every page of which there is a howler'. When his old tutor, H. W. B. Joseph, lay on his deathbed, Bowra noted that 'Joseph has been very ill, but is, I am sorry to say, a little better, though he still enjoys considerable pain … I feel he will not trouble us much more as he can hardly move.' He then coined one of his sour little witticisms: 'While there's death there's hope.'

His biographer, Leslie Mitchell, has a schoolmarmish habit of discreetly censoring the names of some of Bowra's Oxford victims, even though they can easily be identified by looking elsewhere. For instance, in one sentence he writes that 1949 was a terrible year: Balliol elected 'a fearful bore' as its Master, with a wife 'who gives herself airs'. Along with others their existence made Maurice 'vomit with rage and shame'. We are not told their names, but a swift look at today's Balliol College website reveals that the man appointed Master of Balliol in 1949 was Sir David Lindsay Keir.

---

* *Maurice Bowra: A Life* by Leslie Mitchell (2009).

Bowra spread malicious gossip about his enemies with all the doggedness of a farmer spreading manure. He once claimed, for instance, that the American critic Edmund Wilson hated the English because he had visited an English prostitute and caught 'a disgusting disease ... the facts are beyond dispute'. And when the Profumo Affair broke in the early 1960s, he was as pleased as punch ('I look forward to a series of such scandals'), putting it about that 'Mr Marples [the Transport Minister] is said to be next for it, as he is a keen transvestite.'

Yet, in his day, Bowra was considered to be rather more than just a poisonous old queen. Time and again, his biographer talks of people in his inner circle 'falling off their chairs' and/or 'choking with laughter' as Bowra cracked his jokes or gossiped about the sex lives of his colleagues. Alas, gossip is a dish best served piping-hot: from this distance in time, it is hard to care about which long-dead don was getting up to no good. Similarly, jokes cracked in the hubbub of after-dinner conversations seem a good deal less funny now than they must have done then: calling the Hilton in Pisa 'the Tilton Hilton' might have set the Wadham high table a-roar fifty years ago, but now seems no better than one might find in a budget-priced Christmas cracker. How odd that this most sophisticated of men should tell such babyish jokes! I trust the high table came equipped with its fair share of highchairs.

Like flowers, there is a certain kind of wit that withers and dies as time passes. Bowra is one of those (Jonathan Miller is another) whose brilliance in conversation does not transfer on to the page, so is denied permanence. Even his reverential biographer confesses that, in his opinion, Bowra's prose fails to sparkle. Instead, it is 'cautious and flat'. Harold Nicolson said Bowra's prose reads 'like a man writing luggage labels'. Well, yes and no: Bowra's autobiography, *Memories*, seems to me full of good things, with many sharp and touching portraits in it, generally ill-served by the kind of precis dished out by Mitchell. For instance, Bowra's twelve-page portrait of W. B. Yeats offers an excellent idea of what it was like to be in the same room as that charismatic poet, but Mitchell deadens the whole thing by reducing it to just a sentence or two.

Bowra was in many ways a force for good. He was a great classical scholar and put a lot of energy and talent into enthusing his students. He led a lifelong war against the dry-as-dust pedants who tend to populate academia. 'Undergraduates learnt that life could be about what was possible, rather than what was allowed,' writes Mitchell, nicely encapsulating what all good teaching should be about. Bowra was also a brave champion of free speech, speaking out against Oswald Mosley's bully boys and the Soviet Union's persecution of writers.

But this is not the stuff of which legends are made. Bowra remains famous only as a wit and a snob. His wit now seems vaguely on a par with Larry Grayson's, and Mitchell takes pains to deny his snobbishness. 'To label him a snob ... was unfair,' he protests. 'Bowra's snobbery was intellectual, not social.'

Odd, then, that he made such a beeline for society hostesses Emerald Cunard and Sybil Colefax, that he applauded the decision to raise the fees for overseas students ('it means we shall have far fewer of them, and high time too') and that as a guest at a Foyle's lunch in the 1960s he looked with contempt at the general public and concluded: 'There seemed to be no reason why they should be there or indeed why they should exist.' If this isn't snobbery, what is?

Twenty One Clerihews for the *New Statesman*'s Centenary

Beatrice Webb
Refused to be a deb.
She thought life much lusher
In Soviet Russia.

The reputation of Sidney Webb
Continues to ebb
As they look through his files
Under 'Stalin's show trials'.

A. C. Grayling
Has only one failing:
Given the green light he
Holds forth like God Almighty.

John Maynard Keynes
Helped workers lose their chains
And by way of relaxation
Wrote *The Inflation of Currency as a Method of Taxation.*

David Hare
Takes special care
To ensure his plays don't lack
A very long speech about the state of England delivered by a
    disillusioned character, generally dressed in a mac.

Hugh Grant
Said, 'Shan't!'
When told to shut up:
Naughty pup.

Malcolm Muggeridge
Gave a thug a fridge;
He was naturally contrarian
When confronting the barbarian.

Harold Pinter,
Outraged the *Statesman* wouldn't print a
Poem called 'Fucking Yankee Shit Wank Jerk',
Boomed, 'But it's a hugely important work!'

Jemima Khan
Coos: 'Wow, it's so much fahn
Associate-editing The Staggers,
One of my absolute fave glossy maggers!'

Alastair Campbell
Took a gamble
On WMD, and lost;
To our cost.

Eric Hobsbawm
Took Soviet rules as the norm
And didn't react
To the Ribbentrop–Molotov pact.

Cyril Connolly
Would eat and drink bonnily,
Causing him to shout
'In every fat man a thin one is signalling to be let out.'

John Major
Went into rage a
Day after the *Statesman* laid bare
The wrong affair.

Martin Amis
Wasn't cast in *Les Miz*
Though they should have found room: he
Is sufficiently gloomy.

Richard Dawkins
Favours radio talk-ins
'Prof, we're putting you through
To God on Line 2.'

J. B. Priestley
Was rarely beastly
He preferred to sit on the fence
Of plain common sense.

Denis Healey
Has gone all touchy feely,
Recently paying homage
To Nigel Farage.

Bruce Page
Had a talent to enrage
Declaring, 'Evelyn Waugh
Is a writer we deplore!'

Arthur Marshall
Proved too partial
To darling Mrs T.
(Oh deary, deary me!)

George Orwell
Didn't tour well
He'd regularly murmur
Rude remarks about Burma.

Kingsley Martin
Took no part in
'God Save the King':
It wasn't his thing.

With only modest reservations, the founders of the *New Statesman*, Beatrice and Sidney Webb, supported Stalin through the Great Purge, the show trials and the Hitler–Stalin pact. One of A. C. Grayling's pieces for the *New Statesman* began: 'What religious people mean by "god" means nothing to me beyond an incoherent cluster of concepts …' John Maynard Keynes was the chairman of *The Nation* when it merged with the *New Statesman* in 1931, and remained a guiding force. The playwright David Hare, a regular contributor, accepted a knighthood in 1998. Despite heavy criticism, the actor Hugh Grant proved resolute in his campaign to curb press freedom, for which he used the *New Statesman* as a platform. In 1955 Malcolm Muggeridge wrote a pioneering article against the 'tedious adulation' of the Royal Family. Harold Pinter would be sent into a fury whenever a magazine or newspaper turned down the opportunity to publish one of his poems. Jemima Khan is Associate Editor of the *NS*. Alastair Campbell, the former Director of Communications for Tony Blair, guest-edited the magazine in 2009. The late historian Eric Hobsbawm remained a dutiful member of the Communist Party even beyond the invasion of Hungary. Cyril Connolly was a regular contributor to the *NS* in the 1930s. While still Prime Minister, John Major sued the magazine after it printed rumours of an extramarital affair (though not the affair he had earlier enjoyed with Edwina Currie). Martin Amis was Literary Editor in the late 1970s. Richard Dawkins guest-edited the Christmas edition in 2011. J. B. Priestley was a regular contributor; one of his articles led to the foundation of CND. In an interview with the *NS* the nonagenarian elder statesman Denis Healey spoke fondly of Mrs Thatcher, Nick Clegg, David Cameron and Nigel Farage. When he was editor, the Australian Bruce Page declared Evelyn Waugh his least favourite author; he also fired his regular columnist Arthur Marshall, allegedly for saying 'Cooee! Isn't Mrs Thatcher doing well?' when visiting the *NS* offices. George Orwell, author of *Burmese Days*, fell out with *NS* editor Kingsley Martin, who refused to publish his reports on the Spanish Civil War. In 1962, Martin himself wrote *The Crown and the Establishment*, an argument for British republicanism.

THE BIG QUESTIONS

The Great Issues That May
Hang from a Bootlace

Sigmund Freud was born in 1856, just two years after that other great detective, Sherlock Holmes. There is, of course, an essential difference between the two men. One of them was fictitious but has the aura of reality; the other was real but has the aura of fiction.

In many other respects, though, they loom over us in strikingly similar ways.

'You know my method,' says Holmes in 'The Boscombe Valley Mystery'. 'It is founded upon the observance of trifles.' This was the foundation of Freud's method, too. In his essay on 'Lapses' – slips of the tongue, tunes that stick in the mind, misplaced things – he observes that 'an unsuspected wealth of meaning usually lies hidden behind their apparent harmlessness'.

Elsewhere, in one of his most famous case studies, Freud declares that it doesn't matter if someone is withholding the truth because 'anyone with eyes to see and ears to hear will be convinced that mortals cannot hide a secret'. His view is shared by Sherlock Holmes. In 'A Case of Identity' Holmes says, 'I can never bring you to realise the importance of sleeves, the suggestiveness of thumb-nails, or the great issues that may hang from a bootlace.'

Of these two contemporaries, Sherlock Holmes is now seen as the cosier figure, his multitude of peculiarities and his penetrating intelligence both rendered reassuring by the misfortune of his fictitiousness. But even 150 years after his birth, Sigmund Freud remains creepy and threatening, a dark shadow looming up through the fog, ready to prise open our secrets.

I would guess that those who have never read a word by Freud are still aware of his key insights: the Oedipus Complex is as much a part of the language as the Freudian slip, or the Id, or indeed psychoanalysis, which is a term he himself coined. One has only to look at the most banal discussion on afternoon telly to see how many of his pronouncements, shocking at the time, are now part of our mental furniture – the significance of our dreams, for instance, and the dominance of the subconscious in our day-to-day lives, and the notion that adult neurosis is built on a childhood trauma.

Just the other day, I was watching a TV programme in which a criminologist was pointing excitedly to the high statistical correlation between children who wet their beds at a late age and adult arsonists. Yet here, in a footnote first published in 1918, Freud is already expounding on the connection between incontinence and fire.

'To us he is no more a person now but a whole climate of opinion,' observed W. H. Auden in his poem 'In Memory of Sigmund Freud'. Yet still we want to keep him at bay: more often than not, his unavoidable silhouette fills bystanders with a sense of foreboding, or its close relation, scorn. 'I refuse to endure months of expensive humiliation only to be told that at the age of four I was in love with my rocking-horse,' said Noël Coward, the elegant cheerleader of the unconverted. Yet which of us would not be fascinated to read Freud's case notes on Coward?

Freud has taken something of a battering from the experts, too, in recent years. Some have accused him of falsifying evidence, others of cribbing from his peers, still others of simply getting things wrong. Liberals who, fifty years ago, would have trumpeted his cause now join the chorus of tut-tutters: feminists disapprove of his phallo-centric solutions, gays disapprove of his view of homosexuality as an abnormality, and left-wingers disapprove of his emphasis on the neurosis of the individual.

Recently, one critic doubted whether Sigmund Freud had ever cured anyone of anything; even some of those who would call themselves Freudians remain sceptical about many of the cures in his case histories. They suggest that some of the illnesses he loosely attributed to hysteria could nowadays have been cured by conventional medicine, their cause being physical rather than psychological.

The first thing that strikes one about Freud's essays is that, 100 years on, they still possess an extraordinary power to shock. In the space of a single case history of the Wolfman – so called because of his recurrent nightmare involving opening the window to be confronted by half a dozen wolves sitting in a walnut tree, staring back at him with terrifying intent – the reader is confronted by virtually every form of neurosis, from obsessive-compulsive behaviour to childhood seduction, from castration complex to anal eroticism, all described in meticulous detail, much of it unrepeatable here. Within a single page, the reader may at one moment yawn at the long-winded technical language, and at the next moment reel back in horror at the certainty of Freud's stark pronouncements ('faeces are the first gift, the child's loving sacrifice'), only to find himself once again exhilarated by Freud the storyteller.

At one point, for instance, the Wolfman recalls that when his governess was handing out sticks of barley sugar, she playfully told him that they were chopped-up pieces of snake. This causes him to remember that his father had once come upon a snake when out for a walk and had chopped it into pieces with his walking-stick. This in turn makes him remember the fable of the wolf who tries to catch fish in the winter by using his tail as bait, but the tail freezes in the ice and snaps off. 'He was thus preoccupied with the thought of castration,' deduces Freud.

Just as the Sherlock Holmes stories, with their meticulous accumulation of detail, often seem real, so Freud's case histories, with their emphasis on nightmares and strange memories, often seem wholly illusory, dreams within dreams within dreams. But if the fact-checkers continue to pick away at them, and they are found to be acts of the imagination, this may well prove their salvation. If Freud's standing as a scientist declines, perhaps this will serve to liberate his standing as an artist. Science eschews conjecture; art feeds upon it.

You certainly emerge from an essay by Freud feeling moved by a work of art, rather than intrigued by a work of science. For a time, you see the world through his all-consuming vision, at once clinical yet wild, unsparing yet profound. In his determination to establish psychoanalysis as a proper science he couches his essays in cool, slightly stuffy prose, but, every now and then, the poet in him breaks cover. When his patient Dora decides to leave him after years of analysis, just weeks short of reaching some sort of breakthrough, Freud expresses a cry of human anguish, not unmixed, one suspects, with the pain of love: 'Anyone who, like myself, awakens the most wicked demons that dwell untamed in the human breast in order to do battle with them must be prepared to suffer some damage in the course of that struggle.'

I was surprised, upon rereading him, to find how defensive Freud is towards the sceptics of his day: this may also be a reason for his almost tabloid overstatement of the unproveable and the improbable ('probably no male is spared the horror of castration at the sight of female genitals'). He seems constantly aware of the timid or disapproving reader raising an eyebrow. 'I fear that ... the reader will abandon his faith in what I have to say,' he interjects, halfway through his account of the Wolfman.

But he finally acknowledges that there is little point in arguing with sceptics. He is divided from them, he says, by an unbridgeable ocean. 'The polar bear and the whale cannot wage war ... because each is confined in his own element and is unable to make contact with the other.' Is Freud himself the polar bear or the whale? As the years roll by, and his influence grows ever wider and ever deeper, sometimes it seems as if he's more like the ocean.

In a Nutshell:
Vivienne Westwood Has the Answers

Is the government right to raise VAT?

This is very much a question. I do feel nevertheless that what I am saying is. On the other hand, we have this government at the moment and I'm not afraid to call it a government. But this at the moment government really shouldn't call itself a government it has no right to call itself a government but on the other hand it has every right to do so in my opinion. Because that is after all what it is namely a government.

Fourthly, to answer the second part of the question first, I would refer you to the first part of the question and how we should set about answering that. Because that's what we've all got to do if we are to get our country out of this terrible, terrible mess that we find ourselves in, whatever that mess may be. Secondly, I'm not saying that it is necessarily a mess it might be something much better than a mess, it might be a tess or a less or a dress that but this is what we are told and that's all we have to go on.

Firstly, I think it's very very very important for us all on this planet *as human beings* because after all that's what we are to realise that VAT is another way of saying Value Added Tax because unless or until we all realise this then that's what I think.

What should we do about global warming?

Well this is again the whole question, I mean you have to see things all together not just as little bits and pieces you have to take a more what I call Zen approach. Firstly, there's no point sorting out the climate unless you secondly sort out the change. And that's why I think it's not just important but very very important, perhaps even very very very important, and I frankly believe you can't get more important than that.

So what I am saying is that this is what I am saying. We all want to make this world a world in which we live in and the only way we *as human beings* can live in this world is, as I say, to make this world a world in which we live.

On the other hand, and I believe this very strongly, this warming isn't just global and nor is the global just warming. That's what our politicians refuse to understand. I mean I'm not denying that Abraham Lincoln was a great man and I've always really really loved that look he created, sort of urban-stroke-country-puritanical-stroke-statesmany, but he lived in the olden days and there was no reason no reason at all for him to get involved with the whole global warming thing especially as VAT in his day was then at an all-time low or at any rate not very high, as I understand it.

So the answer to the question is in a nutshell and it's up to each and every one of us *as human beings* to try to open that nutshell. And engage with it in a magnificent great big massive ethical nutshell-type debate sort of thing.

Two plus two equals what?

First of all, I'd very much like if I may to answer the second part of this question first. 'Equals what?' is the second part of the question but without the first part it means nothing whatever really so it becomes impossible for me to answer. And this is what I mean when I say that this is what I mean.

Those of us living on this planet among which I include myself must recognise the fact that numbers are very very very complicated and fascinating things. But I truly believe that we *as human beings* have a real duty on ourselves to treat them as numbers. By which I mean that if they are numbers we have got to recognise them as numbers and talk to them with respect and not think that they are just ordinary people like the rest of us because they are not, they are numbers.

So in answer to the question, I think it's very important that there should be a great big debate on it and a debate not just restricted to politicians but to all the electrical too. And we must broach that boundary when we come up against a brick wall or else we'll all drown.

What is the answer to the Middle East question?

There's no doubt at all in my mind. There are lessons to be learnt but the question is what those lessons are because until we know the lessons we're never going to comprehend the question, are we? When we say 'Middle' what do we mean? As a designer and activist, that's what I really really want to know.

I mean, there's middle and there's middle. There's my middle, which would include my waist and surrounding areas and then there's the middle of the road, where the white lines are and then again there's pig-in-the-middle, which is a game we used to play when I was young, it didn't involve a real pig, that would have been very very unethical unless the pig was treated very, very humanely with his own dressing room and such.

So when we talk about the Middle East we've got to understand that we're talking about quite a number of different things, really. From my point of view, East isn't really in the middle at all, it's slightly to the right, that's as you're looking at it, with West to the left and so on, i.e. North above and South below. Middle is in the middle, otherwise it wouldn't be called middle, it would be called something else, something like, I don't know, 'Walrus' or 'Apache' but it's not, it's called Middle.

Where was I? I've lost my thread. And that's really what I mean – we should all of us make much more effort *as human beings* to lose our threads if we want to save this planet we live on. Though on the other hand we need our threads to hold our clothes together so perhaps it's all for the best if we don't lose them too often or our trousers will fall down and that's not a good thing.

Which came first – the chicken or the egg?

The chicken by which I mean the egg.

When you come to think about it, it's very, very hard to separate them. I mean, it's very important we have both. And that's what greatly concerns me about President Obama in the current state of currents. Because frankly it's my strong belief that you can't throw out the egg with the bathwater if you want to hold on to the chicken, though nevertheless *as human beings* we have every right to try but then again you never know, do you?

Four Horsemen

As I was reading this transcript* of four clever men congratulating one another on their own atheism, the phrase that kept entering into my head came, inappropriately enough, from the Bible: 'Vanity of vanities! All is vanity!'

Their discussion took place twelve years ago, in 2007. It was led by Richard Dawkins, on behalf of The Richard Dawkins Foundation for Reason and Science, and was, writes Professor Dawkins, 'filmed by our resident cinematographers'. Unlike God, he has never been backward in coming forward.

It was, he says, 'a memorable evening'. First, the four intellectuals were 'plied with cocktails', then they had their conversation ('the two hours seemed to fly by'), and this was followed by 'a memorable dinner'.

The subtitle boldly calls it 'the discussion that sparked an atheist revolution'. As the book seems to have been commissioned by The Richard Dawkins Foundation for Reason and Science ('a division of the Center for Inquiry'), we are going to have to take this as an article of faith: the publishers offer no rational explanation for such a bold assertion.

The video of the two-hour discussion has been watched by 2,086,061 people on YouTube: an impressive figure, but does it really amount to a revolution? At the last count, Fenton, the tearaway Labrador that chased deer in Richmond Park back in 2011, had clocked up 19,870, 824 views, which makes him nine times more popular than Dawkins and Co. Even a talking cat which seems to be saying 'Oh long, Johnson'

---

* *The Four Horsemen: The Discussion That Sparked an Atheist Revolution* (2019).

has had over ten million views, and so far 1,842,794,076 people have watched Ed Sheeran singing 'Perfect'. Before he next thinks of declaring a revolution, perhaps Professor Dawkins might look to his laurels. In fact, if I were his marketing manager, I would certainly endeavour to persuade Fenton, Sheeran and the talking cat to sign up for his next high-powered discussion.

The book comes with a suitably reverential foreword by Stephen Fry. In it, he bigs up the 'Four Horsemen' of the title in the extravagant terms in which he used to announce the actors on the short list for BAFTAs. They are, he says, 'four people who have thought hard and fought hard (for they have been publicly battered and battled like few intellectuals in our time) without losing their wit, humour and sense of proportion'. Isn't this putting it a bit strong? In the media/academic circles in which they circulate it would take far more courage to say, 'I am a Christian' than 'I am an atheist'.

The men Stephen Fry further characterises as 'The Fearless Four' are Dawkins, the late Christopher Hitchens, Daniel Dennett ('the best-known philosopher alive' according to Fry), and Sam Harris, a neuroscientist. They are, he adds, all authors of 'enormously influential books' with the rather samey titles of *The God Delusion*, *God Is Not Great*, *Breaking the Spell* and *The End of Faith*.

Throughout their 130-odd-page chatathon they agree with each other so much that their discussion has all the hard-hitting fearlessness of four men stroking each other with feather dusters. 'Absolutely!' 'Oh, and how!' 'I could not possibly agree with you more!' And so it goes on. Will the gush never stop? At times one longs for Abu Hamza to pop his head around the door, just to give their agreeable little discussion a bit of a boost.

A sizeable part of their conversation is given over to bitching about Christians, who, when challenged by the Fearless Four, are prepared to stand up for themselves. 'There's this peevish, and tribal, and ultimately dangerous response to having these ideas challenged,' complains Harris. Dennett calls them 'people of breathtaking arrogance', and Hitchens huffs, 'We just can't hope to argue with a mentality of this kind.'

As their talk enters its second hour, Hitchens, who, in the video of the event, is accompanied by a large glass of Scotch and a string of cigarettes, grows more and more extravagant in his abuse of the enemy, and increasingly pompous too. 'It's unconscionable. I don't really mind being accused of ridiculing or treating with contempt people like that. I just, frankly, have no choice. I have the faculty of humour. I'm not going to repress that for the sake of politeness.'

Their central points are straightforward, and much as one would expect: for them, belief in a God does not stand up to rational scrutiny; religion is a source of much misery, such as wars and terrorism; and without the illusion of a God, mankind could live a fuller, more enriching life. 'The universe is a grand, beautiful, wonderful place, and it's petty and parochial and cheapening to believe in jinns and supernatural creators and supernatural interferers' is the way Professor Dawkins puts it: for all his eloquence and learning, there has always been an element of Nanny Knows Best about him.

All the way through, the Four Horsemen come back to the aspect of religion that most irritates them: it is irrational and does not stand up to scientific scrutiny. But of course, almost by definition that is its point: it transcends the limits of rationality. This means that, from a religious point of view, Dawkins and Co. are like four deaf men who have convinced themselves that the whole world is soundless.

Even when they acknowledge the limitations of science, they somehow turn it to their own advantage. In his introduction, Dawkins lists four major questions that science is still unable to answer, the last of which is 'Why is there something rather than nothing?' But rather than accepting this as a flaw in the rationalist argument, he parades it as a strength. 'The fact that science can't (yet) answer these questions testifies to science's humility.' Oh, yes? He allows no such loophole for religion.

Similarly, at one point in the discussion, Daniel Dennett says of believers, 'I don't think many of them ever let themselves contemplate the question which I think scientists ask themselves all the time: "What if I'm wrong?" It's just not part of their repertory.' At hypocritical moments like these, you wonder if the book might not have been better retitled *The Four Black Pots*.

Over the course of two hours, the four men occasionally run into minor points of disagreement, or at least differences in emphasis: by and large, the two Americans, Harris and Dennett, show more understanding towards believers, while Dawkins and Hitchens are less forgiving. Harris mentions an interesting weakness in how atheism tends to present itself. 'I think there's something about the way we, as atheists, merely dismiss the bogus claims of religious people that convinces religious people that there's something we're missing. And I think we have to be sensitive to this.' But this does nothing to deter Hitchens, who is soon even ranting against the Dalai Lama ('repulsive … he runs a crummy little dictatorship') and the pacifism of Quakers ('they're all equally rotten, false, dishonest, corrupt, humourless and dangerous, in the last analysis').

Hitchens's contrarian voice delights in its almost manic overstatement; the other three are, by and large, more measured and nuanced. Every now and then, one of them even makes a concession to the Christian tradition, though they get in a bit of a tangle over the question of whether a world limited by rationality could ever have produced a Bach or a Michelangelo or a Chartres Cathedral. They are also unsure as to whether a perfect world would include no religious faith at all. On this point, Hitchens is in two minds. 'I wish they would stop it, but then I would be left with no one to argue with.'

It's a book that bounds along quite happily, but adds little to the video available on YouTube, which has the benefit of letting you watch their rather stilted physical interaction, and Hitchens's fidgetiness. And their discussion is not without its humour, both acknowledged and unacknowledged. A particular highlight for me comes when Professor Dawkins pipes up, out of nowhere, 'I have not the *slightest problem* with Christmas trees.' But does he still believe in Santa Claus? Who knows?

Four Hoarse Men:
The Transcript

RICHARD DAWKINS: I think I'm right in saying that we're all four of us highly intelligent people, with many things to do, most of them hugely important.

CHRISTOPHER HITCHENS: Absolutely. I couldn't agree with you more.

DAWKINS: Exactly. It's simply wonderful, Christopher, that you couldn't agree with me more. I feel extremely touched and honoured.

DANIEL C. DENNETT: I was wondering if I might just add a few short words to that most excellent encomium?

DAWKINS: Oh, by all means!

DENNETT: It is, I think, remarkably brave of the four of us to come here today to talk about –

HITCHENS: Absolutely. I have not the slightest problem with that. We feel duty-bound to speak out, even when others would seek to interrupt us

DENNETT: – and might I just –

HITCHENS: – and to hell with the consequences!

DAWKINS: This might be a good moment to come back to something I regularly say, to immensely impressive effect, in discussions and conferences around the world. Yes, it takes tremendous courage, but, nevertheless, I intend to carry on saying it.

The atheistic world view, which we all espouse, has the unsung virtue of intellectual courage. As an atheist, one has the moral courage to live to the full the only life one's ever going to get: to fully inhabit reality, to rejoice in it, particularly on social media, for example on Twitter, where I have upwards of two million followers. And I wonder if you've noticed, as I have, that Jesus Christ never ever tweets, and nor does his father – even though so-called 'believers' insist that they are both 'alive'! Proof positive, I would have thought, that they do not exist! I mean, my own tweets, read by many millions – or so I am told – constitute proof of my existence, so their non-tweets, or, if you want, absence of tweets, is surely proof of their non-existence! Father and son claim to have followers – but how can you have followers if you don't tweet??!! And, conversely, if you don't tweet, you can't have followers. Yet theologians refuse to talk about this, point blank!

SAM HARRIS: Yes, and –

HITCHENS: Did someone just say theologians? Of all the human beings on this planet, they are the most singularly corrupt, revolting, rotten, false, –

HARRIS: might I –

HITCHENS: – humourless, obnoxious, bogus, cowardly, egregious, awful, gross, abhorrent, degenerate, dangerous, despicable,

DENNETT: Yes, and –

HITCHENS: – disgusting, depraved, dishonest, degenerate –

HARRIS: – on a point of information, Christopher, I think you said degenerate –

HITCHENS: grotesque, contemptible, heinous, loathsome and, let's face it, degenerate. And, what's more, they never listen. And as for the Dalai Lama! [*takes long slug of Scotch*].

DAWKINS: The thing about religious people is that they persist in believing in something that highly intelligent and informed people like us – people who have achieved very high status in universities and upon the global stage, and, at least in some cases, highly influential positions on radio and television, have proved to be false. Yet even though their persistence constitutes further proof of their stupidity, they still go on!!!

DENNETT: None of them ever let themselves contemplate the question which scientists ask themselves all the time: 'What if I'm wrong?'

DAWKINS: Interestingly, that's not quite the same, is it, as asking 'What if I'm Ron?' Because it is perfectly conceivable that a proportion of them – admittedly a small proportion, but a proportion nonetheless – a proportion of them may well be called Ron. And, in such a case, they would be perfectly justified in asking, 'What if I'm Ron?' because the only valid answer would be, 'Yes, I am Ron'. I think we can all agree on that.

HITCHENS: Absolutely.

HARRIS: I think there's something about the way we, as atheists, dismiss the bogus claims of religious people that convinces religious people that there's something we're missing.

DAWKINS: That's because they're stupid.

DENNETT: I'm sure you're right. Religious people gain enormous strength in their ignorance just by agreeing with one another all the time.

HITCHENS: Absolutely.

DAWKINS: You're so right there. Now, I thought we might move on to examine, calmly and without prejudice, that simply ludicrous old bugbear that secularism has never produced a Bach or a Michelangelo [*laughter*]. It strikes me as perfectly obvious that if Michelangelo were today commissioned to do the ceiling of, to pick an example at random, a Richard Dawkins Museum of Science, then he would produce something every bit as wonderful.

I mean, the figure of God would obviously no longer be God, but it might instead be a learned Oxford professor, internationally renowned in his field, with a variety of influential books to his name, and he might nowadays have a mobile telephone in his right hand, and that would be the most marvellous, exciting thing! A real affirmation of the power of science and rationality over mumbo-jumbo superstition! And with his left hand, he might be looking something up on his laptop – perhaps the responses to his latest tweet from one of his two or three million followers … though obviously that would be merely one of several options.

DENNETT: And it's both easy and appealing to imagine Bach composing a Mass in B Minor in praise of a giant airliner created by dedicated scientists, with the capacity to lift not just its own weight plus passengers and cargo but also the 120 tons of fuel it takes for a thirteen-hour journey of 7,000 miles.

DAWKINS: And, fascinatingly, one can tweet on transatlantic flights these days, so that one's followers can be kept up to speed on one's every move! It really makes all the 'achievements' ascribed to so-called 'God' seem remarkably inferior! And, forgive me if I'm wrong, but I'm sure he never had a foundation named after him!

DENNETT: And just think of all the wars religious people have started!

HITCHENS: Too right. If I had my way, we'd – hic! – bomb them all to smithereens.

DAWKINS: Unfortunately, we're running out of time. I think we've just witnessed a wonderful debate between hugely articulate friends, with everyone in complete agreement about everything.

DENNETT: Unlike religious types, whose faith forces them into the most abject form of self-congratulatory homogeneity.

DAWKINS: Absolutely.

HARRIS: Absolutely.

HITCHENS: Absolutely.

The First Briton in Space:
Tim Peake's Tweets

Tim Peake @astro_timpeake 14 Dec 2015
Looking forward to tomorrow's space launch. Should be literally indescribable!

Tim Peake @astro_timpeake 14 Dec 2015
Wondering what song to hum to myself during space launch tomorrow. Wow! So many to choose from!

Tim Peake @astro_timpeake 14 Dec 2015
Currently favouring something truly catchy by Eurovision winners the great Brotherhood of Man.

Tim Peake @astro_timpeake 15 Dec 2015
Setting off in nine minutes. Has to be 'Save Your Kisses for Me'.

Tim Peake @astro_timpeake 15 Dec 2015
Successful launch fifteen mins ago. As exhilarating as putting your foot on accelerator of really really fast car. Fantastic feeling.

Tim Peake @astro_timpeake 15 Dec 2015
Up in space now. Amazing. Can't get Bee Gees' 'Night Fever' out of my head. Great song.

Tim Peake @astro_timpeake 15 Dec 2015
RIP Maurice and Robin Gibb. Glad you're still with us, Barry.

Tim Peake @astro_timpeake 15 Dec 2015
Have to pinch myself to remind myself I'm still in space! So dark out there! Unbelievable!

Tim Peake @astro_timpeake 16 Dec 2015
Just completed twenty-four hours in space! Keeping busy! Just brushed my teeth!

Tim Peake @astro_timpeake 17 Dec 2015
Taking a 'Peake' out of spacecraft window. Forgive terrible pun! i.e. 'Peake' = 'Peek'. Sorry, guys!!

Tim Peake @astro_timpeake 18 Dec 2015
Still very dark out there. But nevertheless literally amazing, indescribable.

Tim Peake @astro_timpeake 18 Dec 2015
Suppose if you had to compare it to anything you'd say it was like an exceptionally dark tunnel.

Tim Peake @astro_timpeake 18 Dec 2015
But TBH even darker than that.

Tim Peake @astro_timpeake 19 Dec 2015
Very sorry to hear of the death of Jimmy Hill. Tremendous contribution to 'the beautiful game' i.e. football.

Tim Peake @astro_timpeake 20 Dec 2015
Just passed Great Wall of China. Only one word for it. Great.

Tim Peake @astro_timpeake 21 Dec 2015
Done bit of emergency repair work on Twitter feed. Otherwise nothing much happening.

Tim Peake @astro_timpeake 22 Dec 2015
Took selfie.

Tim Peake @astro_timpeake 23 Dec 2015
Looking forward to Xmas in space! Two days to go. Different from Xmas at home but still great.

Tim Peake @astro_timpeake 24 Dec 2015
Just saw Rockies from space. Funny – they look very small from this distance! Must be the perspective. One more day to go.

Tim Peake @astro_timpeake 25 Dec 2015
Merry Xmas to all on Planet Earth! Sorry to miss Queen's speech.

Tim Peake @astro_timpeake 25 Dec 2015
But will make sure to catch up with it on my return.

Tim Peake @astro_timpeake 25 Dec 2015
Have had Slade's 'Merry Christmas Everybody' in my head all day. Great song.

Tim Peake @astro_timpeake 27 Dec 2015
Privileged to perform space somersault for *Good Morning Britain* breakfast show. Big fan of Susanna Reid.

Tim Peake @astro_timpeake 28 Dec 2015
Monday. My day to do the bins, worse luck!

Tim Peake @astro_timpeake 31 Dec 2015
New Year's Eve today. Which can mean only one thing. New Year's Day tomorrow. Great!

Tim Peake @astro_timpeake 1 Jan 2016
Wishing all on Planet Earth a Happy New Year. Sorry to be missing 1st of new series of *The Voice* but wish best of luck to all involved.

Tim Peake @astro_timpeake 2 Jan 2016
Hovering over Paris. Once had very pleasant weekend there, went all way up Eiffel Tower, pleasant lunch too, but forget name of restaurant.

Tim Peake @astro_timpeake 3 Jan 2016
Brasserie Something, I think. But that's probably not much help. Hoping it'll come to me later.

Tim Peake @astro_timpeake 4 Jan 2016
Name of that Paris restaurant still bugging me.

Tim Peake @astro_timpeake 5 Jan 2016
Just had tweet from fantastic Gary Barlow!! Thank you! Always been a big fan, Gary.

Tim Peake @astro_timpeake 5 Jan 2016
Fave Take That song of all time? No question. 'Relight My Fire'. Or possibly 'Could It Be Magic'. Hard to choose, really.

Tim Peake @astro_timpeake 6 Jan 2016
Took selfie.

Tim Peake @astro_timpeake 7 Jan 2016
Took another selfie.

Tim Peake @astro_timpeake 10 Jan 2016
Starry, starry night. Great song by Don Maclean.

Tim Peake @astro_timpeake 11 Jan 2016
Whoops – should have spelt it Don McLean! Even astronauts make mistakes!

Tim Peake @astro_timpeake 12 Jan 2016
Performed space somersault for *BBC One Show*. Big fan of Alex and Matt.

Tim Peake @astro_timpeake 13 Jan 2016
Glad to hear Michael Douglas and Catherine Zeta-Jones back together after brief marriage split.

Tim Peake @astro_timpeake 13 Jan 2016
Romancing the Stone definitely one of my top ten films of all time.

Tim Peake @astro_timpeake 14 Jan 2016
Looking forward to spacewalk tomorrow. Hoping it will be totally indescribable.

Tim Peake @astro_timpeake 15 Jan 2016
Just back from spacewalk. Indescribable.

Tim Peake @astro_timpeake 15 Jan 2016
Closest I can come to describing it is by saying it's a bit like you always imagined floating in space would be.

Tim Peake @astro_timpeake 16 Jan 2016
Took selfie of self performing space somersault. One for the photo album!

Tim Peake @astro_timpeake 17 Jan 2016
Looking down on USA from space. Unforgettable.

Tim Peake @astro_timpeake 18 Jan 2016
Took selfie of self looking down on USA. Huge country.

Tim Peake @astro_timpeake 19 Jan 2016
Return to Planet Earth scheduled for 5 June 2016. Only 137 days to go!

Tim Peake @astro_timpeake 21 Jan 2016
Took selfie. Posted this tweet.

Mysterious Ways:
God and A. C. Grayling

Over the past few years, evangelical atheists have switched places with fire-and-brimstone Christians: where once it was the Christians who brooked no disagreement, now it is the atheists; and it is the atheists, too, who perform cartwheels on the heads of pins. Christopher Hitchens once even managed to argue of the Rev. Martin Luther King, of all people, that 'In no real as opposed to nominal sense … was he a Christian.'

A weaselly self-righteousness is now the hallmark of the celebrity unbeliever. Meanwhile, it is the Christian who nods diligently in any discussion, taking pains to reassure the atheists how very much he respects their point of view.

In *Prospect* magazine, the philosopher A. C. Grayling writes another of his pieces in support of atheism. In it, he exhibits a deft sleight of hand which, viewed close up and in slow motion, looks more and more suspicious. For instance, he complains that 'In England where 3 per cent of the population go regularly to services in the state-established Church, 26 bishops (plus a number of life peer ex-bishops) can sit in the House of Lords.'

It seems a fair point, but is it accurate, let alone fair? There are currently 775 members of the House of Lords. Three per cent of 775 is 23.25. This means that, even by Grayling's own demanding calculations of what constitutes an Anglican, the House of Lords has just two and three-quarter bishops above its fair share.

But Grayling is highly selective with his statistics, and only manages to whittle the percentage of Anglicans down to 3 per cent by defining as an Anglican someone who goes regularly to services. In fact, a recent survey showed that 22.2 per cent of people in the UK describe themselves as Anglican (and 59.3 per cent of people in England and Wales call themselves Christian).

If Grayling demands church attendance as the measure of Christianity, then surely the equivalent should be required of atheists? Yet the British Humanist Association, of which Grayling is Vice-President, has just 28,000 members, or a meagre 0.052 per cent of the UK population as a whole, and I doubt many of them are regular attenders.

Elsewhere, Grayling's footwork is even more deft. At one point, he counters those who point out that Hitler and Stalin were atheists by sighing 'The usual replies have wearily to be given,' as though those who disagree with him are being pig-headedly dim-witted. Almost as an afterthought, he adds that 'Incidentally, Hitler was not an atheist – "Gott mit uns" (God with us) said the legend on Wehrmacht belt buckles – and Stalin was educated in a seminary, where evidently he picked up a few tricks.'

It is true that Stalin was educated in a seminary, but that does not make him a Christian, any more than being confirmed as a teenager makes Dawkins a Christian, or living in my house makes our West Highland Terrier a human being.

In his book *The Dictators*, Richard Overy, Professor of History at King's College, London, writes: 'It is sometimes argued that Stalin, a former seminary student, still harboured residual religious sentiment which might explain the periodic lapses in an otherwise unremitting campaign against the religious world view. There is no evidence to support such a conclusion. Stalin remained a consistent advocate of the scientific and materialist base of all knowledge. His concessions to religion were tactical and opportunistic ...'

So there we have it: Stalin WAS an atheist, or as Grayling's colleague Richard Dawkins himself once conceded, 'There seems no doubt that, as a matter of fact, Stalin was an atheist.'

And so, too, was Hitler. 'Gott mit uns' predated Nazism by 300 years. It was employed for the first time by the Teutonic Order in the seventeenth century, and was inscribed on the helmets of German soldiers in the First World War. For Hitler, it represented the historic rallying cry of the German nation. Even Dawkins, in *The God Delusion*, concedes that this reference to God on Nazi buckles 'does not prove anything'.

Professor Overy also points out that Hitler's private views on Christianity 'betray a profound contempt and indifference ... Hitler, like Stalin, took a very modern view of the incompatibility of religious and scientific explanation'.

Here are a few of Hitler's remarks on the subject, recorded by Martin Bormann within hours of the Führer having uttered them:

'The heaviest blow that ever struck humanity was the coming of Christianity.' (11–12 July 1941)

'The best thing is to let Christianity die a natural death.' (14 October 1941)

'The war will be over one day. I shall then consider that my life's final task will be to solve the religious problem ... The organised lie must be smashed.' (13 December 1941)

All in all, it's hard not to avoid the conclusion that, rather like his old arch enemy, A. C. Grayling works in mysterious ways.

Three Interviewers

David Dimbleby
Remains nimble – he
Displays consummate ease
Saying, 'Next question, please!'

Jon Snow
Is full of get up and go,
But I'd avoid setting eyes
On those ties.

Evan Davis
Knows the way to behave is
Not to act so
Cross as Paxo.

Not All Pants Are Religious:
Richard Dawkins' Tweets

Richard Dawkins @RichardDawkins 2 Sept
Ice Bucket Challenge a loathsome reminder of the sheer unabashed cruelty of religious belief.

Richard Dawkins @RichardDawkins 2 Sept
Predictable tsunami of stupidity greets my condemnation of Ice Bucket Challenge. OK, pouring icy water over a human being might not be conventionally 'religious', but it is irrational enough to be logically described as such.

Richard Dawkins @RichardDawkins 2 Sept
No, I would be happy to subject an unborn foetus to the Ice Bucket Challenge. But that is not the point.

Richard Dawkins @RichardDawkins 2 Sept
Can't you listen? I did not say that every foetus should be subjected to the Ice Bucket Challenge. On other hand, it would probably teach it a valuable early lesson in religious barbarity.

Richard Dawkins @RichardDawkins 2 Sept
RIP Dickie Attenborough. A great admirer of mine.

Richard Dawkins @RichardDawkins 2 Sept
Lalla and I off to *Doctor Who* convention in Birmingham. Taking back seat, but will be available to sign latest book, appear on local TV, radio, etc.

Richard Dawkins @RichardDawkins 2 Sept
Do I detect the hand of 'Pope' Francis behind the Ice Bucket Challenge?
He clearly knows that only by freezing our brains can he force humans
into irrational beliefs.

Richard Dawkins retweeted
Sam Burke @sam burke
The God Delusion by Richard Dawkins is my absolute fave book. The
guy's a total genius.

Richard Dawkins @RichardDawkins 2 Sept
X pours freezing water over head of Y. Y gets cold and wet, X remains
dry. Z stands by, doing nothing. Z is bad, but X is worse. Sorry but my
sympathy as a sentient human being is with Y.

Richard Dawkins @RichardDawkins 2 Sept
See me on YouTube explaining position on Ice Bucket Challenge in
greater philosophical detail to Jon Snow@Channel4news.

Richard Dawkins @RichardDawkins 2 Sept
Ice Bucket Challenge worse than mild paedophilia but better than date
rape. If you think that's an endorsement of mild paedophilia, go away
and learn to think logically.

Richard Dawkins @RichardDawkins 2 Sept
I didn't say that mild paedophilia was BETTER than Ice Bucket
Challenge. I said Ice Bucket Challenge was WORSE than mild paedo-
philia. If you think that's the same, you need your brain mending.

Richard Dawkins @RichardDawkins 2 Sept
RIP Robin Williams. Terrific sense of humour. Only met him once, but
I made him laugh out loud.

Richard Dawkins @RichardDawkins 2 Sept
Not ALL Muslims are mass-murdering child rapists. Of course not. But enough are to justify one's deepest fears.

Richard Dawkins retweeted
Katie@KatiePS 2 Sept
LOVING your autobiog, Richard! Talk about BRAINY!

Richard Dawkins @RichardDawkins 2 Sept
Religion is pants.

Richard Dawkins @RichardDawkins 2 Sept
But not all pants are religious.

Richard Dawkins @RichardDawkins 2 Sept
It is as illogical to believe that a pair of Y-fronts could hold religious beliefs as it is to believe that a pair of boxer shorts could be an atheist.

Richard Dawkins @RichardDawkins 2 Sept
But, if Y-fronts or boxer shorts WERE to be proved capable of rational thought, then the boxer shorts would clearly be right.

Richard Dawkins @RichardDawkins 2 Sept
Therefore it follows that Y-fronts are much more stupid than boxer shorts. Question: how many Y-fronts have been awarded the Nobel Prize? Answer: none.

Richard Dawkins @RichardDawkins 2 Sept
RIP Tommy Ramone. I myself never appeared onstage with The Ramones, but their music remains undeniably excellent.

Richard Dawkins @RichardDawkins 2 Sept

Am I the only person who finds it truly extraordinary that in the twenty-first century a SELF-CONFESSED Christian should be allowed to appear on the BBC (in *The Great British Bake Off*) without first recanting?

Richard Dawkins @RichardDawkins 2 Sept

Parents who buy children My Little Pony should be prosecuted. Do they truly believe that any pony is a) pink b) three inches high c) has hair extensions? NO? Then why force irrational belief upon children?

Richard Dawkins @RichardDawkins 2 Sept

Last night watched *Zulu* movie on TV. Fine, but you could tell it wasn't REAL blood. And could someone please tell me where the orchestra was meant to be?

Richard Dawkins @RichardDawkins 2 Sept

Already my calm, scientific approach to the despicable My Little Pony conspiracy has provoked sanctimonious, absolutist caterwauling from the perpetually offended. Why are these people so offensive?

Richard Dawkins @RichardDawkins 2 Sept

Some Muslim idiot criticised me on Radio 4 *Today* prog this morning. Why can't these towel-head pea brains ever listen to honest criticism without resorting to name-calling?

Looking to Heaven:
Stanley Spencer

Was there ever an artist as lovable as Stanley Spencer?

Love is also what gives most of his paintings their enduring quality. They are infused by love: love of nature, love of people, love of God, each form of love flowing into the other. It is only in his paintings of himself with his grim second wife Patricia that love is replaced by lovelessness. They are studies in mutual isolation, a glimpse of hell on earth.

'He that Loveth not Knoweth not God for God is Love' reads the inscription on his memorial stone in Cookham, the village by the Thames which was, for him, the centre of the universe. Visiting China as part of a cultural delegation, he introduced himself to the Chinese Foreign Minister Zhou Enlai with the words, 'I feel at home in China because I feel that Cookham is somewhere near, only just around the corner.' Zhou Enlai was lost for words.

Spencer spent most of his days wheeling an old pram around Cookham, laden with his easel, paints and brushes, conjuring on to canvas the visions that arose from what he saw. His paintings are matter-of-fact in their other-worldliness: in one, Christ preaches at Cookham Regatta, in another, the graves of Holy Trinity Church, Cookham, open up and the dead casually rise again, in a higgledy-piggledy fashion, with only the faintest trace of surprise on their faces, almost as though they had just heard the first bell for tea-time. They then hobnob with old friends before taking the path to the river to catch a boat to ascend to heaven.

His work has all the muddle and jumble of everyday life, even when it portrays the hereafter. Though to less godly eyes his vision of resurrection in Cookham may seem either whimsical or preposterous, to Stanley it was as real as a duck ascending from the river.

He was almost as feverish a writer as he was a painter, planting an estimated two million words into diaries, letters and notebooks. He made repeated attempts at an autobiography, but he had no editing ability: once the words started to flow, he couldn't stop them. 'I wish to include anything that I have ever thought, felt or done … I hate to exclude anything.'

Spencer died in 1959, aged sixty-eight. Other books have quoted from his writings, but now, for the first time, they have been skilfully shaped and edited into a loose autobiography by his grandson, John Spencer.* *Looking to Heaven* is the first of three intended volumes. It covers his childhood, his time at art school, and his experience in the First World War, first as a medical orderly, then on active service in Salonica.

His childhood was idyllic. The son of an organist and piano teacher, Stanley and his eight siblings would do everything together, including walking to the woods on a summer's evening to listen to the nightin-gales. He remembered 'the soft summer air, filled with the honeysuckle smell and how still they all kept until, out of the deep quiet, came the song of the nightingale. All the children, even the very small ones, were very still while the nightingales sang.'

His parents engendered in their children an overriding sense of wonder and curiosity that was to remain with Stanley for the rest of his life, sustaining and diverting him through the First World War and fuelling his paintings.

His memory of those early years was sharp; in some ways, he never stopped thinking like a child, incorporating the magic of childhood into his personal theology. 'I used to blow bubbles of all sorts of sizes and kinds. I can hardly think of any lovelier game … The bubble is gone, yet its presence still is there; it has ceased to be, just there become a spirit. Gone to God and left a drop of soapy water on the grass.'

---

* *Looking to Heaven* by Stanley Spencer, edited by John Spencer (2016).

For all his dreaming, his writings show there was nothing airy-fairy or precious about him. In fact, quite the reverse: he liked to boast of having a friend who could swear non-stop for five minutes, never using any word more than once. 'There's glory for you!'

Spencer came from a family that liked to call a spade a spade. 'My grand aunt Hatch was a character. On the occasion of my Grandma's death, she was asked how the funeral went off. "My dear, delightful, and the sandwiches were delicious."' Humour is an integral part of even his most sacred work: in his paintings, Jesus and the angels look like the kind of people with whom you could share a good laugh.

He found it almost impossible not to say what he thought, regardless of the consequences. His straight talking often got him into trouble. When his admiring fellow painter, Mark Gertler, offered to help his career, Spencer thought it only right and honest to send Gertler a letter making it clear what he thought of his work. 'I was sorry that you gave up painting in your old way, because while you did these things which were dull, you were in a fair way towards doing something good,' he wrote. 'Then you seemed to lose all faith and patience with your work and began trying to paint like Cézanne, and you were incapable of understanding him.'

Gertler considered this 'an outrageous insult'. Spencer was taken aback by such a reaction: after all, he had only been trying to tell the truth. Needless to say, his apology got him into even more trouble. 'If it was insulting, I apologise, but it was not insulting. You owe me an apology. Thank you for any kindness you have done me. Unless you regret sending me that letter, I forbid you to write to me again.'

He was twenty-three at the outbreak of war. Having joined up, he walked to Maidenhead Station, only to find that his father had overtaken him on his bicycle and was already there to bid him goodbye. 'And just as the train started my father called through the carriage window to the man in charge of us, "Take care of him, he's valuable," which made me feel very awkward. Why should I not be left to look after my own affairs now, I thought, like those other young men? Their Pas and Mas have not come to see them safely packed off. I felt so horribly like the curly-headed boy going out into the wide, wide world all by myself.'

His feelings about the war can be seen in what is perhaps his masterpiece, the Sandham Memorial Chapel in Burghclere. Its interior walls are painted all over with day-to-day scenes derived from his experience in the ambulance service. While other artists saw the First World War in terms of horror or glory, Spencer's murals are both more earthy and more heavenly: men happily shave and slice bread, make beds and scrub floors, while, above the altar, dead soldiers are resurrected, stepping out of their coffins and handing back their crosses to the figure of Christ.

His writings show that, throughout his time at war, he was eager, even desperate, to paint what he had seen. 'My desire to get back to painting becomes almost unbearable at times.' But he recognised that art is fed and nurtured by experience. 'Everything I do inspires me. Even emptying bedpans, and that is the truth,' he wrote to a friend, adding 'How much more wonderfully could a man washing plates be painted by me now than before the war?'

Though he acknowledges that he has been 'stiff with horror and dread' – at one point, he bursts into tears in the midst of battle – he is forever on the lookout for signs of wonder and redemption. Sometimes, his letters home from the war are entirely about life in Cookham – recreating a walk down the lanes and through the meadows, watching the white doves 'circling round and round the farm yard: now over the barn, now casting shadows slanting up the side of the roof of the old farm house now rising up, and, nearer and nearer, now they are over our house I can hear their wings going'.

Spencer's prose lacks the consistency of his painting. It can be tangled and opaque, straggly and shapeless. But it shows at all times the profundity of his artistic vision, and contains moments of transcendent beauty. As he himself says, after watching fireflies dancing about in the wasteland of Salonica, 'It makes you believe in fairies.'

PANICS

Taking Umbrage

The town of Umbrage, recently twinned with the towns of Brouhaha in Germany and Pique in France, is famous for its international Sour Grapes festival. For over a century now, Umbrage has been the go-to destination for all the angriest people in Britain.

Along with its outlying villages – Huff, Uppity, Grudge and Peevish – it has established itself as the perfect place to let off steam.

The BBC's *Question Time* programme is regularly broadcast from Umbrage. Gordon Ramsay has his finishing school there, teaching young chefs to berate their apprentices. Local bigwig Lord Prescott was recently appointed President of the Umbrage Trade Association, motto: 'Non Nostra Culpa' ('Not Our Fault').

Arriving in Umbrage last week, I turned right at the Kenneth Noye School of Motoring. I then drove past the Harold Pinter Theatre, renowned for its annual production of *Look Back in Anger*, past the Beggars Belief public house and straight on until I reached the Very Crossroads, with its imposing statue of Henry VIII towering above the sign 'I SAID KEEP OFF THE GRASS', and, next to it, another sign: 'CAN'T YOU READ?'

Upon my arrival at the Umbrage Visitor Centre I was greeted by Chief Tourist Officer Frank Bickering. He was standing outside, looking ostentatiously at his watch and sighing loudly. 'What time do you call this, then?' I apologised for being two minutes late. 'Two? More like three,' he replied. 'And don't forget to wipe those shoes. Heaven knows where they've been.'

Mr Bickering guided me into the centre, telling me that I was entering at my own risk and that any breakages must be paid for. Apparently, the centre was opened in 2015 by John Cleese, in a rousing speech delivered through a megaphone. He began it in a characteristically light note. 'I'm only doing this because I need the money for my divorce,' he said, adding: 'And since you ask, jokes are extra.'

I asked Mr Bickering if he could explain why Umbrage has become the go-to destination for quite so many angry people. 'Angry? Who says we're angry? You've got a bloody cheek.'

He said he preferred the term 'disgruntled'. 'And we've got plenty to be disgruntled about. I mean, the sheer lack of respect these days. It makes you want to kick people.'

I plucked up the courage to ask Mr Bickering if the townsfolk had ever thought of investing in anger counselling. 'Typically stupid question,' he replied. 'We pride ourselves on our Anger Management Centre – and make sure you spell that C-E-N-T-R-E, not C-E-N-T-E-R, which, let's face it, should be banned as a disgusting Americanism.'

He told me that the Umbrage Anger Management Centre (motto: Don't Get Me Started) trained hundreds of people every year. 'If you manage it successfully, you can boost anger by up to 500 per cent. We'll show you how to make a minor irritation blossom into a gripe and from there into a full-scale tantrum. A high proportion of our former students have gone on to become late-night phone-in hosts on leading radio stations. The others are all listeners, even though most of them hate it.'

In these uncertain times of Brexit, Covid, Trump and Cancel Culture, the previously quiet town of Umbrage has been a howling success, with thousands flocking to live and work there. Mr Bickering even told me of plans to annex Umbrage with the neighbouring town of Chipping Sourpuss, which is now acknowledged as a leader in online grievance, supplying up to 22 per cent of the world's insults and complaints.

'Makes you feel proud,' he said. 'Though not you. People like you don't know the meaning of the word.'

I made my way to Umbrage University (Vice-Chancellor: Lord Prescott). This institution, motto: 'Invidiam Meam Superba Portabo' ('I Shall Bear My Grudge with Pride') is renowned for its new John

Bercow Centre, where all the key debates take place. The motion today was: 'This house believes enough is enough.' Proposing it were Jeremy Corbyn, Yasmin Alibhai-Brown and Nigel Farage.

Everything went swimmingly for at least two minutes, when one speaker accused another of looking at her in a funny way, the other speaker replied 'Well, frankly, look who's talking!', and a third speaker got up and screamed: 'Typical!' Before long, most of the Umbrage students were screaming 'Take that back!' at one another.

I took the opportunity to ask a local historian how the town of Umbrage came by its name. 'I don't see what it's got to do with you!' he replied, before bursting into tears and blaming his outburst on the way his parents brought him up. 'They were Umbrage born and bred,' he explained. He then told me the history of the town.

Apparently, when the Romans attempted to capture what was then a small hilltop village in 50 BC, the villagers mounted the ramparts and started casting aspersions on the commander. Aspersions, as you probably know, were a species of stinging nettle grown locally. Soon the commander could bear it no longer, and fled. A deeply touchy character, he sent a message back to headquarters: 'I came, I saw, I took umbrage.'

Misunderstanding him, a messenger rushed to Caesar with the news that Umbrage had at last been taken.

Once the university debate was over – it ended with everyone refusing to apologise – I put my head around the door of the Umbrage Museum and politely told the curator that if it wasn't open, I'd be happy to come back.

'Did I hear you say this is just a load of old bric-a-brac?' he snapped.

'Not at all,' I explained. 'I was just wondering if you are open.'

'How dare you!' he said. 'Why shouldn't we be open, if we want to be?'

Eventually, he let me in. I must say there were some fascinating exhibits on display. I particularly liked the fragments of ancient jug discovered by local archaeologists at nearby Chipping Sourpuss.

'That jug was all in one piece when it arrived here,' the curator confided. 'But I didn't like the way it looked at me, so we had it out. I'm very sorry, but I will not be looked at in that condescending way by a common little jug!'

My walk around Umbrage was nearing its end. Out on the street, one man was remonstrating with another about the way he had parked his car without due consideration ('And don't you dare tell me to calm down!') and a woman was complaining that her husband had just had a heart attack. 'Why is it always me?'

Inside the butcher's shop, one customer was accusing another of jumping the queue. Further along, I passed a man reading the local newspaper, the *Umbrage Advertiser*, which sported the headline: 'They're Out to Get Us!' Apparently, it carries the same headline every week.

Unfortunately, when I returned to my car I found it was clamped and had several parking tickets attached. I jumped up and down in a fury, threatening to take my complaints to the highest authority. 'Don't you know who I am?!' I screamed, shaking my fist at the sky. And at that moment I realised that Umbrage had taken me to its heart.

Clerihews for the Credit Crunch

HM the Queen
Says, 'I'm not being mean
But the next banquet I host,
It's cheese on toast.'

Crispin Odey
Forgot his PIN code; he
Still hadn't planned
On going cash in hand.

Michael Winner
Is looking much thinner:
The returns must be poor
On *Death Wish 24*.

The Fat Controller
Wears a worn-out bowler
And a threadbare suit:
Thomas couldn't give a hoot.

Sir Philip Green
Hasn't a bean;
His next party but three
Is down the local KFC.

Bill Gates
Trusts in the fates
But he'll only agree to kiss you
If you buy a *Big Issue*.

Roger Waters
Leaves his quarters
To beg, 'Brother, spare a dime
To hear "Money – It's a Crime"'.

The Sultan of Brunei
Tries hard not to cry
But it's tough to stay kingly
In the Bradford and Bingley.

Deborah Meaden
Turns down the King of Sweden:
'You've a crown but no clout;
Sorry – I'm out!'

I Woke Up in a Sweat:
The Nightmares of Tony Benn

The late Tony Benn was the most dogged of political diarists. No day was left unrecorded, no meeting left unminuted. His waking life was devoted to certainties – problems identified, solutions supplied, resolutions carried, disputes supported. But his sleeping life was a very different affair. Every now and then, the Benn diaries offer descriptions of his dreams from the night before: nightmares in which all his daytime certainties evaporate, to be replaced by anxiety, muddle and paranoia.

'I slept on the plane,' he writes in September 1989, having flown back from India, 'and had terrible dreams about water overflowing in the bathroom.'

'I have the most hideous cramp, which forces me out of bed,' reads the entry for 24 May 2008, 'then nightmares! I can never remember them, but all I know is that they're always big problems that I have to solve, and I can't solve them.'

If ever they were to be published in a separate volume, Tony Benn's Dream Diaries would serve as a surreal counterbalance to his regular diaries. They are written in the same busy, matter-of-fact voice, but the landscape they describe is topsy-turvy and peculiar, the political equivalent of *Alice's Adventures in Wonderland*.

The very first dream he records, on Wednesday, 2 March 1966, gives rise to one of the loopiest conversations in any political diary. He is chatting to Marcia Williams, Private Secretary to then Prime Minister Harold Wilson.

'I saw Marcia just before I went in to see Harold and told her that I had dreamt about her on the previous night. She told me that she had dreamt that Harold was dead and had not believed it until she had been shown the body. She said she hadn't dared to tell Harold this story. But then Harold had told her this morning that last night he dreamt that Hugh Gaitskell had been sitting in at a committee – all white. What an extraordinary combination of dreams.'

Extraordinary indeed: if everyone was telling the truth, then on one and the same night, Tony Benn dreamt about Marcia Williams, and Marcia Williams dreamt that Harold Wilson had died, and Wilson dreamt that the ghost of Hugh Gaitskell had been sitting in a committee.

Wilson was a regular visitor to the dreamscape of Tony Benn. 'I had a dream that Harold (Wilson) had called me in and said: "I want you to be Vice-Chamberlain of the Royal Household with a seat in the House of Lords in charge of boxing under the Minister of Sport," Benn writes on Friday, 10 October 1975. 'He told me this in the great Cabinet Room which was full of people. "I'm afraid this doesn't mean a place in the Cabinet for you," he said. I replied: "Harold, I must think about it," and Sir John Hunt said: "Boxing is very important. We must preserve the quality and excellence of the Lonsdale Belt."'

As one would expect from this most driven of politicians, most of Tony Benn's nightmares represent setbacks to his career, or important tasks left uncompleted. 'It takes an awful time to unwind after a week's work,' he writes, as Minister of Aviation, on 31 July 1966, 'and I have nightmares in which I am required to see General de Gaulle about the future of Concorde, or arrive late in the office unshaven, not having read my Cabinet papers.'

This type of anxiety dream recurs throughout his life. In July 1993, aged sixty-eight, he dreams that 'I was doing a meeting in Manchester in November, when it was pelting with rain and terribly dark. And there wasn't a train that would get me back, so somebody said: "Why don't you fly a Tiger Moth back? You know how to fly."

'On the face of it, it seemed a good idea. Then I thought: "My God. First of all, do I remember how to fly a Tiger Moth? Secondly, it will be pelting with rain and pitch-dark. How do I get from Manchester to London?" And I got really quite worried.'

Benn was solipsistic without being introspective; he generally records his nightmares with no attempt at interpretation. But he adds these simple thoughts on his Tiger Moth dream: 'I think what the dream was probably telling me was that I am no longer a young man. I've got to recognise my limitations. But it was very vivid.'

Was his wide-eyed self ever truly aware of what his shut-eyed subconscious was trying to tell him? It seems to me that this dream has more to do with the world being far too complex and treacherous for easy navigation than with the limitations of age, though the two are clearly related. As the years went by, Tony Benn was to become the Grand Old Man of British politics; his dreams, on the other hand, were to grow ever more fearful.

Awake, Benn was a stranger to doubt, full of breezy self-assurance, forever setting the world to rights. But asleep, he could be overtaken by terror and doubt. For instance, on 21 April 1977, flying with a delegation on a Boeing 707 back from Riyadh, 'my head rolled all night and I dreamt of awful tortures in Saudi Arabia'.

The next month, he experiences a nightmare that is even creepier. On 18 May 1977, 'I was standing by a deep concrete pit in a prison with a noose round my neck. I swayed over this pit, looking down and knowing that with the drop the rope would break my neck, and there was this tremendous compulsion to jump, but I didn't. I woke up in a sweat and found that it was 3.50.'

Awake, he offers this interpretation: 'Perhaps it meant that I have managed to control my self-destructive urges; or maybe I was visualising in dramatic form the problems of resignation or dismissal from the Cabinet over direct elections.'

It seems likely that his latter diagnosis was correct: his political career was all-important to him, and though his conscience must often have told him to resign, his ambition always won the day. He was a survivor: when he woke from intense nightmares of ruin and despair, it never took him long to snap back into the here-and-now.

'Last night I dreamt that I visited a factory in Kirkby and found that all the equipment had been taken out, and there were wires hanging from the ceiling and gaps in the floor where all the basic machine tools had been torn out,' he writes on 26 October 1979. 'There was just one candle, and by this candlelight fifty workers were trying to turn the rubbish, the old pieces of wood and stuff, into little objects to sell. It was too much for me, and in my dream I burst into tears and put my hands over my eyes and wept uncontrollably before speaking to them.' But, upon waking, he is quick to recover: 'Anyway, the papers this morning are full of the developments in the party. Callaghan is rumoured to be thinking of resigning ...'

Twenty years later, when it comes to the possibility of retiring from the House of Commons, his dreams express his inner fears. His entry for 8 March 1999 sees him preoccupied with the decision: 'I am actually in quite a state about it.' The following night, 'I was absolutely exhausted and had awful dreams. I dreamt of cats and birds glued to bits of rubber so that they couldn't escape.' This nightmare must surely symbolise his twin anxieties over whether to leave or stay put.

As befits an ambitious politician, over the course of his political career each of his party leaders pops up in his dreams. Invariably, they are trying to force him to do something he doesn't want. 'I had a strange dream last night,' he records on 26 December 1998. 'I dreamt that I was parking my car round the corner and Tony Blair came up and said, "You can't park here – the parking restrictions apply on Saturday." I said, "It's a public holiday – Boxing Day." And he said, "I'm sorry, but the parking restrictions apply because it is Saturday – anyway we've got to generate the income to keep the traffic wardens paid."'

Once out of Parliament, his daytime proclamations grow more utopian while his visions at night grow increasingly dystopian. 'I had this dream that I was wrong about everything, and I had to go today to South Africa to see Nelson Mandela,' he writes on 3 August 2007. The following year, on 20 November 2008, 'I have nightmares every morning. I am overwhelmed by the feeling that the world – Britain and the world – is going to collapse through shortage of oil. I visualise circumstances where people at the top of tower blocks would find that the lift couldn't be run because there was no energy; doctors couldn't climb twenty-four flights of steps to look after them if they were ill; and the whole of society comes to an end.'

Where once he dreamt of building a New Jerusalem, he now suffers dreams of powerlessness. 'The nightmares! I can never remember them, but all I know is that they're always big problems that I have to solve, and I can't solve them.'

Over the coming years he has nightmares that he is trapped in Parliament, and that he is dead. Some are truly horrible. On 2 March 2009, 'I dreamt last night that the house was covered in green slime and fungus, and I went upstairs and in the bedroom was Caroline [Benn's late wife] lying on the bed, and the bed was a complete mess of papers and things. She was absolutely white, her eyes were red, and a fattish woman was cutting huge chunks of bloody meat and giving it to her to eat.'

The nineteenth-century French diarist Jules Renard noted the peculiar urgency of the world of dreams. 'How odd is the world of dreams!' he wrote. 'Thoughts, inner speech, crowd and swarm – a little world hastening to live before the awakening that is its end, its particular death.'

Beyond Livid:
Katie Price@MissKatiePrice

Katie Price@MissKatiePrice 7.45 a.m.
Open fridge door. Milk gone well off. Shouldnt call itself milk if its gone off. Life ruined. Thanx guys. ☺

Katie Price@MissKatiePrice 7.46 a.m.
I swear I'm never going to get milk from that rank overweight loser cow again. Total slapper.

Katie Price@MissKatiePrice 7.53 a.m.
So now my toasts gone and burnt itself. First the milk then the toast. Why is it always me? ☹

Katie Price@MissKatiePrice 7.56 a.m.
Husband Kieran comes downstairs starkers, guess what he's after. You're looking well fit Katie he sez.

Katie Price@MissKatiePrice 7.57 a.m.
I tell him no way not til you done the bins.

Katie Price@MissKatiePrice 7.59 a.m.
OK so he done the bins but I tell him sorry I'm not in the mood he sez you promised I say fuck the fuck off and he starts cutting up rough.

Katie Price@MissKatiePrice 8.01 a.m.
So I say if that's the way feel you 2-timing bastard you shouldnt of done it with my best friend on the sunlounger or my second best friend in the Ford

Katie Price@MissKatiePrice 8.02 a.m.
Fiesta or my eyebrows assistant in the disco toilet so he says don't bring that up again and I say its you what brought it up not me

Katie Price@MissKatiePrice 8.03 a.m.
and he says I never and I say yes you fucking did. Girls make your dreams come true with my new Katie Price Sunkist Instant Matte Tan. ☺

Katie Price @MissKatiePrice 8.04 a.m.
@MailonLine says Katie Price is going on holiday in the Maldives. Pissed off. Those guys dont know the meaning of privacy.

Katie Price@MissKatiePrice 8.05 a.m.
Switched on Radio 4. That Jeremy Corbyn aint half full of himself. He come on to me bigtime two years back, up to his old pranks.

Katie Price@MissKatiePrice 8.06 a.m.
I told him Jeremy you can look but no touching. That put him in his place.

Katie Price@MissKatiePrice 8.07 a.m.
CorrXion. It was Jeremy Beadle. Or he said he was, the bastard.

Katie Price@MissKatiePrice 8.09 a.m.
And Jeremy Kyles eyes were all over my boobs too. And Clarksons all hands. What is it with me and Jeremys?

Katie Price @MissKatiePrice 8.10 a.m.
Staying at 5-star @maldivespremierbeachresort next week with Kerry Katona for Channel 5 special *Katie and Kerry Big It Up on the Beach* #awesome.

Katie Price@MissKatiePrice 8.12 a.m.
Headline story in *Sun* claims KP had 'bigger brighter bouncier' boob job yesterday. So totally false like totally made up.

Katie Price@MissKatiePrice 8.15 a.m.
Look in mirror. TBH my boobs ARE bigger brighter bouncier. Suddenly remember. Honestly I'll forget my own head next!!!!!

Katie Price @MissKatiePrice 8.27 a.m.
Still looking in mirror. Second thoughts, theyre a bit too big for new superslimline Katie. What woz I thinking?

Katie Price @MissKatiePrice 8.30 a.m.
Well pissed off with new boobs. Phone boob doctor, demand new pair asap.

Katie Price @MissKatiePrice 8.34 a.m.
Booked in for new middling-size boobs this afternoon at 4pm. Should be out by 6 long as theres no leaking. Livin the dream.

Katie Price @MissKatiePrice 8.35 a.m.
Agent texts asking if I got enough material for new vol of autobiography. Reply not quite enough will work on it.

Katie Price @MissKatiePrice 8.37 a.m.
Checked out the CCTV cameras. Livid? Im beyond livid. Saw Kieran bonking rank minger against back of the new #@LandRover. If its scratched I'll fucking kill him.

Katie Price @MissKatiePrice 8.42 a.m.
Totally lost it told Kieran I seen him shagging fat slag my lifes in pieces facing the abyss pulled his hair kicked him my world shattered. ☹

Katie Price @MissKatiePrice 8.43 a.m.
Texted agent brill news babe autobiography totally on course. ☺

Katie Price @MissKatiePrice 8.45 a.m.
Kieran begs forgiveness I tell him you just gone and fucking ruined my life dont know why we got married piss off. ☹

Katie Price@MissKatiePrice 8.47 a.m.
Thrilled to bits about launch @debenhamsoxfordstreet of new fragrance that combines the mystique of the East with the glam of Rio.

Katie Price@MissKatiePrice 8.49 a.m.
Slap love rat Kieran so hard he confesses he shagged the stripogram girl I gave him for his birthday and slag who brought the cake. ☹

Katie Price@MissKatiePrice 8.52 a.m.
Last time I order a birthday cake from that shop, who cares if the sponge was light as a feather thats not the point.

Katie Price @MissKatiePrice 8.57 a.m.
Kieran says sorry for shagging rank slag, suggests we renew our marriage vows I could dress all in pink with horses and crystal carriage we could sell it to C5 easy.

Katie Price @MissKatiePrice 8.59 a.m.
Booked church for top glam wedding straight after boob job with celeb vicar horse and carriage, 12 bridesmaids, ballgown entertainment by Lee from SClub7. Dream come true. ☺

Katie Price @MissKatiePrice 9.00 a.m.
Tap won't stop dripping. I'll never forgive that plumber. My world is shattered into a million pieces. Tragic breakfast that turned out to be. ☹

Katie Price@MissKatiePrice 9.02 a.m.
Go on girls rush to @debenhamsoxfordstreet treat yourself to sophisticated new fragrance *Intercourse by Katie.* ☺

Downturn Abbey
Act One: Something Rather Terrible

LORD GRANTHAM: Forgive me, my dear, but something … rather terrible … has happened.

LADY CORA: What do you mean, Rawbutt? When you say something … rather terrible … has happened … do you mean that …?

LORD GRANTHAM: Yes, my dear, I'm afraid so. I mean that something … rather terrible … has happened.

LADY CORA: Something … rather terrible …?

LORD GRANTHAM: Yes, my dear.

LADY CORA: … has happened?

LORD GRANTHAM: Yes, my dear. Something … rather terrible … has happ –

CARSON: Might I have a word, milord?

LORD GRANTHAM: Can't it wait, Carson?

CARSON: I'm sorry to bother you, milord, but something …

LORD GRANTHAM: Yes, Carson?

CARSON: … rather terrible … has happened.

LORD GRANTHAM: I see. That only goes to confirm my suspicion, Carson, that something … rather terrible … has happened.

MRS PATMORE: Forgive me, your lordship, but I was just passing when I overheard Carson saying that something … rather terrible … has happened.

DAISY: Crikey!

MRS PATMORE: Daisy! Mind your language!

Daisy: Sorry, Mrs Patmore! It's the shock.

MRS PATMORE: There, there, Daisy. Dry those eyes!

DOWAGER COUNTESS: Is one hearing things? Did I just overhear Mrs Patmore announcing that she had overheard Carson saying that something … rather terrible … has happened?

THOMAS: Forgive me, but I was just passing when I overheard Her Ladyship saying that she was just passing when she overheard Mrs Patmore saying she was just passing when she overheard Carson saying that something … rather terrible … had happened.

LORD GRANTHAM: Well, I suppose it now behoves me to tell you all the awful news. Something … rather terrible … has happened.

CARSON: More coffee, milord?

LORD GRANTHAM [*reading newspaper*]: Thank you Carson. [*Reflects*] Coffee is a warm, dark beverage much favoured at breakfast. It's bad news, I'm afraid. I have just read in today's *Times* that a major earthquake is on its way!

THE DOWAGER DUCHESS: An earthquake! Here at Downton! The presumption of it!

CARSON: More coffee, milady?

LADY CORA: Thank you, Carson. Whithersofore do they say this earthquake might occur, Rawbutt?

LORD GRANTHAM: Let me see [*studies newspaper*]. Oh no!

CARSON: More coffee, milord?

LORD GRANTHAM: Dash it, Carson, this is no time for a warm beverage! There is no cause for alarm, but it says here in *The Times* that a major earthquake is due 'within the next few minutes'. Apparently it will occur at – gracious heavens! – 'Downton Abbey, the historic stately home of the Earl of Grantham'.

THOMAS [*under his breath*]: I like earthquakes.

O'Brien [*under her breath*]: Me too.

CARSON: More coffee, milady?

LADY CORA: I might never have another chance to say this. Just seconds before this earthquake kills us all, I want everyone to know – I love you, Carson, and I'm expecting your baby!

[*EVERYONE GASPS IN HORROR*]

LORD GRANTHAM [*putting on spectacles*]: One second, everybody! I do apologise. I must have misread! It doesn't say 'Earthquake' at all. It says 'Flower Show'.

THOMAS [*under his breath*]: Shame. I hate flowers.

O'BRIEN [*under her breath*]: Me too!

LORD GRANTHAM: I would entreat you all to return to your duties and behave as though nothing untoward had occurred. Life is full of events, many of them unspeakable, and we must learn to ignore them.

CARSON: Very well, milord.

LORD GRANTHAM: Oh, and Carson?

CARSON: Yes, milord?

LORD GRANTHAM: While you're about it, would you make an appointment for Her Ladyship with Dr Crippen? They say he's very reliable.

CARSON: Very good, milord. More coffee, milord?

FASHION

Dee-AHN-ah

These days, the word Genius, like the words Icon and Legend, is scattered with gay abandon. In the past few weeks, I have seen a former Spice Girl described as a legend, a disc jockey as a genius and a runner-up on *Big Brother* as an icon. Quite where this leaves Shakespeare or Isaac Newton, no one seems to know.

The world of fashion has always played fast and loose with its superlatives. In fashion, you only need to wear a silly hat to a smart party to be called an icon, and if you are a designer, the ability to make a pair of trousers which button up at the top guarantees you the status of genius.

In the early 1980s, when I had a part-time job on *Tatler* magazine, these gushy epithets were being pioneered with some frequency. Virtually every afternoon, I would witness someone wearing a pantomime skirt or green hair or shoes three times too big hobbling down the corridor and I would be told in hushed tones that – yes! – this was so-and-so, the legendary fashion icon.

In those distant days, the most legendary icon and iconic legend of them all was, without doubt, Diana Vreeland. I dare say her name doesn't mean much any more – death renders us all unfashionable – but in those days she was the bee's knees, even if, asked to dress a bee, she would undoubtedly have advised it that knees were SO passé, before bundling it into a pair of magenta culottes.

Who was Diana Vreeland? Through the 1960s, she was the all-powerful editor of *American Vogue*, a woman who, according to her breathless biographer, 'helped millions of women with their fashion problems' and who 'wanted all of her readers to find continuous inspiration to be beautiful, well dressed, intellectually stimulated, and to keep their standards high'. She was, then, the Mother Teresa of the leisured classes. In a funny sort of way, she looked a bit like her, too, with her all-powerful nose ruling over a craggy face and her determined manner of dress.

Like the mystics of old, Diana Vreeland espoused what her followers were to term her fashion 'philosophy'. 'Pink is the navy blue of India' she once said. Her biographer* repeats this little aphorism no less than three times, almost as though it might accrue meaning through repetition. Asked the secret of looking great, Vreeland replied, 'simplicity', regardless of the fact that she would spend hours a day polishing herself up in the bathroom, even going to the effort of rouging her earlobes.

Other cherished gems of the Vreeland philosophy include:

- 'The bikini is the most important thing since the atom bomb.'
- 'No lady wears red shoes.'
- 'Peanut butter is the greatest invention since Christianity.'
- 'Why don't you rinse your blond child's hair in dead champagne to keep its gold?'
- 'All my life I've pursued the perfect red.'
- 'The Civil War was nothing compared to the smell of a San Diego orange' and, perhaps most important of all,
- 'If you don't stand on your head for half an hour every day, you will never have an orgasm.'

And so it goes on. This is all snappy, camp, drag-queen stuff, treating the superficial as profound and the profound as superficial, but her biographer hangs on to every word. Most of her iconic, legendary, etc. etc. sayings are neither particularly true nor particularly funny, though I did find myself smiling at her marvellously ruthless comment on hearing that President Kennedy had been assassinated. 'My God,' she said, 'Lady Bird Johnson in the White House. We can't use her in the magazine.'

---

* *Diana Vreeland* by Eleanor Dwight (2002).

But of course they did: there was the new First Lady, in the May 1964 issue, photographed by Horst, dolled up in a deep-red gown with a pearl choker in front of the blue curtains in the White House, along-side the suitably fawning caption, 'Mrs Johnson, a dark-haired, pretty woman with a twenty-inch waist, an easy smile, tense hands, and a direct intelligence, is totally unlike the nation's folksy impression of her ...' *Vogue* had always acted as the maidservant to the rich and powerful, and for all her catchpenny iconoclasm, Vreeland was the last person to think of changing things.

Diana Vreeland was born in 1903 into the very heart of American wealth and power. Her parents mixed with the Vanderbilts and the Astors, went big-game hunting in Africa and spent their summers in Europe. 'I adore the way I was brought up ... My experiences were so innocent and so easy and so charming,' she recalled. 'Banker Marries Heiress' read the newspaper headline at her marriage to the dashing, philandering Reed Vreeland, and as a young woman Diana inherited over $2 million in today's money.

The Vreelands lived in London and Paris before the war. They mixed in circles sprinkled with people with names like Princess Jean-Louis de Faucigny-Lucinge and the Victomtesse Marie-Laure de Noailles, and they threw 'famous' dinner parties prepared by a 'terrific' cook. 'To friends,' concludes her biographer, 'the apartment's ambience was delightful.'

Diana's secret for a happy life was to ignore anything unhappy. Her husband used to send his girlfriends gardenias floating in a bowl, so that when Diana entered a room and spotted gardenias, she knew what was happening. But she never mentioned it. Similarly, and with a kind of justice, when her beloved husband died of cancer in 1966, she neglected to tell their son. 'I don't want to bother him with that,' she explained. 'It's so unpleasant.'

Her first step into the world of fashion was to open a lingerie shop, just off Berkeley Square, where her friend Wallis Simpson bought suitable nightgowns for her first weekend away with the Prince of Wales. The two became lifelong friends. 'The Duchess looked too beautiful, standing in the garden, dressed in a turquoise djellaba embroidered in black pearls and white pearls – marvellous – and wearing all her sapphires,' she wrote in 1967, yet to this dispassionate viewer the Duchess looked more like a spiteful governess who has just emerged embittered from a collision with a jewellery box.

As the book goes on, it becomes clear that all those, like the Duchess, credited with 'impeccable taste' in fact just have impeccable bank accounts, and are able to be dressed, all day, every day, by Chanel, Saint Laurent or Mainbocher. Even so, most of the photographs in this beautifully designed book make Diana Vreeland, with her wretched passion for red – red lipstick, red dresses, red sofas, red chairs, red drapes, red nails – look as daft as a brush. Her simultaneous passion for hanging vast, clumping earrings and bracelets and necklaces from every part of her body ('Diana's trademark was a profusion of accessories,' coos her biographer) lend her the look of a miniature motor mechanic making do without her tool bag.

Back in America (her name now pronounced Dee-AHN-ah), Diana Vreeland went from fashion editor at *Harper's Bazaar* to editor of *Vogue* and finally to head of the Costume Institute at the Metropolitan Museum. She spent her days striding into the office saying things like, 'I have a feeling that bright grass-green is going to be the colour!' and 'Cotton! Cotton! Cotton!' She would then distribute her advice to her readers. 'Why don't you own, as does one extremely smart woman, twelve diamond roses of all sizes? … Why don't you paint every door in a completely white house the color of a different flower – and thereby give each room its name?'

Was Diana Vreeland, as her biographer claims, a 'super-energetic genius' with 'limitless imagination'? Or was she instead one of the great unsung comic turns of the century, Max Wall in a bright red dress and a shiny black wig?

On Gloves

There were a number of puzzling aspects to the late Karl Lagerfeld. For instance, he is said to have owned 150,000 books. He was eighty-five when he died, so to get through them all he would have had to have read 1,764 books a year, or roughly five books a day, every day, starting from the minute he was born.

Even more peculiar were the gloves he always wore, indoors and outdoors, come rain or shine. He tended to favour gloves of the finger-less variety; faced with such a backlog of pages to turn, this was probably wise. Yet they failed to endow him with an aura of bookish-ness. Instead, they called to mind Albert Steptoe, the rag-and-bone man played so memorably by Wilfrid Brambell in TV's *Steptoe and Son*. Albert – invariably derided as 'you dirty old man' by his aspira-tional son Harold – was a lifelong wearer of fingerless gloves. He would wear his gloves to hold a mug of tea, to eat chicken legs, to load his cart, and even, like Lagerfeld, to do his darning. In one episode, he took a bath in them. Yet for some reason he never gained the kudos that attached itself to Karl Lagerfeld. Life can be so unfair.

Personally, I have never managed to keep my hands on a pair of gloves, fingerless or fingerful, for more than twenty-four hours. They are the most losable of all garments. One minute they are there; the next, they are gone. It is almost as though there were a worldwide conspiracy of gloves, nipping away when their owners' backs are turned, as fast as their fingers can carry them.

Last year, I walked the length of the Thames. Every mile or so, I would pass a single lost glove, planted on a stile or a fence, looking lost and forlorn, presumably placed there by a concerned passer-by. What are all these single gloves doing there, languishing on the banks of the Thames? The late Michael Jackson was well known for wearing single gloves. Presumably, he had to order them in pairs, and then get rid of the one he didn't need. Could it be that the world-renowned singer would take time off to walk – or moonwalk – up and down the Thames, dipping into his sack of unwanted left-hand gloves, then distributing them at regular intervals in the puddles and hedgerows? It seems unlikely, until you remember that Jackson was a friend of Uri Geller, who lives on the Thames in the village of Sonning, which is, incidentally, also home to the footballer Glenn Hoddle, the Clooneys, Jimmy Page and Theresa May.

Hoddle was always a midfielder, so had no need for gloves. Mrs May can sometimes be spotted in gloves as she emerges from the church in Sonning on a frosty Sunday, but I've noticed she always makes a point of wearing two at a time, which suggests she never had to make do with Michael Jackson's hand-me-downs.

Long gloves were once an essential part of a woman's wardrobe. But those days are gone. I have a copy of *Debrett's Guide to Etiquette and Modern Manners* from 1982. Under the heading 'Gloves', it advises: 'Once the sign of a well-bred lady, gloves have become optional accessories, largely reverting to their original purpose of keeping hands warm.'

Men, too, have abandoned gloves. Cars still have glove compartments, but there are no driving gloves to put in them: it is the glove that dare not speak its name. Of course, oven gloves, joined in the middle, can come in very handy in the kitchen, but look out of place when worn to a society ball or Hollywood premiere.

With the deaths of Jackson and now Lagerfeld, the glory days of the glove are over. Madonna used to wear black lacy gloves from time to time, but people don't talk about her any more, and can't even be bothered to check whether she still wears them or not. From now on, the most famous gloves in the world must be Sooty and Sweep, though their careers, like Madonna's, seem to be on the wane. Perhaps the three of them might consider joining forces, with Madonna taking to the stage wearing Sooty on one hand and Sweep on the other.

Choupette

When Karl Lagerfeld died in 2019, he left part of his $200 million fortune to his cat, Choupette.

Choupette was already known as the wealthiest cat in the world. In 2015 alone, she earned $3 million from taking part in two campaigns, one for a Japanese beauty product and the other for a German car company. Lagerfeld supplied her with a bodyguard and two ladies-in-waiting. She travelled everywhere with custom-made Louis Vuitton and Goyard trunks, and had her own iPad. Over the years, Choupette has broadened her portfolio. It now includes a make-up collection with Shu Uemura, a book and a fashion line, plus a huge following on social media. Choupette is what is now known as an 'influencer'.

Her late master's munificence has left her comfortably well off. Like Jacob Rees-Mogg, she benefits from a full-time nanny, who sees to her every need. She feeds off designer chinaware, with separate dishes for water, croquettes and pâté. Her croquettes arrive with a choice of turkey or fish sauce. Furthermore, at the weekend her agent released a set of photographs showing Choupette enjoying a three-course meal and snuggling up on a silk cushion.

Choupette is, says her agent, 'a model who's very easy to work with. She's used to having her photo taken and to all the noise. As soon as she sees the camera, she poses.' Is it just me, or does Choupette look dreadfully smug in these new photographs, even for a cat?

Having done little in her life other than purr and pose, she has been welcomed as a member of the international jet set. No doubt she breakfasts with Gwyneth Paltrow, exchanges selfies with Kim

Kardashian and makes impassioned calls for inclusivity at all the major red-carpet events.

Envy is never an attractive emotion, but, by now, one or two down-at-heel followers may have begun plotting to elbow Choupette out of the way, hoping to take her place at the centre of the *beau monde*.

At first glance, it appears so easy: you wait until Choupette's household staff are taking a well-deserved coffee break, then you catch Choupette unawares, bundle her into a bag, throw the bag to a getaway driver, and take her place on the sofa, dressed up as her double. Hey presto! A life of luxury awaits! Which of us would not relish the chance to spend the rest of our days curled up on a sofa, tucking into croquettes in a chic Paris apartment while a furious Choupette is forced to eat Kattomeat and chase mice in a dank basement somewhere off the Edgware Road?

But, on second thoughts, it will never work. If the recent film of Andrew Lloyd Webber's *Cats* has taught us anything, it is how difficult it is for human beings to pass themselves off as cats. We are simply too big and burly. Those who saw James Corden squeezed into a hairy bodysuit tell me he looked more like the Yeti, or a pantomime horse; quite a few audience survivors are being treated for post-traumatic stress disorder. So it looks as though any attempt to swap places with Choupette is doomed to fail. Instead, we just have to hope that Choupette suffers the fate that assails so many celebrities in the world today.

Not content with her life of luxury, she will grow greedy for more and more fame. Before long, she will be photographed coming out of a nightclub in the early hours of the morning, looking wrecked. Then close friends will tell the newspapers that they are 'seriously concerned' at the weight she is either putting on or taking off. On *Celebrity Big Brother*, Choupette will be recorded saying something offensive in an unguarded moment. She will then face a Twitter storm, and early expulsion. Damning profiles in serious magazines will follow. Her fan base will collapse, and she will be barred from appearing on even fairly modest television shows, like *Celebrity Antiques Road Trip* or *Loose Women*. And then, on top of it all, her misery memoir, chronicling her kittenhood on the streets of Montmartre and her recent descent into celebrity hell, will be met with disappointing sales. And in a couple of years' time, Choupette will appear alongside a member of S Club 7 and a Red Setter from *Animal Hospital* in a feature called *Where Are They Now?**

Poor Choupette! For all its outward luxury, life as a celebrity cat has never been easy. Any cat taking her first few steps towards the high life does so at her peril.

---

* Two years later, she is still living in style, celebrating her tenth birthday with a fishcake at the Hôtel de Crillon. She pays monthly visits to the vet, who monitors her heart, liver and diet. Once subject to kidnapping threats, she now lives a quieter life, though she still has 100,000 followers on Instagram, and is transported to modelling assignments by her chauffeur.

Downturn Abbey
Act Two: Wraparound Shades

LADY CORA: Might I have a word, Mrs Hughes? Lady Mary is in a dark place.

MRS HUGHES: A dark place, Your Ladyship?

LADY CORA: Yes, Mrs Hughes. A very dark place indeed. I regret to say she has taken to the coal cellar in a pair of extra-dark wraparound shades.

MRS HUGHES: Wraparound shades! Forgive me, Your Ladyship, but what might they be?

LADY CORA: They are a new-fangled invention, Mrs Hughes. We must learn to move with the times. Apparently, they are all the rage. Lady Mary tells me she wishes to look 'badass'.

Dowager Duchess: 'Badass'? Surely you mean Badedas, the luxurious new bath essence?

CARSON: Badedas, milady? Forgive me, but surely you mean Bandana, a new-fangled colourful kerchief, generally worn on the head or around the neck for protective or decorative purposes?

MRS HUGHES: In my day, we used to EAT bananas. For pity's sake, what is the world coming to?

EARL OF GRANTHAM: Did I hear you mention Baader Meinhof? No daughter of mine shall ever join any new-fangled Marxist-Leninist terrorist faction – and my decision is final!

CARSON: Might I have a word, milady?

LADY MARY: A word, Carson?

CARSON: Yes, milady. A word on a matter of some delicacy.

LADY MARY: A matter of some delicacy, Carson?

CARSON: Yes, milady. It has come to my notice that you are unable to convey any form of expression, but instead simply repeat the words that have only just this minute been spoken.

LADY MARY: Repeat the words that have only just this minute been spoken, Carson?

CARSON: Yes, milady. So I was wondering, milady, whether anything was … wrong.

LADY MARY: Wrong, Carson?

CARSON: Forgive me, milady. But have you, perchance, forgotten the lines?

LADY MARY: Forgotten the lines, Carson?

CARSON: Please assure me, milady, that there's no need to worry.

LADY MARY: No need to worry, Carson?

CARSON: Well, that's a weight off my mind.

LADY MARY: Off my mind, Carson.

Hitler's Hair

It's been a bad hair week,* as far as tyrants are concerned. On Tuesday, a lock of Napoleon's hair was stolen from a museum in Melbourne. Yesterday, the North Korean embassy complained to the Foreign Office about a West London hairdresser exhibiting a jokey photograph of Kim Jong-Un in his window. Meanwhile, a battle is raging over Adolf Hitler's hair.

The cranky historian David Irving claimed that he lent a lock of Hitler's hair to Channel 4, and they failed to return it. In turn, Channel 4 said they bought it off Irving for $5,000. Irving countered that they had paid him the $5,000 for an interview, not for the hair. And now Channel 4 are arguing that DNA tests suggest that the hair is not Hitler's after all. 'The hair was found to be non-European, most likely from the subcontinent,' says a spokesman.

This has angered David Irving. 'I know it was Hitler's because it came from his barber, with a signed letter of authentication,' he thunders. He was, he says, assured that Hitler's barber picked the hair off the floor by means of sticky tape on the soles of his shoes, though to me this sounds unlikely. Anyone who has ever visited a barber knows that even a modest trim produces a great mass of hair clippings. Some hairs stick to the gown the barber puts round you, and the rest fall on to the floor.

There would be no need for sticky tape, which would anyway have made an irritating noise, and alerted the Führer to the purloining of his locks. If the barber in question wished to be discreet, why did he

---

* 13–20 April 2014.

not just gather the hair with a dustpan and brush once the haircut was over?

Hitler's hair was never his strongest point. In photographs, it always looks lank and greasy. Experts might say it lacked body. On the other hand, it is hard to imagine it any other way – a bouffant or a mullet, or even a crew cut – and he certainly wouldn't have suited a ponytail.

Even in the longest, most magisterial biographies, Hitler's hair barely gets a look in. Professor Ian Kershaw's two-volume biography, widely regarded as the most comprehensive, deals with it only a few times over the course of 2,000-odd pages, though each mention is interesting.

In January 1910, the twenty-one-year-old Hitler was living the life of a tramp in a dosshouse in Vienna. At this point he had, says Kershaw, his 'hair over his collar and dark fuzz on his chin'. His appearance 'even provoked his fellow vagrants to remark on it'.

Two years later, still down-and-out, he is 'shabbily dressed and unkempt, wearing a long greyish coat, worn at the sleeves, and battered old hat, trousers full of holes, and shoes stuffed with paper'. By now, he has 'shoulder-length hair and a ragged beard'.

It seems to have been the First World War that made it neater, though as late as 1932 it continued to defy convention. Franz von Papen, the former Chancellor of Germany, noted around this time that Hitler 'had an unhealthy complexion, and with his little moustache and curious hair style had an indefinable bohemian quality'.

The only memoir in which Hitler's hair is covered at any length is *With Hitler to the End*, written by his devoted valet, Heinz Linge. 'Hitler's characteristic lock of hair, which always lay across his forehead – and his moustache – attracted a lot of friendly amusement among the population,' he writes. 'He knew this and took great pride in both. Whether he was copying Napoleon's hairstyle I have no idea. Even as a schoolboy he parted his hair on the right for a while. His moustache was often a clue to his mood. If he was sucking it, this was always a warning for us.' Too much information, as the younger generation would say.

Since we're tackling the theme of Hitler and hair, might I point out a previously overlooked snippet that pops up six lines from the bottom of page 55 in the chapter titled 'Drop Out' in the first volume of Kershaw's biography?

It is February 1910, and the young Hitler has moved to the Men's Home in the north of Vienna. Hitler is scraping a living selling post-card-size paintings, generally copies of works in the famous museums. 'Hitler and his cronies in the Men's Home were at this time prepared to entertain any dotty scheme – a miracle hair-restorer was one such idea – that would bring in a bit of money,' writes Kershaw.

And that is all: disappointingly, Kershaw fails to elaborate on Hitler's miracle hair-restorer and what became of it.

In the past, historians have speculated that a small dose of artistic success might have stopped Hitler from pursuing a career in politics. Might not the same be said of Hitler's singular failure to market a miracle hair-restorer? With his undoubted gift for communication, Hitlercreem could have become as popular as Brylcreem, and then he wouldn't have needed to prove himself in other, more catastrophic ways.

As he nurses his wounds, David Irving might care to chronicle this alternative history in his next book. He might think it batty, but he has written far battier.

Three Toupees

Death has its drawbacks, particularly for those whose toupees survive them. Recently, an auction house in Bristol sold off items that had once belonged to Peter Wyngarde, the smoothie actor who played the moustachioed TV detective Jason King. The lots at the auction included Wyngarde's snakeskin jacket, his purple-shaded sunglasses, his childhood teddy bear and his silk kaftan smoking gown, as well as his trophy for the 'Best-Dressed Personality of 1970', won against stiff competition from Cliff Richard and George Best.

Yet the most memorable item in the auction was Lot 190, sheepishly described by the auctioneer as Wyngarde's 'personal toupee ... with a fine mesh base. Supplied within its original box, addressed to Wyngarde at his personal residence. A rare item from the Peter Wyngarde estate.' One customer was prepared to buy it for £170, so we must trust that it went to a happy home, or even a happy head. But Wyngarde was a fastidious man and not the sort of person who would have wanted his toupee put under the gavel.

I felt the same sense of squeamishness on behalf of Frankie Howerd. In life, the great comedian was always embarrassed by his baldness, so took to wearing a singularly ill-fitting toupee. 'He was the only one convinced that it was practically impossible to see the join,' observed his biographer, Graham McCann. 'Even Max Bygraves, one of his oldest most trusted confidants, had to pretend not to notice every time a gust of wind caused the hairpiece to hover slightly over Howerd's head.' A few years after Frankie died, his house in Somerset was opened to the public. Along with his furniture and his various artworks, his toupee was placed on display, perched on his old dressing table for visitors to gawp at.

The pop artist Andy Warhol, a year younger than Peter Wyngarde, was another closet toupee-wearer. The victim of alopecia, he was always embarrassed at being bald, particularly in the 1960s, when hair was all the rage. He owned four toupees, each slightly different. One of his helpers claimed to be able to gauge Warhol's mood by his toupee. 'The messy one was supposed to indicate he was in a bad mood and not to be approached.'

One day, a friend sneaked a peek into the little case that Warhol took with him everywhere, and spotted a pair of scissors and a roll of Johnson & Johnson medical tape. 'So that's how he attaches his toupee,' he thought. That same friend rode with him on the roller-coaster at Coney Island in 1963, and looked back to see Warhol's toupee lifting off his head in the wind. 'Oh my God!' he thought, 'It's gonna come off!' But it stayed put, thanks to the adhesive powers of Johnson & Johnson.

I remember sitting immediately behind Warhol in a minibus on the way to Oxford in 1980, and being captivated by the tell-tale gap between his hair and his head. His wide-eyed biographer, Blake Gopnik, believes that 'the way he camouflaged his baldness had a touch of genius'. But to me, it seemed more like a touch of ineptitude.

And now, like Peter and Frankie, Warhol must suffer the posthumous indignity of having his toupees on public display. Back in March, Tate Modern in London opened a 'major retrospective' of Warhol's art, which included his four toupees laid out in a display cabinet for all to see. No sooner had the exhibition opened than it closed, due to Covid. But the ghosts of Warhol's blushes have not been spared: you can still see the toupees online, in a short film on the Tate's website.

Between the two curators saying that this-or-that work is 'extraordinarily powerful' – the catch-all term of praise in the art world – they start cooing over his toupees. 'In the late fifties, he starts to wear a toupee,' one of them says, 'which then becomes this very iconic silver wig.'

Toupee or not toupee? Poor Peter! Poor Frankie! And now, poor Andy! Is it not time we let their toupees rest in peace?

The Last Blazer

Alan Whicker may be the last Briton to have worn a silver-buttoned blazer with complete confidence. His demise at the age of eighty-seven tolls the death knell for this most self-confidently middle-class of garments. Which is not to say that the blazer has entirely disappeared from the British wardrobe. There are still those who trot around in blazers – this year's Wimbledon was awash with them – but something tells me their hearts are not entirely in it. They suspect that, deep down, they are fighting a losing battle.

Like the periwig and the bowler bat, the plus-four and the bow tie, the blazer is on the way out; those who persist in wearing it do so with a smattering of self-consciousness, a touch of obstinacy, even a pinch of camp. It is as though they are determined to stand up for a tradition that they know, in their heart of hearts, has already had its day.

With the passing of Alan Whicker, television's other great Alan – Alan Partridge – steps up to take his place as our most famous living blazer-wearer. His green blazer is as much a part of him as his driving gloves and his love of Wagon Wheels. 'It's classic English gentleman abroad,' Partridge observed on a recent trip to Paris. 'It's David Niven, Stewart Granger, Nigel Havers. It's a green blazer. The look? Imperial leisure.' What is it about Alans and blazers? Alan Titchmarsh can often be spotted in a blazer, and I imagine that slipping into a shiny-but-toned blazer while on vacation is just about as relaxed as Alan Sugar ever gets.

In its heyday, the blazer came to symbolise a kind of conventional decency. Yacht club commodores and school bursars wore blazers. People who played bowls wore blazers. And because they wore blazers, you felt you could trust them. A man in a blazer wouldn't pilfer your wallet or run off with your wife. The Major in *Fawlty Towers* was, I think, the consummate blazer-wearer: a little dim, perhaps even a little dull, but the salt of the earth. For this very reason, the blazer was doomed to be targeted by all sorts of ne'er-do-wells, and fast became the preferred uniform of the confidence trickster.

Before long, every bogus Major striding along the seaside promenade at Bournemouth in pursuit of a gullible spinster would be sure to sport a blazer with shiny brass buttons. This meant there came a time when all the fishiest people in public life were wearing them. From Lord Mountbatten of Burma to Arthur Daley, from Hughie Green to the Duke of Windsor, anyone who was the slightest bit dodgy would be sure to hang a selection of well-pressed blazers in his wardrobe.

Years ago, when the Duchess of York's erratic father, Major Ron, was still going strong, I asked a mutual friend what the Major's job description as the Queen's Polo Manager actually meant. 'He's just a jumped-up stable lad in a fancy blazer,' came the reply. Word of this got back to Major Ron, and he was furious, presumably because he knew it to be true. By then, a fancy blazer had become the sign of a cad and a charlatan, of someone who wasn't quite what he claimed to be. Like the firm handshake and looking people straight in the eye, the blazer had originally been a symbol of trust. Because of this, it had been purloined by the less than trustworthy, and became their preferred disguise.

It's no coincidence that Lord Archer of Weston-Super-Mare always makes a point of looking strangers straight in the eye and shaking them firmly by the hand. He is also an inveterate blazer-wearer. Nowadays, whenever I encounter someone in a blazer, I start counting the spoons. Yet, in defence of the man in the blazer, it should also be said that there are limits to his awfulness. He may be a rogue, but he is rarely a monster. The blazer is, one might say, the costume of the small-time trickster rather than the depraved tyrant.

It is hard to imagine Adolf Hitler in a blazer, or Josef Stalin for that matter. Neither man went in for smart-casual, or chose to attend dinner-dances at their local golf club. Might a blazer have discouraged them from pursuing some of their greater crimes against humanity? You can imagine plotting a jewellery heist or a modest piece of blackmail while in a blazer, but for anything more serious you would probably want to slip into something a little more intimidating, like full military uniform.

Of Frocks and Fracks:
Vivienne Westwood

The author is pictured, full length, on the cover, arms and legs outstretched, with slogans pinned all over her dress, rather in the manner of the elderly gent who used to stand on Oxford Street wearing a sandwich-board warning that protein increases the libido.

Vivienne Westwood's opinions are more up to date and of the moment than his, of course. Hanging from her neck is a large head-shot of Chelsea (née Bradley) Manning, with the caption TRUTH in big letters beneath it. Stuck to her stomach are the words 'CLIMATE REVOLUTION'. There are two words attached to her sleeves, but both are at such an angle as to be unreadable. Down one of her legs the word 'REVOLUTION' is repeated.

Since 2010, Dame Vivienne has been keeping an online diary, which a publisher has now reduced by half for a fancily produced book, chock-full of colour photographs.* 'Reading it, you will access my point of view,' she writes, approvingly, 'which is completely heretical to that of the status quo regarding culture and political economy.'

In fact, to see Vivienne Westwood as 'completely heretical' is to over-egg the pudding. Three-quarters of her views will be shared by readers of the *Guardian*, and viewers of *Channel 4 News*. She is against fracking, drones and global warming, and in favour of Wikileaks, the Occupy movement and the overthrow of capitalism. She believes that the world is governed by a conspiracy of the rich, and 'the rich are racing as fast as they can to destroy the world, and the poor are fighting to stop them'. In her mind, this cabal of the well-to-do extends to

---

* *Get A Life! The Diaries of Vivienne Westwood* (2016).

even the most esoteric areas of life, including Santa Claus. 'It is important to our rulers that we believe in him just as we believe the propaganda that the world will carry on as normal.'

The remaining quarter of her opinions is infinitely more traditional, and would find favour with readers of the *Daily Telegraph* and admirers of the Royal Family. She favours classical music over pop, and the Old Masters over Andy Warhol and Tracey Emin. Furthermore, she believes that our monarchy 'gives stability and provides social cement and national identity'.

Her lifestyle, as lovingly documented in these diaries, reflects the contradictions inherent in these conflicting points of view. When she is not blaming the rich for wrecking the planet, she is measuring them for her expensive haute couture, or hobnobbing with them at their expensive private parties.

So she doesn't just sup with the devil; she dresses him, too. Richard Branson is, she declares, 'a businessman who cares. He is tackling the problems of climate change by use of business methods.' She is delighted that his cabin staff all now wear specially designed Vivienne Westwood uniforms. What's more, 'the fabrics are the most eco-friendly'. Yet, as another of her gurus, the ecologist George Monbiot, once pointed out, the Virgin Atlantic fleet produces 13 per cent more carbon dioxide per passenger kilometre than the industry average for long-haul flights, so tends rather more towards the eco-spiteful.

And what of Bill Gates, widely regarded as the richest man in the world? In her diary, Dame Vivienne records meeting a representative of the Gates Foundation. 'He is impressed by our slogan, "Buy less, choose well, make it last", thinks it could have a big effect on changing people's aspirations and could be a most important tool in Climate Revolution.' And so Bill Gates is excused, too.

She may blame the rich for wrecking the planet, but she seldom hobnobs with anyone earning less than half a million pounds a year. One of the most splendid photographs in her book is captioned, 'Mehrangarh fort, Jodhpur, lit up for a party'. The picture shows thousands of bulbs ablaze through hundreds of different windows, all for a party in honour of Naomi Campbell's boyfriend, Vlad.

It emerges that anyone who is anyone has flown out to India to be there, their carbon footprints clothed in the finest silks. 'For the party nights, we were all dressed in Indian costumes. Michael Howard, the creative director for Dior, must have worked for weeks,' coos Dame Vivienne. The guests, she adds, were attended by dozens of drummers, dancers, acrobats, fire-eaters, 'camels caparisoned in mirrors and tassels' and 'ladies throwing rose petals'. Nice work if you can get it. Now that it's party time, there's no need to worry about climate change and global poverty and so on: after all, 'Naomi mentioned that she's going to do some charity work in India about waste recycling.' Three cheers for Naomi! Three cheers for waste!

Dame Vivienne seems convinced that the ills of the world – poverty, disease, environmental catastrophe – can all be cured by a reviving sniff of glamour. One of my favourite of her picture captions goes: 'Ajuma modelling our clothes in a Nairobi shanty town'. On another day, she films the supermodel Lily Cole performing a version of 'Red Shoes', and sends the finished product to the United Nations Secretary-General Ban Ki-moon, telling him it represents 'a metaphor for climate change'. One can only imagine Ban Ki-moon saying, 'Lily Cole dancing away in a costume designed by Vivienne Westwood has finally convinced me to do everything I can to stop global warming.'

Another photograph shows Dame Vivienne in a lush silk gown standing next to Lily Cole at the Met Ball in New York. 'I wore a photo of Bradley Manning on my dress' reads the caption. Sure enough, pinned to her lapel is Bradley in his beret. Unfortunately, she discovers that most of the fashionistas at the Met Ball ($30,000 a head) don't quite recognise the face. 'When I said the name then one or two knew him; when I said Wikileaks they all did. The reaction was guilt that they didn't know already but glad to know when I explained.' Happily, 'they were all sympathetic to Bradley', though I suspect they swiftly changed the subject to something more relevant, such as shoes or handbags.

Every time I think I have located the daftest diary entry, I turn a page and find myself forced to think again. 'I was thrilled to see Lady Gaga wearing a Climate Revolution T-Shirt' looked like a winner, but then I spotted: 'Yoga. Then long talk with Julian Assange.' This in turn was knocked into a cocked hat by 'Naomi Campbell hosted a party at Cipriani's in Mayfair to mark the Olympics … Yes, lots of our friends were there, Kate especially and Sarah Ferguson. She is doing work in the Congo – Sarah's very capable, always doing charity work.'

In a nutshell, Vivienne Westwood's philosophy is that the rich are all destroying the planet, unless they are very, very glamorous and/or are her customers, in which case they are saving it. George Soros, Jemima Khan all gain approving mentions, as do Mark Ruffalo, Colin Firth and Bianca Jagger, because they all signed an open letter to David Cameron condemning fracking. The Queen is also excused ('I'm a great fan') and so too is Prince Charles because, in her view, 'if he'd been world ruler for the last thirty years we would not have climate change'.

If only she could earn air miles for being all over the place, Vivienne Westwood would be flying first-class to the ice cap on a weekly basis. Yet, for all her absurdity, there is something strangely winning about her scattergun enthusiasms, and her unstoppable bossiness. 'Try to visit a hygienist for cleaning twice a year,' she tells her readers. 'This way you will keep your teeth.'

In 100 years' time, this book may be seen to encapsulate the follies and enthusiasms of our era. One or two of her entries are already out of date. Right at the beginning of the book, in March 2008, she reads a report in the *Guardian* that the scientist James Lovelock has estimated that by the end of this century, there will be 'only one billion people left due to climate change'.

'We must tell everyone!' she exclaims. 'What can we do? We must get people talking!'

As luck would have it, on 30 September 2016, just when her diaries were off at the printers, the *Guardian* ran another interview with Lovelock. He's had second thoughts. 'I'm not sure the whole thing isn't crazy, this climate change,' he now says. The Green movement is a religious cult, 'totally unscientific', he says, and he's now all for fracking. Whoops! One can only hope he's not expecting an invitation to the next Met Ball.

M&S

I fear Marks and Spencer
Are a trifle dense, sir:
They still think beige
All the rage.

HISTORY

In Retreat:
The Art of David Jones

David Jones was born in 1895 in the down-at-heel neighbourhood of Brockley in South London, at that time bordered by fields of wheat. It was another country. A man with a dancing bear on a leash was a regular sight on the streets; a peddler could often be heard singing, 'Who'll Buy My Sweet Lavender?'.

Jones died, penniless, in a residential home in Harrow in October 1974, when Damien Hirst was nine years old. In the world of art, there is no such thing as progress. These days, the poetry and artworks of David Jones are revered by a select few, but the very rich remain blind to their beauty: you could still buy one of his paintings for £20,000 or so, and an engraving for much less, whereas a mass-produced Damien Hirst spot painting – of which there are now well over 1,000 – could set you back £1 million.

The art world has long been a sucker for self-promotion. Throughout his life, David Jones was shy and self-effacing, totally uninterested in fame and recognition. He once noted that 'In fifty years, 99 per cent of those world's "important" people will have gone, and it will not have mattered a damn.'

Yet he must surely have been reassured by the admiration of his peers. W. H. Auden told him, 'Your work makes me feel very small and madly jealous,' while Dylan Thomas once said, 'I would like to have done anything as good as David Jones has done.' Kenneth Clark considered him 'absolutely unique, a remarkable genius'.

Jones's life was shaped by the First World War. He was an eighteen-year-old art student when it started, and rushed to enlist. But he had always been a skinny little thing, much prone to illness, and found himself rejected on the grounds of 'deficient chest measurement'.

In an attempt to enlarge his chest, he took to running around Brockley, but by the end of the year the requirements were relaxed and he was able to join the Royal Welch Fusiliers. He was with them from January 1915 until the end of the war, serving longer on the Front – 117 weeks – than any other British writer.

He survived the Somme and Passchendaele, though they caused him lasting psychological damage. For the rest of his life he suffered from agoraphobia, and the sound of a door slamming or a car backfiring would send his mind hurtling back to the trenches. 'The memory of the war is like a disease,' he said towards the end of his life. 'I still think about it more than anything else.'

As an old man, he would walk around in a trench coat, no matter how hot the weather. In 1966, on a visit to see the Bonnard exhibition at the Royal Academy, he experienced a terrible panic attack. When his companion came back from parking her car, an attendant asked her, 'Do you know anything about this tramp? He won't part with his coat.'

David Jones's novel-length work about life in the trenches, *In Parenthesis*, published in 1937, is a beguiling mixture of prose and poetry, a swirling stream of consciousness that is at one and the same time earthy and spiritual, robust and defenceless. It takes you right into the blood and guts of the battlefield, while simultaneously floating above it, like a recording angel. From line to line, it swings between high and low, epic and colloquial, music hall and bible. All the time, the poet's empathy is firmly with the ordinary soldiers, of whom he was one: he found the officers were arrogant and humourless.

In Parenthesis is also remarkably humane: Jones complained that other war writers failed to show 'the extreme tenderness of men in action to one another'. Fittingly, he dedicated it to 'the bearded infantry who exchanged their long loaves with us at a sector's barrier and to the enemy front-fighters who shared our pains, against whom we found ourselves by misadventure'.

Of course, no one at home had an inkling of what life was like in the trenches. His kindly mother reacted to a letter from her son at the

Front by ticking him off for his spelling: 'Really, David, the spelling in your last letter was a disgrace to the family. A child of four would do better.' Returning soldiers were meant to get back to their previous lives, as though nothing had happened. Jones himself returned to Camberwell Art College and lost himself in art.

His paintings have the same jumbled, kaleidoscopic quality as his poetry, with one thing reflecting on to another, and no clear boundaries. But they are essentially joyous, too. His biographer, Thomas Dilworth,* says of them that they have 'a sense of substance being insubstantial'; which gives them a strong spiritual quality, a sense of real life existing beyond the here-and-now.

Dilworth also suggests that, like El Greco before him, David Jones's art may have been helped by an optical malfunction. 'All my life, my retinas retained the image a fraction of a second too long,' he once confessed. This may have encouraged the transparent layering in his paintings, in which flowers, cows, walls, gates, stars and trees all seem to exist on the same plane.

Might it also illuminate the mystical way in which he made no clear distinction between the present and the past? When walking along Hadrian's Wall, he once experienced 'the feeling of the past still living in the present', as though he 'might meet a Roman legionary around the next bend'. In Canterbury Cathedral, he hurt his hand giving a vengeful whack to the tomb of an archbishop who had helped King Edward I conquer Wales.

For all his innumerable complexes and inhibitions, Jones was a tremendously appealing character, with friends everywhere. He was a devotee of shaggy-dog stories, one or two of which Dilworth includes in his biography. He loved James Joyce, *Alice's Adventures in Wonderland*, William Blake and Gregorian chant. Every year, he reread John Collier's sinister comic novel *His Monkey Wife*, a sure sign of someone with a good sense of humour. His dislikes were endearing, too: Salvador Dalì, bullying, *Paradise Lost*, hymns, the Royal Academy, sweet peas.

---

* *David Jones: Engraver, Soldier, Painter, Poet* by Thomas Dilworth (2017).

Right up to the end, he would fall head over heels in love with women. Often it was reciprocated, but there was something in him that buckled at commitment. Love made him come out in a rash. His last great love was a full thirty-nine years younger than he was, and might have consented to a marriage proposal, but he held back. 'I wish I could marry her. If only I could pull myself together,' he observed, mournfully.

Charm is a notoriously difficult quality to render in print, but Dilworth somehow manages it. Unlike most biographers, he has devoted his life to the study and appreciation of his subject; every now and then, it becomes clear that he also knew Jones personally. From all this knowledge, he has constructed a wonderful, sympathetic, multi-layered portrait of the man, while also managing to preserve his elusive quality.

Reading any biography, I always want to know what it would be like to be in a room with the subject. 'Being with David was like playing tennis with a better player,' says someone who knew him. 'He brought from you insights, comments, knowledge that you didn't dream were there. He lifted you up. He always talked to the simplest person as an equal. I shouldn't think he knew how to talk down to anyone. He had an original mind and a depth of mind that is rare, but you never heard big words from him or difficult constructions, highfalutin approaches.'

Famous people flocked to him. Evelyn Waugh, Henry Moore, Stanley Spencer, John Betjeman, Anthony Powell, G. K. Chesterton, Igor Stravinsky and the Queen Mother all sought his acquaintance. He was happy to receive them, but spurned any sort of discipleship.

Hearing of his poverty in old age – by this time, he was employing safety pins to keep his trousers up – the actor Richard Burton donated £1,000. Three days before his seventy-ninth birthday, Jones died in his sleep. His biographer closes by praising him for creating 'so much intelligent beauty during so many years of psychological distress'. And so say all of us.

In Our Time

MELVYN BRAGG: It's been called one of the most crucial ideas in all human history. But it is also a lot more than that. The concept of EMV, or *equum mortuum verberans* – literally, the flogging of a dead horse – has been around since time immemorial. Consciously or unconsciously, we've all done it – but what exactly does it mean, 'flogging a dead horse', and how did it originate?

Charles Darwin, Søren Kierkegaard, Hermes Trismegistus, Baruch Spinoza and Hadron Collider – these are just some of the names that have grappled with this extraordinary theory down the centuries. Yet it is only in recent years that we have been fully able to grasp its profound significance.

With me to discuss the whole question of EMV – in layman's language, that's flogging a dead horse – are Jeff Beardy, Professor of Applied EMV Studies at Queen's College, Oxford; Lynne Nervy, Visiting Fellow in the History of Equine Applications at the University of Surrey; and Gervaise Hedge, Professor of Equine Linguistics at University College, London.

Gervaise Hedge, if I could start with you. EMV is often referred to as a paradigm shift?

PROFESSOR HEDGE: Oh, very much so. It is, to my mind, a key branch of chaos theory, whereby the sensitive dependence on initial conditions in which a small change in one state of a deterministic non-linear system can result in large differences in a larger state. So that, if one starts to, as it were, flog a dead horse, then somehow it is in the very nature of the act of flogging to see the continuing process of, as it were, the act of being flogged.

MELVYN BRAGG: You're going to have to say what you mean by that. Let's start with the horse – is it, so to speak, a real horse that we're proposing to flog? Or is it in some way more symbolic?

PROFESSOR HEDGE: Oh, very much so. At this point, I'd like to backtrack, if I may, and draw your attention to something that we may be in danger of overlooking, namely the human tendency to backtrack just as things are, as it were, 'getting going'. But, then again, what exactly do we mean when we say that someone is 'getting going'? Are they getting, or are they going, or are they doing something that in some mysterious way transcends both these activities? This is an extremely complex question, by which I mean –

MELVYN BRAGG: Well, we'll come back to that in a moment, if we may. But first I'd like to bring you in, Lynne Nervy. Could I ask you to fill us in – briefly – on the history of flogging a dead horse?

LYNNE NERVY: Well, the story really begins around 650 BC, with major developments in the key years of AD 43, 706 – and here I'm reverting to the Gregorian calendar for simplicity's sake – 1491, 1542, and to my mind most crucially, 1736.

MELVYN BRAGG: I see. And – just to be clear on this – what was it that, in particular, happened in those crucial years, in overall terms of dead-horse flogging? Perhaps you'd expand for us, Lynne?

LYNNE NERVY: Let's stay with those key years for a moment. The history of *equum mortuum verberans* –

MELVYN BRAGG: – that's flogging a dead horse –

LYNNE NERVY: Yes, well the history of EMV –

MELVYN BRAGG: – *equum mortuum verberans* –

LYNNE NERVY: Yes, the history of flogging a dead horse –

MELVYN BRAGG: – known as EMV for short –

LYNNE NERVY: – also contains within itself the parallel histories not only of those horses that, once deceased, are flogged, but also, of course, of those humans who, for whatever reason, and I can think of many, have been driven to the act or practice of flogging those very same late horses. So, if I could start with the first date, 650 BC –

MELVYN BRAGG: – and here we're talking a very long time ago, in terms of *equum mortuum verberans* –

LYNNE NERVY: – Oh, very much so – well, the year 650 BC is a keynote date because –

MELVYN BRAGG: We're going to have to move on, I'm afraid. Perhaps I could bring you in here, Professor Jeff Beardy. Let's talk about how this discovery of EMV, this idea, fed into the whole notion of man's capacity to, as it were, eke things out, or in other ways protract them, or, in some sense, draw them out or needlessly prolong them? Just to make it clear: did it perhaps have something to do with the abiding wish to spend an undue amount of time discussing something that would not, in the end, grow any clearer?

LYNNE NERVY: If I could just go back to something I was saying earlier –

MELVYN BRAGG: Well, I hope there'll be time later to go back to what you were saying earlier, but for now, I'd like to put that question to Professor Jeff Beardy. Jeff?

PROFESSOR BEARDY: I'd like to go back to something Professor Hedge said when he talked about the human tendency to 'backtrack' just as things were, as he put it, 'getting going'.

MELVYN BRAGG: I'd like to deal with that a little later, if I may, but for the time being I want to ask something else. Is it significant that the horse is dead? Was it always dead? And would it be equally significant if it were alive? Do you briefly want to come in on this, Jeff Beardy?

PROFESSOR BEARDY: I mean, fundamentally, I wouldn't disagree with that, but, to go back to something Lynne Nervy said a few minutes ago, I would say that the notion of a parallel history in which dead humans are flogged by horses is fundamentally flawed –

MELVYN BRAGG: Lynne, you are waving your hand.

LYNNE NERVY: Well, it's not what I said actually, Professor Beardy.

MELVYN BRAGG: Do you want to say what you were saying, Lynne, or would you prefer to say what you were not saying?

PROFESSOR HEDGE: Could I just say –

LYNNE NERVY: I'd just say that I didn't say what he said I said, and if I had said what he said I'd said I'd just say that he wouldn't have said that I'd said it.

MELVYN BRAGG: But I don't think that is what he's saying, to be honest. Do you want to recap on what you were saying about what Lynne Nervy said you said she said, Jeff Beardy?

PROFESSOR HEDGE: Could I just say a few words on String Theory?

MELVYN BRAGG: Well we've ranged from horses to flogging and back again to death, and the part it played in EMV, or flogging dead horses. So I think this would be an excellent time to see if we can expand on Stringing-It-Out Theory. Lynne?

I've Seen Better:
The Historical Online Archive

A dip into the Historical Online Archive at Kew, where hundreds of thousands of ancient online comments and tweets from ordinary, decent Britons down the ages are lovingly preserved.

4000 BC: Invention of the wheel

It'll never catch on. *P. D., Mesopotamia*

My mate tried it, says it's total rubbish. *Brian, Sumeria*

When I pushed it, it kept on moving. All in all, a very disappointing product. *W. H., Turkey*

2560 BC: Completion of the Great Pyramid of Giza

Eyesore. *P. K.*

More money than sense. *Mr P., London*

They say you can see our house from the very top. *Martin, Tewkesbury*

Lot more impressive the other way up. *@Egghead*

Quite nice but long way to shops. *@gingercat*

1600 BC: Completion of Stonehenge

Eyesore. *Tony, Salisbury, Wilts*

Very draughty come winter. *Ann, Dorset*

1310 BC: The parting of the Red Sea

Not impressed frankly. Literally anyone could do that. *P. W., York*

Moses up to his old tricks again. Typical crowd-pleasing. Give it a rest, mate. *@Daffyduck.co.uk*

240 BC: First recorded sighting of Halley's Comet

Who are they kidding? You could see the strings. *Jeff, Nuneaton*

AD 29: Sermon on the Mount

Political correctness gone mad. *T. B. N.*
Couldn't hear a word. *Jetski*
Typical touchy-feely rubbish. *Reginald K.*
Here today, gone tomorrow. *Sadman*

105: Invention of paper, China

Gimmick. It'll never catch on. *Alan P., London*
What's wrong with carving on stone? Why can't these people leave
   well alone, that's what I want to know. *P. L., Herts*

180: Most Roman roads in Britain completed

The old roads were much better. Why all these straight lines? They're
   defiling the countryside – and all in the name of foreign
   businessmen. *Martin, Colchester*

625: King Raedwald's burial at Sutton Hoo, Suffolk

Waste of a perfectly good ship. *P. T., Ipswich*
We used to do burials so much better in the old days. *Nick, Norwich*

1079: Bayeux Tapestry unveiled

Two stars. Too much gratuitous violence. *Jack, Bigglesworth*
Some nice needlework, if that's what you're into. *P. B., Marlborough*
After all the build-up, I was expecting something more exciting.
   Mandy, Dorking
Typical modern art. Child could of done it. *Bob, Tring*
It's the horses I feel sorry for. *Ann, Maidstone*
I think I spotted my dad on it – 372nd person from the left, the one
   just next to the horse, with his hand in the air. *Davina, Sutton*

1215: Magna Carta signed at Runnymede by King John

Yet more nanny state. *R. L., Cheam, Surrey*

1250–1500: Easter Island statues erected

Second from the left looks a bit like my aunty. *@earlybird*

It's the people next door I feel sorry for. *Angry, Berks*

A child could have done it. *@artlover*

Totally unrealistic. Heads too big 4 their bodies and where's the legs?
 M. T., Great Missenden

1260: Consecration of Chartres Cathedral

It's already running way over budget and not even halfway finished.
 And will someone please tell me where all that money is going to
 come from? *Pierre, Bordeaux*

Stained glass just another fad. Won't catch on. *Cilla, Dover*

I've seen better. *Mike, Darlington*

1348: Black Death

I've seen worse. *Mike, Darlington*

1397: Geoffrey Chaucer narrates the *Canterbury Tales* for the court of King Richard II

Pure filth. *A. M., Middlesex*

1431: Joan of Arc burnt at the stake

That'll teach her to dress like a man. She had only herself to blame.
 Barry, Brentwood

Reminds me of my sister. Anything to be centre of attention. *Mary P.,
 Orleans*

With the BarBQ season coming up, can NE1 recommend the best
 way to stop a fire smoking? *Slim, Puckeridge*

Love that white robe she wuz waring! Could some1 tell me where to
 get one like it puh-lease! *Sandra, Esher*

I disagree with Sandra. If I was going to the stake, I'd wear something
 more summery, maybe shorts with matching top. *Edwina,
 Edinburgh*

Litrully MAD to wear shorts to the stake; go for something loose-
 fitting. *Avril, Southend*

1505: Leonardo da Vinci paints the *Mona Lisa*
She's put on weight. *S. H., Macclesfield*
That top doesn't suit her. *Sue, Cornwall*
Someone should wipe that silly grin off her face. *P. P., Cardiff*
Wish I had time to sit around all day, being painted. Some of us have to work to do. *M. W., Wilts*

1512: Michelangelo completes painting of Sistine Chapel ceiling
Rating: **
Michelangelo only got the job because he knew the right people. These days, it's not what you know, it's who. *Antonio, Florence*
Not bad if you like that sort of thing. *E. W., Venezia*
Totally unrealistic. *Ricardo Dawkini, Oxford*

1533: King Henry VIII marries Anne Boleyn
She looked so happy. This one will last forever. *P. L., Staffs*

1536: Execution of Anne Boleyn
I always said it would never last. *P. L., Staffs*

1595: Premiere of *Romeo and Juliet*
Liked her, didn't like him. *Sally, Barnstaple*
Liked him, didn't like her. *Andy, Exeter*
Didn't like either of them. *BeefyBoy, Grimsby*
Ice cream in the interval a bit melty, otherwise OK, seats comfy. *Sandy, Stratford*

1601: First performance of *Hamlet*
Left after the first act. Woman in front was wearing a big hat and I couldn't see properly. *Nick, Southwark*

1649: Execution of King Charles I
Why all the fuss? He might have had his head chopped off but with his money he can get it sewn back on. *Ann, Manchester*

1659: Vermeer paints *Girl Reading a Letter at an Open Window*

What's she doing with the window open at this time of year? She'll
  catch her death. *Worried, Okehampton*

OK, so you can read. Big deal. Get over it. *@Realist*

Rubbish hairdo. Change your stylist, love. *Sophie, Manchester*

I agree. She needs extensions big-time. *Mandy, Rochester*

1666: Great Fire of London

Sorry but I've seen better flames in my own fireplace. *William,
  Tottenham*

1724 Premiere of *St John Passion* by J. S. Bach

We the undersigned respect Mr Bach's right to his religious beliefs
  but we object to his foisting of them on us in the form of music.
  Most people want their music free from Christian propaganda and
  do not want religions or religious identities to be actively
  prioritised by top composers. R. D., *Oxford and fifty others*

1739: Dick Turpin hanged

That's the last we'll hear of him. *H. P., West London*

1756: Black Hole of Calcutta

Lovely and roomy. Don't know what they're complaining about.
  Dave, Surrey

1807: Slave trade abolished

Political correctness gone mad. *Nigel, Beccles*

Typical chattering classes. Don't these do-gooders realise slaves will
  be worse off? *James, Lancs*

Speak to any slave, and he'll tell you how much he enjoys picking
  cotton in the sun, or rowing the Atlantic. Slave owners have
  contributed a great deal to our economy, and the trickle-down
  effect means slaves have cast-iron employment. Don't get me
  started! *Greg, York*

Two hundred years from now, our ancestors will be shaking their heads in disbelief that we could ever have got rid of such a long-standing British tradition. *Elaine, Surrey*

1824 Premiere of Beethoven's 9th Symphony
Catchy in parts. *P. L. T., Nuneaton*

1830: First steam railway opens, Liverpool to Manchester
Of all the daft ideas. *Bill, Cambridge*
Mark my words, one thing will lead to another. 130 years from now there'll be a Great Train Robbery. *Dave, Sheffield*

1855: Livingstone first sets eyes on Victoria Falls
Very damp. *Pete, Middlesex*
There's a bloke with time on his hands. *Fishfinger*

1864: Brunel's Clifton Suspension Bridge opened
Why can't these engineers leave well alone? Terrible eyesore, built in the face of local opposition. I give it ten years, max, before it falls down. *Mick, Bradford-on-Avon*
If they'd asked me, I'd have advised them to put it somewhere else. *Geoffrey, Bridport*

1872 George Eliot's *Middlemarch* published
Three stars. Too many characters. *Jeff, Hastings*
You can tell it's a bloke writing this tosh. Doesn't understand women at all. Typical. *Sara, North Yorks*
Haven't got round to reading it yet. *Gillian, South London*

1877: Queen Victoria proclaimed Empress of India
The woman has enough on her plate already. *Maddie, London*
To be honest, I've never been to India. *Loserboy*
Me neither. *Maxine, Birmingham*
Has she never heard of dieting? Cut back on the cream buns, love. *Jeanette, Herts*

I met her once. Very down-to-earth. *Gary, Swansea*

1912: Scott reaches the South Pole

Tenerife's much nicer than the Antarctic at this time of year. *Sue, Manchester*

1914: Assassination of Archduke Ferdinand

So? Surely there's more important things worth writing about? @*twitcher, Medway*

Never heard of him. Loser! *Pete, Birmingham*

I feel sorry for the guy. Not nice being assassinated. *Eileen, Dover*

My cousin's friend has a baby called Ferdinand, I think it's a boy but it might be a girl. Can't remember. *Diana, Staines*

Me neither. *Derek, Chorley*

1927: *À la recherche du temps perdu* by Marcel Proust published

Wordy. *P. J., Cobham*

Damn. I was planning to write just the same novel, but never found the time. *Mrs P., Saffron Walden*

1953: Ascent of Mount Everest

Been there, done that. Went halfway up Snowdon summer be4 last. Nothing to shout about. *Mr P., Runcorn*

1961: Berlin Wall erected

As a keen gardener, I'd advise a few well-chosen climbing plants and wall shrubs to brighten the wall up a bit. Clematis, wisteria and honeysuckle are among my personal favourites. Regular pruning highly recommended. *@greenfingers*

Typical modern architecture. *Artlover, Edinburgh*

I blame the BBC. *Gavin, Droitwich*

It'll never come down that's 4 sure. *Laura, Maidenhead*

1963: Martin Luther King's 'I have a dream' speech

We've all had dreams, mate, but we don't bang on about them, boring for everyone else. *Jeff, Chertsey*

Snap! I had a dream last night, too. I was wrestling with this sort of, well, I can only describe it as a THING. And then I woke up. *P. V., Wilts*

I once had to make a speech in front of maybe 50 people. Boy was I nervous. *@jethro*

Political correctness gone mad. *N. G., Manchester*

1969: First Man on the Moon

Tripadvisor rating: 2 stars

All right so long as you don't mind self-catering. *Sortid*

1986: Space Shuttle *Challenger* disaster

To think I might have been on it. The only thing that stopped me was the fact that I wasn't a US citizen, I have poor hand/eye co-ordination and I have no head for heights so never applied. *Mrs P., Saffron Walden*

I once had a near-miss on the A3, as you're coming into Petersfield. *Derek, Portsmouth*

The Greatest Oprah Winfrey Interviews of All Time: (1) Queen Elizabeth I

OPRAH: I'd so love to hug you!

ELIZABETH: That won't be necessary.

OPRAH: A big, big hug! Oh, wouldn't that be just great! Elizabeth, I remember your coronation at the Abbey in 1559. Thanks for inviting me, by the way! I so recall this sense of magic, I never experienced anything like it. When you came through that door, you seemed like you were floating down the aisle. Were you even inside your body at the time?

ELIZABETH: I was aware that this wasn't just my day, this was the day planned for the world.

OPRAH: So, tell me about the narrative of your childhood, Elizabeth. Your mother was … Her Royal Majesty Queen Anne Boleyn, right?

ELIZABETH: Yes …

OPRAH: Wow! That must have been something!

ELIZABETH: … before my father had her beheaded.

OPRAH: [*staring open-mouthed in silence, with her eyebrows raised*] Wh-what? You're kiddin' me? Say that again!

ELIZABETH: My father had her beheaded.

OPRAH: Whoah! Let's get some clarification. Are you telling me your pop had your mom's head chopped off? What with?

ELIZABETH: A sword.

OPRAH: Wh-what? A sword?

ELIZABETH: So it seems.

OPRAH: A sword! Whoah! That must have been so tough. Not only on you, but on her. I mean, no one wants their head getting chopped off. That's not a narrative anyone should have to learn to run with. And you were how old at this time, Bess?

ELIZABETH: Two and a half.

OPRAH: Wh-what? But that's so little! And, tell me, Bess – how did that make you *feel*?

ELIZABETH: Uncomfortable. And my father had his marriage annulled, so that made me … illegitimate.

OPRAH: Wh-what? Hold on. Stop right now. Let's clarify! So first your father beheads your mom, then he declares you *illegitimate*? And did that make you … cry?

ELIZABETH: He didn't want me to be a princess. It was a really hard time, and, yes, it really hurt my feelings, but he was upset about something, and he owned it, he apologised. He brought me flowers and a note to say sorry. He did what I would do if I knew if I had cut someone else's mom's head off. He took accountability for it. So I don't want to get into the details.

OPRAH: OK, Bess. Thank you for having the courage to share that with us. So then your dad marries four more times. That's a helluva lot of stepmoms!

ELIZABETH: I don't want in any way to be disparaging about my father … but I think at least one of them had her head chopped off.

OPRAH: Not a great look.

ELIZABETH: And so … no way am I blaming her, but she lacked communication skills. She wasn't great to talk to. And another one died. Another, he divorced.

OPRAH: And how do you remember your father now? In a word?

ELIZABETH: Compassionate.

OPRAH: So let's fast-forward. Your half-brother, Edward VI, becomes king, even though he's younger than you.

ELIZABETH: I know.

OPRAH: That's so unfair! Nobody should have to go through that. And then he dies, and your half-sister, Mary, gets the throne. And Mary never reached out to you. How did that make you feel? You must have been in a very dark place.

ELIZABETH: I was in a very dark place. It was a prison.

OPRAH: Wh-what? Whoah!

ELIZABETH: The Tower of London. I'm just telling you what happened, Oprah. I wasn't planning to say anything shocking.

OPRAH: Whoah! I am shocked! And how do you feel about Mary now?

ELIZABETH: I feel so much compassion for her. And that's why when I became Queen I reached out to so many of her most fervent followers … and set fire to them. It was for their own good. And I did it with so much compassion. You see, they had been perpetuating falsehoods. And no one wants to perpetuate falsehoods.

OPRAH: That must have been so hard on you.

ELIZABETH: I still grieve. But at a certain point, you're going to go, 'But, hey, you guys, someone just tell the truth!' And that comes with the risk of losing things. Like, your heads. But I'm still standing, and my hope for people in the takeaway from this is to know that there's another side.

OPRAH: Your fairy tale has a happy ending. So thank you for trusting me to share your story. We are going to take a break, y'all. See you in a few minutes!

An Historian

Peter Hennessy
Is a bit of a menace; he
Has done more to bore me than
Any other historian.

Study Notes for A-Level Cultural Studies 2044: Boris Johnson – The Legacy

HISTORICAL BACKGROUND: Now aged eighty, Boris Johnson has been the recipient of many prestigious honours and awards in the field of entertainment. Examiners will be looking for a detailed knowledge of all these prizes.

Remember to mention The Bruce Forsyth Award for his hosting of *The Great British Bake-Off* (2025), The *TV Times* Viewers' Choice Award for his acclaimed appearance on *I'm a Celebrity ... Get Me Out of Here!* (2026) and The Laurence Llewelyn-Bowen Prize for Best Lifestyle Programme for his work on the long-running series *Carrie and Boris Go Wild with Wallpaper* (2022–30).

In 2038, Johnson received a BAFTA nomination for his series *In the Footsteps of Portillo*, in which he traced the routes taken by mysterious presenter Michael Portillo throughout his thirty-five years of being filmed getting on and off trains clutching a little book.

FUN FACT: It is often forgotten that Boris Johnson was Prime Minister of Great Britain from 2019 to 2022. The examiner may well ask you to expand on this extraordinary detail.

If so, you may wish to mention that he came immediately after Theresa May (2016–19) and before the Coalition Government of Truth and Reconciliation led by Sir Alan Titchmarsh and Dame Mary Berry (2022–29).

Mentioning this in passing will suggest to the examiners that you have really mastered the subject.

PUBLICATIONS: Books written by Boris Johnson include *The Dream of Rome* (2006), *The Churchill Factor* (2014), *Piffle and Balderdash: The Downing Street Diaries* (2024), as well as *The Prison Diaries* (2027).

More recently, Johnson published the successful TV tie-in *Countdown: The First 60 Years*, a celebration of the long-running words-and-numbers game show which he has hosted for the past ten years, having taken over from veteran presenter Michael Gove.

FUN FACT: In summer 2022, Boris Johnson's dog Dilyn announced on the doorstep of 10 Downing Street, that 'after a hugely enjoyable stint with Boris and Carrie' he was 'setting off to pastures new in search of fresh challenges'.

Three days later, Dilyn announced on Twitter that he had accepted 'a key advisory role' with Sir Keir Starmer.

In 2022, Dilyn published a controversial memoir, *Barking Mad: The Downing Street Years*, which included the shock revelation that Boris Johnson used to upset staff by scratching the carpet and chewing the furniture.

In 2026, Dilyn was runner-up on *Celebrity Pet Big Brother*, having been narrowly beaten by Lady Beckham's short-haired labradoodle, Stella.

TV APPEARANCES: Boris Johnson started his career with regular guest appearances on *Have I Got News For You* (currently on its 231st series). After his sudden retirement from a three-year stint starring in *Prime Minister's Questions*, a number of reported 'financial difficulties' resulted in appearances on *Celebrity Coach Trip*, *Celebrity First Dates* and *Celebrity Naked Attraction*.

But he re-emerged to co-present popular home decoration shows such as *Boris and Carrie's Grand Designs* and *Boris and Carrie's Complete Sitting Room Makeover for Under £100,000*.

His long-running gameshow *Boris's Great Big Inverted Pyramid of Piffle* was a Saturday-night staple for fifteen years. 'Tell a Whopper – Win a Million' was the show's slogan. Examiners for the Advanced

Level may wish you to explain in no more 200 words the Meaning and Origin of the Inverted Pyramid of Piffle.

In 2036, shooting of *Three Old Men in a Boat* was postponed half-way through the first episode after a pleasant chug past Henley-on-Thames descended into a pitched battle between the three elderly presenters, Boris Johnson, Dominic Cummings and Alastair Campbell.

Some time later, police divers recovered the body of Dominic Cummings, best known for his starring role as the evil Professor Yana on TV's *Dr Who*, opposite Ann Widdecombe as Widders the Wicked. Following an intensive investigation, foul play was ruled out owing to lack of evidence.

Over the years, Boris Johnson has appeared in documentaries about more recent prime ministers. These include *Titchmarsh at Number 10* and *The Schofield Years*, a ten-part series on legendary former Prime Minister Phillip Schofield.

KEY AREAS FOR GENERAL REVISION: The examiner will wish to assess your working knowledge of Johnson. He will expect a working knowledge of key Johnson catchphrases.

In the Language Comprehension Paper, you should expect questions on familiar expressions such as 'Them's The Breaks', 'Get Brexit Done', 'Paid for It Myself' and 'Bodies Piled High'. What did they ever mean, if anything?

In a Nutshell:
Histwee with Lucy Worsley

Lucy Worsley: Lots and lots and LOTS of people remember their histwee lessons from school as being about kings and queens

Cut to Lucy dressed in crown and robes

– and battles

Cut to Lucy dressed in chain mail, swinging a sword

– and dates.

Cut to Lucy dressed up as a raisin

You might think histwee is a record of what happened – but actually it's not that AT ALL! As soon as you do a bit of digging –

Cut to Lucy in wellingtons with a spade, pretending to wipe sweat off her brow

– you discover it's more like …

Lucy pretends to be looking for the right word

… a TAPESTRY woven by whoever was in power at the time!

Cut to Lucy dressed up as Queen Elizabeth I, weaving a tapestry

INTERIOR, LIBRARY

Lucy: Here I am in a DUSTY OLD LIBRARY talking to a man with a beard who really knows lots and lots and lots about the WARS OF THE ROSES! So, man with a beard, am I right in thinking that the WARS OF THE ROSES was not actually a series of battles between one rose –

Lucy produces a red rose in one hand

– and another rose?

Lucy produces a white rose in the other hand, and then bashes them together

Man with beard: That's right, Lucy. The Wars of the Roses were in fact between the House of Lancaster and the House of York.

Lucy Worsley: Fascinating! But are we talking about two ACTUAL HOUSES MADE OF BRICKS AND MORTAR fighting each other –

Cut to Lucy wearing boxing gloves, dressed up as a house, with her head where the chimney would be

– or are we in fact talking about something REALLY RATHER DIFFERENT?

Man with beard: Yes. Very different.

EXTERIOR, LUCY STANDING ON TOP OF WHITE CLIFFS OF DOVER DRESSED UP AS A BLUEBIRD

Lucy: So there we have it, in a nutshell –

Lucy dips into a packet of pistachio nuts, and starts shelling them

– the so-called WARS of the ROSES were VERY VERY DIFFERENT
from what we've been taught!!!! They were in fact like a real-life
Game of Thrones, or *Emmerdale Farm*, but without a tractor –

Cut to Lucy driving a tractor through a field

– because back in the olden days, they didn't have tractors – they had
horses and carts!!!

Cut to Lucy dressed as Tudor milkmaid driving a horse and cart

So now let's take a look –

*Cut to Lucy dressed up as Admiral Nelson, taking a look through a tele-
scope*

– at how William Shakespeare, the greatest storyteller of them all,
portrayed King Richard III!

Cut to Lucy dressed up as King Richard III, with hunchback, etc.

Lucy: 'Now is the winter –'

Snow starts falling in studio, Lucy as King Richard builds snowman

'– of our discontent, Made glorious summer –'

Cut to Lucy sunbathing on a summer beach in Victorian swimsuit

'– by this sun of York'

Cut to Lucy in a cloth cap, feeding a Yorkshire pudding to a whippet

*EXTERIOR, BOSWORTH FIELD. LUCY WORSLEY DRESSED AS
KNIGHT IN ARMOUR.*

Lucy: But what, you may ask, was the TRUE HISTWEE of the Battle of Bosworth? Alas, there was an awful lot of bloodshed –

Cut to a pool of blood
Cut to a garden shed

– that day. First the Yorkists were chased –

Lucy runs along the field, a look of mild alarm on her face, as she continues talking to camera

– all the way to this hedge. And then the Lancastrians started to massacre them, so that they all fell over –

Lucy falls over
Close-up of Lucy with a little bit of mud daintily smeared on both cheeks

– and it was the slaughter was HORRENDOUS –

Close-up of Lucy putting on sad face

– and the battle was lost!

INTERIOR, MEDICAL LAB. LUCY DRESSED AS MORTUARY ATTENDANT.

Lucy: I'm now holding an old skull from the battle.

Lucy puts on 'yucky' face

Lucy: And so, Dr Tompkins, I suppose this proves that whoever this skull belonged to is now dead?
Dr Tompkins: That's right, Lucy. And he's probably been dead quite some little while.
Lucy: Super! Smashing! Goody-goody-gum-drops!

INTERIOR, TOWER OF LONDON

Lucy: Here I am dressing up as a real-life Yeoman of the Guard!!!! Golly gosh, what an awful lot of buttons there were to do up! What you never see in the histwee books is that in the olden days there were no such things as zips – which is probably why all those kings and queens were always losing their tempers!!!So, Keith, you've been a Yeoman for these past forty years, is that right?
Keith the Yeoman [*proudly*]: That's right.
Lucy: So could you do me up at the back, please? Super!

EXTERIOR, TOWER OF LONDON. LUCY IN HER YEOMAN'S OUTFIT WITH HER HEAD ON THE EXECUTIONER'S BLOCK.

Lucy: So what we've learnt is that, as far as histwee goes, there's really an awful lot at stake.

Close-up of a steak and chips

Next time, I'll be exploring the Legend of Robin –

Close-up of a little bird

– Hood.

Close-up of Lucy in a hood

And we'll be asking ourselves – who was the REAL FRIAR TUCK?

Dressed as Maid Marian, Lucy mounts a white horse and gallops away into the sunset, looking back over her shoulder, whimsically

The Match with St Trinian's Has Been Postponed: Ronald Searle's War Years

Think of Ronald Searle, and you smile. He is most famous, of course, for drawing the girls of St Trinian's, but they were just a tiny part of an output that is brimful with wicked delight. You would struggle to name a more sprightly cartoonist of the twentieth century, or, indeed, of any century.

He died in Provence at the end of 2011, still drawing at the grand old age of ninety-one. Yet for four years in his youth it was touch and go whether he would live or die. In 1939, he was, he says, 'a mildly talented nineteen-year-old', though he was clearly very talented indeed, as he had been a regular cartoonist for the *Cambridge Evening News* since the age of fifteen. A scholar at the Cambridge School of Art, he was well on his way to an illustrious career as a graphic artist when the war broke out.

As an art student, he had been trained to sketch whatever was around him, whenever he could, and he kept up this practice. His drawings from the early war years show troops on the move, with soldiers having haircuts, or writing letters home, or peeling potatoes. But at the same time, he continued to find his style as a comic illustrator: a cartoon he drew in 1941 shows a gang of plaited schoolgirls with hockey sticks staring peevishly at the school noticeboard. 'Owing to the international situation,' reads the notice, 'the match with St Trinian's has been postponed.'

The girls of St Trinian's would have a long wait before their next match. The following year, Searle was taken prisoner by the Japanese in Singapore. From that moment on, he made it his mission to make a pictorial record of everything he witnessed. He wanted, he says, 'to reveal to the world something of what happened during those lost and more or less unphotographed years'. He describes the 400 or so pictures he drew in secret on pieces of scrap paper as 'the graffiti of a condemned man, intending to leave a rough witness of his passing through'.

These war drawings have now been republished, with a brief, self-effacing commentary by Searle.* Like so many soldiers, he underplays his courage. Has there ever been a more persistent artist? Despite working eighteen hours at a stretch on the infamous 'Death Railway' from Siam to Burma, he made himself sketch every morning at first light before setting off.

'It was often very hard to force myself to continue when all I wanted was to forget and escape into the reality of sleep,' he recalls, almost as though he were just facing a hard day at the office. Yet over 100,000 men died building those 273 miles of railway track – one man dead for every sleeper laid – and Russell Davies's tremendous 1990 biography of Searle shows all too clearly how close to death he came.

His friend Russell Braddon told his biographer: 'When the line was finished he was a sick boy. I remember that there was nothing much of him, that he was like a baby or a monkey or something. We thought he was dying and we – some of his remaining friends – used to put him out on a groundsheet in the sun. I don't know why, but we felt that the sun would do something. He could barely move, and we had no food, he had dysentery, malaria and was covered in running sores, and each day we expected him to die ... If you can imagine something that weighs six stone or so, is on the point of death and has no qualities of the human condition that aren't revolting, calmly lying there with a pencil and a scrap of paper, *drawing*, you have some idea of the difference of temperament that this man had from the ordinary human being.'

Anyone who has read Eric Lomax's moving autobiography *The Railway Man* will already be familiar with some of the revolting hardships and tortures undergone by Allied prisoners during the

---

* *To the Kwai – And Back, War Drawings 1939–1945* by Ronald Searle (2006).

construction of the Burma railway. Yet each new description opens one's eyes to fresh horrors. Searle's abiding memory is of one prisoner tipping his basket of rocks over the edge of the cutting who was so weak that he fell with his basket, 'and we weren't allowed to go near him, we weren't allowed to touch him. They had to go on tipping their rocks over the edge of this cutting, until the man was buried by his fellows.'

One of the first drawings in the book is simply captioned 'Siamese jungle, 1943. Prisoner dying of cholera.' With a scattering of thin lines, it depicts a virtual skeleton staring out towards the artist in horror, his eyeballs blacked in like stones. In fact, the plight of the man was even worse than it looks. 'I desperately wanted to put down on paper the unbelieving horror that this man felt when he knew that the fly had landed on his rice and not on someone else's,' Searle told Davies. Every prisoner knew that flies carried disease, and that if a fly landed on your rice you had to throw it away and continue to starve for another twenty-four hours. 'The footprint of one of those filthy flies was enough to bring about a swift and agonizing death,' writes Searle. 'We hated them and even today I am neurotic about being in the same room with one.'

Paradoxically, it was the threat of cholera that allowed Ronald Searle to hang on to his drawings throughout his four years as a prisoner. Had they been discovered, they would have been destroyed, and so would he. But the guards were terrified of catching the disease, which meant that the best place to hide them was beneath the bodies of the dying. That the drawings are still with us, a unique testament to their suffering, is, says Searle, thanks to the selflessness of these cholera victims.

His drawings from those years are, for the most part, as grim as can be: skeletal young men, their heads bent low, walking up and down bearing rocks, or trudging through mud; a roomful of amputees; a random prisoner forced to hold a heavy rock over his head for the amusement of the guards, knowing he would be beaten with bamboo sticks the moment he dropped it. Much is made of the pain of the creative artist, but it is hard to conceive of a collection of sketches that ever arose from a pain more acute than this. Yet it is noticeable that

Searle's sketches are never self-absorbed: he is always turning his gaze outwards towards others; even his rare self-portraits look stoical rather than self-pitying.

Four years spent in a prisoner of war camp, then on the Burma railway, and then in the notorious Changi Gaol (where 10,000 men were crammed into a building designed for 600) were not, you might have thought, a likely training ground for one of our most nimble humorists. But there is evidence that his sense of humour never deserted Searle, and may even have provided him with a lifeline.

In Changi, he drew cartoons for a prison magazine called *The Exile*, which had a print run of just one copy for 10,000 potential readers. The cartoons may have been inspired by captivity, but they remained miraculously light-hearted. One of them shows two goldfish in a bowl. One says to the other, 'Maybe it would be better, darling, if we didn't see each other again.'

And Searle's second St Trinian's cartoon saw the light of day in Changi, too. 'Hand up the girl who burnt down the East Wing last night' says a quizzical headmistress to a classroom of beaming school-girls.

One of the last sketches in the book is of an Allied B-42 plane flying over Changi Gaol in August 1945, dropping leaflets confirming that the war was finally over. The prisoners are waving their arms in the air. 'We all began to cry,' writes Searle. Those who returned had one advantage over those who never had to go: 'We now had in our grasp a thorny, but true, measuring-stick against which to place the things that did or did not matter in life.' And perhaps this is the clue to why Searle forged his life's path in comedy rather than in tragedy: for those who have languished in the deepest, darkest abyss the only way is up, towards the light.

Nothing is Real:
The Slippery Art of Biography

One of the longest biographies of recent years, the ill-fated *Philip Roth* by Blake Bailey, runs to 800 pages, which takes a total of thirty-one hours and forty-six minutes to listen to on audiobook. Roth was eighty-five when he died, so his real life ran to a total of 750,000 hours or so. Even the longest biography is but a tiny fraction of the life it is intended to chronicle.

Robert Caro's biography of President Johnson is so vast that it makes Bailey's *Roth* look like a haiku. Caro has been working on his biography of LBJ since the mid-1970s. Each volume is roughly 800,000 words; he published Volume Four in 2012. The audiobook for that volume alone takes thirty-two hours and forty-five minutes. Caro is still trying to complete the fifth and final volume, which will take LBJ from 1964 to his death in 1973. Caro himself is now eighty-five. Will he live long enough to reach the end?

John Richardson published the first volume of his biography of Pablo Picasso in 1991. It was 548 pages long, and took Picasso up to the age of twenty-five. Volume Two appeared in 1996; Picasso was thirty-five years old at its close. Volume Three arrived in 2007; Picasso was still only fifty, but his biographer was by now eighty-three. After 1,500 pages, Richardson still had forty-one years of Picasso's life to cover. In 2019, the biographer lost his race against his subject, dying at the age of ninety-five, with Picasso still going strong.

Describing Richardson's biography, reviewers would regularly use the adjective 'exhaustive', which is often a euphemism for 'exhausting'. Certainly, his *Life of Picasso* tells you all you need to know, and perhaps more than you need to know, about the exterior circumstances of the life of Picasso. It will tell you, for instance, the exact day he checked into the Savoy Hotel in 1919 (25 May) and the number of his room (574) and the number to which it has since been changed (536) and the person who booked it for him (Sergei Diaghilev), and so on and so forth.

These day-to-day biographical details, dropping like heavy snow, can often blot out the subject. And what is lost, above all, is the art. Writing the biography of a writer or a painter can be like pulling down a great building in the hope of uncovering the secret of its creation; or like shooting a bird to find out how it used to fly. 'Collect all the facts that can be collected about the life of Racine,' observed Paul Valéry, 'and you will never learn from them the art of his verse.'

An entirely comprehensive biography would last as long as its subject's life – or infinitely longer, given all the other lives that would have intersected with it. A truly scrupulous biography would thus be the equivalent of Borges's complete map of the world, which is, of necessity, exactly the same size as the world itself.

In 2003, at the age of forty-five, Mark Lewisohn began researching a history of The Beatles. Ten years later, he published the first volume. The extended version runs to 1,698 pages, and only takes The Beatles up to the end of 1962 and the recording of 'Love Me Do'. Lewisohn is now sixty-two, and expects to be well into his seventies before his trilogy is complete. It is, by any measure, an extraordinary achievement, but the detail sometimes threatens to smother the whole. For instance, you may well want to know that George Harrison's first car was a Ford Anglia. Fair enough. But do you really need to know that it was a second-hand two-door blue Ford Anglia 105E Deluxe, bought by George from Brian Epstein's friend Terry Doran, who worked at a car dealership in Warrington?

There are those of us who will be intrigued to learn that Ringo's stepfather Harry Graves bought Ringo his first set of drums in Romford for £10 in 1957. But are we as eager to know the exact route taken by Harry (born in 1937, favourite football team West Ham, favourite singer Sarah Vaughan) when he was lugging it back to Liverpool (Romford to Liverpool Street, then Circle Line to Euston

Square and walk to Euston Station for the train to Lime Street, followed by a taxi to Dingle)?

Lewisohn is so conscientious that he even includes the details he has failed to find out. For instance, of one of John, Paul and George's earliest incarnations, Japage 3, he informs us that 'History doesn't tell if Japage 3 sang "Three Cool Cats" when they performed at La Scala Ballroom in Runcorn on Friday 8 May.'

Quite clearly, however indiscriminate or exhaustive any biographer may be, there is still far more that must be left out than put in. No life can be recaptured in its entirety. It follows that not even one single minute of any life could ever be recaptured as a whole, as there is not a minute in the life of the brain that can be isolated from the rest of its life. We live in the present, but we think in the past and in the present and in the future, and often all at the same time.

Biography as a form is necessarily artificial. In the end, all biography is a form of fiction. As Peter Ackroyd once said, 'Fiction requires truth-telling, whereas in a biography one can make things up.' Introducing *Burning Man*, her extraordinary new book covering ten years in the life of D. H. Lawrence, Frances Wilson writes: 'Just as writers of fiction might provide a disclaimer declaring that what follows is a work of imagination not based on real characters, and writers of non-fiction might provide a disclaimer declaring that what follows is not a work of imagination and very much based on real characters, I should similarly state that *Burning Man* is a work of non-fiction which is also a work of imagination.'

Biography is at the mercy of information, and information is seldom there when you want it. Or occasionally there is a wealth of information, but most of it is window-dressing: the shop itself is shut, visible only through the front window, its private offices firmly under lock and key. This is what makes biography the most sheepish and constrained of the arts, and the least like life.

The deepest part of any life lies within the head. Thomas Wright, author of *Oscar's Books: A Journey Around the Library of Oscar Wilde*, wrote: 'I felt that his biographers had placed undue emphasis on the dramatic external episodes of his life, and not enough on the inner world of his intellect and imagination. It seemed to me that the great events of Wilde's biography, to adapt his own phrase, had taken place in his brain.'

This is, of course, the trouble with all literary biography, and most other biography besides. The real life of anyone takes place largely in the mind, yet it is only the secondary, external stuff – people met, places visited, opinions expressed, and so forth – that is accessible to the biographer. Unless they are spoken or written down, an individual's thoughts evaporate into nothing. The subject's head is, you might say, a closed book. This has not, of course, prevented certain biographers from counterfeiting entry into the heads of their subjects. In the very last sentence of her vast biography of Mao Tse-tung, Jung Chang somehow finds access to Mao's dying thoughts: 'His mind remained lucid to the end, and in it stirred just one thought: himself and his power.' To which one is bound to ask: how do you know?

Royal biographers regularly follow the same practice. In her biography of Princess Diana, Tina Brown makes no division between knowledge and conjecture. In fact, she goes one step further than Jung Chang, claiming to reproduce not only what Diana thought she thought, but what she would have thought, had she been honest with herself: 'As she entered her thirty-seventh year, Diana told herself she was looking for love. But what she was really seeking was a guy with a Gulfstream.'

Similarly, in the first paragraph of his biography of the Queen, Robert Lacey describes Her Majesty at Balmoral on the Thursday after the death of Princess Diana, reading the newspapers, 'digesting their angry sermons with the long-practised pensiveness which caused her eyes to narrow. Her jaw would firm slightly as her thought processes started, shifting her chin forward a fraction – a signal to her staff to think one more hard thought before they opened their mouths.'

This passage raises any number of questions. Was the intrepid Mr Lacey in the Balmoral breakfast room that September morning, perhaps hiding under the table with a periscope to hand? If not, how could he know that the Queen's reading 'caused her eyes to narrow'? And how does anyone, let alone the Queen, set about practising pensiveness? And since, presumably, Lacey was crouching in her brain, like one of the Numbskull cartoon characters in *The Beezer*, could he please explain what, if anything, was going on in the Queen's brain before she firmed her jaw and 'her thought processes started'?

This sort of intrusion can be much more pernicious. In 1975 Primo Levi published his uncompromising book *The Periodic Table* as a testament to the primacy of truth. A professional chemist, he saw chemistry as truth, and unverifiable creeds (not least Nazism) as enemies of truth. For him, each element in the periodic table represented the primacy of fact. 'There is trouble in store', he writes with his engagingly cool understatement, 'for anyone who surrenders to the temptation of mistaking an elegant hypothesis for a certainty.'

This might be a good motto for biographers to pin on their office walls. However recent and well-documented a life may be – and Primo Levi's life was both – there will always be blank areas where there is a lack of proper information to feed the biographer's curiosity. Few of us can recall in any detail what we did on each day of last month. How much harder it would be to gather what a friend of ours was doing during the same period – and harder still to find out what a complete stranger was up to. And how can you hope to work out what went on in anyone's head on a particular day, years ago? The biographer craves certainty, but in its absence will often be tempted by the elegant hypothesis.

It is creepily ironic, then, that one of Levi's biographers should have such a shifting relationship with the truth. 'Where I can, I tell Primo Levi's story straight', Carole Angier writes in her introduction to *The Double Bond: Primo Levi, A Biography*. 'Where I cannot – because I cannot betray my sources, or because I have felt and imagined the past from a story, or from an encounter – I simply give you the story of the encounter. That is why this book is on two levels: a rationally tested, known or knowable one; and the other. Perhaps I needn't say that the felt and imagined level seems to me equally true, and even more important.'

This, it soon emerges, is gobbledegook for 'What I couldn't find out, I made up.' Calling him 'Primo' throughout, Angier spends an awful lot of time empathising and emoting ('my heart sank to the dusty floor', 'I can feel my heart beating', 'half of me wants to burst into laughter, and the other half wants to burst into tears') but often sounds as though she has learnt psychology from binge-watching *The Oprah Winfrey Show*: 'Primo's mother did not love him either. How could she? He was the fruit of the first terrible days of her marriage, and he was male.'

She re-enacts Primo Levi's life as a neurotic melodrama, without nuance or shade. 'At school', she writes, 'he rarely spoke or smiled; he was serious, unsporty and solitary.' Yet, after interviewing many of his contemporaries, Levi's other biographer, Ian Thomson, formed a very different impression: 'Though he was a model pupil, Levi managed to be popular … No one I spoke to had a bad word for the schoolboy.'

Again, when Angier puts her head round the door of the school changing room, she finds him 'so pathologically shy that he really did undress with his back to the other boys'.

In my experience, this makes 95 per cent of schoolboys 'pathologically shy'. But then 'pathological' is one of her words: at one point, she even notes that she herself has 'a pathologically detailed knowledge of everyone he ever met' – an assertion that is not only daft but hateful, given the hundreds of people Levi met at Auschwitz who now lie in unmarked graves.

Of course, more scrupulous biographers eschew such conjecture and rely on first-hand accounts: what do those who were there at the time remember? But this method raises problems. Are first-hand accounts reliable? In real life, people change their memories almost as regularly as they change their minds.

In his book *The Irish Story*, the historian Roy Foster examines the accounts of Irish emigrants at the time they embarked for America and compares them with accounts given by those same emigrants in retrospect. At the moment of departure, they explained that they were leaving Ireland because of unpleasant neighbours or debts or the weather or various runs of bad luck. But given time their memories altered: decades later, having learnt what Foster calls 'the language of exile', they put their exodus down to the cruel English driving them from their homes.

'One would expect people to remember the past and imagine the future,' wrote the historian Lewis Namier, 'but in fact, when discoursing or writing about history, they imagine it in terms of their own experience … they imagine the past and remember the future.'

What of those who wrote it all down at the time, without a view to public show? Surely they can be trusted? I wonder. Who is to say that Pepys's memory never played tricks on him, or that he never misheard a conversation, or that his interpretation of events was not warped by his own imagination, or his desire to shape a good story?

The journals kept by the novelist John Fowles are particularly revealing in this respect, as they sometimes contain their own corrections, added by another hand. Fowles regularly chronicles the rows he has with his beleaguered wife Elizabeth after she has read their contents, but it is not until 1987 that Elizabeth actually starts scribbling her own objections in the margins. Thus, writing about the death of Elizabeth's aunt, Fowles observes that, as she lay dying, Elizabeth 'wouldn't touch her'. Elizabeth reads this, then writes: 'I touched her hands. I fondled her hands. You see nothing. You feel nothing.' On another occasion, when Fowles records that he has made Elizabeth go to the doctor, she scribbles in the margin: 'You do not MAKE me. I telephone. I make my own choice … You are inept. But imagine yourself all-powerful.'

From time to time, the lives of two diarists coincide, and each describes meeting the other. On Wednesday, 21 November 1990, the evening before Margaret Thatcher resigned, two political diarists bumped into each other. Edwina Currie had voted for Heseltine, Alan Clark for Thatcher. In her diary, Currie records that 'Wednesday ended in tears for me, though no one saw them.' She had, she writes, been walking past a group sitting behind the Speaker's chair. The group consisted of Tristan Garel-Jones, Alan Clark and Richard Ryder. 'Everything all right?' Ryder asks her, as she walks past.

'Prat, I thought, vacuous unctuous prat,' she writes. Edwina turns on him. 'No, it isn't,' she snaps. 'The party is falling apart and you're just sitting there grinning.' After a little more banter, she records Alan Clark saying, angrily: 'Why don't you apply for the Chiltern Hundreds right now? Then you can have a different career.'

'Snob, I thought, and turd with it,' she writes in her blunt style. She then turns on Clark. 'I have other things I do now, Alan, and you don't need to be insulting to me: I'm not going to insult you. But we cannot win the election on the basis of safe seats in the south alone. We have to win my seat, and others like it in the Midlands and the north.' She then exits: 'I will not be faced down by these men, I thought, and walked off to the car park, where I cried in my car for ten minutes.'

Oddly enough, not a single word of dialogue in Clark's diary entry for that same meeting coincides with Currie's. Clark's version makes no reference to the presence of Richard Ryder, though he does mention sitting with Tristan Garel-Jones, who 'had little to say'.

'Then along came Edwina. "Hullo, aren't you Edwina Currie?"

"Now then, Alan, there's no need to be objectionable."

"If that is who you are, I must congratulate you on the combination of loyalty and restraint that you have shown in going on television to announce your intention to vote against the Prime Minister in the leadership election."

"Alan, I'm perfectly prepared to argue this with you, if you'll listen."

"Piss off."

Which she did.

Tristan said: "She's not a bad girl really."'

Which of the two diary entries comes closest to the truth? Clark wrote his diary only a few hours later, in an Indian restaurant around the corner from the House of Commons. Clark's account was thus hot off the press. As for Currie, she waited until the following Sunday to write up her diary, while sitting in a hotel in Bangladesh. In the same entry, she covered the whole of the rest of the week, including attending an aerobics class and dancing around her flat at the news of Mrs Thatcher's resignation.

The authenticity of recorded speech is often best judged by reading it aloud. In Clark's dialogue one can hear his authentic camp acidity and the pert, flouncy tone of Currie, though both could be said to carry a hint of caricature. But I would defy even the most skilled actor to speak the line Currie gives herself – 'But we cannot win the election on the basis of safe seats in the south alone. We have to win my seat, and others like it in the Midlands and the north' – and make it sound natural.

In the end, we will never know which of the two diarists to trust. It can't be both, and may well be neither. But posterity will favour Alan Clark, for posterity has no means of verification, and so opts instead for style, preferring the good writer to the bad.

In a letter to Arnold Zweig, who had just suggested writing his biography, Sigmund Freud wrote: 'Anyone turning biographer commits himself to lies, to concealment, to hypocrisy, to flattery, and even to hiding his own lack of understanding, for biographical truth is not to be had, and even if it were it couldn't be used.'

This may be too severe, but the artificiality of the genre is helped neither by the slippery nature of memory, nor, indeed, by the slippery nature of biographers. Everyone who has ever written non-fiction will know that, from paragraph to paragraph, perhaps even from sentence to sentence, one is always obliged to pick which version of the truth to tell: every available source has a slightly different slant. It would be tedious to present each different version of each event, or the finished book would be impossibly long, and impossibly boring. So which to choose? And how do you know if it is the right one?

I have examined the randomness of this selection process at various points in my last three books. My book *One on One* presented a daisy chain of 101 meetings between well-known figures ranging from Leo Tolstoy to Michael Barrymore. In one chapter I set out to describe the meeting that occurred on 19 May 1922 at the Hôtel Majestic in Paris between four of the most powerful artists of the twentieth century – Igor Stravinsky, Pablo Picasso, Marcel Proust and James Joyce.

The four men had been brought together by wealthy art patrons called Sydney and Violet Schiff. As we all know, encounters at parties are subject to the vagaries of memory, and further obscured by layers of gossip and hearsay and inaudibility, the whole mix often further muddled by alcohol. This meant that when it came to the conversation between Proust and Joyce – who had never met before, and were never to meet again – I found there were at least seven different versions, each of them standing in contradiction to the others.

The briefest version was told by Joyce's friend Arthur Power. It goes:

PROUST: Do you like truffles?
JOYCE: Yes, I do.

The next version, almost as brief, was told by the Duchesse de Clermont-Tonnerre:

PROUST: I have never read your works, Mr Joyce.
JOYCE: I have never read *your* works, Mr Proust.

A third version was told by Joyce himself, many years later, to Jacques Mercanton:

'Proust would talk only of duchesses,' he said, 'while I was more concerned with chambermaids.'

Joyce offered another version to his close friend Frank Budgen:

'Our talk consisted solely of the word "No". Proust asked me if I knew the duc de so-and-so. I said "No". Our hostess asked Proust if he had read such and such a piece of *Ulysses*. Proust said "No". And so on. Of course the situation was impossible. Proust's day was just beginning. Mine was at an end.'

According to another friend of Joyce, Padraic Colum, Joyce wished to undermine the Schiffs' hope for a legendary occasion, so he tried to stay as silent as possible.

PROUST: Ah, Monsieur Joyce, you know the Princess …
JOYCE: No, Monsieur.
PROUST: Ah, you know the Countess …
JOYCE: No, Monsieur.
PROUST: Then you know Madame …
JOYCE: No, Monsieur.

However, in this version, Joyce clearly wrong-foots himself, as his silence becomes part of the legend.

Version six was told by the modernist poet William Carlos Williams:

JOYCE: I've had headaches every day. My eyes are terrible.
PROUST: My poor stomach. What am I going to do? It's killing me. In fact, I must leave at once.
JOYCE: I'm in the same situation. If I can find someone to take me by the arm. Goodbye!
PROUST: *Charme!* Oh, my stomach.

And version seven was told by the author Ford Madox Ford, who had a reputation for tall stories:

PROUST: As I say, Monsieur, in *Du côte de chez Swann*, which no doubt you have –
JOYCE: No, Monsieur. [*pause*] As Mr Bloom says in my *Ulysses*, which, Monsieur, you have doubtless read …
PROUST: But, no, Monsieur.

[*pause*]

Proust apologises for his late arrival, ascribing it to malady, before going into the symptoms in some detail:

JOYCE: Well, Monsieur, I have almost exactly the same symptoms. Only in my case, the analysis …

And from then on, for a number of hours, the two men discuss their various illnesses.

I offered a similar chart in my book about Princess Margaret, this one concerning the gangster and occasional actor John Bindon, with whom she became acquainted in Mustique in the 1970s. Despite a CV encompassing walk-on roles in *The Sweeney*, *Quadrophenia* and *Softly Softly*, and being put on trial for, among other offences, murder and grievous bodily harm, at his death in 1993 Bindon was probably best remembered for a party trick with his penis. But the exact nature of the trick, and the scale of his penis, was open to as much historical dispute as the causes of the First World War. Among the Princess's previous biographers, Noel Botham stated that what he called Bindon's 'unique cabaret turn' involved 'balancing three half-pint glasses on his erect penis'. Tim Heald was more vague, and was convinced that it involved dangling rather than balancing. Bindon was, he said, 'best known for a party trick that involved hanging beer tankards from his erect penis'.

Theo Aronson didn't mention a party trick with glasses or tankards, but just wrote that 'Bindon was apparently very proud of his "enormous penis" which he would display in the palm of his hand.' He added that there had been talk on the island that he had once 'flashed it for Princess Margaret'. And beyond the enclosed world of royal biographers, accounts also vary: *Brewer's Rogues, Villains and Eccentrics* claims that Bindon entertained Princess Margaret 'by balancing six glasses of beer on his penis', while his obituarist in the *Daily Telegraph* argued that 'He was justly famed for a party trick which entailed the balancing of as many as six half-pint mugs on one part of his anatomy.' In his autobiography *Confessions of a King's Road Cowboy*, Johnny Cigarini, a contemporary of Bindon, confidently states that 'His party trick in pubs was to put empty pint glasses on it and put his penis through the handles,' before going on to estimate the final count as 'ten at one time, or something ridiculous'.

And so it goes on, this whirligig of conflicting accounts. In her autobiography, Christine Keeler, best known for her role in the Profumo scandal, says that Bindon would 'balance five half-pints of beer on his penis'. Bindon's own biographer, Wensley Clarkson, agrees with her on the number, but not on the method: he suggests that Bindon would 'hang five half-pint beer glasses from it'.

In his *Private Eye* diary for 15 November 1979, Auberon Waugh dismissed this estimate as 'ludicrous' and 'preposterous', stating firmly that 'sources close to Princess Margaret' had assured him that Bindon 'never managed to balance more than one small sherry schooner in this way'.

How to make sense of all these contradictions? In *Ma'am Darling* I presented them in chart form:

BOTHAM: three half-pint glasses (balancing)
BREWER'S: six glasses of beer (balancing)
CLARKSON: five half-pint glasses (hanging)
DAILY TELEGRAPH: six half-pint glasses (balancing)
HEALD: unspecified number of 'tankards' (hanging)
CIGARINI: ten pint glasses (hanging)
WAUGH: one small sherry schooner (balancing)

Writing *Ma'am Darling*, I would spend hours puzzling over the same not-very-interesting anecdote told about the Princess by different people, each one contradicting the next. Should I go for the most likely, the funniest, the most interesting, or even, as part of my noble effort to write a serious work, the dullest? And which was which? I found it increasingly hard to judge. Should I favour one version of events over the other, or should I risk boring the reader by relaying every variant?

To pick just one more example, here are two different versions of a humdrum little story concerning Lord Snowdon, Princess Margaret, a cigarette and a cushion. The first is from *Of Kings and Cabbages* (1984), a memoir by Peter Coats, partner of Chips Channon and editor of *House and Garden* magazine, widely known by the nickname 'Petti-Coats': 'Tony Snowdon was having a mild argument with his wife, Princess Margaret, and, having lit a cigarette, flicked the match towards an ashtray and it fell into Princess Margaret's brocaded lap. HRH brushed it off quickly and, rather annoyed, said, "Really, Tony, you might have burnt my dress." To which came the reply, "I don't care. I never did like that material." The Princess drew herself up and said very grandly, "Material is a word we do not use." I admit to having told this story several times, and it always arouses a storm-in-a-cocktail-glass of discussion. What other word? Stuff, perhaps?'

So there we are. Now take a look at this second version of the same event, which comes from *Redeeming Features* (2009), an enjoyably baroque memoir by the interior decorator and socialite Nicky Haslam: 'We joined a party at Kate and Ivan Moffat's, where the growing distance and determined one-upmanship between Princess Margaret and Tony Snowdon was all too evident. Bored, Tony played with a box of matches, flicking them, lit, at his wife. "Oh, do stop," she said. "You'll set fire to my dress." Tony glowered. "Good thing too. I hate that material." Princess Margaret stiffened. "We call it stuff."'

Who is telling the truth? It can't be both. The Coats version is milder, the Haslam version more extreme. Coats has Snowdon lighting a cigarette and flicking a single match with the intention of making it land in an ashtray; Haslam has him playing with an entire box of matches out of boredom, and aiming and flicking the lit matches, one by one, at Princess Margaret. According to Coats, the Princess says, 'Material is a word we do not use.'

We will never know which version is true, or truer, or if both are false, or half-true and half-false. If you could whizz back in time and corner both men as they left the Moffats' house, I imagine that each

would swear by his own story, and someone else emerging from the same party – Lord Snowdon, or Princess Margaret, or one of the Moffats, for instance – would say that both of them had got it wrong, and the truth was more mundane, or more civilised, or more complicated, or more outrageous.

Even if we agree on a judicious mash-up of these two accounts, we are still obliged to embark on an investigation of late-twentieth-century royal linguistics. Both accounts agree that 'material' was a word offensive to Princess Margaret, and perhaps even to the entire Royal Family. But why? As words go, it has a perfectly good pedigree: it dates back to 1380, and was employed by Geoffrey Chaucer. On the other hand, though 'stuff' may sound more aggressively modern, coarse and general, it in fact predates 'material' by forty years. 'Stuff' originally meant fabric – in particular the quilted fabric worn under chain mail. It was centuries before it was demoted into a catch-all term applied to anything you couldn't quite remember the right name for. So the Princess's etymological instinct turns out to have been spot on.

But that's not all. Might her preference for 'stuff' over 'material' be an unconscious throwback to her family's Germanic roots? The German for material is '*Stoff*', so it's perfectly possible that the Royal Family's liking for 'stuff' has been handed down from generation to generation, its basis lost in time.

And what of all the other words Princess Margaret didn't like? She loathed 'placement' and 'scrambled eggs', for instance, insisting on '*place à table*' and 'buttered eggs' instead. Should the dutiful biographer investigate the deeper meanings beneath all her peculiar preferences?

So a biography of Princess Margaret – or, indeed, anyone else who ever lived – is set to expand like the universe itself, or, in more graspable terms, like a cheese soufflé, every reference breeding 100 more references, every story 1,000 more stories, each with its own galaxy of additions, contradictions and embellishments. You try to construct a hay bale, but you end up with a haystack. And the needle is nowhere to be seen.

In my most recent book, *One Two Three Four: The Beatles in Time* I presented a chart of fifteen accounts – from both onlookers and historians – of John Lennon's fight with the Cavern MC Bob Wooler at Paul McCartney's twenty-first birthday party at his Auntie Gin's house in Huyton on 21 June 1963.

Everyone seems to agree that Wooler provoked John by teasing him about his recent holiday in Spain with Brian Epstein, and that Bob Wooler had ended up in hospital. But eyewitnesses differ over the nature of the assault and the extent of the injuries. Tony Barrow, who was present, reports simply that John 'punched Wooler'. Tony Bramwell, also present, says he 'assaulted Bob', leaving him with 'broken ribs and a bloody nose'. Another eyewitness, Peter Brown, describes it as a 'pummeling', and remembers taking 'three men to pull John off, but not before he managed to break three of the man's ribs'. Cynthia Lennon says John 'leapt on Bob' and gave him 'a black eye and badly bruised ribs'. To The Beatles' authorised biographer, Hunter Davies, John said, 'I broke his bloody ribs for him.' John's old school friend Pete Shotton recalls John 'repeatedly clobbering him in the face with a shovel', adding that 'the damage to Bob's visage was so extensive that an ambulance had to be summoned to rush him to hospital'.

Rex Makin, The Beatles' solicitor, who had to deal with the matter, suggested that Bob Wooler had made a pass at John, and that in return John gave Wooler a black eye and a broken nose.

Versions of the incident offered by Beatles biographers are yet more varied: Ray Connolly gives John a stick to beat Wooler, whereas Bob Spitz says John 'leapt on Wooler, beating him viciously with tightly closed fists' before grabbing a garden shovel and whacking Wooler with the handle. Spitz quotes one observer as saying, 'Bob was holding his hands to his face and John was kicking all the skin off his fingers'. As to Wooler's injuries, Spitz's final reckoning was 'a broken nose, a cracked collar bone and three broken ribs'. But even this grand total was surpassed by the most unforgiving of John's biographers, Albert Goldman, who, miraculously, also seems to have direct access to John's thoughts at the time: 'seizing a shovel that was lying in the yard, Lennon began to beat Wooler to death. Blow after blow came smashing down on the defenseless man lying on the ground. It would have ended in murder if John had not suddenly realized: "If I hit him one more time, I'll kill him." Making an enormous effort of will, Lennon restrained himself.'

No other episode in the lives of The Beatles illustrates quite so starkly the random, subjective nature of history, a form predicated on objectivity but reliant on the shifting sands of memory. As Paul McCartney himself once said: 'In an earthquake you get many different versions of what happened by all the people that saw it. And they're all true.'

Another shortcoming of biography lies in its bias towards coherence. In their drive to create a coherent narrative, biographers are forced to conceal the randomness of life, the contrived nature of 'character' and the unpredictability of human beings. 'Every schoolboy could understand each thing as it happened,' wrote the novelist Robert Musil, 'but as to what it all meant in general, nobody really knew except for a few persons, and even they were not sure. Only a short time later it might well have happened in a different sequence, or the other way round, and nobody would have known the difference.'

Biography is written with hindsight: from the start, the biographer knows how the story will unfold. But human beings exist in the present tense. We live our lives without knowing the future. We hurtle forward, but the front window is blacked out: we are only ever able to see out of the back and side windows.

How to overcome these obstacles? When I was a schoolboy, *Jackdaw* folders were all the rage. They consisted of individual reproductions of original documents about a particular person or event – Alfred the Great, the Gunpowder Plot, the English Civil War – all contained within a colourful folder. You could juggle these documents at will. The documents were self-contained, with no connecting narrative to pull them all together. For a schoolchild, the joy lay in sifting through them at random, before alighting on one – say, a copy of King Charles I's death warrant – that seemed particularly captivating. In a strange way, this made *Jackdaws* closer to real life than many a grander, grown-up history: they were free from the constraints of chronology, free from embellishment, free from bogus threads linking one event to another.

Every few years since that time, I have read a biography that presented an original way of piercing through the artificiality of the conventional form. *Brief Lives* by John Aubrey, written at the end of the seventeenth century, is a celebration of the colourful detail that orthodox historians prefer to pooh-pooh. The dogged trawl through achievements and appointments is banished in favour of gossip, impure and simple. Who can forget Aubrey's description of sex up against a tree between Sir Walter Raleigh and a young lady friend? At first, 'fearful of her Honour, and modest' she says: 'sweet Sir Walter'. But then, 'as the danger and the pleasure at the same time grew higher, she cried in ecstasy, "swisser Swatter, Swisser Swatter!"'

Or again, Aubrey writes of Edward de Vere, Earl of Oxford: 'The Earl of Oxford, making of his low obeisance to Queen Elizabeth, happened to let a Fart, at which he was so abashed and ashamed that he went to travel, 7 years. On his return the Queen welcomed him home, and said, My Lord, I had forgot the Fart.'

Was Aubrey accurate? He offered no learned references to authenticate his claims but, then again, he would have expected his readers to take his anecdotes with the same freewheeling, comical spirit in which they were offered. Similarly, Lytton Strachey eschewed the sombre and the judicious for something sharper and more overtly subjective. He may have swapped fairness for laughter, but he always got a terrific exchange rate. Bertrand Russell read *Eminent Victorians* in Brixton Prison and laughed so loud that an officer felt obliged to remind him that prison was a place of punishment.

In one of the most beautiful and memorable passages of his biography of Queen Victoria, Strachey imagines the thoughts running through the mind of the old Queen on her deathbed: 'she herself, as she lay blind and silent, seemed to those who watched her to be divested of all thinking – to have glided already, unawares, into oblivion. Yet, perhaps, in the secret chambers of consciousness, she had her thoughts, too. Perhaps her fading mind called up once more the shadows of the past to float before it, and retraced, for the last time, the vanished visions of that long history – passing back and back, through the cloud of years, to older and ever older memories – to the spring woods at

Osborne, so full of primroses for Lord Beaconsfield, to Lord Palmerston's queer clothes and high demeanour, and Albert's face under the green lamp, and Albert's first stag at Balmoral, and Albert in his blue and silver uniform, and the Baron coming in through a doorway, and Lord M. dreaming at Windsor with the rooks cawing in the elm-trees, and the Archbishop of Canterbury on his knees in the dawn, and the old King's turkey-cock ejaculations, and Uncle Leopold's soft voice at Claremont, and Lehzen with the globes, and her mother's feathers sweeping down towards her, and a great old repeater-watch of her father's in its tortoise-shell case, and a yellow rug, and some friendly flounces of sprigged muslin, and the trees and the grass at Kensington.'

It might be argued that, just as Jung Chang presented us with the dying thoughts of Chairman Mao, Strachey has here strayed into areas out of bounds to the biographer. Yet there is a clear difference between the two. Jung Chang simply asserts that Mao's dying thoughts were solely about himself and his power. Strachey, on the other hand, heralds his imaginative leap into the unknown by saying 'Yet, perhaps, in the secret chambers of consciousness, she had her thoughts, too.' He then self-consciously summons forth a stream of poetic images from the life – and The Life – he has just created. This is biography at its most playful and imaginative, biography that stresses, rather than hides, the inarguable but so often unacknowledged link between the mind of the writer and the life of his subject.

There are numerous examples of other biographies that have broken through the genre's dull and dogged obeisance to available information. These biographies pursue a sense of pattern and aesthetic purpose more usually found in a novel. They tend to stress, rather than to hide, the inarguable but so often unacknowledged link between the mind of the biographer and the mind of the subject. Alethea Hayter's *A Sultry Month* (1965) focuses on a single month – June 1846 – in London. Within a mile or two, Robert Browning and Elizabeth Barrett, Dickens, Wordsworth and Tennyson are all milling around; meanwhile, the depressive Benjamin Haydon, painter of increasingly unfashionable historical canvases, has his latest exhibition upstaged and outsold by General Tom Thumb's show next door.

In *The Quest for Corvo*, subtitled, *An Experiment in Biography* (1934), A. J. A. Symonds pursues his subject, the deeply eccentric and unreliable Frederick Rolfe, as a detective might pursue a prime suspect, describing all the witnesses he interviews along the way. In *Out of Sheer Rage* (1997), Geoff Dyer created a book about not writing a book. Ostensibly a biography of D. H. Lawrence, it is really a book about never quite getting round to writing a biography of D. H. Lawrence.

In his attempt to break through the barrier of available fact and into Oscar Wilde's inner world, Thomas Wright set about reading all 2,000 books in Wilde's library. Fifty of them he read in their original volumes, some of which had Oscar's own marginalia, marks, tears and stains still on them. A number were torn here and there, testament to Wilde's eccentric habit of tearing off the top corner of a page as he read it, rolling the paper into a ball and then popping it into his mouth. Reading one volume, Wright came across a jam stain on its pages, and laughed with delight: 'I imagined Wilde ... holding the volume in one hand and a slice of bread and jam in the other.' Other volumes, from his time in prison, had dirt smudges still on them, poignant finger-print memorials to two years of hard labour. The result of Wright's labour, *Oscar's Books* (2008), is, like those others I have mentioned, an exhilarating experiment in biography. But, like the others, it is an experiment so perfectly suited to its subject that it would be impossible to emulate.

This suggests that, to be entirely fresh, each new biography must create a template of its own. The tidily chronological, omniscient, cradle-to-grave biography, however dutifully rendered, may serve a purpose as a sort of magnified CV, but, in the words of John Updike, it will struggle to 'convey the unearthly human innocence that attends, in the present tense of living, the self that seems the real one'.

CELEBRITY

What's My Line?

Our new 'smart' television offers such a vast archive of programmes, all queuing to be watched, that real life has been forced to take a back seat. The other day, I stumbled across yet another hidden treasure. Buried deep on BBC4 there is a stash of ancient quiz shows, chosen, or, to use the vogue word, 'curated', by Richard Osman.

I made a beeline for an edition of *What's My Line?*, broadcast on 19 January 1974, and introduced with tinkly saloon-bar piano music. Our host is the suave David Jacobs, dapper in a slightly-too-large black bow tie and dinner jacket. Having welcomed us to the show, he introduces us to the panel, the women in evening dresses, the men in dinner jackets. 'Let's meet them straight away – Lady Isobel Barnett, Kenneth Williams, Nanette Newman and Bill Franklyn! Well, that's the team, and this is our first challenger!'

Never is the inexorability of human mortality demonstrated more starkly than when watching old TV shows. The only one of those five beaming, easy-going celebrities still alive is Nanette Newman. Two of them – Lady Isobel Barnett and Kenneth Williams – were destined to kill themselves.

The quiz gets under way. A pleasant-looking woman in her thirties comes on and signs her name – Charlotte Murtagh – on a blackboard. 'And now, for the benefit of those of you at home, this is what she does for a living!' A sign pops up on the screen saying 'Detective Constable'. The audience hoots with laughter. This is 1974, when the idea of a female detective constable was too silly for words.

The panellists on *What's My Line?* then quiz the challenger about what she does for a living. If she says 'No' ten times, they lose. Charlotte

Murtagh hasn't joined in with the audience laughter, so, after saying 'Good evening', Bill Franklyn asks: 'Am I right in thinking that you don't find your job particularly amusing?' 'It can be, but not as a rule,' says Charlotte.

The panellists continue with their questions:

'Something to do with medicine?'

'No.'

'Are you in a domestic job?'

'No.'

It's Kenneth Williams's turn. 'You're not ordained, or anything like that? No, obviously ... you couldn't have a woman priest, could you?' Finally, he gets it right. 'A lady policeman or a woman detective?' The audience applauds, and Kenneth Williams looks pleased with himself. He then asks Charlotte: 'A man is called a detective, but what is the correct title for a lady?' 'Woman detective, just woman detective,' replies Charlotte. The past is another country.

Next up is a man who describes himself, on the blackboard, as a 'Burglar Alarmist'. From the questions, it emerges that this profession is very new. The panel is baffled. They fail to get it in ten, so David Jacobs presents the challenger with his prize – modest by today's grabby standards – of a printed diploma. He exits, to be replaced by a taxidermist, who ends his session by showing the panel one of his creations, a stuffed lion cub. 'It's a pity the poor thing's not alive, but thank you for bringing it with you,' says David Jacobs, politely bidding him farewell.

The panel now put on big black blindfolds. 'Will our guest celebrity sign in please?' It is the impressionist Mike Yarwood, as famous in 1974 as Stephen Fry or Peter Kay are now, but today unknown to those under the age of fifty. Yarwood adopts a funny husky voice to answer the panel.

'Have you got laryngitis?' asks Lady Isobel Barnett, which wastes one of her questions.

'You're Dick Emery!' says Kenneth Williams, wasting another of his.

But by now they have narrowed him down to the world of entertainment.

'I know the voice … are you David Nixon?' asks Bill Franklyn.

They eventually identify him, and then David Jacobs invites him to do his impersonation of Robin Day. Mike Yarwood, Dick Emery, David Nixon, Robin Day: so big in their day, now all but forgotten.

The final challenger is Betty Lees, described as 'Electrolygist (Removes Hair)'. After a few questions, the panel establishes that her job involves treating people in some way.

'Do you touch them?' asks Lady Isobel Barnett.

David Jacobs moves closer to her, and smiles lasciviously.

'She hasn't touched me yet!' he smirks. It is a joke no one would dare make in our more cautious times, fifty years on.

It's Siiiiiiimon Deeeeeee!

By happy chance, on the same day the BBC revealed its payments to its top stars, I tracked down a volume for which I had long been searching: *The Simon Dee Book*, published over half a century ago, in 1968.

In those days, Simon Dee was the highest-paid TV personality, with his own twice-weekly BBC chat show, *Dee Time*, which used to start with a film of him driving an open-top E-type Jaguar around London, accompanied by a glamorous blonde in the passenger seat.

He was the Jonathan Ross of his day, but, at thirty-three, younger, leaner and – to employ a once-fashionable phrase – more 'with-it'. Roughly two million viewers tune into Jonathan Ross's current chat show, but Simon Dee gathered audiences of eighteen million for *Dee Time*.

For three years he embodied the 1960s dream, hosting his own show ('It's Siiiiiiimon Dee!'), dashing up and down the King's Road in his own Aston Martin DB5,* compering the Miss World competition, enjoying an affair with Joanna Lumley, presenting an award to The Beatles, and numbering Michael Caine ('Mike') and Roger Moore ('Rog') among his famous friends.

The Simon Dee Book is like a time capsule, or, perhaps more accurately, a black box. How cool he seemed then, how crusty he seems now. In a questionnaire, he is asked what he thinks of working wives. 'Only in the bedroom,' he replies.

Throughout, he calls women either 'dolls' or 'birds'. He talks of his early days as a door-to-door salesman. 'I never found much trouble in

---

* Bought in cash from the actor Robert Shaw.

chatting up the housewives. Actually women are their own worst enemy. A little bit of flattery and they're ready to believe anything. Believe me, it never ceased to make me laugh!'

He talks about himself in the third person as he describes the effect on the other shoppers as he enters his local supermarket. 'It's a hint of glamour having Simon, the big TV star, right among them to brighten their suburban lives – and I don't mean that unkindly either.'

Part of *The Simon Dee Book* is taken up with his diary ('Dee Days') of a typical week. It starts with his drive into work and reveals his contempt for the commuters he passes. 'The faceless ones are on the march, folks, crawling with deadly purpose into the metropolis, eyes half-closed.'

He drives down Chelsea's then-trendy King's Road. 'Float my way past "Countdown", "Fifth Avenue" and "Dandie Fashions" … past "Bazaar", where Mary Quant launched her famous dolly gear … Arrive at Vidal Sassoon's, am ushered in by young dolly, have my coat taken by another and a coffee brought up by a third.'

After meeting his lawyer – 'Actually, he's a pretty swinging fellow: not at all the stuffed owl you might expect' – Dee is interviewed by a journalist who asks: 'How much do you earn?' 'Currently, around 30 grand,' he replies. This means that he was on the equivalent of £364,000, placing him roughly in line with the broadcasting grandees of today.

In his next diary entry, he boasts of going out to lunch with 'the casting director of a major film company'. He wants to get into films. 'Mike Caine's had a good run for his money. So it's time he moved over for a younger lad. Not to say prettier!'

The book presents a picture of a man at the height of success; it is illustrated with full-page photographs of Dee with the big names of the era: A. J. P. Taylor, Davy Jones of The Monkees, Twiggy, Donovan and Vanessa Redgrave (in a psychedelic trouser suit).

He had been born Cyril Henty-Dodd, and attended Shrewsbury public school, alongside John Peel, who was born John Ravenscroft. One of his old schoolmasters recalls him as 'Absolutely charming. But he also had this unpredictable side to him which nobody seemed able to control.'

After a year, young Cyril was expelled from Shrewsbury after being caught stealing money from his friends. He moved to Brighton College, which he left with just one O-Level, and so to the RAF, where he worked in aerial reconnaissance.

He left the RAF aged twenty-three, and for the next few years flitted between fifty different jobs, sweeping leaves, putting shoes in boxes, driving lorries, letting flats and selling vacuum cleaners door-to-door. He might have carried on with this hand-to-mouth existence had it not been for an amazing stroke of luck: working as a builder, he paid to go to acting class once a week, and while there he bumped into a fellow student, Ronan O'Rahilly, who was then the manager of Georgie Fame.

It so happened that O'Rahilly was planning to start Britain's first pirate radio station, Radio Caroline (named after President Kennedy's daughter), and was on the lookout for cheap and cheerful disc jockeys. Cyril Henty-Dodd joined, changed his name to the catchier Simon Dee, and proved an instant success. His on-air repartee with his fellow DJ Chris Moore sounds eerily close to Smashy and Nicey, or Alan Partridge and Dave Clifton, with an uncomfortable mix of public chumminess and private contempt:

Chris Moore: And here's the next record – Dave Brubeck and 'Take Five'.

Simon Dee: Take Five what?

Chris Moore: 'Take Five'.

Simon Dee: Yes, but Take Five what?

Chris Moore: Don't listen to him, people! 'Take Five' is just the name of the record! And here it is …

Thus Simon Dee became one of the pioneers of talking nonsense for hours on end; his skill in that peculiar new profession roped in ten million listeners a week. Yet his colleagues had already spotted a couple of fatal flaws in his character: a lightning temper and a paranoid belief that everyone was out to get him.

After fifteen months, he had a furious row with O'Rahilly and stormed out. By now he was thirty-one years old. He then kicked around the BBC, occasionally compering shows such as *Thank Your Lucky Stars*, and recording pilot shows for series that weren't commissioned. And so he may have remained, just another former disc jockey grubbing around for spare work, had he not experienced another stroke of luck: the wife of Bill Cotton, the BBC variety chief, spotted him on a Smith's Crisps advertisement and mentioned him to her husband, who was looking for a new chat show host.

Hey presto! *Dee Time* was born, a groovier British version of *The Johnny Carson Show*, with big names galore. But how many of those big names can we still remember? A biography includes lists of everyone who was ever a guest.* Roughly one in five of these names remains big, or at least biggish, today (Lulu, Lionel Blair, Cliff Richard, Des O'Connor), and others have faded somewhat (Lance Percival, The Tremeloes, Scott Walker) but at least half (The Cuff-Links, Vi Reed, Annette Day, Monte Crick, The Warm Sounds) have disappeared entirely, and now exist on a plane of celebrity several rungs below Simon Dee, so obscure as to be invisible.

If, as these lists suggest, there are so many people, once famous, now obscure, why is it Simon Dee who has been singled out for special attention? His downfall, when it came, was swifter, more extreme and more public than most, but it was also self-inflicted, which makes his story the closest the world of telly will ever come to a Greek tragedy.

As chat show hosts go, he was just as talented as his exact contemporary Michael Parkinson, and in many ways less irritating. These days, Simon Dee could easily be sitting in Parky's chair, smarming up to showbiz folk on Saturday nights, were it not for the fact that, backstage, he was almost pathologically inclined to wind everyone up the wrong way.

Behind the scenes at *Dee Time* he was increasingly rude to his writers, rude to his bosses, rude to his studio audiences. His megalomania grew and grew: he even started issuing a Messiah-like newsletter called *Dee-spatches*, with a Dee-code, imparting his wisdom to his fans ('parents come in all sizes, from square to stream-lined').

---

* *Whatever Happened to Simon Dee?* by Richard Wiseman (2005).

As his fame grew, so did his ego and his demands. He began to insist on choosing his own guests, and would threaten to walk out when he didn't get his own way. Eventually, Billy Cotton called his bluff: when the time came to renew his contract, he offered Dee less money rather than more. His pride hurt, he left for London Weekend Television, where he was soon to find himself sidelined in favour of David Frost, who was part-owner of the company.

Things went from bad to worse, culminating in an interview with that other forgotten 1960s figure George Lazenby, the one-time James Bond, in which he encouraged Lazenby to read out a long list of American senators he claimed had conspired in the assassination of President Kennedy.

Dee was sacked from LWT, and subsequently fell out with everyone who offered him the chance of a comeback. By the end of 1970, he had signed on at his local Labour Exchange. 'How the mighty have fallen,' observed the clerk who served him.

He walked out of the Radio 4 *Today* programme after just two broadcasts, from a Fairy Liquid commercial during lunchtime on day one, and from a Reading radio station on his very first morning, having refused to interview the lowly Alvin Stardust.

Over the next thirty-five years, Dee's life was a series of downhill bumps. He found himself in various courtrooms for, successively, shoplifting a potato peeler, non-payment of rates, smashing up a loo seat in a shop, and assaulting a Buckingham Palace policeman who had refused to let him speak to the Queen. In 2003, Channel 4 offered him a one-off live chat show. He gave researchers a list of his old 1960s chums – Mike Caine, Rog Moore, etc. – but none of them wanted to appear alongside him. 'Did you tell him that it was me, that it was my big comeback show?' Dee asked the researchers. Yes, we did, they replied. 'At which point,' recalled one of them, Richard Wiseman, 'Dee said nothing and simply looked very sad.'

On the big night he blew it, his fatal lack of preparation causing him to be tongue-tied with his guests. After three minutes interviewing the elderly Peter Wyngarde (born Cyril Goldbert), he dried up. After a long pause, he finally came up with his next question: 'Seen any good shows recently?'

Dee died aged seventy-four in 2009, in a modest flat in Winchester, surrounded by twenty-six scrapbooks stuffed with his newspaper cuttings, beginning in 1964 and ending in 1972. By the time of his death, he had come to personify the frailty of fame, the ghost of TV past.

Simon Dee is buried on the outskirts of Winchester under his real name, Cyril Henty-Dodd; his tomb a monument to that most modern of paradoxes, the celebrity who is remembered for having been forgotten.

Eight Things You Didn't
Know about Bears

1) In *The Revenant*, Leonardo DiCaprio wrestles with a grizzly bear. Among those who auditioned for the supporting role was Britain's own Rupert Bear, but director Alejandro González Iñárritu decided to go for a more rugged look. 'Rupert is one of the old school and refused point blank to take off his yellow-check trousers for the cameras, so Alejandro was forced to look elsewhere,' reports one source.

2) Tony, the bear finally chosen for the role, was a virtual unknown. Originally spotted prowling in Canada's Kluane National Park, he had previously only played walk-on parts in bear-based amateur dramatics. 'I literally thought myself into the part, and just adored my little grapple with Leo,' Tony says of his famous scene in *The Revenant*. 'He's an absolute poppet and we had the most marvellous giggle about it afterwards.'

Tony now wants to turn his hand to a stage musical – Jean Valjean in *Les Miz* or Maria in *The Sound of Music*. He currently lives with his partner, Bruno, in a mock-Tudor mansion in Beverly Hills, where he boasts an unrivalled collection of scented candles and is rumoured to be a Scientologist.

3) Confronted by a grizzly bear, what's the best course of action? It's a question that continues to divide the experts.

Some say scramble uphill, so as to appear superior, while others argue that it is best to scoot downhill, so as not to represent a threat. However, a spokesman for the Canadian National Federation of Bears considers neither method to be fool-proof. 'Show-offs and cowards both taste equally delicious to us,' he says.

4) For some years, Winnie the Pooh is said to have nursed a grudge against Paddington Bear. 'It all stems from envy,' confides a mutual friend. 'For decades, Winnie was the go-to bear for all British publishers and film-makers. Then Paddington suddenly arrived on the scene, the new kid on the block with his suitcase and sou'wester, and Winnie was hopping mad.

'Of course, when they meet on chat shows, awards ceremonies and so forth, they greet each other like long-lost friends. But, behind the scenes, it's a very different story. Winnie often rants for hours on end about how Paddington stole all his best ideas and that he's got no right to be here.'

5) Early last year, rumours began to surface that Pooh had secretly reported Paddington to the immigration authorities, but it is an allegation he strenuously denies. 'Absolutely not – I would never ever do such a thing,' he says, before adding: 'But the fact remains that, for all his very real talent, Paddington arrived in this country as an illegal stowaway from Peru. Frankly, if he does not have valid papers about his person, then it is only right and proper that the relevant authorities should be alerted.'

6) Experts warn that brown bears and grizzly bears can be highly dangerous, but teddy bears less so. 'There have been only three reported attacks by teddy bears in North America in the past two years,' says a senior spokesman for the Stuffed Animals Consortium. 'And, let's face it, they were all reacting to extreme provocation. How would you like your head to be twisted around 360 degrees, and then tossed across a room like a deck quoit?'

7) For centuries, bears have caught salmon by dipping their paws into rivers, but in certain parts of North America they have begun to favour fishing rods. 'A decent rod is so much more convenient and stops your paws getting sopping wet,' says a leading bear.

8) Brown bears regularly catch human beings by quietly letting themselves in through the back door, then lying down and acting like rugs. 'It's easier than roaming around in the freezing cold on the off-chance,' reveals one bear. Many also stick their heads through walls and pose as hunting trophies for days on end until it's time to pounce. 'We generally say "Boo!", just to keep the whole thing light-hearted,' adds the bear.

Fifteen Clerihews for
Strictly Come Dancing

Edwina Currie
Left in a hurry
After the judges watched her lumber
Through the rumba.

For Vanessa Feltz
Len's tender heart melts
But he still finds faults
With her waltz.

Craig Revel Horwood
Isn't backward in coming forward
Which is why he's a master
At braying 'Dis-aaaaaster!'

Kelly Brook
Has the look
That makes every man go
Mad for her tango.

Anton du Beke
Looked a wreck
When Ann Widdecombe
Bid he come.

Lisa Riley
Was ever so smiley
Before being called Roly Poly
By Bruno Tonioli.

Russell Grant
Turned can-can to can't-can't,
Though he couldn't have tried harder
At the polonaise and lambada.

Pixie Lott
Excels at the gavotte
But for something more low-key
She might try the hokey-cokey.

Gary Rhodes
Mastered all the dance modes
But considered the pogo
A no-go.

Gregg Wallace
Seeks solace:
'It's cooking I miss –
Dancing doesn't get tougher than this.'

Julian Clary
Said 'It's ever so scary!'
Though, then again,
He got a ten from Len.

Judy Murray
Refuses to worry
Though it took her a while
To master Gangnam Style.

Martina Hingis
Said, 'The thing is
I prefer to rock'n'roll
With Brendan Cole.'

Carol Vorderman
Yelled 'You're well out of order, man!'
On being given a low five
For her samba and her jive.

Claudia Winkleman
I don't think'll scan
So I'll call her Claudia W.
(Sorry to trouble you.)

To Hell and Back with Katie Price

1

We may be used to celebrities not writing their own autobiographies, but Jordan takes the process one stage further. Just after I had finished reading *Being Jordan*, I heard the author promoting it on *Woman's Hour*.* To my surprise, halfway through she happened to say, 'I don't know if they mentioned this in the book, but ...', thus letting slip that not only had she not written her own autobiography, but she hadn't even got round to reading it either.

Jordan was born Katie Price in Brighton in 1978, the daughter of an antiques dealer. Her grandmother had once earned her living as a topless mermaid, but got the sack for smoking.

Katie's mother signed her up for modelling classes when she was eleven years old, 'but they were well dodgy'. Aged thirteen, she used to be dropped off by her mother at a photographer's home. There she would pose in a black-velvet catsuit, or dressed up as a schoolgirl sticking her tongue out or sucking a lollipop. Neither Katie nor her mother thought anything of it at the time, but the photographer was eventually sent to prison. 'We didn't realise that the whole cheeky schoolgirl look was fuelling his depraved fantasies ... What a sick bastard.'

By the age of fifteen, she had already developed what she calls 'my own unique style. Even at that age, I loved outrageous outfits – the tighter and more revealing the better.' On her sixteenth birthday she gave herself to her first boyfriend, Jeff, but sadly it made her feel 'dirty,

---

* *Being Jordan* by Katie Price (2006).

impure and sore'. It was never really a fairy-tale relationship. For one thing, Jeff's mother didn't approve of her ('she threatened to throw battery acid in my face if she caught me round her house again'), and for another Jeff became 'eaten up with jealousy'. One night, he came round to Katie's house and started screaming and threatening. It took eight policemen to restrain him. Jeff, too, ended up in prison, for non-payment of fines.

Katie's next boyfriend was Kieran, who was 'something in property'. But Kieran wanted her to get on all fours, 'then he got on his back and started pushing against me. What the hell was that all about? So I got shot of him pretty quickly'.

Next came Gary, an electrician. 'Our sex life was OK,' she reveals, but 'I did think his willy was a bit of an odd shape though'. Things came to a head when Katie put him to the test by suggesting she watched him having sex with her best friend. Gary went ahead with her plan, whereupon Katie got furious. 'If he could behave like this in front of me, God knows what he was capable of when I wasn't there. All right I had encouraged him, but he hadn't thought twice ...'

By this time, she had become a successful Page 3 girl and, now renamed Jordan, was booked to shed her clothes across a whole week to tie in with the film *Striptease*. 'I was only just eighteen, and there I was: famous.' Her new status as Jordan meant that she could do better than an electrician, so she set her cap at a footballer, Teddy Sheringham ('I had fancied him for ages'). In a chapter called 'Oh, Teddy, Teddy!' she outlines a golden rule she claims to have stuck to, with the odd blip, ever since. She will get into bed with a man on their first date, and she'll let him kiss and cuddle, but he mustn't go too far. 'I always make men wait at least a month, just to prove that they're interested in me for myself'. Like all the others, Teddy 'was obviously desperate to make love ... but I wasn't having it'.

Sadly, before the month of abstinence was out, their romance had hit the headlines. Teddy thought Jordan had tipped off the press, and stopped returning her calls. So Jordan was driven into the arms of a TV Gladiator called Ace ('he was gorgeous') whose real name is Warren. After the statutory month was out, Ace took a bit of getting going ('I tried every trick in the book but nothing would get him hard'), but eventually he came up trumps. However, Ace's mum hated Jordan ('it really pissed me off') and Ace's house in Essex, which he had boasted was a mansion, turned out to be 'just a normal house, nothing special'. Alas, like so many before and after, Ace became 'jealous for no reason' and 'my gentle giant was beginning to show a nasty streak'; so it was time to give him the push.

By now, despite popular opposition ('80 per cent of *Sun* Readers Say No'), Jordan had enlarged her bosoms, each to roughly the same size as a football, perhaps in the hope of attracting another footballer. But first she had a racing driver, Ralf Schumacher ('he seemed to have everything') in her sights. She got him into bed, but, mysteriously, he wasn't in the mood ('I'm not used to getting into bed with a man who doesn't at least try and kiss and cuddle me'). Unfortunately, before the week was out, the mystery of Ralf's indifference had hit the headlines ('Jordan Got Schumacher in Pole Position, But He Kept Passion Idle') and he stopped answering her calls.

After a flirtation with another footballer, John Scales ('in case you're wondering, no, we didn't have sex'), Jordan teamed up with Dane Bowers ('he was gorgeous') from a boy band called Another Level. At this point in her book, Jordan treats the reader to a Compare and Contrast between Ace and Dane, with Dane scoring highest ('True, he had the smallest willy, but … he was better with his hands'). But the romance didn't last. Dane was pictured kissing a footballer's wife, and then a lap dancer sold a kiss-and-tell story about him cheating on Jordan ('I was devastated … I hit the bottle big time').

From Dane, Jordan moved to a footballer called Dwight ('What is it with me and footballers?'). Unfortunately Dwight 'was very selfish in bed' and a bad kisser, but 'to give him his due he did try different positions' and 'he had quite a big willy'. In retrospect, 'I should have realised that Dwight was only after a quick shag with Jordan the glamour model, that he was never going to be interested in getting to know Katie,' and so they broke up.

From Dane to Dwight and from Dwight to Dwayne ('drop-dead gorgeous'), and so to a flingette with an anonymous soldier ('We only cuddled, nothing more … I think he might have touched my boobs, but that was that'). At this stage Jordan turned on her television and glimpsed seventeen-year-old Gareth Gates on *Pop Idol* ('the bloke was gorgeous!'). Her make-up artist obtained his phone number, and for the first time Jordan broke her own one-month rule. 'After two weeks of all this heavy petting, I thought it was time we went further … I can definitely say I took his virginity.' Though poor little Gareth 'didn't seem to know where to put his hands or what to do with them', Jordan has 'no complaints about the size of his willy. It was all right – it wasn't the biggest or the smallest, just average'.

Once again, the press somehow got hold of the news of their affair, but Gareth, from a churchgoing family, denied it. 'I can never forgive him for making me look a fool,' says Jordan. For a while, Jordan found consolation in a tanning salon assistant called Matt, who had 'the biggest willy I've ever seen' but who soon 'seriously started to get on my nerves'. Her career was soaring, though, with a *Playboy* session ('the positions were all tasteful: no spread legs').

Next came Scott Sullivan, who didn't have any particular job but was 'into motocross racing'. Like others before him, 'he let me down badly', but by now Jordan was in the Australian rainforest, competing in *I'm a Celebrity … Get Me Out of Here!*. There she met pop singer Peter Andre ('I was bowled over by his good looks, gorgeous body and warm personality') and that's all for now, folks.

Phew! It is all eerily reminiscent of Pauline Calf. Besides a few well-aimed biffs at Victoria Beckham ('I remember how rough she looked without her make-up'; 'I don't know why she denies it … I can spot a boob job a mile off') and a reassuring word or two about her own bosoms ('When I lie down they naturally fall to the side, they're not all rock-hard and rigid'), Jordan's interests do not extend much beyond footballers, gladiators and pop singers. But then, it would not be to Jordan that one would turn for descriptions of the countryside or appreciations of early English music, and, as she admits herself, 'let's face it, I was never going to be a brain surgeon'.

2

'I thought, he's got a well-fit body, I wouldn't mind some of that.'

Jordan's second memoir, *A Whole New World*, returns to her initial get-together with Peter Andre on *I'm a Celebrity ... in 2004.**

As she emerged from the jungle, her boyfriend Scott was there to greet her, but Jordan had already made other plans. 'Scott was history. It seems really harsh that I could go off him so suddenly and so totally but I didn't want him anywhere near me ... there was no sexual chemistry between us.'

After the briefest of hellos to her baby Harvey ('I scooped him up in my arms, showered his face with kisses and held him close to me. "Mummy's got some sorting out to do," I told him, reluctantly putting him down and picking up my phone to check my messages'), she makes a beeline for the salon ('the natural look was all very well but I wanted to knock him dead') in preparation for Peter's jungle exit.

But – would you believe it? – the salon lets her down. 'They hadn't blow-dried my hair straight, how I like it, and I thought I looked a complete mess ... to cap it all I was wearing the wrong outfit and the wrong make-up.'

As the book goes on, it becomes increasingly apparent that part and parcel of Being Jordan is Being Let Down. The reader is battered with a litany of disappointments, past, present and future. Her old manager lets her down ('I thought, actually, I don't know how much longer I want you representing me'). Her present manager lets her down by wanting the usual percentage for the wedding deal with *OK!* magazine ('which really pissed us off'). Her *OK!* wedding photographer lets her down ('I don't get on with him'). And the photos themselves are a let-down ('they hadn't been airbrushed for a start').

In fact, most of the fairy-tale wedding is a let-down, including her old nan. 'She moaned to me, saying she was appalled about where she had been sitting. "Thanks a lot, Nan," I said. "Now you're ruining my

---

* *Jordan: A Whole New World* by Katie Price (2007).

day as well."' Presumably this is the same Nan from Volume One, who, in her youth, worked as a topless mermaid before getting the sack for smoking.

Of course, all Jordan's old boyfriends – Dane and Dwight and Dwayne (and that's just the D's) – let her down in Volume One, but this doesn't stop her nursing the familiar grievances again in Volume Two. 'Warren, my Gladiator, was far too inhibited in the bedroom to fully satisfy me … My pop idol, Gareth Gates, was too young and inexperienced to know how to satisfy me … Dwight only seemed to care about HIS pleasure … Frank was very flirtatious with me and really tried it on but kissing and the odd blow-job was as far as it went …'

From time to time, she steps out of the author's role to give one of her exes a Vicky Pollard-style dressing-down direct. 'I'm sure that sometimes he must wonder whether we could get back together, but if you're reading this, Dane, no you couldn't have, because as far as I'm concerned you had nothing going for you.' Oddly enough, this isn't what she said in Volume One, where she gave Dane full marks as a lover ('he'd take me from behind, on top, me on top – you name the position, we tried it. It was mind-blowing').

Just in case Dane hasn't got the latest message, a few pages later she puts the other boot in: 'Well, I'm pretty pleased with where I've got to, but I don't imagine Dane is quite so pleased about where he's ended up … Dane who?'

Since she chucked him in the jungle, poor old Scott has also let her down, first by selling a story about her to the newspapers and then – worse – by going out 'with that wannabe me, Jodie Marsh'. The thought of the two of them together is, she says, 'kind of gross', but 'I did think it was ironic that he ended up with her because he had told me that he thought she was rank.'

To date, though, her greatest disappointment is her failure to realise 'my lifelong dream of becoming a singer'. She has always been convinced that 'there was more to me than being paid to get my tits out', but no one else has been able to see past them, as it were.

Her former manager ('I can't say any more about this as we're locked into a legal battle') kept promising ('as so many had before him') to get her a record deal, but had failed. Her new manager 'kept saying a million per cent that the deal was in the bag', but 'what a surprise, I've been let down again'.

As a way of attaining that elusive record deal, Jordan agreed to join the shortlist for Britain's entry to the Eurovision Song Contest. She wore 'my all-time favourite outfit – a rubber catsuit' for her performance. She left the stage convinced that she would win, her performance notwithstanding. 'I think that after that first hiccup where I was slightly out of tune, I actually did OK, though I forgot the dance routine, but it didn't seem to matter.' Alas, her deadly rival Javine won instead. 'I thought, *You bitch* ...'

As it happens, Javine came third from bottom in the Eurovision proper ('I felt embarrassed for her'). Later, when the pair of them bumped into each other at the Soap Awards, the two Js indulged in a slanging match. 'I'm successful without Eurovision and at the end of the day all you'll ever be is a one-hit wonder,' Jordan told Javine. 'And for good measure I added, "F*** off you slag!" I was so angry.'

Her disappointments continue, even when she goes into a swanky private hospital to have her new baby ('I had a tiny TV in my bedroom and it didn't even have Sky'). At least she manages to get the better of the nurse. 'The nurse had told me I might need to shave *down there* and I replied, "don't worry, it's bald as a badger".'

But she then rows with Peter, who wants a Greek name for his baby ('"Look!" I screamed back, having lost my rag, "I don't f***ing like the name Savva!"'). Which of us would swap places with Peter Andre? The phrase 'we ended up having a massive row' recurs like a catchy chorus throughout the book. They row about the babysitter, about their wedding vows, about what she should wear to meet his Jehovah's Witness parents, and about one of his exes being allowed to come to the wedding ('I don't give a shit, Pete. You should have thought about that before you shagged her').

Jordan ends this, her second volume of autobiography, which covers the eighteen months that have gone by since the first, with the news that she is about to undergo 'boob job number four'.

'This time,' she says, 'I am going for a reduction. I want my boobs to be smaller and more pert.' She plans to auction the discarded XXXL silicone implants on eBay.

3

The combustible four-year marriage of Katie Price and Peter Andre is chronicled across nine fly-on-the-wall TV series and a third autobiography, *Pushed to the Limit*.*

Her next husband is a cage fighter called Alex who seems 'rugged and manly', but how wrong you can be. 'I soon discovered that in private he liked to dress as a woman.' One day, she enters her house 'to find that my bedroom had been transformed into a sex dungeon'. She doesn't want to be sucked into his 'sick and sordid' world, so she leaves him.

After a fling with rugby player Danny Cipriani, 'who turned out to be a liar and a womaniser and ... left me a broken woman', she has an affair with someone she will refer to only as Mr X because 'I'm not a kiss-and-tell person.'

Mr X proves energetic but insensitive. 'He was like a cordless drill on a multi-speed setting.' She then gets engaged to an Argentinian model called Leandro, but it turns out that Leandro has 'a jealous, angry streak', so Katie exchanges him for a course of antidepressants.

By now, anyone expecting Jane Austen will be suffering a measure of disappointment. Of course, Jane once observed that 'There are as many forms of love as there are moments in time', but, then again, she lived in the days before topless models, tanning assistants, TV gladiators and transvestite cage fighters.

One joyous day, love comes a-calling in the unexpected shape of Kieran Hayler, a former plasterer turned male stripper. After five weeks, Kieran – 'my knight in shining armour' – asks Katie to marry him. 'I felt like the luckiest woman in the world,' she recalls, even

---

* *Jordan: Pushed to the Limit* by Katie Price (2008).

though in the back of her mind she is already entertaining doubts. 'I know what strippers are like … They'll shag anything with a pulse.'

Regrettably, her suspicions prove accurate. Her latest volume of autobiography – by my reckoning, her seventh – covers Katie Price's remarkably rocky three-year marriage to Kieran, a period during which she not only 'hit rock bottom' but also went 'to hell and back', a return journey now so regular that she might almost qualify as a commuter.*

The source of most of her misery is her (former) best friend Jane Pountney, who had always been so attentive. 'For example, if I need an outfit for a court appearance she would help choose it.' The source for the rest of her misery is her ebullient (former) second-best friend, Chrissy Thomas. 'A chef, actors, footballers. You name it, she's had it.'

The trouble starts when Katie notices that Jane, who 'isn't glam in the slightest' but 'an average-looking mumsy dumpy housewife', is beginning to copy her style. First it's her hairpiece, then her eyebrows, then her make-up, then her ponytail, then her extensions.

And Jane copies her home furnishings too, buying curtains and rugs like Katie's 'and similar light fittings only in a much cheaper version'. On holiday with Katie and Kieran, Jane dons a skimpy glittery bikini 'which didn't even suit her', and Katie can't help noticing that, just like her, 'she'd had everything waxed off'. Previously something of a shrinking violet, Jane takes to dancing on the table-top in front of Kieran, 'wiggling her bum in the air, showing off her cleavage. It was pure cringe.'

And then it happens. One evening on a tropical holiday, five months pregnant, Katie peers into the darkness and sees her husband and her best friend kissing passionately in the moonlight. Not only that, but Jane's hands are slowly reaching down towards Kieran's shorts. Something snaps. 'Without a moment's thought, I reached out and grabbed Jane's hair from behind. She had no chance to hear or see me before I dragged her from the sunbed … I yanked her hair tighter … I punched her hard in the face and watched her reel backward.'

---

* *Reborn* by Katie Price (2016).

'It isn't what you think it is, Kate,' whimpers Jane.

'Shut the f*** up, you bitch!' replies Katie, brusquely.

The next day, Katie's temper is unabated. Once again, she grabs Jane's hair and repeatedly bangs her head against her raised knee. 'I punched her with the other fist too, cracking a nail as I made contact.'

Back home, Katie writes Jane a strong letter, calling her, among other things, 'an evil, twisted woman' and a 'disgusting human being'. She advises her to 'take your baggy, haggard face, tea-bag ugly tits and remember you're fifty years old'. She is saddened when Jane fails to reply.

Kieran swears they never went the whole hog, but Katie is determined to get to the bottom of it. To this end, she calls in the man who conducts the lie detector tests for the *Jeremy Kyle Show*. The results come through. The polygraph confirms that Kieran is lying.

But still he won't come clean. At a cost of £2,500 a day Katie hires a therapist for Kieran ('apparently, he'd worked with serial killers and psychopaths'). Eventually, Kieran confesses to having sex with Jane six times. Katie thinks that's an underestimate, so she gets the lie detector man back. This time, Kieran admits to having sex with another woman, too. 'I couldn't control myself,' recalls Katie. 'I grabbed the nearest thing to me, which happened to be a hardback copy of my sixth autobiography, and lobbed it straight at Kieran's head.'

Kieran confesses that he and Jane had an affair for ten months, 'mainly ... in her Ford Focus'. This disturbs Katie. 'How could I even look at a Ford Focus again?'

She then does what anyone would do, given the circumstances: she tweets her heartbreak to her two million followers. 'Sorry to say me and Kieran are divorcing, him and my best friend Jane Pountney have been having a full-blown sexual affair.'

A few weeks later, Kieran admits that the other woman was her second-best friend Chrissy. 'Livid? I was beyond livid!' She reacts by selling the story to the *Sun*. 'I figured I might as well benefit from my own misery.' A great many other authors have trod this path before.

For no apparent reason, she decides to give Kieran a second chance. By now, they have had a second baby. They toy with the names Disney,

Bambi, Duchess and Precious but finally settle on Bunny. Katie thinks of spelling it Bunni 'with a heart above the "i"', but Kieran thinks a heart above the 'i' is not part of the English language.

She has her sixth boob job – 'I adore that round, uniform, all-American stuck-on look' – then a seventh, this time a reduction, but it goes pear-shaped – 'it swelled like an angry toad' – so she is obliged to have an eighth.

Early last year, Katie and Kieran renewed their marriage vows. Before the ceremony, the congregation were obliged to watch a video of Katie running through the ups and downs of the past two years. 'I caught Kieran on the beach kissing my best friend and interrupted their sex session,' she explained, candidly.

But now, she says, they are a happy couple once more, and she is 'the luckiest woman in the world'. 'It just goes to show,' she concludes, 'the dreams that you dare to dream really do come true.' I hate to be a wet blanket, but might the same not also be true of nightmares?

'The more I know of the world, the more I am convinced that I shall never see a man whom I can really love. I require so much!' It is Marianne Dashwood who says this in *Sense and Sensibility*, but, in many ways, it might just as well be Katie Price.

The First Shall Be Last:
Perky and Pinky

After all these years, Andrew Lloyd Webber has explained why his name always comes before Tim Rice's in their song-writing credits. The reason, it transpires, is neither alphabetical nor hierarchical. 'The fact is Lloyd Webber and Rice is easier to say than Rice and Lloyd Webber,' he told the *Mail on Sunday*. 'Just as Sullivan and Gilbert would have sounded awful.'

Is that so? Sullivan and Gilbert may sound a little peculiar to us now, but that is surely because we have grown so used to saying Gilbert and Sullivan.

There's not much in it, but it seems to me just as easy – or as difficult – to say Rice and Lloyd Webber as it is to say Lloyd Webber and Rice. If one member of a duo is more talented and harder-working than the other, then clearly he or she has the right to be first in the pecking order. Was this the real reason Lloyd Webber wanted to be first?

The same must surely have been true of Batman and Robin. When the crime crusaders first got together, it would have been impertinent for weedy little Robin to have insisted on top billing. He was quite clearly the sidekick, the number two, the hanger-on. Without Batman, Robin would have had no hope of forging a career as a caped crusader, unless it was as some sort of junior store detective in the fancy dress department of the Gotham City Walmart. So it was quite right that they called themselves Batman and Robin, not Robin and Batman.

The same goes for many other unequal partnerships. There is no point in putting the duff partner first, otherwise we would have Wise and Morecambe, Watson and Holmes, Joseph and Mary. The weaker partner should always come last, hence David and Goliath and – harsh but true – Barbie and Ken.

But what of partnerships that operate on a completely equal footing, with no clear superior? It is in the nature of duos to fall out, so the best way of avoiding an early contretemps is to stick to strict alphabetical order. This is what the most successful and democratic duos have done, or else we would now be talking of Dec and Ant, Dave and Chas, Sweep and Sooty, Jerry & Ben, Jill and Jack and Spencer & Marks.

When alphabetical order is reversed, sceptics rush to judgement. We immediately assume that the first-named insisted on signalling his or her precedence over the second-named. Personally, I consider Paul Simon perfectly within his rights to force the less talented Art Garfunkel into second place, but it can't have done much to help their already scratchy relationship. They have been squabbling for the past sixty years or more about everything, even toupees: a recent biography revealed that because Simon wanted to wear a hairpiece at their 1981 gig in New York's Central Park, he insisted Garfunkel must wear one too, in solidarity. Needless to say, an argument ensued.

In some billings, there is a clear gender bias: Hansel precedes Gretel, Samson precedes Delilah, Peters precedes Lee, Terry precedes June. Even though Cher always had much more to offer than Sonny, it was always Sonny and Cher, never Cher and Sonny.

Other billings are more baffling. Within the piggy puppet community, why did Perky let Pinky go first, defying the alphabet, when their stage roles were the same, their genders indeterminate and their skills interchangeable?

Personally, I feel sore on Perky's behalf. I have no inside knowledge, but Perky's downgrading must surely have been down to Pinky's pushiness, and Perky's yearning for the quiet life. It was Pinky who pulled the strings. The same must also be said of quite a few other duos where alphabetical order is reversed, for no clear reason.

In a fair world, we would have Little & Osborne, Hutch and Starsky, Edgar & Swan, Large and Little, Peller & Rigby and Ben and Bill. But, then again, when was the world ever fair?

Behind the Scenes at
The Life of Mammals

The plan had been to visit the set of the latest David Attenborough series, but my flight to Africa had been delayed. When I arrived, they were all packing up for the night. Thankfully, I was allowed into the VIP enclosure. 'You might find one or two of the stars hanging around,' said the programme's publicity officer. 'They like to unwind in the lounge after a hard day's filming.'

In a corner of the bar, with their feet up, were two young hippos, swapping tales over a couple of pints. 'Mind if I join you?' I said.

'Not at all, old boy,' said the first hippo, who had an unexpectedly posh English accent. His name was Adrian. It turned out he'd spent much of his youth on secondment to Chessington Zoo in Surrey. 'One didn't set out to upgrade my accent,' he said. 'It just sort of rubbed off on one, as these things do.'

He told me he was 'literally exhausted', after some pretty gruelling filming. 'David was desperately keen to film us having a scrap with a lion or a crocodile. I put him in touch with an old lion pal of mine called Geoffrey, who's got a CV as long as your arm, and, I might add, won an Emmy for his work on *Daktari*.

'Geoffrey's always popping up on wildlife documentaries, chasing this, that and the other. Producers simply LOVE him. He'll always go that extra mile, is relatively inexpensive and, of course, still devilishly handsome. Oh, look – there he is!'

Adrian the Hippo waved in the direction of a lion sitting at the bar, nursing a pina colada. In return, the lion blew him a kiss.

'I never imagined you'd be such good pals,' I commented. I had seen

YouTube footage of a hippo and a lion fighting by the water's edge, and it had all looked very real to me.

'Don't be daft!' said Adrian. 'Once the cameras are turned off, we're all the best of friends! I mean, take a look at that little gang!'

He pointed towards the far corner of the lounge. A group of hyenas were sharing a laugh with an antelope.

'Just an hour ago, they were out on location, coming to blows for the cameras,' said Adrian the Hippo. 'But the moment David shouted "Cut!" they stopped, and were congratulating each other on their performances. Believe me, you can't survive in this business without a real sense of teamwork.'

Geoffrey the Lion strolled over. 'I was just telling Craig how much I admired your performance today!' said Adrian. 'And I simply ADORED that very, very slight hesitation you made before leaping on top of me and baring those gorgeous teeth of yours! It ratcheted up the tension quite beautifully! Pure genius!'

Geoffrey affected indifference at this compliment, but you could tell he was lapping it up. 'You were marvellous, too, Adrian,' he replied. 'You put on that WONDERFUL scared expression of yours – always an absolute winner, darling!' He turned to me. 'No one, but NO ONE does scared better than Adrian.'

I moved over to the group of hyenas in the far corner. They were reminiscing about their early work on *Wildlife on One*. 'It was all very primitive,' said one of them. 'The lighting was DESPERATELY unsympathetic, and the make-up was as crude as can be – one had to get on one's knees and BEG for even the faintest DAB of blusher!'

'Tell me about it!' chipped in another. 'And they barely rehearsed us! David, lovely David, would simply point to the darling little antelope and tell us to improvise – first we'd have to surround him and then, on cue, we'd have to make our trademark funny little noises! One FELT one's way into the part – it was all very "Method" in those days!'

As the hyenas continued to chuckle at the memory, the antelope wiped the fake blood off his fur. 'I suppose we overdid it, if I'm honest – but, then again, there's nothing the viewers appreciate more than a proper bloodbath.'

At this point, I spotted Sir David himself near the entrance, congratulating a crocodile and a wildebeest on the day's shoot. 'You really looked as if you were going for him!' he told the crocodile, who laughed self-deprecatingly.

'In fact, we're old mates,' the wildebeest chipped in. 'We first met on the set of *Out of Africa* with Meryl Streep and Robert Redford, lovely guy. Do you know Bobby?'

In Make-Up, I came upon a young elephant, Ellie, sitting in front of the mirror. 'For today's shoot I'm playing an elderly elephant, so they need me to look suitably lined,' she told me.

As we spoke, Sally – a make-up artiste who has worked with the likes of TV legends Joan Collins and Cap'n Birdseye – was applying extra wrinkles all over Ellie's body, a job she expected to take three hours or more.

Alongside Ellie was Leo the Lion, veteran of over thirty wildlife documentaries. 'To be brutally honest, I'm basically playing myself, so I don't require much make-up, other than a light dusting of powder and perhaps the merest touch of eyeliner,' he explained. 'But I do insist that my mane is at its best, and that involves endless blow-drying and back-combing. One owes it to one's fans.' In 2016, Leo won an Emmy for Best Hairdo in a One-Off Wildlife Documentary.

Next to Leo sat movie legend Gillian the Giraffe, who was last seen on our screens being brutally attacked by a crocodile near a swamp. 'It was all shot at Pinewood, darling,' Gillian told me, 'and of course the croc and I go back thirty years, all the way to *Animal Magic* with Johnny Morris, who was an absolute darling.'

For the famous croc-attack scene, Gillian required a lot of stage blood smeared over her legs, but on the day of my visit she needed only a dab of mascara. However, the make-up process required a complicated system of scaffolding, and the roof above her chair had to be raised 20 feet or so.

At 8 a.m., filming commenced. I watched as a cheetah and a zebra rehearsed a chase sequence over and over again. 'Simply super, darlings!' shouted the fight director after they had completed their umpteenth quarter-mile sprint. 'But could we try it just once more, and this time, Zebra, sweetie, would you try looking back over your shoulder? Give the cheetah a nasty look as he bites into your ankle, darling!'

After the shoot was over, I shared a cappuccino with the zebra. He loved appearing in David Attenborough's shows, he explained, but he sometimes yearned to play something other than the victim. 'These wildlife directors are always stereotyping zebras,' he said, unwrapping a KitKat with his hoof. 'If I've been chased once, I've been chased a hundred times. But there's so much more to me than that! I can do aggressive, romantic, happy, heartbroken, heroic, the lot – but all they ever ask for is victim!' 'Tell me about it, love!' chipped in a passing antelope.

That afternoon, I watched the filming of a fight between a warthog and a porcupine. 'It can take anywhere between four and five hours to ensure all the tiny little protectors are in place on the porcupine's quills,' said the health and safety officer. 'For us, the well-being of the warthog is paramount.'

Finally, I was invited to watch Sir David shoot a very intimate scene between a male and a female black mamba. 'I only ever agree to do these scenes if I consider them artistically valid,' explained the female, as the lighting director busied around her. 'And never without an intimacy coach to hand.'

I Con Hic

St Pancras Station. Rachmaninoff's Piano Concerto No. 2, Opus 18 plays portentously.

ALAN YENTOB [*voiceover*]: Do you remember the first time you saw the iconic work of Tracey Emin? The wild abandon with which she first broke through has given way to a more mature, reflective voice. A voice that has something vitally important and iconic to tell us all.

Workmen in cranes at St Pancras erect a large neon sign saying 'I want my time with you' in squiggly writing.

ALAN YENTOB: Tracey, this strikes me as one of your most powerful and iconic pieces, both painful yet curiously hopeful. What exactly were you trying to convey with it, what was on your mind when you conceived it?

TRACEY EMIN: It's like this is a famous station and since childhood I've always like had this I don't know kind of real feeling that stations and platforms and whatever are like places where trains go in and out of and people are on them or off them depending whether they've like bought tickets or not and that's a feeling that's never left me.

YENTOB continues to nod, looking surprised and intrigued.

YENTOB: So who is the real woman behind this painfully honest and iconic confessional work and does she still have the power to SHOCK and INSPIRE like she did when she first came to our attention twenty-five years ago?

Old footage of Tracey Emin drunk in studio discussion.

TRACEY: I don't give a fucking fuck about the fucking – oh, what the fuck, fuck this for a fuck –

WOMAN FROM TATE: There's at least three Traceys. There's the Tracey you meet when you meet her. And there's the Tracey you don't meet when you don't meet her. Yes, there's at least two Traceys.

SERIOUS ART CRITIC: It's impossible to ignore Tracey and that's, in a very real way, why she's impossible to ignore. You have to engage with her on her own terms, which are, in a very real way, the terms upon which you have to engage with her.

Yentob and Tracey walking along street in Margate. Birds are flying around.

YENTOB [*voiceover*]: It's June 2018 and I'm receiving an iconic tour of Margate from its most famous daughter.

TRACEY: That's the sea and that's a house and that's more sea and that's a road and that's a shop and that's an amusement arcade.

YENTOB: An amusement arcade! Did you go in there much?

TRACEY: Not much, no.

YENTOB: Hey! What on earth is that? It looks ... extraordinary. And powerful. Powerful and extraordinary. And ... strangely unsettling.

TRACEY: It's a seagull.

YENTOB: There's something ... iconic ... about its wings. And the way it flies. It's clearly some sort of bird. Have you always felt this, I don't know how you'd describe it ... connection ... with what you call 'seagulls'?

TRACEY: You like get used to them I s'pose like the way they're sort of gulls so they fly but they're also SEAgulls, so they swim too or like not exactly swim but sort of paddle about a bit.

YENTOB [*voiceover*]: Emin shares her instinctive affinity with Margate with that most quintessential of British artists, J. W. M. Turner. And now, Turner is receiving the ultimate accolade of having his works exhibited as a backdrop to Tracey Emin's powerful and iconic bed. For me, it's quite uncanny to observe the symmetry between Turner's seascapes and Tracey's bed.

TRACEY: Like you have the white of the sheets well off-white more like then you have the white of the waves and then there's blue in the sky and there's a bit of blue [*Yentob nods enthusiastically*] on that box of Kleenex or whatever by the bed I mean I can't really believe all these like connections it's just brilliant.

YENTOB [*looks sympathetic*]: And – as I understand it – the bed's got an awful lot of pain in it.

TRACEY: Yeah there's a lot of pie in it I was really into Fray Bentos steak and kidney back then so that's like definitely what that mark must be.

Cut to Nicholas Serota.

SEROTA: *My Bed* is a tremendously … *powerful* … piece, calling to mind Goya and Van Gogh and Schiele. And if you get up very close to it, you can see these splashes that can best be described as *human evacuations*, and they have a sort of … *raw urgency* … about them which is, to my mind, really compelling. When one looks at the bed, one sees the bed looking back at one, asking one where one is in the world, and who one is, and why one exists, and one thinks to oneself she's not only pressed the button and pushed the envelope but also – in a very real way – she's changed the sheets, or, paradoxically, not changed the sheets, and that is, to my mind, every bit as powerful.

YENTOB [*voiceover*]: In the late 1980s and early 1990s, the British art scene experienced an iconic renaissance when a group of Young Turks were busy reconfiguring the very definition of art. From now on, they wanted it to combine the searingly honest with the powerfully intellectual.

Old footage of Tracey disco-dancing in a T-shirt with the slogan 'Have You Wanked Over Me Yet.'

TRACEY: So like I made a tent with everyone I'd ever slept with in it like it was so important because it was saying like I had sex with all these people and everyone I could think of was on that list and what it was saying was that I had sex with them all not all at the same time but all at different times and like that was a really important statement because those times are never going to happen again so they're in the past and not the future so it was a way of saying that the past and the future are not the present so there was all these different like layers that people could relate to.

YENTOB [*nods*]: And how many names were in that iconic tent, Tracey? How many men had you actually … slept … with?

TRACEY: A hundred and two.

YENTOB [*nods vigorously*]: A hundred and two? That's very iconic, very urgent, very … numerous.

TRACEY: My vision my thoughts and my whole nature want to connect with something not only in me but not in me by which I mean outside me so what I'm doing is really a dialogue between myself and whatever it is that isn't myself, or at least would be myself if it was myself which it is in a way like it's really personal.

YENTOB: A hundred and two … Imagine!

Back to St Pancras Station. Tracey Emin surrounded by photographers.

YENTOB: She's been made a CBE, is Professor of Drawing at the Royal College of Art and was in the vanguard of guests at the recent prestigious marriage of Princess Eugenie at St George's Chapel, Windsor. Like William Blake and Johann Sebastian Bach, William Shakespeare and Plato, Tracey Emin's searingly honest work has explored this rich seam of human existence for three iconic decades now, tracing the line that connects our primal passions with our deepest desires. And, for me, there's only one word for it. Iconic.

Closing titles to Rachmaninoff's Prelude Opus 2, No. 5.

BORES

See It, Say It, Sorted

In this warm weather, you are advised to keep a bottle of water with you at all times.

If you see someone without a bottle of water, please contact a member of the Transport Police.

See it, say it, sorted.

You must wear a face covering over your nose and mouth at all times on the station concourse and on our trains unless you are exempt. If you are exempt, you must be prepared for scowls from your fellow passengers.

Any bottle of water kept in your pocket must be securely fastened. Failure to comply may result in damp patches, which in certain areas may lead to embarrassment.

Customers found with bottles of water blocking doorways, aisles or vestibules may be liable to a penalty.

Avoid the toilet in Coach D. See it, say it, sordid.

Pouring a bottle of water over your neighbour's head may result in an altercation.

The first stop will come before all the other stops. The intermediate stops will come after the first stop and before the last stop. If you do not wish to get out at the next stop then remain in your seat. After the final stop, there will be no further stops. You are reminded to treat other passengers with respect. Poking, pinching or punching our staff and/or other passengers is not permitted unless you are exempt, see terms and conditions.

In bright, sunny weather a pair of sunglasses may help to prevent squinting. A woolly hat is not advisable in hot weather. If your belt is too tight, why not let it out a few notches.

This is Emma, your customer host. A full range of hot and cold coffees and teas, alcoholic beverages, soft drinks and a choice of snacks, sandwiches, pasties, biscuits, cakes and light meals are available from the buffet.

The buffet closed five minutes ago.

You may only remove your face covering to eat or drink snacks and hot or cold beverages. Please put your face covering back on once you have finished eating. Resuming snacking with your face covering still on may result in a filthy mess.

Always plan ahead and consider travelling at quieter times. Remember: you only have yourself to blame. If you had planned ahead, you would not be travelling at a time like this.

We offer a full range of hot and cold snacks, including tepid, reheated and lukewarm.

If you see or hear anyone coughing and/or sneezing, be sure to cast them an angry glance and text TUT-TUT-TUT to British Transport Police.

Wearing socks with shoes may help prevent blisters. A baggier shirt is recommended for those with a fuller figure.

Brush your teeth twice a day. Remember to floss. Neither a borrower nor a lender be. The early bird catches the worm.

Passengers are not permitted to travel on the roof or undercarriage, unless exempt.

We operate a No Smoking policy on all of our trains, including the vestibule.

Passengers are not permitted to leave their vests in the vestibule. Or their boules.

Customers are advised that the baseball cap worn the wrong way round is not a good look, never has been, never will be.

Any customer sitting in the wrong seat is advised to move to the right seat.

Customers in the right seats are advised to start feeling anxious that they may be in the wrong seats but they will only find out for sure once it is too late.

Customers are reminded that Coach G is a dedicated quiet carriage.

Those travelling in Coach G are requested to listen to the frequent onboard updates reminding them that Coach G is a dedicated quiet carriage.

A full list of station stops past, present and future will be recited in the quiet carriage in a loud voice at regular intervals.

For their added safety, customers in Coach G will be reminded every few minutes that they are not permitted to employ mobile phones, personal stereos, hammers, nails, squeaky toys, fog horns, loud hailers, trombones, dental drills, whoopee cushions, duck calls, party crackers, machine guns and/or bagpipes.

Customers in Coach G who are attempting to read books or go to sleep are reminded that Coach G is a designated Quiet Zone.

This is another reminder for Customers in Coach G that Coach G is a designated Quiet Zone.

Furthermore, customers in Coach G are reminded that Coach G remains a designated Quiet Zone.

Customers with advance Happy-Days Super-Discount Off-Peak Steady-As-You-Go Travelbuster Anytime Special Rover Two-For-One tickets are advised to think carefully before travelling as these tickets are not valid on any train at any time, day or night.

Doors will not open until the train has come to a full stop. Customers are advised to avoid commas and semicolons.

Upon alighting from this train, be sure to take your belongings with you. Passengers are advised to take the down escalator unless they wish to travel up.

Due to unforeseen circumstances, we are now approaching our final station stop.

Customers planning to use the platform stairs at the next station stop are reminded while ascending or descending to ensure they lift their left and right legs in succession or face serious injury.

You are reminded that armed robbery is a crime.

Customers wishing to travel on must be in possession of a valid packet of crisps from the buffet.

See it, say it, salted.

We apologise for the late arrival of this train. This is due to the late arrival of this train.

For those travellers wishing to make their connection, the train standing at Platform 6 has just departed.

Red Faces All Round: Cricketing Anecdotes

Applause

BLOFELD: Good evening, my dear old things. I'm Henry Blofeld – but my friends call me Blowers, after I suffered a bout of tummy trouble out at the Second Test in Madras!

Laughter, applause

Well, all I can say is it has been the most TREMENDOUS fun! But all good things must come to the proverbial end, and so, after forty-odd years, I've decided to pull my stump – whoops! Deary me! What a howler!!

Laughter, applause

I'll never live it down! Marvellous! And to assist me on my trip down the proverbial Memory Lane is the dear fellow who was my producer on *Test Match Special* for goodness-knows-how-many years, Peter Baxter – better known to one and all as the immortal Backers!!

Laughter, applause

BAXTER: Good evening, Blowers. Tonight, we're going to tell you of some of the most extraordinary and uproarious episodes that ever happened to us.

BLOFELD: Talking of which, my dear old thing, one is instantly reminded of the simply marvellous time when Johnners – that's the inimitable Brian Johnston, to the uninitiated! – when Johnners was commentating on the 1977 Test Match from Lord's! Well, being Johnners, he rather fancied a sandwich during an over which was, let's face it, inching along pretty bloody slowly, if you'll pardon my proverbial! Much to my utter astonishment, while I was busy commentating Johnners simply reached into his bag, or baggers, as he always called it (!) pulled out the most delicious ham sandwich – AND TOOK A BITE OF IT!

Laughter, applause

True story! Of course, the listeners hadn't the foggiest that he was tucking into a ham sandwich live on air – he was always the consummate professional – but I need hardly tell you the rest of us simply cracked up. Well, needless to say, I never let him live it down, and I ribbed him about that simply hilarious incident for absolute yonks!

'Johnners,' I would say, 'I rather fancy a ham sandwich – HOW ABOUT YOU?' Result? Collapse of stout party! Wonderful!

Laughter, applause

BAXTER: For my money, Blowers, that's one of the best – if not THE best – stories about dear old Johnners and his ham sandwiches! But I wonder if I might try to cap it with my classic tale of Johnners and the egg roll!

BLOFELD: Oh, good gracious, Johnners and the egg roll! One simply can't WAIT to hear that one again!! As I remember it –

BAXTER: No, Blowers, hang on, old thing, as I remember it, Johnners had just arrived at Lord's –

BLOFELD: Or was it The Oval?

BAXTER: No, Lord's. Well, either Lord's or The Oval.

BLOFELD: – at any rate, one or the other –

BAXTER: When he was suddenly overcome by a sudden and unassuageable craving for, yes, would you believe it – an egg roll! Not just any old roll, oh no – it simply HAD to be an egg roll!

Laughter, applause

BLOFELD: As I remember it, England were playing India, and India were all out for 116 –

BAXTER: Or were England playing Australia, with Australia at 132 for 6? At any rate, one or the other, and then, as I say, Johnners was overcome by this sudden and unassuageable craving for an egg roll! So what does he do? Well, luckily he had brought one with him, so he simply dipped into his famous bag, pulled out the aforesaid egg roll – and enjoyed a jolly good tuck-in!!!

Laughter, applause

BLOFELD: And of course the wireless audience at home were none the wiser!

BAXTER: No, none the wiser! Talking of egg sandwiches, Blowers, I'm sure we'd all relish another opportunity to hear your evergreen anecdote concerning, if I'm not much mistaken, the legendary John Arlott –

BLOFELD: – The immortal Lotters! –

BAXTER: – and the egg sandwich that went for a Burton!

Laughter, applause

BLOFELD: Here goes! It was 1980 or thereabouts, and the Test Match was well under way, with the Aussies all out for 343, if I remember –

BAXTER: Or was it 342?

BLOFELD: No, I think you'll find it was 343 – and Boycott having made an impressive 66 with only two wickets down.

BAXTER: So the scene is set, though I could swear it was 342.

BLOFELD: Yes, the scene is indeed set. Being Lotters, he'd always make a point of bringing along a bit of grub, and on this immortal occasion his tasty morsel of choice was the most almighty egg sandwich, which Lotters duly began to consume at an opportune moment when play was slow. But, as luck would have it, he'd only managed a couple of bites when, blow me down, if he didn't drop it on the studio floor! Result: all-round hilarity, and giggles a-plenty! True story!

Laughter, applause

BAXTER: And – Ha ha ha! – I'll never forget the time we drove with the great Johnny Woodcock –

BLOFELD: – Ah, dear old Wooders!

BAXTER: – to Southampton.

BLOFELD: – Ah, dear old Hampers!

BAXTER: And Wooders, who was sitting either in the backers or in the fronters, one forgets which, suddenly turned to you and said –

BLOFELD: 'I trust we're in no danger of running out of petters!'

BAXTER: Yes, he had just caught sight of the petrol gauge, and, never one to hold back, he was expressing the fear, in his own inimitable way, that we might soon run out of petrol!

BLOFELD: Needless to say, I was at pains to inform him that there was a petrol station in three or four miles, and so there was absolutely no cause for alarm!

BAXTER: And, sure enough, we arrived safely at our destination with something over half a tank to spare! But, my word, there would have been red faces all round if we hadn't, and that's for sure!

Laughter, applause

BLOFELD: Personally, I'll never forget that simply marvellous occasion when Johnners was commenting on the Testers at Lord's and he made the immortal comment, 'The bowler is blowing the batsman's cock.' Or words to that effect! Ha ha ha! Red faces all round! Ha ha ha!

BAXTER: Or that legendary time you said, 'The bowler's ramming his penis up the batsman's BTM!' Ha ha ha!

BLOFELD: Easy mistake to make! Splendid! And did I ever tell you about the time Johnners reached into his bag for the most ALMIGHTY ham sandwich?

John Cleese and Eric Idle:
Our Twitter Diary

john cleese @JohnCleese Mar 14
Eric and I are hugely enjoying our tour of Australia. 100 per cent sell-outs in Brisbane. So much for biased UK press saying we are 'unfunny'!

eric idle retweeted
john cleese @JohnCleese Mar 14
Eric and I are hugely enjoying our tour of Australia. 100 per cent sell-outs in Brisbane. So much for biased UK press saying we are 'unfunny'!

eric idle @EricIdle Mar 13
Sorry to hear news of untimely death of would-be comedian Graeme Bostock. Auditioned for Python back in 1960s, but didn't get in 'cos not funny enough! Classic!

eric idle retweeted
Sausage Man @SausageMan Feb 22
eric idle still very funny.

eric idle retweeted
Kylie Silvey @KylieSylvie Mar 12
Absolutely brilliant Idle/Cleese show in Perth last night. Still the same old magic.

eric idle @EricIdle Mar 9
So sorry to hear news of George Martin's death. Heard he was big Python fan. Nudge, nudge, wink, wink! RIP.

john cleese @JohnCleese Mar 7
Seriously, we all know what happened to John Lennon, Princess Di and Martin Luther King when they tried to stand up to Murdoch.

john cleese @JohnCleese Mar 7
Great opportunity for brave satirists like Yours Truly to make jokes about recent Murdoch wedding. If we dare!

john cleese @JohnCleese Mar 7
Jerry Hall marriage to R. Murdoch straight out of Python. Couldn't make it up!

eric idle @EricIdle Mar 7
Deeply sorry to hear of death of former First Lady Nancy Reagan. Anyone know if she ever said she watched Monty Python?

eric idle @EricIdle Mar 6
True story. Fan came up to me this morning, asked for autograph. Off the cuff, I quipped 'I didn't expect the Spanish Inquisition!' Hilarity all round.

john cleese @JohnCleese Mar 6
So *Daily Mail* claims I'm 'not funny any more'. Are they really saying 3,500 people in Hobart weren't laughing at our Spam sketch last night? Next lie, please!

john cleese retweeted
@PythonFan Mar 6
Brill show in Hobart last night, @JohnCleese. Spam, spam, and more spam! Know all the words! Even funnier fiftieth time round!

eric idle retweeted
john cleese @JohnCleese Mar 5
Old pal eric idle on brilliant comic form in Hobart tonight. Perfect timing saying 'Nudge, Nudge, Wink, Wink' brought house down.

john cleese @JohnCleese Mar 5
Bitterly disappointing news for humourless hacks in the British press – *Life of Brian* described as 'hilarious' in *Sydney Morning Herald* today. Sorry chaps!

john cleese @JohnCleese Mar 5
I'm not watching CNN again till they stop showing Donald Trump every night on the news. The man's a 100 per cent nutcase. Do they want him to win?

eric idle retweeted
Sausage Man @SausageMan Feb 22
eric idle still very funny.

john cleese @JohnCleese Mar 4
For information of @DailyMail: our Sweden, Denmark, Holland and Belgium shows in April and May are almost sold out. So who's not funny now?

eric idle @EricIdle Mar 3
Sorry to read of the death of Tony Warren, creator of *Coronation Street*. Corrie used to be on TV two hours before Monty Python. I hope he found us worth the wait!

john cleese @JohnCleese Mar 3
My autobiography *So, Anyway* now into its 7th reprinting in paperback in Fiji.

john cleese @JohnCleese Mar 3
So, Anyway at no. 5 on the North Carolina Bestseller List, and no. 4 in New Hampshire. Who said our American brethren had no GSOH?

john cleese @JohnCleese Mar 2
Am I the first to notice that Donald Trump is the proud possessor of one of the silliest hairstyle in the world ever? Take note, young comedians!

john cleese @JohnCleese Mar 1
When overpaid Murdoch hacks suggest my autobiography is 'not funny' – real quote!!! – they are wilfully ignoring fact that sales now top 400,000. Do I detect an agenda?

john cleese @JohnCleese Mar 1
Eric and I went into a restaurant tonight and – totally unprompted – asked for 'spam, spam, spam and spam'. Waiter fell about! Aussies have GSOH!

eric idle @EricIdle Feb 28
Shocked to learn of death of TV's Jimmy Hill. I immortalised him with a mention in a classic Python 'chinny chin' sketch back in 1972. Hilarious! He never looked back!

eric idle @EricIdle Feb 27
Thanks for great interview with lovely lovely Bruce and Sally on *Good Morning Canberra* today! Pythonesque satire lives! Wink, wink, nudge, nudge!

eric idle retweeted
Sausage Man @SausageMan Feb 22
eric idle still very funny.

eric idle @EricIdle Feb 26
Still missing David Bowie RIP. Great bloke, huge Python fan, sadly missed. He used to fall around with laughter at my jokes! GSOH. RIP.

john cleese @JohnCleese Feb 26
FACT. Went to buy a blazer at Harrods last year. They couldn't fit me. Repeat: Harrods hadn't got a SINGLE blazer my size. Never happened before in 48 years. Very sadly, UK going down plughole.

eric idle @EricIdle Feb 25
True story. Python fan accosts me for autograph in Melbourne street. Totally off the cuff, I say, 'I didn't expect the Spanish Inquisition!' Result? Tears of uncontrollable laughter.

john cleese @JohnCleese Feb 24
Donald Trump reminds me of my ex-wife. Yes, he may be better-looking. But she's richer, as she's got all my money!

john cleese @JohnCleese Feb 24
If filthy Rothermere/Murdoch hacks could have heard the laughter in Adelaide last night they would have cut their throats. Lighten up!

eric idle @EricIdle Feb 23
Good morning, Adelaide! Feeling as fresh as Daisy – whoever she is! Nudge, nudge, wink, wink! And now for something completely different!

eric idle retweeted
Sausage Man @SausageMan Feb 22
eric idle still very funny.

Nonversation

Do you know what a nonversation is?

Hmmm? Hang on. Sorry, I was just …

Do you know what a nonversation is?

Fine, thanks. How are you?

I was just wondering if you'd ever heard the expression 'a nonversation'? Hello?

Sorry?

A 'nonversation'. It's a new word for when one person is trying to have a conversation and the other person is –

Yeah.

– and the other person is pretending to listen but is really doing something else. It happens a lot when you are on the telephone and the person on the other end is on the internet –

… internet …

– but it can also happen when you are in the same room and the other person has a mobile phone or a BlackBerry. So it means that while you are talking, they are only half-listening –

… half-listening …

– because their mind is chiefly occupied by texting, or playing a computer game –

… computer game …

– and they vaguely think they can cover it up simply by repeating the last thing you said and signalling their agreement with it.

… the last thing you said and signalling their agreement with it. Yeah, quite, I know.

So that's what having a 'nonversation' means. It's a new word. I just thought you might like to know.

Like to know. Right.

And the odd thing about these nonversations is that even though the person trying to speak suspects that the person on the other end of the telephone isn't really concentrating on what's being said because he's checking his e-mails, or watching a man bicycling off a cliff on YouTube, or texting another friend saying he'll be roughly half an hour late for a meeting, there is an unspoken rule for nonversations which means that you aren't allowed just to come out with it and say: 'LOOK, HAVE YOU BEEN LISTENING TO A SINGLE WORD I'VE BEEN SAYING?'

Sorry? Oh yes. Definitely. Yes, I've definitely been listening. As you say, it's erm … yes, absolutely, I quite agree.

These days, there are so many other things going on to divert every-one's attention from the subject in hand that ... Hello? Are you still there?

Yes. Sorry. I see they're expecting more snow next week.

What do you mean?

The weather people are expecting more snow next week. It says so on the BBC website.

But I was just trying to tell you about nonversations.

Nonversations?

Yes. That's right. Nonversations.

Oh. That sounds interesting. What are nonversations?

You know. What I was just saying. They're when you're talking to someone, maybe on the telephone, and as the conversation progresses it dawns on you that they're not paying attention because they're being distracted, probably by something on a screen.

Sorry. What were you just saying?

I was saying how annoying these nonversations are. And strangely humiliating, too, because you soon realise that whatever you are saying, no matter how serious or funny, is less important to the other person than whatever they happen to be staring at on their screens. Like the weather.

Hmmm. Whether what?

So they're only half-listening, even though what you're saying may be infinitely more interesting than what they are taking in from the screen.

Oh dear. It looks like England are all out for 175. Alan Titchmarsh has a new novel out in the autumn. And Peter Andre has gone on a winter break to Antigua. Without the kids.

And that's why I thought I'd just get back in touch and tell you all about nonversations. Because a lot of people haven't heard about them. And even those people who have just been told what a nonversation is may still not realise when they are taking part in one.

Yeah, great. Nonversations. Lovely talking to you.

In the end, most nonversations just peter out. And when you put down the phone, you've got no idea whether the person you've just been speaking to has taken in a single word you've said ... Well, so now you know what a nonversation is.

Yes. Right. Hey, can you believe it? They're predicting more snow next week. Or did I just say that?

Bye for now!

Very well. How are you?

Elf Club

A few years ago, the book dealer Rick Gekoski wrote a funny book of reminiscences called *Tolkien's Gown*. In the title essay, he discussed the amazing prices commanded by J. R. R. Tolkien in the world of rare books. Apparently, a signed copy of *The Lord of The Rings* can now fetch £50,000, and a signed copy of *The Hobbit* £75,000.

Tolkien was Merton Professor of English Language and Literature at Oxford University, and one of Gekoski's earliest sale items, back in 1982, was Tolkien's old gown, which he billed as 'original black cloth, slightly frayed and with a little soiling'. He sold it to an American academic for a comparatively modest $1,000, but now thinks he could have got a lot more: 'An added attraction, not evident in those innocent times, was that from one of its many DNA-rich stains one might eventually hope to clone a small army of Tolkiens, and fill a senior common room full of professors brandishing epics.'

Oddly enough, since Tolkien's death aged eighty-one in 1973, he has had more new books published than he ever did when he was alive. *The Father Christmas Letters* came out in 1976, *The Silmarillion* in 1977, *Unfinished Tales* in 1980, *The Letters* in 1981, *Finn and Hengest* in 1982, and so on and so forth, up to *Roverandom* in 1998. It is almost as though Murdoch, The Dark Lord from Down Under and All-Commanding Master of The Busy Elves of HarperCollins, had succeeded in cloning hundreds of those little Tolkiens from that stained gown, and had forced them into a hole in the ground, where they beaver away on new publications.

Another year, another new work by J. R. R. Tolkien.* *The Children*

---

* *The Children of Hurin* by J. R. R. Tolkien, edited by Christopher Tolkien (2013).

of Hurin, or, to give it its full name, *Narn i Chîn Húrin: The Tale of the Children of Hurin*, for with Tolkien everything has to be translated from the original gobbledegook, runs to 313 pages. These are fleshed out with a preface, an introduction, a note on pronunciation ('U in names like Hurin, Turin, should be pronounced *oo*; thus '*Toorin*' not '*Tyoorin*'), three separate genealogies, two appendices, a long, long list of names of characters and places ('*Hador Goldenhead*: Elf-friend, lord of Dor-Lomin, vassal of King Fingolfin, father of Galdor father of Hurin and Huor slain at Eithel Sirion in the Dagor Bragollach, *House of Hador*, one of the Houses of the Edain'), a little map, plus a little note on the little map.

The book itself has been pieced together by Tolkien's third son and literary executor, Christopher, who is eighty-three years old. In his prefaces and appendices, Christopher explains how the book came to be, though, even after repeated readings, I'm still not sure I've managed to take it all in. From what I could gather, J. R. R. Tolkien started the book in the First World War, but put it down unfinished, took it up again in the 1920s, this time in Anglo-Saxon verse, and then, after six years and 4,000 lines, put it down once more. Thirty-four years after his father's death, Christopher has knocked the various storylines into some sort of shape, and so off we go …

But not so fast, or – as Tolkien might put it – fast not be but so so thus! First, Christopher provides what he calls a 'very brief sketch' to fill us in on the background of the hero's childhood. Are you sitting comfortably? Then I'll begin: 'In the north the boundaries of Beleriand seem to have been formed by the Ered Wethrin, the Mountains of Shadlow, beyond which lay Hurin's country, Dor-lomi, a part of Hithlum while in the east Beleriand extended to the feet of the Blue Mountains …'

A page later, and the brief background sketch is still going strong: 'the prime mover in the rebellion against the Valar was Feanor, "Spirit of Fire": he was the eldest son of Finwe, who had led the host of Noldor from Cuivienen …'

And on it goes ('the second son of Finwe was Fingolfin, the half-brother of Feanor, who was held the overlord of all the Noldorl') and on ('the eldest son of Finarfin was Finrod, who …') and on ('the other sons of Finarfin, Angrod and Aegnor, vassals of their brother Finrod, dwelt on Dorthonian, looking northwards over the vast plain of Ard-galen …') and on and on and on, through a vast, thorny, impenetrable forest of fourteen long pages.

I let out a sigh of relief when I eventually arrived at the start of the book on page 33. At last! – Chapter 1: The Childhood of Turin! I had been praying for something simple and straightforward, like the famous first sentence of *The Hobbit*: 'In a hole in the ground there lived a hobbit.' But instead this came: 'Hador Goldenhead was a lord of the Edain and well-beloved by the Eldar … His daughter Gloredhel wedded Haldir son of Halmir, lord of the Men of Brethil; and at the same feast his son Galdor the Tall wedded Hareth, the daughter of Halmir.'

To my horror, the book went on in this relentless vein – like someone playing silly buggers with a bagful of Scrabble letters – until it reached the end. I have never been particularly fond of either fantasy or pedantry, but the combination of the two induced a terrible feeling of claustrophobia in me, almost as though someone had wrapped that bag of Scrabble letters over my head, and then abandoned me in a hole.

Tolkien specialises in a strange sort of back-to-front prose, designed, I suppose, to lend period gravitas to his repetitive imaginings. Thus, we learn that the hero, Hurin, is 'strong in body and fiery of mind', that his mother is 'somewhat stern of mood and proud', and that, pursued by Orcs, his relations 'knew not the way to go on or return' but finally came to reside in the King's house 'for well nigh a year'.

Not for Tolkien a simple phrase like 'the cat sat on the mat'. Under his stewardship, it would come out as: 'Pussykins, son of Felix, daughter of Paddy-Paws, of the House of Number 39, in the month of Gob El Digook, made much haste on his four legs towards the mat, and thereon placed his feline weight for eight years long and comfortable.'

The story of *The Children of Hurin* is packed to the rafters with different characters, but, like the 'Aram begat Aminadab and Aminadab begat Naason and Naason begat …' passage in the Bible, the more that pop up, the duller the story grows. The basic plot involves Turin, son of Hurin, pursued by Orcs and Easterlings, briefly adopted by King Thingol (surely one of Tolkien's all-time silliest names), and later taken in by Mim the Dwarf ('so began the abiding of Turin son of Hurin in the halls of Mim, in Bar-en-Danwedh, the House of Ransom …') before encountering any number of pitched battles, hidden staircases, caves, and great big stones rolled across secret passageways. This may all sound very exciting, but I can assure you it is not: all the characters, Orcs and Kings, Elves and Dwarfs, speak like drunken chatterboxes in a pantomime ('Thither after wandering I came to seek welcome'), and any natural event comes shrouded in topsy-turvy saloon-bar verbiage ('night is a cold counsellor'), generally expressed as though someone has been arsing around with the fridge magnets ('But grass came there and grew again long and green upon that hill').

Eventually, Turin gets his own back on the baddy ('Die now and then darkness have you! Thus is Turin son of Hurin avenged!') before coming to grief himself. Halfway through, I thought things might be perking up a bit when 'an Elvish band' put their heads around the door. Could this be a band of Elvish Impersonators, all the way from Lash Vegas, singing 'Huirt Breg Hoe Tel' and 'Allshoo Qup' in their white spangly jumpsuits? Alas no: they were just the usual band of Tolkien elves, or 'elven folk', as he insists on calling them.

C. S. Lewis and J. R. R. Tolkien once had an awkward encounter. The two children's authors used to meet every now and then to read their latest writings to each other. Once, when Tolkien finished reading his first paragraph, Lewis sighed, 'Oh no, not more ELVES again!'

Perhaps Lewis was being a bit churlish: in the right place, elves, like shelves, can serve a purpose. But enough is enough: someone should tell that secret army of Tolkien clones to call it a day. The largest stone in Middle Earth could then be rolled over the entrance to their cave, allowing us, the liberated readers, to tiptoe quietly away.

The Ongoing Debate

EVAN DAVIS: What's the cost of us staying in, and what's the cost of coming out? We could discuss these points until the cows come home. But just how long will it be before the cows do, in fact, come home? Professor Barry Dullard?

PROFESSOR DULLARD: Well, if Brexit has its way, and we are forced to leave, then it's a fact that the cows will never be able to come home. It's as simple as that.

EVAN DAVIS: Could you answer that particular point about the cows, Sue Blather?

SUE BLATHER: This is yet another scare tactic, Evan. Of course the cows can come home if we leave. It's a simple fact that, even on the lowest estimates, up to 72 per cent of cows in 82 per cent of non-EU countries come home 58 per cent of the time – and that's not even taking into account the –

EVAN DAVIS: I'd like to stop you there if I may. Professor Dullard, do you agree with the statistics Sue Blather has just offered us?

PROFESSOR DULLARD: No. I find them deeply misleading. In 63 per cent of the cases over the past twelve years, 32 per cent of the cows were simply in a neighbouring field, so to all intents and purposes they had never left home, so had no reason to come back. If the Leave camp have their way, the cows will come home when pigs might fly.

SUE BLATHER: That's my point entirely. It's the simple truth that British pigs would fly perfectly well if they were allowed to, but under EU regulations pigs are prevented from flying, so they just stay put, grunting and groaning and refusing to move. This means they have to be transported to market by road, which is highly expensive, as well as ruinous for the environment. All we want is a level playing field.

EVAN DAVIS: Barry?

PROFESSOR DULLARD: Well, 61 per cent of the pigs we've asked are highly satisfied or reasonably satisfied with the levelness of their playing fields under the existing EU settlement. It's as simple as that!

EVAN DAVIS: Which brings us neatly to the whole level playing field debate. How level should a field be before it is played on? Or, to put it another way, if you level a field, does it automatically become fit for playing? Barry?

PROFESSOR DULLARD: I think you have to look at the whole playing field issue in the wider context of Europe as a whole.

SUE BLATHER: Let me make this quite clear, this is not an issue, it's a topic.

PROFESSOR DULLARD: I'm very sorry, but I really can't let that go unchallenged. It's not a topic. It's an issue. Or at very least a concern. And a major concern, at that.

SUE BLATHER: Sorry, but independent experts have confirmed that it's neither a concern nor an issue. It's a topic. Case closed!

EVAN DAVIS: Forgive me, but I don't want us to get bogged down in the issue of what's a topic or what's an issue. If we could move on to …

SUE BLATHER: It's not an issue!

PROFESSOR DULLARD: It's an issue!

SUE BLATHER: Topic!

EVAN DAVIS: Let's not get bogged down …

PROFESSOR DULLARD: But we are in fact 76 per cent more than likely to get bogged down if we leave, Evan, because the EC Bog Standard Commission is our only guarantee that anything up to 46 per cent of British citizens will not be swallowed up in a bog by the year 2027. I'm very sorry, but that's a fact!

SUE BLATHER: That's nonsense. British bog farmers put in £2,250 a year and receive £1,253 in return, giving them a net loss of …

PROFESSOR DULLARD: There's no question of a net loss! If they lost their nets, they'd simply apply to the EU Emergency Net Loss Fund, and under the present system they'd get a rebate.

SUE BLATHER: Sorry, but you're talking of high-mesh nets, which aren't suited to covering anything beyond 37 per cent of British lowland bogs, rising to a lower figure in the winter months.

EVAN DAVIS: I'll have to interrupt you there, if I may, as I really want to get down to the nitty-gritty. What about you, Sue? Where do you stand? Are you nitty – or gritty?

SUE BLATHER: Nitty. No question about it, Evan. If we stay in the EU, we'll be forced to build an estimated 240 warehouses every single day for the next seventy-five years just to store all the unwanted gritty, and we simply can't afford it.

PROFESSOR DULLARD: If we leave, we'll find we're worse off by up to four tons of nitty per household per year, and there's no telling what will happen to the gritty. I'm sorry, but those who say we'll be self-sufficient in either nitty or gritty are frankly living in cloud cuckoo land.

EVAN DAVIS: Yet most reputable economists believe that by the year 2028 the cost of clouds will overtake the price of cuckoos, which may leave cloud cuckoo land extremely vulnerable. So that raises the vexed question of when the birds will come home to roost. Barry?

Mrs McGinty's Dead Bored

We all know the moment. We have enjoyed a variety of murders in any number of exotic locations. At the beginning, we thought it was the doctor who did it. Then we changed our mind and suspected the elderly spinster. But the elderly spinster turned out to be the next victim, so we had to reconsider, and settled on the dashing young sportsman. But now we are starting to think it might just have been the doctor all along.

With twenty pages still to go, Monsieur Poirot gathers all the suspects into the drawing room.

'As you say, Miss Twittering was a perfectly harmless creature who wouldn't hurt a fly! Why, then, was she deliberately and brutally murdered?' he asks the assembled company. It's a conversation-stopper. He then does one of his knowing looks. 'Well, I will tell you what I think.'

Oh, no! Monsieur Poirot is never more boring than he is when delivering explanations. They don't just go on: they go on and on and on and on and on.

'It is my belief that Miss Twittering was murdered because she knew not too much – but too little.'

You pray that he will end it there. But no! At this point, one of the key suspects leans forward. As a viewer, you find yourself shouting at the screen: 'Whatever you do, don't ask him for an explanation!'

But it's too late. The suspect has already raised an eyebrow.

'What are you suggesting, Monsieur Poirot?'

'I am suggesting, Dr Chance, that things are not quite what they seem.'

And he's off!

'On that Sunday night, Miss Chadwick was restless, so she got up. She saw the light on in the ballroom and there found Miss Twittering looking through the bag that you, Dr Chance, had so carefully placed there just two hours before. But none of them had reckoned with Professor Nobbs, who was at that very moment passing by on his way to the shrubbery to meet ... Mademoiselle Bulstrode! And who should he bump into on his way to the shrubbery but ...'

And so it goes on. Give Poirot an inch and he'll take a mile. Even the explanations have explanations. On television, you can almost see the poor actors thinking: 'We haven't got all day! If we wrap it up in the next few minutes, we could just catch the 18.26 back to London. Oh, do please get on with it!'

As viewers, all we want is the finger pointed at the murderer, and the murderer led away, cursing. But Poirot always assumes we are desperate for a full rehash of every character's movements from day one, now with added motives.

'Of course, she could never forgive him for what had happened to her so long ago, so she was determined to have her revenge, and that is what brought her to the shrubbery on that fateful night – but little did she realise that Professor Nobbs was not Professor Nobbs at all, but Mr Cedric Anstruther, whose first wife, Mirabella, was better known as Amelia Plaistow, lady's maid to Miss Twittering!'

For all his much-vaunted omniscience, Poirot never notices all eyes glazing over, suspects and viewers alike. Who cares who went where when with what and why? We just want to know who did it, and be done with it. Once he's into his stride, Poirot becomes a self-generating machine, specially calibrated for boring the pants off bystanders. For every question he answers, another ten spring up. Take this, from *Mrs McGinty's Dead*. A few minutes into a Poirot borathon, the principal suspect stupidly asks: 'Why me?'

Fatal question! Hercule Poirot replies: 'Why were you so interested in Broadhinny? Why, when you went over there, did you ask Robin Upward for an autograph? You are not the autograph-hunting type. What did you know about the Upwards? Why did you come to this part of the world in the first place? How did you know that Eva Kane died in Australia and the name she took when she left England?' He then takes a full seven pages to answer his own questions, one at a time, each in stultifying detail.

Given that he or she will shortly be facing the hangman's noose, the accused never seems particularly bothered. They just say something a little bit testy – 'You can never stop meddling in other people's business, can you, Poirot?' – before being led away. Have they perhaps twigged that Poirot's preposterous explanations will never hold up in court and that any sane jury will leap at the chance to declare the accused Not Guilty?

POLITICS

Skin-a-Rabbit!:
The Diary of Jacob Rees-Mogg

'Good morning, Nanny!'

  'Good morning, Master Jacob!'

  'Good morning, children!'

  'Good morning, Pater!'

  The breaking of one's fast, or to employ the dreadful modern jargon, 'breakfasting' (!) with one's family is surely one of the great pleasures of existence on earth.

The silver gleaming on the dining table; the children smartly lined up in their buttons and bows ready with their pewter dishes as they anticipate the arrival of our esteemed Cook with her doughty ladle; the vittles and viands awaiting our earnest attentions, and presiding over us all, one's estimable Nanny, ever on the lookout for the tooth unbrushed and the ear unwashed: all in all, a most welcome start to every spring morn, as one prepares to do battle with the buffoons, rapscallions and ne'er-do-wells who take the shilling of the 'European Union'.

Under the expert guidance of Nanny, the children fill up their bowls. They then sit in silence while Nanny delivers two hearty thumps with a teaspoon to my boiled eggs, and sets about unpeeling them.

'It's high time you learnt to do this by yourself, Master Jacob!' she says.

'Oh, Nanny!' I reply, 'Do not berate me so, for my mind is at present filled with the more pressing concerns of Queen and Country!'

'I was but jesting!' replies Nanny, with her abundant good cheer. I look down at the egg cups in keen anticipation, and she has only one or two little bits of eggshell to remove before the eggs are ready to eat.

I peruse the *Financial Times*. It is as well to know what the ordinary people, if may one use such a term, are up to, so as better to represent them in Parliament. I also like to make sure that the international markets are behaving themselves. I am delighted to see that my own shares, and those of my clients, are performing commendably. Our wealth has, once again, increased while we slumbered – and yet, in spite of all the evidence, Messrs Corbyn and Co. continue to insist that our great nation has, in some unfathomable way, failed to benefit from the firm smack of austerity!

'A drop in our overseas markets – that's good news for us!' I say.

'Ooh, you're so sharp, you'll cut yourself!' chuckles Nanny.

'Elbows off the table, Master Jacob!'

Nanny draws up a chair and takes her knife to the toast. She butters it, then cuts each slice up into lovely straight lines.

'The soldiers have arrived, Master Jacob!' she says, 'and they're queuing up for their dipping!'

With that, she dips my first soldier into the yolk. This is the sign for me to open my mouth as wide as I possibly can.

'In he pops!' says Nanny, placing him in my mouth. 'What a good boy!'

'Mmmm!' I exclaim. I notice that shares in Consolidated are down a couple of points, though no cause for immediate concern.

'That face of yours could do with a good wipe!' says Nanny, spitting on to her napkin and dabbing at a bit of stubborn yolk on my cheek.

With heavy heart, I turn to the editorial pages of my *Financial Times*. It never ceases to surprise me that so many of our 'experts' (and, believe me, I use the term lightly!) continue to believe that this great trading nation of ours, birthplace of Handel and Prince Albert, will fail to rise to the challenge of independence!

'Please, Nanny, may I have a little extra butter on my last soldier?'

'Those who ask, don't get, Master Jacob!' says Nanny. And then she chuckles, says, 'Oh, get on with you!', and adds a dollop of butter.

'Open wide! And down the big red road! All finished! That's a good boy!' My children applaud me as I take up my napkin and wipe my own mouth. I am, I need hardly say, a firm believer in self-reliance.

I believe, too, in traditional meals, partaken in a traditional way. I sometimes worry that the British have lost the ability to fend for themselves. Where is our backbone? Our Empire was built neither on casual eating nor on sloppy manners.

'Let's be getting you dressed, Master Jacob!' says Nanny. 'Time you were out of those jim-jams!'

Together, we climb the stairs to my dressing room.

The sound of that marvellous tune, 'Land of Hope and Glory', can be heard. It is my mobile telephone. It is Iain Duncan Smith, a wonderful little man, asking if I'd be prepared to go on *Newsnight* to argue the case for No Deal.

As I am sorting out the schedule and so forth, with her eagle-eye Nanny notices that I have a runny nose. She dips into her pocket for a hanky. We gave it to her some years ago, a reward for long service.

'There! Big blow! All better!' she says.

'I'm sorry, what did you say?' says Iain.

'It was only Nanny,' I say, reassuringly.

'Skin-a-rabbit!' says Nanny, pulling off my jim-jam tops. She lets me take my bottoms off by myself.

'Let's get you on the bed, and we'll see to you,' says Nanny.

I dutifully lie on the bed. Nanny unpins my nappy. I put my legs high in the air. This makes it so much easier for Nanny to give things a really good wipe 'down there'.

These ancient traditions, dating back generations, lie at the very heart of Rees-Mogg family life.

Nanny unpins my towelling nappy.

'Who's been a messy boy, then?' laughs Nanny. 'Someone's in need of a good wipe-down, Master Jacob!'

While Nanny sets about her business, I leaf through the latest issue of the *Spectator*. It's as well to keep in touch with what ordinary, decent people are thinking, and a period of silence from me helps Nanny get on with the job in hand.

'Good boy!' announces Nanny. 'All lovely and clean!'

It is a Tuesday, so she lets me pick my own suit. I always go for something double-breasted. Within reason, one should keep 'up to date', and triple-breasted might be going too far.

Nanny wheels me the 500 or so yards to the Commons, but I always insist on making my own way into the Chamber. This country must learn to grow up and stand on its own two feet, and it's so important to set an example.

Prezza

First, the good news: he didn't write it himself.* John Prescott's publishers had the bright idea of asking Hunter Davies to write it for him. Davies has already succeeded in ghosting full-length autobiographies for Paul Gascoigne, Wayne Rooney and Dwight Yorke, the writerly equivalent of surviving a month naked on Dartmoor in December, so he had certainly got in training for Mount Prescott.

The result is a political autobiography like no other. It is written in a version of Prescott's own voice – bluff and bossy and blokeish – but skilfully manicured, so that absolute gibberish is kept to a minimum, a fair proportion of the words are in roughly the right order, and for most of the time it just about makes sense.

Full of 'let me thinks' and 'by the ways' and even the odd 'er' ('I wasn't quite as, er, hefty in those days'), it reads like a conversation with Prescott after he has been heavily sedated. The spluttering and slightly sinister aggression he recently displayed to John Humphrys on the radio is, for the most part, replaced with a folksy calm, rather as though an actor togged up to play the role of John Prescott has just nipped offstage for a bit of a breather.

Maybe it's because he so closely resembles the chubby comic actor Terry Scott, who regularly played one of the Ugly Sisters come Christmas time, that I have long detected something of the pantomime dame about John Prescott. Perhaps sensing this, Hunter Davies, like the most expert theatrical make-up artiste, has not attempted to gloss the chips on his shoulders; rather, he has chosen to camp them

---

* *Prezza: Pulling No Punches* by John Prescott with Hunter Davies (2008).

up, so they emerge as his character's trademark, like the humps on a camel.

In fact, *The Chip on My Shoulder* might have made a snappier subtitle, since it's a phrase that pops up throughout the book. Young John fails the Eleven-Plus: 'Perhaps that was when I got the chip on my shoulder.' Later, he goes to Scout camp with homemade scones, not shop-bought ones: 'I felt ashamed ... the chip on my shoulder got bigger.' In government, he discovers Tony and his cronies have been meeting secretly without him, 'stirring up my chip-on-the-shoulder sense of inferiority'.

At Ruskin College, Oxford, one of his reports said he was 'pathologically sensitive to criticism'. His autobiography is a lengthy catalogue of slights followed by fury. As a young steward on a liner, he unpacks his new pyjamas. 'They didn't half take the p*** ... They all thought I must be gay.' In Hull University library he meets Philip Larkin, but the stand-offish poet looks down his nose at him. In an official painting of the House of Commons, he finds he has been removed from the front bench and placed a row further back. Time and again, he throws a hissy fit whenever anyone draws attention to his butter-fingered handling of the English language.

He attributes all criticism to snobbery, but senior politicians from humbler backgrounds (Callaghan, Major, Kinnock, etc.) have been perfectly articulate, while the Tory grandee Willie Whitelaw blathered away just as incoherently and was teased about it just as mercilessly. Prescott argues that muddle with words has nothing to do with muddle in the head, but I doubt this is so. 'I think my main problem is that my brain works faster than my mouth,' he says. But I suspect he has got it the wrong way round: his mouth gabbles away and his brain finds it hard to keep up.

Language is inseparable from intelligence. Prescott's own book highlights, more cruelly than any of his critics, the limits of his intelligence. Although he paints a vivid and comical portrait of his gambling, two-timing, freeloading father, he seems to have noticed very little about anyone else. His other character assessments are so limited and repetitive as to suggest rank stupidity. We learn that Dennis Skinner is 'a very decent bloke', that Norman Lamont is 'a decent enough bloke', that Peter Shore was 'a great bloke', that his stepson Paul is also 'a great bloke', that Jim Callaghan was 'a nice enough bloke', and that Lord Longford was also 'a nice enough bloke'. On a more general level, he found the Chinese 'very easy to deal with'. Might this be because they had the benefit of an interpreter? He is keen to present himself as a class warrior, but somehow all his battles seem to end up with him marching in step with the conquering forces.

He likes to call it fighting to change things from the inside, but I'm not so sure. On first meeting the Queen, he vows not to bow, but then she craftily whispers and – what do you know? – he finds himself forced to lean over. Of course, he's always been dead against the snooty, etc. etc. monarchy, but when it comes to summing up his many achievements he can't help bragging that 'I've also got some nice letters from Prince Charles, many of them handwritten'. Once on top, it takes him about a second to acquire an old-fashioned sense of hierarchy.

When he finally gets to be a Secretary of State, he notices that a senior civil servant lets a junior sit in the better chair. 'That gave me an insight into his character. The top men should always act like the top men. I thought then that … I wouldn't want him as my permanent secretary.' So much for the class warrior! He is a great one for the defiant gesture followed by total capitulation. For instance, he prides himself on being Old Labour, and boasts that he has never used the phrase New Labour ('I just couldn't bear those words to come out of my mouth'), but at the same time he has faithfully pursued the New Labour agenda, even at its most breezily Thatcherite.

Will he now join the House of Lords, the institution that he once so despised? 'Will I go to the Lords? Pauline would like me to,' he says, which I take to mean: 'Yes, but blame the wife.' When he gets there, he might think of selecting 'To Have My Cake and Eat It' as a suitable motto for his coat of arms.* He reveals that the only time he actually threatened to resign was over the inclusion of a Lib Dem in the Cabinet. Iraq, the Dome, Europe, the vast increase in surveillance, his

---

* He was to become Lord Prescott of Kingston upon Hull in 2010.

forsaken promise to renationalise the railways: he has hoovered it all up without so much as a burp.

Which brings us to his vomiting. If they have any hope of selling, political memoirs need a headline-grabbing revelation. His publishers must have been delighted when John Prescott coughed up, so to speak. His revelation is, of course, that he suffered – although from the sound of it there wasn't much suffering involved – from bulimia. 'So what I did was stuff my face with anything around, any old rubbish – burgers, chocolates, crisps, fish and chips, loads of it, 'til I felt sick … There would be a weird kind of pleasure in vomiting and feeling relieved.' Apart from attributing it to the general stress of high office, he won't analyse his reasons for succumbing to this curious disorder. Instead, he tries to laugh it off – the chapter is called 'Getting Stuffed' – as though it were just one of those funny little things. Yet earlier he has confessed to slipping out of an official dinner in 1976 and bursting into tears. 'I went to the toilet and sat there crying. It was uncontrollable.' His autobiography often hints at inner turmoil; at a strange sort of Norman Bates personality, at odds with himself and the world. 'One day I went to my mother and said, "Mum, I've broken off my engagement to Pauline." "Oh, John," she said, "I'm so pleased." "No, I haven't," I said. "I was just seeing how you'd react. Now I know what you really think."'

'It might sound like a nasty trick,' adds Prescott, 'but it's always been part of my character to find out the truth.' Am I the only one to find this passage slightly creepy?

Twelve Politicians

Vince Cable
Is exceptionally able
But a book I won't read twice is
The World Economic Crisis.

Liam Fox
Remains tox-
ic; but to his credit he
Stays in touch with Adam Werritty.

John Bercow
Is a bit of a jerk; oh,
And nor am I pally
With his wife Sally.

Harriet Harman
Would make a rotten barman:
As you were shooting the breeze
She'd call: 'Time, gentlemen, please!'

Were James Cleverly
To be called Beverly
He'd be Beverly Cleverly
So he'd lose heavily.

Jo Johnson
Is Mick Ronson
To Boris's Bowie
(i.e. duller, less showy).

Liz Truss
Thinks 'If Boris falls under a bus
It might just be me
Who'll be the next leader but three.'

Chris Grayling
Has only one failing:
Try as we might,
We dislike him on sight.

Philip Hammond
Says, 'Damn and
Blast!
My day is past!'

George Osborne
Was born
To rule; with a touch of lard he
Styles his hair like Oliver Hardy.

Jacob Rees-Mogg
Looks on agog:
'Things have gone badly downhill
Since the Great Reform Bill.'

Chris Huhne
Is over the moon:
'Within a year or two
I'll be known as Chris Who?'

Hoon but Not Forgotten

Legend has it that Ernest Hemingway once bet a tableful of friends $10 each that he could write a story using just six words. He then wrote on a napkin 'For sale: baby shoes, never worn', and picked up his winnings.

Short stories – very short stories – may be found in the least likely places, and often the most poignant are true. I came across one at the weekend. As I was composing a clerihew about Chris Huhne, I found myself wondering what had happened to his near-namesake Geoff Hoon.

Hoon is, you may remember, the former Labour Defence Secretary who fell from grace just before the 2010 general election, having been caught in a Channel 4 sting operation offering his services for money. This resulted in his being banned from Parliament for five years.

Where is he now? The most unlikely people have taken to Twitter, so I typed 'Geoff Hoon Twitter' into the search engine, on the off-chance. Up came: 'Rt Hon Geoff Hoon MP: @GeoffHoonMP', which appears to be his official Twitter account.

The first thing I noticed was the extraordinary modesty of his online presence: tweets: eleven, followers: ten. Disgraced he may have been, but how could he possibly have attracted so few followers?

On closer examination, Hoon's paucity of tweets and followers is explained: his first and last tweets both took place on exactly the same day, 5 April 2010 – a fortnight after the revelations – very, very early in the morning, in that nightmarish half-hour between 2.51 a.m. and 3.21 a.m.

The first, tweeted at 2.51 a.m., reads, somewhat plaintively: 'Please don't believe everything you read about in the press. They have a tendency to exaggerrate [*sic*]. I'm not a bad chap really!'

As with his other ten tweets, it contains misspellings and the odd word left out. The next, sent two minutes later, at 2.53 a.m., is addressed to his former colleague Harriet Harman. Sweetly, it reads: 'Hello Harriet. Didn't know you were on here! Just signed up myself!'

This is the first indication that he imagines tweeting to be a private form of communication, addressed from one person to another, with no one else looking in. As with his other tweets, there is no sign of any reply.

Hoon sends his third tweet just one minute later, at 2.54 a.m. Again, it is to Harriet Harman. 'Just wanted you to know I am still available to help the party in an [*sic*] I can during election period, despite everything.' Again, no reply.

Before his downfall, Hoon had been involved in an abortive coup against the then Labour leader, Gordon Brown: perhaps this explains Harman's reluctance to get involved.

He is now tweeting at the furious rate of one a minute. At 2.55 a.m. he tweets: 'Please vote Labour on May 6 and help your local partyas-sosciation [*sic*]. Volunteers are always welcome!'

He then pauses for four minutes before tweeting Jim Sheridan MP. 'Hello Jim. Best of luck with the campaign. Big day tomorrow!'

He waits a further three minutes before tweeting John Prescott, at 3.02 a.m. Once again, he appears to believe he is communicating privately. 'I've signed up to Twitter to try and get the proper story re recent events out to the people. I hope I have your support John.' No reply.

At 3.07 a.m. he tweets Ed Balls. This one has an air of defeat about it, a tweet expecting the answer no. 'I am always available to help the party, despite everything. I'm sure you know that. Right now we need to have all hands on deck.'

Three minutes later, at 3.10 a.m., he tweets Balls again. He seems to have got a bit of fight back in him. 'We must keep the pressure on Chris Grayling. We have to force Cameron to back him or sack him.'

At 3.13 a.m. he tweets John Prescott: 'We must remember a lot of people will have sympathy for Graylings [*sic*] position re rights for business owners to discriminate.' And a minute later, another to Prescott: 'How is the recruitment of celebs like @chrisdjmoyles and @fearne cotton to help the campaign going. Any luck?'

Finally, at 3.21 a.m., Geoff Hoon writes his last tweet. It is to Angela Eagle MP: 'It will be a tough fight with polls going the way they are, but I have every confidence you will prevail. Best of luck!'

And there we have it: a sad little short story, full of dashed hope, with a tinge of desperation. Who would have wished to be Geoff Hoon, at that time of that day?

'At three o'clock in the morning, a forgotten package has the same tragic importance as a death sentence ...' wrote F. Scott Fitzgerald, 'and in a real dark night of the soul it is always three o'clock in the morning, day after day.'

Stars in His Eyes:
The Twilight Years of Tony Benn

1

However fixed our beliefs, we are all adrift on the tide of history. In the 1970s, when Tony Benn was to be found behind the loudhailer at every demonstration and picket line, no one would have imagined that his first diary entry for this, his eighth volume of diaries,* would be: 'Sunday 24 June 2001: Saffron Burrows came and we had a talk about *Harpers & Queen*, which wants to interview us together.'

It reads like a particularly random game of Consequences, but is real. Tony Benn is now part and parcel of our celebrity culture, hobnobbing with actresses and TV presenters, courted by the glossy magazines. Four years on, *Vogue* wants a slice of the action: 'Wednesday 26 January 2005. I had a phone call saying that David Bailey, the well-known society photographer, wanted to take a picture of Saffron Burrows with me, for *Vogue* … David Bailey is a funny man. He used to be married to Catherine Deneuve, a glamorous French actress.'

The Benn diaries used to be full of beefy trades unionists and duffel-coated activists. But the world has moved on, and it has taken Tony Benn with it. Now the index reads more like the production manual for *Stars in Their Eyes*. Nigel Havers, Joan Collins, Nicholas Parsons and Bianca Jagger all pop up, and so too does the loopy fashion designer Vivienne Westwood, earnestly calling for the withdrawal of British troops from Vietnam. His new best friends are Saffron Burrows

---

* *More Time for Politics* by Tony Benn (2007).

and Natasha Kaplinsky ('very professional and exceptionally beautiful'). Even the world statesmen he bumps into try to steer the conversation towards more glamorous things than politics. Bill Clinton wants to talk about their mutual friend Saffron Burrows; when Benn kicks off a conversation with Gorbachev by saying he was in Parliament for fifty years, Gorby simply replies, 'How boring that must have been!'

When Tony Benn stopped being an MP in 2001, he said that he would now have 'more time for politics', hence the title of this latest volume of the diaries he has been keeping since 1940. On his eightieth birthday, he boasts that, since leaving Parliament, 'I've made 555 speeches in around 130 towns and cities. Did 1,089 broadcasts (683 radio and 416 television).' He has always been very trainspotterish about his own career, but the fact that he feels the need to tot up all these appearances suggests that somewhere in the back of his mind he knows that, as far as politics is concerned, he has become a marginal figure. He may have more time for politics, but does politics have any more time for him?

Like an old figure in a short story by William Trevor, he is struck by sudden flashes of self-awareness, realising with a terrible pang that he is no longer at the hub of events: 'I'm a bit depressed, I have to be honest ... You know, you've had a very active life, and been in the forefront of things, and then gradually you slip into the background.'

He is, it transpires, a key member of a kind of mutual-support society of former political grandees. They are now on the outside, their noses pressed to the window of power, but they do their best to convince one another that they are still on the inside, looking out. Edward Heath phones Benn to ask, 'How can we get rid of Blair?' The disgraced former Liberal leader Jeremy Thorpe summons him to his study, decorated with photographs of himself with Kissinger, Mandela and Nixon, in the hope of organising an international conference on the Middle East.

A sizeable portion of Tony Benn's media work now involves passing judgements on old comrades or opponents for TV obituaries, either after they die, or, in some cases, before. 'If you survive,' he reflects, 'your main function is to do obituaries of people you know.' Barbara Castle is taken ill, so he agrees to record her obituary for telly; they then ring again. Will he do Jim Callaghan at the same time – and why not throw Denis Healey in too?

One man's death is another man's airtime. 'Monday 18 July 2005: Got up at 5.30, picked up at a quarter to seven and did a whole series of interviews: first with Jim Naughtie of the *Today* programme and Lord Armstrong, about Ted Heath, who has died.' Note the order of priorities: the interviews are mentioned first, then, almost as an afterthought, the death.

Adherents of the previous volumes of the Benn diaries will be delighted to recognise many of the familiar old jingles, brought back for another blast. Here again are the classic conspiracy theories involving The Establishment ('the British Establishment desperately wants to keep the monarchy going') and The Media ('there is an absolute press blackout on Parliament'). Small wonder, then, that his favourite new film is *The Da Vinci Code*. 'It could be true,' he muses. And his boundless enthusiasm for ever more unlikely people has now soared beyond parody: Ted Heath is 'an attractive old boy', Lord Young of Graffham 'very agreeable', Gerry Adams 'immensely sensitive', Tariq Azis 'a nice guy' and even Saddam Hussein 'very friendly'. His eye-popping fury has greatly dwindled, and is now reserved almost exclusively for the architects of New Labour, including Mandelson ('such a nonentity'), Byers ('a really slippery guy') and, above all, Blair ('the man is absolutely hysterical! … He doesn't understand anything – he doesn't listen to anybody! … It's all gimmick, gimmick, gimmick, gimmick, gimmick'). Oddly enough, for all his enviable ability to forgive and forget, the mutual antipathy between Benn and Michael Foot still seems to be going strong.

But behind the familiar Bennite drones and drumbeats, a more plangent and haunting melody can be heard. It is the eternal tune of old age, loneliness and grief. Straight away, he misses being an MP. 'Came home. I was very lonely,' he records on 22 July 2001. 'There will be lots of days like this – no Parliament.' But more than this, he misses his wife Caroline, who died in 2000. His grief is constant, bravely borne, and desperately affecting. Every now and then, something reminds him of her, and he bursts into tears. 'Not only do I miss her terribly,' he writes on the first anniversary of her death, 'but also I'm still riddled with guilt, the things I should have done with her that I didn't ... I think Caroline would have been pleased at the way I'm tackling being on my own.' The next day, 'I went shopping and came home and had a cry. I just sobbed on the couch for a bit.' Later that month, this elderly man whose life has been so informed by certainty finds himself confronted by the ultimate uncertainty: 'I was listening to cassettes in the car, and I began crying, and I sobbed and sobbed ... It just comes back to you all of a sudden, and I wondered where Caroline was. Had she disappeared into thin air? What does death mean? Is it a complete and absolute end?'

Yet he keeps going, and it is this keeping going that is so heroic, and so moving. He suffers aches and pains; at one point he collapses in the gents, and is taken away in an ambulance. But he retains a zest for living: yes, he may get knocked down, but he always gets back up again.

He watches the films of his youth and cooks himself pizza and plays solitary word games. He is blessed with a large and devoted family, and where once there were causes and amendments and statements, there are now children and grandchildren, and family visits to the theatre. In one entry in the last volume he confessed, 'I can't say that politics is my main interest at the moment. What I have learnt recently is the tremendous importance of personal relations.'

It is this realisation that shines through every page of these later diaries. In earlier volumes, he only really came alive when talking about mankind as a whole. Now, despite his best efforts, his interest in politics has transmuted into an interest in individual human beings. And through all the pain and sorrow, there is a new kind of freedom in his thoughts and in his writing. He may not have achieved the liberation of mankind, but perhaps he has liberated something almost as difficult: himself.

2

Throughout his political career, Tony Benn had a gift for seeing the sunny side. When Chairman Mao died in 1976, he wrote in his diary: 'In my opinion, he will undoubtedly be regarded as one of the greatest – if not the greatest – figures of the 20th century.' Twenty years later, when it had become clear to the rest of the world that Mao was in fact one of the greatest – if not the greatest – mass murderers in history, Benn mentioned a meeting with the Chinese Ambassador: 'I said, "I'm a great admirer of Mao. He made mistakes, because everybody does, but it seems to me that the development of the countryside and so on was very sensible …"' As it happens, forty-five million died as a result of Mao's enforced famines in the countryside.

Benn hit upon the title of this book* back in 2007. 'Although I may never publish another volume of diaries, if ever I did, I think the best possible title would be … A Blaze of Autumn Sunshine.' But is it the best possible title? He is now ninety years old, so autumn is long gone. Nor is there much sunshine. The one phrase that crops up more than any other is 'I'm depressed'. The runner-up is 'I'm very depressed'.

It remains a remarkable document, perhaps all the more so for having a title so at odds with its content. From the moment he embarked on his diaries in 1940, they were underpinned by an astonishing sense of certainty towards matters both global and personal. You would never catch him saying: 'On the one hand … but on the other.' He was a stranger to self-doubt. But these last diaries read like something out of Samuel Beckett. His legs are wobbly, his hearing has gone; he gets cramp when he tries to write; he finds it a struggle to get upstairs. His old certainties are falling apart; his self-confidence is crumbling; the mind that once outlined a glorious future for the world is now turning, more and more, towards its own death.

One morning, he wakes up choking and thinks: 'Well, this is the moment when it happens, you know … the end.' Another night: 'I had an extraordinary dream that this was the time to die, here and now,

---

* *A Blaze of Autumn Sunshine: The Last Diaries* by Tony Benn (2013).

and I lay wondering if I was going to die, and how long it would be before my body was discovered.'

On New Year's Eve 2007, he writes: 'I feel totally out of sympathy with the Labour Party on civil liberties, on the war, on Europe, and perhaps the only answer is to die, which is an extreme thing to say, but I don't quite know how I'm going to cope.'

Premonitions of death and doubts about the new radicalism are juxtaposed with frequent bouts of celebrititis. When he retired as an MP, he ventured, albeit with protestations of reluctance, into that strange nether world of celebrity, a world in which former Cabinet ministers are happy to act as spear-carriers to the titans of showbiz.

On the very first page, he receives an invitation from Richard Branson and Peter Gabriel to join a meeting of 'Elders' in Africa: 'Mandela's going, Carter's going, Mary Robinson's going.' Oprah Winfrey is someone else who might be there; Richard Branson informs them that he thinks he can persuade Gordon Brown to abandon Trident.

And the celebrities keep on coming. At Hay-on-Wye he meets Mariella Frostrup and Harry Hill; at Tina Brown's launch for her Princess Di book he spots Melvyn Bragg and 'just tons of celebrities'. Along the way he meets Michael Palin, Joan Collins ('caked in make-up'), Jarvis Cocker, Dickie Attenborough ('couldn't have been nicer!'), Annie Lennox, Brian Eno and Gore Vidal ('I think he's gay').

In the foyer of the BBC he spots Liza Minnelli, 'so I went up to her and said, "Can I shake your hand?"' One of his most bizarre encounters is with Bill Clinton, whose book-signing he has queue-barged. First, 'I reminded him of our mutual friend, Saffron Burrows.' Then he tells Clinton that he is thinking of standing for Parliament again, 'and he said, "What a good idea!" Well, I had slipped into my pocket a tape recorder, and I haven't heard it yet, but I think I've got a record of him saying, "What a good idea!" That was a wicked thing to do, but still!'

The next day, there is a ring at the door. 'I opened it up and there was Saffron Burrows! So I gave her a huge hug, and then another hug, and then a kiss and another hug, and she gave me a hug. She said she was going to the Cannes Film Festival.'

For decades, he has tape-recorded his diaries at the end of each day. Until he retired from Westminster, these diaries were all busy, busy, busy, packed with things done and things to do. They were singularly short on self-reflection. But now, like King Lear on the blasted heath, he comes face to face with himself, as if for the first time. 'When I look back on my life, I've been so obsessed with myself all the time – Benn, Benn, Benn, Tony Benn – and actually I'm just not interesting.'

So what have all these millions and millions of words been for? 'I fear that perhaps my diary and my archives are an attempt to prolong my life in some way … I realised – reading it all – that I'm an angry old man. I have been very abusive, and despite all I say about not making personal attacks, my diary is full of them: "he's an awful man", "I loathe him", "he's pompous", "he's arrogant".'

But then, a couple of weeks later, he is at it again, calling Piers Morgan 'that awful man', and, a month later, avoiding the journalist Simon Hoggart, 'whom I loathe'. And some less predictable targets get it in the neck too. He finds Richard Dawkins 'offensive', for instance, and 'I don't really like Jesse Jackson … I don't know why.'

He is also, for the first time in his life, out of touch with some of the key causes of the radical Left: 'I find the general panic which is going on about climate change a bit of a puzzle.' The sweetest moments in these diaries, and the only times when Benn seems truly to feel that blaze of sunshine, are all with his family. 'My thoughts increasingly incline, very simply, towards being the best grandfather that I can be.' Before Christmas 2007, he wraps 140 presents for twenty-eight family members. 'It's an utterly exhausting job and I had to pause and have a rest on the couch.' One day, when he is feeling particularly depressed, his daughter Melissa says: 'You always get depressed in the holidays because you don't get enough attention.'

In the old days, he would never have recorded such an adverse comment in his diaries, which were really a form of glorified CV. But now in it goes, and he even agrees with her ('a very shrewd analysis!'). Melissa then goes on to say, 'Your nanny, Nurse Parker, spoilt you and you've been looking for attention ever since, all the time, and you only get it when you make speech,' and he puts this in, too, adding: 'Well, out of the minds of babes and sucklings cometh forth wisdom ...!'

Is Melissa right? Were all those barnstorming speeches, all those rallies, all those forthright appearances on *Question Time* really nothing more than a yearning for his old nanny's attention? Years ago, Harold Wilson said of Benn that 'he immatures with age'. It was a cruel jibe, but perhaps he had a point. In extreme old age, he has become as defenceless as a child. Only the hardest of hearts could not be moved.

Tony Benn died on 14 March 2014, a month before his eighty-ninth birthday, surrounded by his family. His funeral service at St Margaret's, Westminster finished with the singing of 'The Red Flag'.

Resorting to Jane Austen:
The Diaries of Harold Macmillan

Even in his own day, Harold Macmillan seemed like a throwback to an earlier age. He was Prime Minister when The Beatles were topping the charts, yet he was born in 1894, and severely wounded in the Battle of the Somme.

Like every Conservative Prime Minister since, he gave the impression of embracing change, but his heart lay elsewhere. The modern world was alien to him, and, when times got tough, he would retreat into the literature of an earlier age. 'Sometimes the strain is so awful, you have to resort to Jane Austen,' he once confessed to his colleague Rab Butler.

The beginning of 1962 – the year of the spy scandals and the Cuban Missile Crisis – finds him 'In bed all day, writing, reading, dozing.'* The book he is reading is an 'old favourite' by George Meredith. Its appeal lies in its nostalgia for a time before the First World War, 'for it reminded me all the time of ... the old dead world, in which I had just begun to live and move before it crashed.'

He avoided anything as modern as television. 'I have not looked at any TV,' he confides to his diary. 'Happily, we have not got the instrument ... (except in the Servants' Hall).' Space travel, too, left him cold. 'The Russians have put another man in orbit round and round the Earth and brought him safely back,' he notes in August 1961. 'He seems to have gone round 17 times. It is a wonderful feat of science and technology, altho' I shd have thought it rather dull for a man.'

---

* *The Macmillan Diaries Volume Two: Prime Minister and After 1957–1966* edited by Peter Catterall (2013).

Staying at the White House in 1959, he was obliged to sit through the latest blockbuster movie, *The Big Country* starring Gregory Peck. He could barely contain his boredom: 'We had a film called "The Great Country", or some such name. It was a "Western". It lasted three hours! It was inconceivably banal.'

Reading this diary entry now, I particularly like those stand-offish inverted commas around the word 'Western'. Much of the rest of the language he employs is wonderfully cobwebby. He talks of 'motoring' and 'luncheon', and, on a visit to Africa, finds a couple of African leaders 'unprepossessing'.

Apart from reading (even when he is Prime Minister he gets through two books a week, and he even reads *Catch-22*), his deepest pleasure comes from shooting grouse.

'Yesterday was very fine – just a little wind – a perfect shooting day,' he writes on 19 November 1961, after a week of intense discussions with President Kennedy and General de Gaulle. 'We got 320 pheasants – all very high, many birds were really out of shot. It was wonderful sport. Duke of Roxburghe; Duke of Marlborough; Lord Sefton; Col W. Sterling; Lord Carnarvon; Lord Porchester made together as fine a team of guns as you cd get together in this island.'

It's interesting to compare all this with Tony Blair's autobiography, published last year. 'Wow, I was really freaked out,' Blair writes at one point. This would have read like a foreign language to Macmillan. How strange to think that for three years (1983–6) these two men were both sitting in the Houses of Parliament!

Macmillan's years in Downing Street coincided with the growth of satire, much of it directed at him. The young satirists portrayed him as tweedy and blundering and hopelessly out of touch with the modern world. One of Peter Cook's impressions of him in *Beyond the Fringe* had Macmillan talking about his recent meeting with President Kennedy: 'We talked of Great Britain's position in the world as an honest broker. I agreed with him when he said that no nation could be more honest, and he agreed with me when I said that no nation could be broker.'

One evening, Macmillan went with his son to a performance of *Beyond the Fringe*. 'Very amusing and satirical, tho' not malevolent,' he writes in his diary. 'There were two skits of me and my presence to enjoy them drew applause from the audience.'

Politicians' diaries are as interesting for what they leave out as for what they put in. This entry is particularly telling, because Macmillan makes no mention at all of a little bit of improvisation that Peter Cook tacked on to his monologue the moment he saw Macmillan looking back at him from the audience: 'When I've a spare evening,' he said, in Macmillan's doddery voice, 'there's nothing I like better than to wander over to a theatre and sit there listening to a group of sappy, urgent, vibrant young satirists, with a stupid great grin spread all over my silly old face.'

His fellow cast member Alan Bennett recalled that evening some years ago: 'Macmillan buried his face in the programme, and the audience, out of embarrassment, gradually froze. But this didn't stop Peter. On he plunged.' So why does Macmillan neglect to mention this almost entirely malevolent assault, and pretend that his own squirming reaction was purely appreciative?

He doesn't seem to have written his diary with a view to publication, but more as an aide-memoire for his six-volume autobiography. This suggests that he was hiding the truth of his embarrassing evening at *Beyond the Fringe* from himself as much as from anyone else.

In the same year, the US Ambassador to London wrote a secret character analysis of Macmillan in which he observed that 'His inmost thoughts are seldom open to penetration.' Other entries in these diaries offer further evidence that his easy-going, fuddy-duddy character was almost entirely theatrical, a mask against the world. But what lay beneath?

The US Ambassador added that 'He is a political animal, shrewd, subtle in manoeuvre ... His opponents think him a cold-blooded but formidable individual.' His opponents may have been right. There is a particularly odd diary entry for the historic day of 22 November 1963. Macmillan starts by saying he has read Macaulay's *Essays* ('extraordinary how readable they still are'), and also his *Life and Letters*. He then compares Macaulay to another bachelor, his Cabinet colleague Sir

Edward Boyle ('He knows everything and is a large, boisterous, and rather attractive bachelor – or, shd i say?, maiden aunt').

So far so good. But he mentions going to 'a nice party' at Petworth, and then, almost as an afterthought, adds that 'Just before dinner, we heard the stunning news – overpowering, incredible – of President Kennedy's assassination in Dallas City, Texas.'

And that's that. He devotes much more time and space to musing about a Victorian historian than to the assassination of a President to whom he was, apparently, deeply attached.

This same iciness is evident in his entry for his infamous 'Night of the Long Knives', during which, to save his political skin, he sacked no fewer than seven members of his Cabinet with singular brutality: 'so we set to. In the end, things worked out pretty well,' he begins. After zipping through the multitude of sackings, he concludes, 'Well, it's all over. I am in bed, in mother's old bedroom, looking out into the garden and the woods. It is all very peaceful.' Anyone might think he was writing about a spot of spring-cleaning.

There is virtually no introspection in his diaries. Nor does he ever mention his wife Dorothy's long affair with the caddish Bob Boothby. But every now and then one catches a glimpse of a deep, dark crevasse beneath the thin ice of his charm. On 27 July 1963, when President Kennedy phones him to tell him that the Test Ban Treaty on which 'we have worked so hard and so long' has been ratified, he writes that 'I had to go out of the room ... and burst into tears.'

Three months later, on 14 October 1963, he records: 'I had a rather better night, but very confused dreams and ideas. It seemed to me that everyone was trying to destroy me and were all marching on the Palace, with that purpose. The Queens were protecting me.' Reading this, it occurred to me, not for the first time during these 700-odd pages, that, beneath his unflappable, world-weary persona, Macmillan might just have been scared stiff.

Seventeen Prime Ministers

Tony Blair
Is reluctant to declare:
'I was foolish to embark
On the invasion of Iraq.'

Sir Anthony Eden
Never invaded Sweden;
Thank goodness he knew his
Stockholm from his Suez.

Sir Robert Peel
Had nerves of steel,
Braving schoolboys' snores
To repeal the Corn Laws.

Earl Grey
Was a giant in his day.
No PM achieved more than he –
Yet he's still remembered as a tea.

Benjamin Disraeli
Had a touch of Arthur Daley
Which helped him achieve his goal
Of reaching the top of the greasy pole.

Though John Major
Did his best to assuage her
Edwina Currie
Remained a worry.

Lord North
Called forth
The opprobrium that awaits
Those who misplace the States.

Lord John Russell
Never moved a muscle
To charm; hence,
Offence.

Gordon Brown
Was inclined to frown
Though once an hour
He preferred to glower.

Pitt the Younger,
Prone to hunger,
Says: 'I could eat one of Bellamy's veal pies.'
Seconds later, he dies.

The Earl of Aberdeen
Went from kingpin to has-been
After they got the idea
To blame him for Crimea.

Alec Douglas-Home
Was too polite to fume,
But he disliked being called 'Home'
To rhyme with 'comb'.

Lord Bute
Was condemned as a brute.
The British can't abide a
Tax on cider.

The Marquess of Rockingham
Had a talent for shocking 'em
By nipping off to gamble
Without any preamble.

Theresa May
Had this to say:
'You'll not see me off
Cough! Never! Never! Cough!'

Boris
Seldom quotes Horace
But quote him I must:
'We are but shadow and dust.'

As for Spencer Perceval,
Let's be merciful,
Since it was his lot
To be shot.

Notes: Tony Blair (1997–2007) lost his popularity over the invasion of Iraq; Sir Anthony Eden (1955–7) was undone by Suez; Sir Robert Peel (1834–5 and 1841–6) forced through the repeal of the Corn Laws; Earl Grey (1830–34) introduced the Great Reform Bill, abolished slavery and regulated child labour; Benjamin Disraeli (1868 and 1874–80) said of himself: 'I have climbed to the top of the greasy pole'; John Major (1990–97) had a secret affair with the talkative Edwina Currie before he became Prime Minister; Lord North (1770–82) lost the American colonies, and has remained unpopular ever since; throughout his life, Lord John Russell (1846–52 and 1865–6) demonstrated, in Andrew Gimson's words, 'a capacity for giving needless offence'; Gordon Brown (2007–10) was not known for his sunny disposition; the last words of Pitt the Younger (1783–1801 and 1804–6) were: 'I could eat one of Bellamy's veal pies'; the Earl of Aberdeen (1852–5) had his premiership cut short by the disaster of the Crimean War; Sir Alec Douglas-Home (1963–4) was 'the best-mannered and most unexpected of all Tory prime ministers'; according to Gimson, Lord Bute (1762–3) was 'the most hated Prime Minister of all time', not least for raising taxes on cider; the Marquess of Rockingham (1765–6 and 1782) was an inveterate gambler; Theresa May (2016–19) has never been celebrated for her oratory; Spencer Perceval (1809–12) is the only PM to have been assassinated.

Yankee Doodle Dandy:
The Diaries of Ronald Reagan

There is a fascinating story in the authorised biography of President Reagan, published in 1999. Years before he entered the White House, Reagan went to his adopted son Michael's school for the graduation ceremony. As the students gathered round this famous film star-turned-politician, Reagan would genially hold out his hand and say, 'My name is Ronald Reagan. What's yours?' Walking along a corridor, introducing himself to everyone, he bumped into his Michael by chance. Immediately, he held out his hand and said, 'My name is Ronald Reagan. What's yours?'

Ronald Reagan was one of the most amiable and popular of all the American presidents, but also one of the most remote. In public and in private he radiated bonhomie, but, according to his biographer, he had no real friends other than his adoring wife Nancy. The former Republican Senator Paul Laxalt, one of his oldest allies, remembered Reagan phoning him to thank him for all his help on his successful 1984 re-election campaign, only to pause mid-sentence and audibly turn over the next page of his script.

In her 1992 autobiography, Reagan's daughter Patti wrote that 'Often, I'd come into a room and he'd look up from his notecards as though he wasn't sure who I was. Ron [his youngest son] would race up to him, small and brimming with a child's enthusiasm, and I'd see the same bewildered look in my father's eyes, like he had to remind himself who Ron was.'

On his very first day of his presidency, 20 January 1981, Ronald Reagan started keeping a day-by-day diary – the only diary kept by a twentieth-century president. By the end of his eight years he had written half a million words, of which this hefty volume is a representative selection. 'In these writings Ronald Reagan's true nature is revealed,' writes his editor in his introduction.* 'His uncomplicated and humble notations are on display in these pages: genuine, thoughtful and caring.'

Well, yes and no: his reflections are certainly uncomplicated, but aren't they just a little TOO uncomplicated, too blind to the complexities involved in leading the world's most powerful nation?

This was, of course, the central enigma of Ronald Reagan: how could such an apparently naive, all-American guy not only have made it to the White House, but also become one of the most popular presidents in history?

His diaries certainly do nothing to contradict his image of simplicity. If all the names and events were changed, you would think you were reading the diary of a twinkly old gent in charge of the neighbourhood store. Each day, he doggedly ploughs his way through his

---

* *The Reagan Diaries* by Ronald Reagan, edited by Douglas Brinkley (2007).

list of meetings and speeches before relaxing in front of an old black and white movie with his wife Nancy, whom he calls 'Mommie' throughout. He then catches an early night ('It was a great evening. Then beddy bye').

He invariably seems much more interested in his bedtime movie than in his day's work. He is much keener on old favourites – Errol Flynn in *Robin Hood*, Cary Grant in *Gunga Din*, John Wayne in *Stagecoach* – than in anything more up to date.

He finds *An Officer and a Gentleman* a 'good story spoiled by nudity, language and sex'. *Star Trek III* 'wasn't too good'. Jack Lemmon's *Missing* turned out to be 'a pretty biased slam at Chile and our own government'. *Nine to Five* with Dolly Parton was enjoyable, 'but one scene made me mad'. This was the scene in which the girls get high on pot.

His favourite film of all – he watches it twice in six months – is the patriotic, feelgood *Yankee Doodle Dandy*, starring Jimmy Cagney. It is probably best remembered for the moment when the old vaudevillian Cagney says, 'Where else in the world could a plain guy like me sit down and talk things over with the head man?', to which President Roosevelt replies, 'Well, now, you know, Mr Cohan, that's as good a description of America as I've ever heard.'

In these diaries, the influence of *Yankee Doodle Dandy* on Ronald Reagan's outlook is palpable: as the head man, he is always phoning good, plain guys he has never met, wanting to talk things over with them. These entries find him at his most endearing: he will read a story in his newspaper about a passer-by who has rescued a blind man from between the rails in a subway, or a woman who has managed to catch a baby who has fallen from a second-floor balcony, and then, unprompted, he will pick up the phone to wish them well. Nor does he shirk the more awkward calls: he phones all seven bereaved families in turn after the space shuttle Challenger has blown up. At one point, he phones to comfort a nice black family who have been in the news after being harassed by racists. 'There is no place in this land for hate-mongers and bigots,' he reflects in his diaries, and you feel that this is Reagan at his best, the humble fellow in the White

House wanting to make the world a happier place, a place fit for the movies of his youth.

Homespun folksiness came to him as naturally as breathing. In between talks on the crisis in Lebanon, he goes out on to the White House lawn and picks up acorns. 'I'm going to give them to the squirrels outside the Oval Office,' he writes. Sweetly, he always mentions his birthday ('Happy Birthday to me') and seems genuinely taken aback by each surprise birthday party, even though Nancy lays one on almost every year. Whenever Nancy is away for the night, he complains about feeling lonesome and watches *The Waltons* or *Hart to Hart* before going to bed. (Sleep was always high on his agenda: on the morning of his inauguration, his aide Michael Deaver found him still fast asleep at 9.00 a.m.).

He was also deeply God-fearing, in a way that only an American can be. When Nancy's elderly father, an agnostic, falls ill, he writes: 'I believe this is a moment when he should turn to God, and I want so much to help him do that.'

The day-to-day business of politics failed to excite him in the way that it excited a busy bee like Margaret Thatcher. Each day he records with a kind of bored exasperation the budget overview meetings, the talks on foreign affairs, the committee meetings and greetings of dignitaries. 'I'm getting d--n sick of cramming like a school kid,' he writes before a meeting with the Soviet Foreign Minister. It is only in charting his ovations at public meetings that he really comes alive. Otherwise, there is no zest to these daily lists; they are as dogged and to-the-point as stage directions.

Endearingly, after three years of such routine entries – and this book is, by and large, very, very dull – he confesses that 'I think I've been doing wrong in these diaries.' He has, it emerges, just discovered that the White House already has a record of the schedules he has been so conscientiously listing. 'I guess I should be noting other things so I'll start now.' But in fact he goes on just the same, not really differentiating one meeting from another: President Zia is 'a good man', Jacques Chirac 'a good, sound and charming man', Mother Teresa 'a most remarkable little woman', the Pope 'a great man', Charles and Diana 'very nice', and so on.

These cheery, dozy diary entries would seem almost eerily two-dimensional were it not for the brief glimpses of a third dimension populated by his deeply dysfunctional family. Whenever he mentions his children, it is as though the Corleones were peeping their heads round the front door of the Little House on the Prairie. 'Insanity is hereditary – you catch it from your kids,' he quips, following a screaming match with his daughter Patti. 'I'm not talking to him until he apologizes for hanging up on me,' writes the seventy-two-year-old President, after yet another row with his youngest son. 'She's nuts,' he writes of Patti, while Mike is 'a really disturbed young man'. These glimpses of discomfort are made all the more ominous by the frequency in the text of dots (…) indicating excisions requested by Nancy.

But Reagan never lets his children get to him, just as he never lets the day-to-day problems of his presidency – scandals, invasions, betrayals, bombings, disasters – get to him. He sails through it all with a smile and a wave. And how could you be a successful President if you weren't able to cushion yourself against the impact of real life? In his autobiography, *An American Life*, Reagan recalled his happiness as a young actor on his first day of filming. 'I was completely surrounded by a wall of light,' he wrote, nostalgically. For the rest of his life, he somehow managed to keep that wall of light around him, and the American people were happy to sit back and bask in it.

Titter Ye Not

Who does he remind me of? Watching Donald Trump on television, this question kept nagging me. His strange hair, like an airplane on a launch pad; his camp gestures; his over-expressive eyebrows, so at odds with the rest of his face; his rambling non-sequiturs; his habit of constantly interrupting himself, mid-flow; the way he uses catch-phrases like stepping-stones, to manoeuvre from one topic to the next; his oddball face, part donkey, part chipmunk.

Who does he remind me of?

And then there is the content of his speeches, their defiant outrage borne along on an undertow of self-pity, and the way all his complaints of being got at are underpinned by the conviction that everything is going downhill, and the world is out to get him.

Woe, woe and thrice woe!

Yes, of course! It suddenly struck me that Donald J. Trump* is the reincarnation of the late Frankie Howerd. The two men certainly share a strong physical resemblance. Barry Cryer once memorably described Frankie Howerd's peculiar hair: 'He used to scratch the back of his head when he was talking to you sometimes, and the hairpiece would go up and down like a pedal bin.'

Donald Trump's hair is, in many ways, even more remarkable. So much care and attention has been lavished upon it, and all to such unintended comical purpose. Like Frankie Howerd's, it resembles a

---

* At that point, the 2016 Republican candidate for the presidency of the United States of America.

pedal bin, but a pedal bin that for some reason has been granted the prime spot in the kitchen.

And, for all his boundless self-confidence, Trump shares Frankie Howerd's habit of looking ill at ease in his own clothes. 'Loosen something! LOOSEN SOMETHING!' Howerd would say, tugging the seat of his trousers in the middle of a speech, in a fruitless bid to rejig them. 'There's nothing worse than your knickers out of focus.'

The speeches of the two men share a stop-start quality. They embark on a rambling shaggy-dog story but interrupt their own flow, and then interrupt their interruption. Here is a transcript of Frankie Howerd talking about taking a pair of elephants on the London Underground: 'So I got a bit of string. And, I, um, tied it round their necks, y'see, and I led 'em out into the street! Oooh, I did feel a ninny! I tried to look as if I wasn't with 'em! Anyway. Well! No! But the way people stared! You'd think they'd never seen two elephants going down the Underground before! And I had a shocking – listen! 'Ere! Listen! – Yes! Ye may titter. Titter ye may! – I had a shocking time with 'em down this Underground!'

Compare and contrast this elephant speech with the transcript of a recent rally speech by Donald Trump. Talking at a conference centre in Roanoke, he interrupted his own call to make America great again and suddenly rounded on the venue, saying: 'Everyone's sweating and soaking wet, right? Here's the difference. It's not supposed to be so hot, so what they do is they turn the air con down to save money. But here we are in a ballroom, right, and, right, right, so I don't know what hotel this is but we're not going to get you paid, am I right? It's hot. Just to let you know, I'm really good at this business, you'd be surprised, but this is ridiculous ...'

These two monologues share the same jerky rhythm, the same tone of faux outrage, the same sense of jeopardy: at any given point, the speaker looks like losing the plot.

The politician has his catchphrases, just like the comedian. Donald Trump's include 'I have to be honest' and 'Apparently' and 'You know what?' and 'By the way' and 'It's frightening'. He also pronounces the word 'huge' in a funny way ('Yuge').

Similarly, Frankie Howerd says, 'Oh, please yourselves!' and 'Titter ye not' and 'Shut your face' and 'Not on your nelly!' and 'Nay, nay and thrice nay!' He also pronounces 'Ooh no missus' in a funny way ('Ooooooh! Nywo! Missussss!').

Trump has published a number of books, as did Howerd. Trump's include *The Art of the Deal* and *Think Big and Kick Ass in Business and Life*. The title of Frankie Howerd's autobiography – *On the Way I Lost It* – is just as straightforward, though less forthright. Oddly enough, both the politician and the comedian produced self-help books with the words 'How To' in the title. Donald Trump's was called *How to Get Rich*. And – strange but true – Frankie Howerd's just happens to have been called *Trumps: And How to Come Up*.

POP

In Bowie's Footsteps

Once upon a time, the archetypal professor was an elderly, bespectacled figure who favoured a corduroy jacket with leather patches on the elbows and a bicycle with a wicker basket and no gears. More often than not, he would spend his days puffing on an erratic pipe and shambling about in carpet slippers.

But times have moved on, and so have professors. Last week, Professor Will Brooker, a 'film and cultural studies expert' from Kingston University, popped up on morning television to tell viewers about his latest project. Professor Brooker revealed that he is hard at work on an academic monograph on the subject of David Bowie, to be called *Forever Stardust*.

He told Eamonn Holmes of his research. For a start, he will be reading 'between four and six biographies' of Bowie. By my reckoning, this means five. So, on the reading front, the professor will not be overstretched. But this, it turns out, is only the start. On top of his reading list, he plans to 'live his life as David Bowie for a year to gain a better understanding of the pop icon's mind'. To this end, he will be eating the food Bowie ate, reading the books Bowie read, wearing the clothes Bowie wore and visiting the places Bowie visited.

'The idea', he explains, 'is to inhabit Bowie's head space at points in his life and career to understand his work from an original angle, while retaining a critical and objective perspective at the same time.'

This approach to biography is not entirely new. As the novelist Graham Greene's authorised biographer, Norman Sherry, 'Mitchell Distinguished Professor of Literature at Trinity University in San Antonio', spent twenty-nine years trying to do much the same thing.

Greene had a sadistic sense of humour, and many people now believe that by appointing the dogged Professor Sherry as his biographer he was indulging in a bit of a tease. Early on, he sent Sherry a map of the world with all the places he had ever visited carefully marked in red ink. The gullible professor spent the next seven years travelling to some of the most unpleasant places in the world, among them Haiti and the Congo. He went temporarily blind in Africa and contracted gangrene in Panama. 'I do hope I am not going to be the death of him,' chuckled Greene.

In 2004, the final volume of Sherry's 2,500-page biography was published, to decidedly mixed reviews. Unkind critics wondered whether all that rushing around the world in the footsteps of his subject had resulted in anything more than a mountain of doctor's bills. Ian Thomson in the *Observer* described the finished work as dim, repetitive and 'ludicrously self-aggrandising'.

In many ways, Professor Brooker's trail of David Bowie seems destined to be even more futile. So far, according to the *Guardian*, 'he has been to Brixton, Bromley and Beckenham and plans to go to Berlin next month'. Renting a spiky red wig, Brooker has togged himself up as Bowie's alter ego, Aladdin Sane, complete with lightning-flash make-up all over his face.

Bowie once admitted to having lived on 'red peppers, cocaine and milk' for a few years in the 1970s, so Professor Brooker has attempted to follow suit. He dutifully ate red peppers and drank milk for a couple of days, but chickened out when it came to the cocaine. 'The levels of cocaine Bowie was consuming are not just illegal for a professor like myself,' he explained, 'but it's much too expensive – as well as unhealthy.' Instead, he bought himself a six-pack of energy drinks, and downed them over a weekend. This proved more than enough. 'It made me very jumpy,' he reported.

It's all a bit half-hearted, as though a biographer of Scott of the Antarctic hoping to 'inhabit Captain Scott's head space' had opened the fridge door and stuck his hand inside it for five minutes, or a biographer of Napoleon had donned a French beret, placed a string of onions around his neck and marched up and down the street looking triumphant.

My advice to Professor Brooker would be to change the subject of his academic monograph to someone less tricky. There are plenty of other people born in 1947 – Lord Sugar, for instance, or Camilla Parker Bowles – whose lives would be less demanding in the reliving.

My own choice for Professor Brooker's new subject would be the stocky former Conservative MP Ann Widdecombe, just a few months Bowie's junior, who, like Bowie, used to live in Kent and South London. This would at least mean that Brooker's travels to Bromley and Beckenham wouldn't have been entirely wasted. Widdecombe's no-nonsense, locally styled frocks look more affordable than Bowie's, her make-up and wigs infinitely more straightforward.

Her lifestyle, too, remains a lot less edgy, though in the past few days she has admitted to wearing goggles when frying eggs, a curious practice that might in itself be worth an academic monograph all of its own.

Blinky and The Boss:
Bruce Springsteen

Whether they are written by politicians, pop stars, comedians, novelists or footballers, autobiographies have a tendency towards self-glorification. Most of them tell roughly the same story: Little Me takes on the rest of the world, with the noble, plucky, visionary underdog finally succeeding against all the odds. If it hadn't been for the poor example set by Adolf Hitler, 'My Struggle' might be one of the most popular titles for an autobiography: *My Struggle* by Keith Richards, *My Struggle* by Nick Clegg, *My Struggle* by Katie Price, and so on.

And what of Bruce Springsteen? Born in 1950, he grew up in a working-class town in New Jersey, the son of a sullen, alcoholic car factory worker. The family home had no hot water. As a child Bruce was so nervous that he would blink uncontrollably, leading the other kids to call him Blinky. According to his own account, his voice has always been average, his guitar-playing rudimentary. But for the past forty years or more he has been one of the most successful and dynamic rock stars in the world. It would be strange if there were not a touch of self-glorification, of Little-Me-ism, of My Struggle, within the 500-odd pages of his autobiography.*

Yet *Born to Run* is one of the most unforgiving autobiographies I have ever read, and the person Springsteen finds it hardest to forgive is himself. Within the pages of this book he describes himself as, successively, a control freak and an egotist, gross, bullying and violent, full of rage, fear, distrust and misogyny, self-centred, narcissistic and

---

* *Born to Run* by Bruce Springsteen (2016).

manically insecure. And just when you think that, as he enters old age, he may have found peace and happiness with his wife and three children, he reveals that he has been on antidepressants for the past fifteen years, and his sixties have in fact been 'a rough, rough ride' dogged by black moods when 'I can be cruel: I run, I dissemble, I dodge, I weave, I disappear, I return, I rarely apologise.'

Has any author ever unpeeled his own easy image with such brutal deliberation? To his fans he has always been The Boss, rough, tough, democratic, straight-talking and full of confidence and joy, happily playing for three, four, five hours in his jeans and his cowboy boots, his bandana and his cut-off T-shirt. And he makes clear that this image is no affectation: onstage, he really does turn into The Boss, everyone's favourite brother, the benign master of the universe, just as offstage he reverts, however unwillingly, to Blinky.

He writes with brilliance about the way performing can release you from confusion into a world of joy. Pop stars are, he says, 'strong, addictive personalities, fired by compulsion, narcissism, license, passion and inbred entitlement'. The stage is their oasis, a refuge from the regrets and complications of the world beyond. Onstage, he feels safe; he knows that he can do exactly what is expected of him. 'The shows are an insane high. The adulation, the touring company, the fact that it's all about you … That's why at our shows you just can't get rid of me.' In this respect, if no other, he reminds me of Ken Dodd, who only really felt fully alive onstage, and so was always determined to stay there for as long as he possibly could. Last week in Philadelphia, Bruce Springsteen played for four hours, three minutes and forty-six seconds, breaking the record he had set only the week before. He is sixty-seven years old, and is currently on a seventy-five-venue tour.

In several respects he resembles his hero, Bob Dylan. Both men have an obsessive interest in the roots of popular music, particularly Woody Guthrie and Pete Seeger; both are avid readers of American history; both had serious accidents on motorbikes; both portray themselves as compulsively ambitious men who always felt at odds with the easy-going generations they were meant to represent. By the time he signed his first record deal, Bruce Springsteen, the ordinary downtown, working-class guy, had still never touched a drop of alcohol. Once, when his band came late onstage because they were playing ping-pong, he banned ping-pong, a ban that still holds.

Dylan's memoirs were good as far as they went, but never went as far as they might. He barely mentioned his motorbike accident, for instance, or his childhood and schooldays, or his children, or his religion. It was not until page 230 that he let on that his father ('the best man in the world') worked as an accountant for Standard Oil.

Springsteen, on the other hand, is unflinching in his determination to deal with everything, however uncomfortable – or, rather, the more uncomfortable, the better. Aged seventeen, he crushes his leg in a motorbike accident, and is unable to move for some weeks. His father, who hates his long hair, seizes the opportunity to have a barber come in and give him a short-back-and-sides. 'That was the last straw. I screamed and swore at him. It was the only time I told my dad I hated – HATED – him.'

His father casts his shadow over the entire book, an impotent colossus of silent resentment and frustration and paranoia, a man who believed that the love songs they played on the radio were part of a government ploy to get you to marry and pay taxes. He was, says Springsteen, 'a misanthrope who shunned most of mankind'. He would sit in the corner saying, 'Nobody's any good, and so what if they are.'

Theirs was an Oedipal struggle, the father brimming with 'hostility and raw anger toward his son, the only other man in the house. He felt we competed for my mother's affection. We did.' After drinking, he would unleash 'a flood of self-pitying rage and ferocity that turned our home into a minefield of fear and anxiety'. Springsteen's burning need to seize the day, to take control of his own life and to succeed is a direct reaction to his father's bitter failure.

Some of the most moving passages in the book are those that deal with their attempts at reconciliation. In his late teens, already a jobbing musician, Bruce agrees to accompany his father on a trip to Long Beach, California, to see the *Queen Mary*, the ship that had carried him and his fellow soldiers to the Second World War. 'I was a punk, grumbling my way through the whole *Queen Mary* tour. My dad's journey on this ship was probably the most meaningful of his life and I couldn't respect it. I'd pay anything now to be able to walk that ship with my father again.'

Years later, just before the forty-year-old Bruce, at the peak of his success, has his first child, his elderly father turns up on his doorstep, having driven 500 miles. 'Bruce, you've been very good to us … And I wasn't very good to you,' he says. To which Bruce replies, 'You did the best you could.'

At the height of his fame, he would return obsessively to his home-town of Freehold, NJ. 'I would never leave the confines of my car. That would've ruined it. My car was my sealed time capsule … I rolled through its streets, listening for the voices of my father, my mother, me as a child.'

Half-Irish, half-Italian, Springsteen was raised a Roman Catholic, educated by nuns and priests. 'I know somewhere, deep inside … I'm still on the team,' he says. Immersed in his boundlessly interesting autobiography, it struck me that his songs, with their forceful choruses and their emphasis on suffering and redemption, could be seen as modern-day Catholic hymns. 'In Catholicism, there existed the poetry, danger and darkness that reflected my imagination and my inner self. I found a land of great and harsh beauty, of fantastic stories, of unim-aginable punishment and infinite reward.'

His narrative, too, is quintessentially Catholic: deeply confessional, forthright, labyrinthine, purgatory, sometimes overblown, and awash in the theology of transubstantiation: 'A lot of what the E Street Band does', he writes, 'is hand-me-down shtick transformed by will power and intense communication into something transcendent.' I can't think of a more honest or revealing memoir by any rock musician; in comparison, it makes the efforts of Patti Smith, Keith Richards and Bob Dylan seem buttoned-up and humdrum.

A Gentleman's Life:
Keith Richards

To those born in the 1940s, Keith Richards occupies the same place in their hearts as the Queen Mother did for those born in the 1900s. He is a symbol of stability, the embodiment of easy living, a reminder, in these uncertain times, that some things never change.

He is at least half-aware of his position in public life. 'People love that image. They imagined me, they made me, the folks out there created this folk hero. Bless their hearts. And I'll do the best I can to fulfil their needs. They're wishing me to do things that they can't. They've got to do this job, they've got this life, they're an insurance salesman ... but at the same time, inside of them is a raging Keith Richards.'

Soon to celebrate his sixty-seventh birthday,* Keith actually lives an infinitely more conservative life than most of those who idolise him. He has been off drugs for thirty years. When in London he resides at Claridge's. He has lived in the same house in East Wittering for forty-four years. His ex, Anita Pallenberg, now a doting granny, sometimes pops by with the garden clippers to tidy up the ivy. 'I live a gentleman's life,' he reports.

He is full of nostalgia for his days as a Boy Scout, even jumping to attention when a photo of Baden-Powell comes on the hotel television during a Rolling Stones tour. 'All alone in my room, I stood up, made the three-fingered salute and said, "Patrol leader, Beaver Patrol,

---

* I wrote this in 2010. He is now soon to celebrate his seventy-ninth birthday; he has been off drugs for forty-two years. Anita Pallenberg died in 2017. Marlon Richards is now in his mid-fifties.

Seventh Dartford Scouts, sir." I felt I had to report.' He relaxes by listening to Mozart and reading the historical seafaring novels of Patrick O'Brian. And he employs an Old Etonian, James Fox, as his ghostwriter. Who knows? Perhaps he keeps an Old Harrovian to polish his shoes. He is the Bertie Wooster of rock'n'roll.

'This is my life. Believe it or not I haven't forgotten any of it,' he writes in a red-ink scrawl on the back cover.* In fact, he seems to have forgotten a great deal, though some readers may wish he had forgotten a whole lot more. At getting on for 600 pages, his autobiography proves a bit of a slog, one description of being out of it on heroin (or, as he puts it in his unexpectedly arch, saloon-bar prose, 'consuming substances with more than usual dedication') being much like another.

Now and then, he remembers how much he has forgotten. For instance, on page 206 he struggles to recall 'an acid-fuelled road trip' in 1967 through the West Country with John Lennon and a girl called Kari-Ann. He – or at least his ghostwriter – asked Kari-Ann for her memories, but they turned out to be 'quite different from mine. But hers were at least not almost a total blank, like mine.' On another occasion he left a tape recorder running, only to discover when he woke up that he had written 'Satisfaction' in his sleep.

Though it is larded with the quaint rock'n'roll argot of a bygone age – 'every copper wanted to bust us' etc. etc. – in key respects Keith Richards' *Life* most resembles the memoirs of a major-general, recalling, at interminable length, forgotten raids and fallen comrades. When reminiscing about the battlefield of the 1960s, he is no stranger to self-glorification. He is in love with the idea of himself as the lone commando, single-handedly taking on the enemy forces. 'I'm a guitar player in a pop band and I'm being targeted by the British government and its vicious police force, all of which shows me how frightened they are. We won two world wars, and these people are shivering in their goddamn boots,' he writes, pompously. And later: 'I could never believe that the British Empire would want to pick on a few musicians. Where's the threat? You've got navies and armies, and you're unleash-

---

* *Life* by Keith Richards (2010).

ing your evil little troops on a few troubadours.' All this, after an overnight stay in an English prison!

Keith knows that his doughty band of retired middle-management fans expects him to be laid-back, so laid-back he is, though from time to time he admits to a temper. He once threatened a keyboard player with a knife for drowning out his guitar, and on another occasion beat up the producer Robert Stigwood ('he got the knee, one for every grand he owed us – sixteen of them').

But get him on the topic of Mick Jagger and he becomes almost pathetically un-cool. He claims that Jagger doesn't trust anybody, that he has 'fallen in love with power', that he is too big for his boots, that his singing and dancing have grown 'unnatural' and 'plastic', that he has 'blown his credibility' by accepting a knighthood and even that he has 'a tiny todger'. He even tut-tuts at his promiscuity. His envy is transparent. How it must pain him to realise that Mick Jagger is the main reason most people will buy a book by Keith Richards!

The success of each is, of course, entirely dependent on the other: their solo careers have come to nothing. 'Mick's album was called *She's the Boss*, which said it all. I've never listened to the entire thing all the way through. Who has?' sneers Keith. But which of us could name any of Keith's solo albums?

It is impossible to imagine The Rolling Stones without Jagger, but not so very hard to imagine them without Richards. Even though their last big hit came thirty-odd years ago, they have somehow managed to retain their reputation as the greatest rock'n'roll band in the world. This is all down to Mick Jagger's extraordinary energy and business acumen: had sleepy old Keith been left in charge, they would now be reduced to headlining 1960s revival tours with Herman's Hermits and The Swinging Blue Jeans.

At times, Richards's resentment of Jagger is eerily reminiscent of Gordon Brown's resentment of Tony Blair. It is the envy of the plodder for the thruster, of the back-room boy for the front man. And just as Brown tried to undermine Blair's leadership, so Richards tried to sabotage Jagger's. At the beginning of a concert, Keith would sneak his own musicians onstage; when Jagger arranged for thirty-five dancers to accompany them on tour, Keith fired them all at the last moment, at a total cost of £100,000. 'Sight unseen, I sent them all home. Sorry, girls, go hoof it somewhere else.' It is characteristic of his self-importance that this is a boast, not a confession.

By the end, Keith Richards's claim to remember everything seems very hollow. His character sketches are notably thin. Of Marianne Faithfull, he remembers that she had 'two beautiful jugs' and that she was 'a naughty lady, bless her heart'. Well, fancy that! Small wonder that his Jeevesian ghostwriter has farmed out several pages to those blessed with sharper recall.

The most vivid and moving of these contributions comes from Keith's son Marlon, now in his early forties. His account of surviving a bizarre topsy-turvy childhood is on a par with Esther Freud's *Hideous Kinky* and J. G. Ballard's *Empire of the Sun*. Everything he says is poignant and fascinating.

Aged seven, he was put in charge of waking his father before concerts, because the adults were too frightened of Keith's temper. When Keith was forced by the courts into rehab, Marlon was farmed out to a right-wing religious family. One winter, he stayed with Keith in a vast house on Long Island; the elevator broke, so they stopped going downstairs. When they eventually went down, they saw that the front door had been open, and the whole floor was frozen, with icicles hanging from the chandeliers and his two pet frogs frozen in their tank.

And Marlon was there when the seventeen-year-old boyfriend of his mother, Anita Pallenberg, shot himself dead. Marlon survived car crashes and any amount of neglect (though, tellingly, Mick Jagger was always kind). 'I found the drugs repulsive,' he says. Eventually he decided to get himself an education, emerging with four A-Levels.

Marlon's tale is infinitely more extraordinary and unexpected and genuinely rebellious than the tale of his dreary old dad. Did they ask the wrong member of the family to write the book?

Under My Tum

Over the years, Keith Richards's fans have argued that he is twice the man Mick Jagger ever was. At long last, they have the proof. Much as I enjoyed watching The Rolling Stones live from Glastonbury, I was distracted by the size of Keith Richards's new tummy.

The whole concert was, in its way, like an old-fashioned Spot the Ball competition: viewed head-on, Keith looked his usual self, lean and moody, but every time he moved sideways there was the bump, like a football, or even a Space Hopper, hiding beneath his great tent of an XXL shirt.

On Saturday, Mick looked as skinny as can be; had Keith come onstage before him, I might have guessed that Mick was plotting a surprise entrance by hiding beneath the folds of Keith's shirt, tucked up in there like a baby wallaby.

This overnight tubbiness wouldn't matter with other stars. From its earliest days, pop has always reserved a place for the fuller figure. Bill Haley, who is generally credited with having the first rock'n'roll hit, was always very portly, and the first hit by Fats Domino was 'The Fat Man' (1950), with its chorus claiming that all the girls loved him because he weighed 200 pounds. Closer to our own time, no one expects Elton John, say, or Van Morrison, or Brian Wilson to be svelte. In fact, it would be rather shocking if any of them were to lose weight, just as it was shocking when tubby old Nigel Lawson went on a binge-diet only to emerge, a few weeks later, looking just like Lester Piggott.

But there are one or two rock stars for whom being thin is the be-all and end-all. It would be deeply upsetting, for instance, were Sir Cliff

Richard to start piling on the pounds, as it would suggest that this most self-disciplined of characters had suddenly spun out of control. At the other end of the rock spectrum, Keith Richards has always been treated as the coolest of the cool because he seemed immune to everything – drink, drugs, imprisonment – that life could throw at him. But life at last seems to have caught up with him, after throwing him a bumper pack of pork pies.

Will Keith Richards bring his considerable weight to bear on updating the Rolling Stones back catalogue? With only a little tweaking, the list of tracks on the back of their next Greatest Hits collection might read like this:

1. Sympathy for the Breville
2. Ain't Too Proud to Bake
3. Roast This Joint
4. As Beers Go By
5. Under My Tum
6. Fool to Fry
7. Gimme Shellfish
8. Cherry Cake Oh Baby
9. Can't You Hear Me Slurping?
10. Batter Move On
11. I Wanna Be Your Flan
12. Slumping Jack Flash
13. Let It Burst
14. Big Red Rooster
15. Eggs Benedict on Main Street
16. Sticky Toffee Fingers
17. Far Away Pies
18. Midnight Rumbler
19. Harlem Truffle
20. Sit Me Up
21. Miss Stew
22. You Got the Sliver
23. We Love Chew

24. Tumbling Rice
25. Gooseberry Fool to Cry

Over the weekend, the BBC turned into the GBC, or Glastonbury Broadcasting Corporation, with unavoidable hours and hours of Glastonbury on BBC 2, 3 and 4. At one point, I switched on the television to see what was happening, only to be confronted by a very, very fat man with a red face screaming at the top of his voice, wearing the sort of floaty, silhouette-defying top favoured by Dame Barbara Cartland in her declining years. It turned out to be Johnny Rotten, aka John Lydon, now looking just like the late Sir Cyril Smith would have done had he ever asked his barber in Rochdale for a Mohican, or like the equally late Demis Roussos, if he had shaved off his beard and painted his face bright red.

Might he be the victim of too many extra dollops of all that Country Life butter he used to advertise? He is, alas, another of those rock stars whose image is entirely dependent on skinniness. Now that he has quadrupled in size, he looks less like an angry young rebel than a livid old colonel. Time, I think, for a reworking of those old Sex Pistols hits. 'God Save the Cream' would be an appropriate curtain-raiser, with 'Apple Crumble in the UK' his closing number.

Sixteen Clerihews for Rock's Senior Citizens

Prince
Sports a blue rinse
And grows a little hazy
Singing, 'Let's Go Crazy!'

Madonna
Has new lyrics thrust upon her
For: Hanky Panky
Insert: Cranky Clanky.

Michael Jackson
Has grown so Anglo-Saxon:
Out for a ramble,
He could be Wilfrid Brambell.

Sting
Says of the Police thing:
'If I'd stayed in the public sector
I could have been a Chief Inspector.'

Richard, Cliff
Complains his back's a little stiff
But his ears, he has found,
Can be Wired for Sound.

Richards, Keith
Has several loose teeth
And suffers sore knees
When he falls out of trees.

Richard, Little
Is free with his spittle.
He slooshes the room
Singing Awopbopaloobopalopbamboom.

Mick Jagger
Is prone to stagger;
After an all-night bash,
He becomes Slumping Jack Flash.

Chuck Berry
Likes to make merry
Yelping, 'We sho' havin' fun!'
At the age of eighty-one.

Johnny Rotten
Is gone and forgotten
One might almost say
It's Amnesia in the UK.

Tom Jones
Still moans
'Sex Bomb' at seventy-seven;
And his fans are in very heaven.

David Cassidy
Is a bit of a hazard: he
Can be a world-class bore
Asking, 'How Can I Be Sure?'

Leonard Cohen
Says, 'I must be goin'!
It's four in the morning …
And I can't stop yawning.'

Lou Reed
Has gone to seed:
He was recently spied
Taking a Walk on the Wide Side.

The Bay City Rollers
Switched their baby strollers
For transport which glimmers:
They look great on their zimmers.

Pete Doherty
Puts his hand in his pocket; he
Pulls out some powder
And starts to sing louder.

I wrote this in 2007. Lou Reed, Leonard Cohen, Little Richard, Michael Jackson, Chuck Berry, David Cassidy, Prince and two of the Bay City Rollers have since died.

Orft We Jolly Well Go:
Jimmy Young

The disc-jockey autobiography is a literary genre ignored by literary critics – I don't think I've ever seen one reviewed, anywhere – yet I find myself strangely drawn to them, rather in the way one is drawn to books about fraudsters or serial killers.

'The reward of radio is the total control,' is a revealing aside delivered by the former Radio 1 disc jockey Simon Bates in his autobiography *My Tune* (1994). Disc jockeys share the creepy ability to spend their lives sitting alone in a padded room for up to three hours a day, talking to invisible people who may be listening or not.

Their reward – total control – often spins into their private lives. In his autobiography *The Living Legend* (1985), Bates's former colleague and bitter rival Tony Blackburn writes of splitting up with his wife Tessa. 'I wanted to possess Tessa mind and body, and for her it was all too much. From Tessa I wanted the complete fusion of her life into mine but it wasn't to be … I was short-tempered at work and at home I became like a Jekyll and Hyde character so evil was the spit and malice which spewed out of me.'

Later, Blackburn expresses a preference for jabbering away alone in a padded room over any form of real contact with other human beings. 'I'd like nothing better than to broadcast all day if someone would let me. To me a microphone is another human being I'm holding a conversation with – hopefully an attractive woman.'

When Radio 1 was first launched, Tony Blackburn's show used to precede Jimmy Young's. Blackburn confesses that the two of them did not socialise. 'Jimmy was a lonely character,' he writes, 'and, I was told, a terrible worrier … He knows all the right people but that doesn't stop him worrying that someone will step into his shoes when he goes on holiday.'

In his autobiography, Jimmy Young unwittingly confirms Blackburn's character sketch of him as a neurotic loner.* The book comes steeped in paranoia. 'People who were hired as replacements', he writes, 'were largely figures who would give their eye-teeth to take over my programme, and most of them didn't bother to hide the fact.'

Eighteen years after Blackburn wrote his prophetic remarks, one of Jimmy Young's holiday replacements, Jeremy Vine, did finally step into his shoes, and Young left the BBC in a terrific bate. For all its attempts at merriment, Young's autobiography continues to bubble over with fury at the unfairness of it all. Indeed, the very first words of the book are 'Did I jump or was I pushed?'. True to his disc-jockeying roots, Young then immediately replies to his own question. 'I was pushed … you certainly don't leave 5.75 million listeners who are asking you not to go.'

This statement strikes me as a little shaky. I myself was, from time to time, one of Young's 5.75 million listeners, largely because his counterparts on Radio 1 are so moronic. But that doesn't mean I would ever have thought of asking him not to go. In fact, now that he HAS finally gone,† I find myself much preferring Jeremy Vine – who remains steadfastly unnamed in his book.

Though Jimmy Young boasts of his own 'sense of humour and warmth' and his 'nice soft burr that sounds warm and friendly', I always found him a wee bit creepy, with the kind of automatic warmth reminiscent of those old episodes of *The Avengers* in which Olde Englishe villages come populated with counterfeit grinning locals in yokel smocks, while their real-life counterparts are tied up in a dungeon below. It is just about permissible, I suppose, to say, 'So orft we jolly well go' once or twice in one's life, but were any one of us to repeat it once a day for forty-odd years we, too, might finally crack.

---

* *Forever Young – The Autobiography* by Jimmy Young (2003).

† Gone forever; he died in 2016, aged ninety-five.

Jimmy Young was born in 1921 in the Forest of Dean. This was also the birthplace of the playwright Dennis Potter, and the setting for his masterpiece, *Pennies from Heaven*, which is about a solitary sheet-music salesman who lives a fantasy life, lost in dreams of showbusiness.

Jimmy Young, too, dreamt of showbusiness and found it hard to come to terms with normal life, leaving his first wife and daughter in order to live alone in Surbiton ('I found close relationships very claustrophobic'). Though he had stints helping his baker father with his bread deliveries, and later working for his brother-in-law, Marcel, as a hairdresser, he always longed to be a singer. Eventually, he was taken on by the Northern Variety Orchestra, and his co-singer, Sally Douglas, became his second wife.

In 1955, he became the first British singer to reach number 1 in the hit parade twice in a row. He then left Sally for Jane ('a stunner – a head-turner wherever she went'). But Jane left him when the hit records dried up. 'I took it very badly. I began to drink far too much, and by the beginning of 1960 I was back at rock bottom.'

At this point, he went to an astrologer called Katina who told him that he was due for a change of career. 'You are going to be interviewing people, and you are going to be a tremendous success.' Weeks later, he was invited to present *Housewives' Choice* on the wireless for a fortnight; one disc-jockeying job led to another, and another, and another.

'By the end of 1960,' he recalls, 'the music trade papers were saying such things as "Jimmy Young is beaming with justifiable delight over his recent emergence as an extremely successful and much sought-after disc jockey".' From the evidence of this autobiography, Young is diligent in maintaining a library of all the praise he has ever received from even the most obscure magazines.

Nor, it seems, does he bother to throw away cuttings that have had harsh words for his rivals. He recalls, for instance, how Terry Wogan's television show 'was described by one critic as "dear old Terry, over-exposed and ill at ease in his thrice-weekly television borathon".' Did he cut this out and keep it or – odder still – did he commit it to memory? He does not say, but adds, chummily, 'I'm still convinced that his natural medium is radio.'

There is, it must be said, a strong element of Alan Partridge in Jimmy Young. Both men combine relentless self-advertisement ('I became the first person, on either radio or television, to present a programme live from Dartmoor Prison ... On Christmas Day, I got twice the audience of the person opposite me on Radio 2') with the nagging fear that someone, somewhere is trying to do them down.

Early on, Young jokily remembers how, during his otherwise uneventful military service, he was often picked on ('little Corporal Young was usually the first victim'). But, he adds, 'one such trouble-maker lived to regret it. In the mess there was a stove, and when you stoke up a service stove you work at it until the top is glowing red and almost transparent with white-hot heat ... I uplifted this particular visitor and planted him on the stove. He had to be taken to hospital, but a good time was had by all, as they say in the local papers.'

Jeepers Creepers! Asides such as this make one wonder whether a film of the book might not be forced to carry an 18 certificate. As well as chirpiness and chippiness, Young also shares Alan Partridge's love affair with cliché. All hell breaks loose, there are different strokes for different folks, and 'putting bums on seats is the name of my game'.

Throughout his life, Jimmy Young has met fascinating people and visited fascinating places, but he has precious little to say about them. Japan, we learn, is 'an intensely competitive nation' and Mrs Thatcher was a 'complete professional', while David Blunkett 'has certainly not allowed his blindness to hold back his career'. Of his private life after 1960, he is notably unforthcoming. I suspect that, like Tony Blackburn and the rest of them, he never felt truly alive unless at least 5.75 million people were listening to him.

Blackburn vs Peel:
The Forty-Year Feud

The tiff that has been rumbling between Gordon Brown and David Cameron may simply be a ploy to divert the media's attention from a more seismic rift that has been in danger of splitting the nation these past forty years. I am referring, of course, to the long-standing feud between the followers of Tony Blackburn and the followers of the late John Peel.

Many must have assumed that, following Peel's death in 2004, Tony Blackburn had decided to let bygones be bygones. But far from it: in his new autobiography *Poptastic! My Life in Radio*,* he delivers yet another slug at his deceased rival. 'There I was, waking up the nation with the most uplifting sounds you could possibly hear,' he writes, 'and there was John, bless him, sending them to sleep at the end of the day with a load of old codswallop dressed up as something clever and arty.'

Don't be fooled by that chummy 'bless him'. The wounds are still raw. And he doesn't stop there. Instead, he goes so far as to suggest that Peel knew that it was all 'a load of old codswallop' right from the start, identifying a market niche, and then feigning enthusiasm for the next thirty-six years. 'He chose early on to stay out of the mainstream and build a career on playing esoteric records to a small number of listeners. I remember coming across him once in 1967, sitting alone in a studio surrounded by records. "Have a listen to this," he said in his customary drawl, "What a load of crap!"

'But he seemed to undergo some kind of instant revelation, because he added, "Hey, I think I can make a programme out of this lot." Days

---

* *Poptastic! My Life in Radio* by Tony Blackburn (2007).

later, he was hosting a new, late-night show called *The Perfumed Garden*, in which he spoke in a soft, monotone voice and read out the blurbs from the back of record sleeves. I thought the stuff he played was almost without exception completely awful. I'd call it ELP – as in Extremely Loud and Pretentious.'

At the Sony Radio Awards, John Peel was posthumously awarded the preposterously grand title of Broadcaster's Broadcaster, beating every other broadcaster who ever lived – Alastair Cooke, all the Dimblebys, Alvar Lidell, even Winston Churchill, when you come to think of it. As Peel's widow came to the stage to collect the award, everyone in the hall gave her late husband a standing ovation – among them poor old Tony Blackburn. I was sitting only two tables away, so had a clear view of his face: I can report back that his grin was never more energetic, or so strained.

Perhaps it was the trauma of having to perform this act of obeisance to his sainted rival that led Tony Blackburn to exact revenge in his autobiography. But his irritation has been simmering for much longer.

I must be one of the few people in the world to have read both of Tony Blackburn's autobiographies. In 1985, he published *Tony Blackburn: The Living Legend*, which covers, as one might expect, much the same ground as the new one and is, in most respects, strikingly similar. In it he pioneers his accusation that Peel actually disliked the music he pretended to espouse. The words may be a little different, but the drift is just the same: 'One day I dropped by and heard him playing this new music in the studio and certainly at the time he couldn't make head or tail of it. He kept taking records off the turntable because they sounded so terrible. But that was the start of a cult show John called *The Perfumed Garden*. It wailed through the night hours and in the morning the studio smelled of the incense he burned. He had the same interesting voice then but a good deal more hair.'

But it takes two to tumble: Blackburn was never the sole combatant. In *Margrave of the Marshes* (2005), an autobiography started by John Peel and then finished, as a memoir, by his widow, we discover that 'John used to regard Tony as the anti-Christ, and would do whatever he could to disrupt his programmes.' His widow then recalls that, back in 1970, Tony Blackburn told the *Wellingborough News* that Peel's show spoilt his weekend listening: "'I really think it should be taken off the air," he complained, before condemning the kind of bands favoured by John as "hairy, scruffy individuals, unsociable towards everyone". Perhaps the most striking thing about this reminiscence is that Peel should have kept an obscure cutting from the *Wellingborough News* in a drawer for all that time.

Thirty-seven years later, the war continues. In his most recent autobiography, Blackburn complains that Peel 'never missed any opportunity to snipe at me ... but to me our disagreement was about aesthetics, whereas John continually personalised it. Our strained relationship was a perfect metaphor for what was happening in the pop world: John was on the side of the long-haired, the drop-outs, the students – all those who regarded the three-minute pop single as a blot on the face of culture. I was the happy-go-lucky dispenser of the kind of song that an audience only had to hear once before rushing out to buy it.'

Strange, in a way, to be reading Tony Blackburn on the subject of aesthetics, but he has certainly hit the nail on the head. From the start, the two men stood for two entirely different and opposed types of music. Peel favoured the rough, Blackburn the smooth; Peel the difficult, Blackburn the easy; Peel the ironic, Blackburn the straightforward; Peel the gloomy, Blackburn the catchy; Peel the clever, Blackburn the silly. The groups listed in the index of Peel's autobiography include Half Man Half Biscuit, Captain Beefheart and his Magic Band, Swarm, Napalm Death and Pink Floyd (of whose album *The Piper at the Gates of Dawn* he once said, 'it evokes the sound of dying galaxies'). The groups listed in the index of Blackburn's first autobiography, on the other hand, include The Supremes, The Temptations, The Honeycombs and The Bee Gees.

Comparing those lists, it seems inarguable that posterity will crown Tony Blackburn the surprising victor. Groups like The Supremes and The Temptations which, back in the 1960s, were scorned by Peelite hippies as 'commercial rubbish' are still played by us all, whereas Napalm Death and Captain Beefheart lie untouched in cardboard boxes at the back of the cupboard beneath the stairs. This is the moral: stupid people often get it right. A catchy tune and a simple lyric are at the heart of pop. Anything else dates dreadfully, and the more cutting-edge it seems, the quicker it dates.

And so there our story might have ended, with Peel winning most of the battles, but Blackburn the overall winner in their forty-year war. But hold! We have seen it happen in countless Agatha Christies: just when the villain thinks he's got away with it, he becomes a little too cocky, and inadvertently blurts out some dreadful revelation that leaves the crowd in no doubt as to who the real baddie is.

'If I'm being perfectly honest,' writes the cocky Tony Blackburn in his latest autobiography, 'I'd say that seeing Bobby Vee perform was far more enjoyable than watching The Beatles in their prime. I was never big on Elvis – I prefer Perry Como – and I'll take Alvin Stardust over David Bowie any day.'

How Peel must be chuckling to himself, up there in disc-jockey heaven! Those two short sentences have set the Blackburn cause back some twenty years. If he wishes to regain the ground he has just lost, Tony Blackburn has no choice: working flat out, he might just get that third volume of autobiography into the bookshops by the spring.

The Fragile Life of Mr Epstein

With his polite side-parting, unflashy suits, diffident manner and public-school accent, Brian Epstein appeared much more mature than The Beatles. In interviews he would call them 'my boys' or 'the boys'; they, in turn, would always refer to him as 'Mr Epstein'.

So it comes as a surprise to realise he was only six years older than John and Ringo. In April 1964, when he embarked on this memoir, he was twenty-nine. That same month, the top five places in the American Top 10 were all occupied by The Beatles, and there were a further seven Beatles' singles in the Top 100, along with two songs about them – 'We Love You Beatles' by The Carefrees and 'A Letter to The Beatles' by The Four Preps.

Since February, they had become the four most famous young men in the world. Even Ringo Starr, the least prepossessing of The Beatles, had been made the subject of a song, 'Ringo, I Love You', written and produced by Phil Spector and sung by Bonnie Jo Mason, soon to become more famous as Cher.

Having engineered all this fame, Epstein was clearly in no mood to play it down. In *A Cellarful of Noise* he describes The Beatles as 'a world-wide phenomenon, like nothing in any of our lifetimes, and like nothing any of us will ever see again'. Mixing condescension with a dash of hyperbole, he writes: 'The haunted, wonderful wistful eyes of little Ringo Starr from Liverpool's Dingle are more instantly recognisable than any single feature of any of the world's great states-men.'

A Cellarful of Noise is a period piece. At times the period seems much earlier than the 1960s, exhibiting the muscular snobbery of John

Buchan or Baden-Powell. At one point, Epstein declares that The Beatles 'never sit while a woman stands', and at another that 'their naturalness ... wins them the admiration of people like Lord Mountbatten'. Of one of his artistes, Gerry Marsden, he boasts that 'Princess Alexandra twice requested him for cabaret at society balls'.

Many of his observations about the world of pop are now as dated as the National Milk Bar in Liverpool where he and the boys tucked into four packets of biscuits to celebrate the promise of a recording session at EMI. 'The disc charts cannot stand very many girls,' he writes, 'however gorgeous they may look onstage.'

Nearly sixty years on, The Beatles are still part of the air we breathe, but some of Epstein's other artistes, as he always called them, have vanished without trace. Who remembers Tommy Quickly? Epstein confidently predicts 'he is going to be a star', but, alas, he never was. Taken up by Epstein, he left his job as a telephone fitter, changed his name from Quigley to Quickly, took part in three Beatles tours and recorded five singles, all flops. He retired from the music business in 1965.

Michael Haslam – 'he is, I believe, going to be very big' – had been part of The Beatles' Christmas Show at the Hammersmith Odeon for three weeks in 1963. He recorded two unsuccessful singles, both produced by George Martin, the last of which was to be called, ominously, 'There Goes the Forgotten Man'. Eventually, he fell out with Brian Epstein over an expenses claim for a pair of socks. Epstein let him go, and in 1966 Haslam returned to his £15 a week job on a fleshing machine at Walker and Martin's tannery in Weston Street, Bolton. His fellow workers greeted his return with a jaunty banner that read: 'Welcome Back Mike. Top of the Flops.'

In contrast to the devil-may-care merriment of The Beatles, Brian Epstein cultivated a reserved, fastidious air. He wore a Burberry raincoat, well-polished buckled shoes, gold cufflinks, a monogrammed shirt and a Christian Dior silk tie or a polka-dot cravat. 'He was immaculate from head to toe, like Cary Grant,' recalled Cilla Black. 'He was everything you wanted a posh fella to look like.' His Liverpool tailor, George Hayes, maintained that he always looked as if he'd just stepped out of the bath.

Epstein would have preferred Godfrey Winn or Beverley Nichols, well-manicured household names, to ghostwrite his memoir, but his publisher, Ernst Hecht, vetoed them for being 'far too pricey and the wrong image'. In the end, Epstein settled for Derek Taylor, then a showbiz journalist on the *Daily Express*, but soon to become The Beatles' press officer.

The two men motored down to the Imperial Hotel, Torquay in Epstein's chauffeur-driven Rolls-Royce. Taylor was particularly impressed by the electric windows. 'I'd never seen such a thing.' They got on well. In their first session, Epstein opened up about his uneasy childhood and troubled adolescence, but he hesitated before revealing his deepest secret. There came a point when he realised he would have to broach the subject. Over lunch he suddenly asked, 'Did you know that I was queer?' 'No, I didn't,' replied Taylor. 'Well, I am, and if we're going to do this book I'm going to have to stop buggering about saying I was with this girl when I would not be with a girl, it would be a boy. Does that make any difference?'

It must have been an agonising confession – in 1964 homosexuality was still an imprisonable offence – but Taylor was unfazed. 'No,' he remembered saying, 'it does not make any difference. It'll make it a lot easier. So you mustn't worry any more, difficult as it may be to convince you perhaps, but I won't ever let you down.'

Between the two of them, they conspired to render everything seemly. The book makes no mention of Epstein's sexuality, or the deep torment it caused him. Of his time in National Service, for instance, we hear simply that he was 'the lousiest soldier in the world'. Wearing a pin-striped suit and a bowler hat, he was charged with impersonating an officer and confined to barracks. This caused his nerves to become 'seriously upset'. Psychiatrists decided he was 'a compulsive civilian and quite unfit for military service', so he was 'discharged on medical grounds'.

The truth is both more fraught and more interesting. Stationed at the Albany Barracks in Regent's Park, Epstein had hated his 'hideous' private's uniform and had asked his tailor to run him up a rather more elegant officer's outfit, which he had then worn to cruise the West End in search of young men. At the Army and Navy Club on Pall Mall military police arrested him, and charged him with impersonating an officer. His parents employed lawyers who succeeded in saving him from a court martial. He was eventually discharged for being 'emotionally and mentally unfit' – code for homosexuality.

Elsewhere in the book, Epstein claims: 'I lost a girlfriend called Rita Harris who worked for me and who said, "I'm not going to compete with four kids who think they're entering the big time."' In reality, 'Rita' was a boy.

In unpublished diaries he was much less guarded, confessing that, after leaving the army, 'My life became a succession of mental illnesses and sordid, unhappy events bringing great sorrow to my family'. It now seems probable that his sexuality led to his torment and his torment led, eventually, to his death. John Lennon's schoolfriend Pete Shotton noted: 'Not only was Brian homosexual; he was sexually aroused by precisely those traits that otherwise most affronted or menaced him: qualities like vulgarity, insolence, callousness and aggressiveness, all so abundantly on display in the persona of The Beatles' rhythm guitarist … Brian Epstein was irredeemably mesmerised by the one whose demeanour most resembled that of a caged animal.'

True to character, John Lennon taunted him about the memoir. When Epstein was wondering out loud what to call it, Lennon said: 'Why don't you call it "Queer Jew"?' Later, when Epstein said it was called 'A Cellarful of Noise', Lennon replied that he would be better off calling it 'A Cellarful of Boys'.

The self-portrait in *A Cellarful of Noise* may be partial, but it is not untrue. Epstein portrays himself as lonely, businesslike, scrupulous, obsessive, shrewd, awkward and pernickety, all of which he was. Now that we know how his story ended, the odd phrase flashes on the page like a fork of lightning. Quite late in the book, he confesses that the strain of being in sole charge of management 'continues and increases and thrives like a malignant disease'. On the next page, he talks of the pressures he is under. 'The chief of them is loneliness, for ultimately I must bear the strain alone, not only in the office or the theatre, but at home in the small hours.'

He was fanatical, in both senses of the word. When he writes, 'I can think of no warmer experience than to be in a vast audience at a Beatles concert', he is guilty only of understatement. The four Beatles were everything he could never be. He told an interviewer in 1964 that The Beatles 'represented the direct, unselfconscious, good-natured, uninhibited human relationships which I hadn't found and had wanted and felt deprived of. And my own sense of inferiority evaporated with The Beatles because I knew I could help them, and that they wanted me to help them, and trusted me to help them.'

Simon Napier-Bell, the manager of The Yardbirds, Wham and many others, once recalled Epstein telling him that at a Beatles stadium concert in America 'he went into the crowd of girls and he just screamed like one of the girls, which he said is what he'd always wanted to do from the first minute he'd ever seen them. He had spent his

whole life being restrained and wearing suits and suddenly he just screamed and became the mad fan he wanted to be.'

John, Paul, George and Ringo sometimes went wild, and sometimes behaved foolishly, but they were always able to adapt and move on. They were survivors. Each of them was equipped with a safety valve. But for all his extraordinary abilities, for all his carefully buttoned-up exterior, Brian Epstein was not. He could manage others, but he could never manage himself; he lived in perpetual jeopardy. He took drugs – uppers, downers, acid, heroin, coke – far more recklessly than his boys, and was known to gamble away £20,000 in a single night. Nor could he resist picking up the type of young man who would steal from him and beat him up and blackmail him.

'Eppy seems to be in a terrible state,' John told Pete Shotton one night. 'The guy's head's a total mess, and we're all really worried about him.' John then played a tape. Pete described it as 'one of the most harrowing performances I've ever heard', adding, 'The recording was barely recognisable as that of a human voice, alternately groaning, grunting and shrieking words which, even when decipherable, made no apparent sense whatsoever. The man on the tape was obviously suffering from great emotional stress, and very likely under the influence of some extremely potent drugs.'

'What the fuck's all that John?' I said incredulously.

'Don't you recognise the voice? That's Brian. He made the tape for me in his house. I don't know why he sent it, but he's trying to tell me something – fuck knows what. He just can't seem to communicate with us in his usual way any more.'

Three years after the publication of *A Cellarful of Noise*, on Sunday, 27 August 1967, Brian Epstein was found dead in the bedroom of his house in Belgravia. Two brief suicide notes were discovered, hidden away in a book, but they were both dated several weeks before. At the inquest his psychiatrist, Dr Flood, reported that 'his main complaint was insomnia, anxiety and depression'. Epstein had, he said, 'always shown some signs of emotional instability ... The patient was homosexual, but had been unable to come to terms with this problem.'

Recording a verdict of accidental death, the coroner said that it was due to poisoning by the sedative Carbatrol, caused by an incautious self-overdose.

Together, The Beatles went round to comfort Brian's mother, Queenie. They wanted to attend his funeral, but Queenie dreaded it turning into a media circus, and thought it best if they stayed away. 'They were like four lost children,' she recalled.

In the vast Beatles Story Museum in Liverpool, just around the corner from a cabinet containing the four Sgt Pepper costumes, and housed in a glass case of its own, stands a dapper knee-length blue coat with three shiny buttons. It dresses a headless mannequin. A little triangle of sharp white shirt and a Paisley tie poke out through the top. The caption on the cabinet reads: 'Brian's wool and cashmere coat made by Aquascutum of Regent Street'.

Had he lived, Brian Epstein would now be pushing ninety. He would probably have controlled The Beatles Story Museum, and ensured The Beatles a decent share of the profits. He would undoubtedly have expanded his empire. Over the past fifty-odd years, society's misgivings about his homosexuality would have transformed into qualifications. By now he would be Sir Brian Epstein, or perhaps even Lord Epstein of Belgravia, a valued board member of the Garrick Club, Tate Modern and the Liverpool Institute for Performing Arts.

Instead he lies buried in Everton cemetery, while his Aquascutum coat, spick and span as ever, retains a life of its own, resplendent under a spotlight in a smart glass case, admired by 300,000 people a year. It is a modern relic, or, in sacramental terms, an outward sign of inward grace. In gold letters, embossed on the bottom of the case, is a quote from Paul McCartney: 'If anyone was the fifth Beatle, it was Brian.'

BAD HATS

The Man Who Wasn't There:
John Stonehouse

November 1974 was the month to vanish. On the 7th, Lord Lucan went missing, and a fortnight later John Stonehouse MP disappeared from a beach in Miami. Lucan was never found, so remains prominent in our national mythology. Nothing endures like a mystery. Stonehouse, on the other hand, was discovered in Melbourne six weeks later, living under an assumed name. His vanishing trick, so carefully rehearsed, had unravelled – partly due to Lucan, as it happened. Having been alerted to a suspicious Briton by a beady bank clerk, the Australian police thought he might be Lucan. Their first act after arresting their suspect was to lift his trouser leg to look for the missing earl's telltale scar.

Stonehouse had long had a tendency to vanish. In a diary entry written five years earlier, Barbara Castle complained that, just when she needed him, Stonehouse had 'disappeared'. Eventually he was tracked down, and Castle told Roy Hattersley not to let him out of his sight. Stonehouse remained, she wrote in the same entry, 'smooth and enigmatic as ever'.

There was something ghostly about him, something not-quite-there, as if he might put on a fresh identity as others might put on a new suit. I first met him in the House of Commons, after he had returned from Australia under police escort to face trial on twenty-one different charges of theft, fraud and deception. As an ambitious teenager reading drama at Bristol University, I had been in touch, suggesting I write a play about him. By this time he had left the Labour Party, and was identifying as a victim of the Establishment. In his resignation letter to the Leader of the House, he explained that 'the long traumas I suffered were caused by a deep disillusionment with the state of English society and the complete frustration of the ideals I have pursued in my political and business life'.

His supporters being thin on the ground, he invited me to meet him in the House of Commons. As we walked along the corridors of Westminster, he greeted passing colleagues with an ostentatiously chummy 'Hello, Bill' and 'How are you, Jim?'. In return, they kept staring straight ahead and said nothing. It was like being with a ghost only I could see or hear. To them he was the spectre at the feast, the MP who had pursued the common middle-aged fantasy of living another life in another place as someone else. And now the vanishing man had come back to haunt them.

Yesterday upon the stair,
I met a man who wasn't there.
He wasn't there again today,
I wish, I wish he'd go away.

The next time I saw him was at the Old Bailey. He was conducting his own defence, cross-examining a series of bank clerks, forever referring to himself in the third person ('and when did you first encounter Mr Stonehouse?'). Once again, this added to the impression that he wasn't really there, or that he was there, but as someone else. His closing statement from the dock – the longest in British legal history – lasted six days.

The gist of his defence was contained in the title of the memoir he had rush-released a few weeks earlier: *Death of an Idealist* (1975). If he did anything wrong, it was the result of a mental breakdown, a split personality, caused by the clash between his own lofty ideals and the moral turpitude of a sick nation. 'This country!', as Alan Partridge once complained, having just stubbed his toe.

In *John Stonehouse, My Father* (2021) his eldest daughter, Julia, loyally embraces this offbeat defence. She won't hear a word against her late parent, describing him successively as 'tolerant, supportive and amusing', 'highly conscientious and hard-working' and 'a hero'. If his businesses, which had shady catch-all names such as Export Promotion and Consultancy Services and Ambulant Finance, were in a dodgy state, that was because he had been too charitable, too trusting, too keen to keep them afloat for the good of mankind. Those who took against him – journalists, the police, MPs, the Old Bailey judge – were motivated by malice. At one point she suggests that his parliamentary colleagues envied him because he was so attractive to women – and 'jealousy all too easily turns to hate'.

The Stonehouse family endured a terrible shock. For six weeks they were grieving for him, only finding out he was alive when the *Daily Mirror* phoned them with the news on Christmas Eve. But Julia barely mentions herself or her feelings at the time. Instead, she offers a clear, dispassionate and selfless chronicle of the full extent of her father's crimes and misdemeanours, while simultaneously absolving him of all blame. The more devious his behaviour, the more she finds it so 'completely out of character' that it is proof of a mental breakdown, brought on by the purity of his ideals, all crushed by the moral corruption of virtually everyone else.

But has anybody ever prepared for their own mental breakdown with such diligence, such attention to detail? Copying the methods employed by the hired assassin in Frederick Forsyth's *The Day of the Jackal*, Stonehouse had phoned a hospital in his constituency, saying that he wished to distribute money to young widows. Could they give him the names of married men who had recently died? He then dropped in on two of these widows, Mrs Mildoon and Mrs Markham, and with his soft-spoken, sympathetic manner wheedled enough information out of them to apply for passports and bank accounts in the names of their late husbands. 'It's so out of character for the John Stonehouse we knew, we can only attribute it to madness, one symptom of which is that the person does mad things,' explains Julia, employing dizzying, Escher-like circular logic.

She charts her father's meticulous preparations – countersigning passport photos with the forged signature of a dying colleague, siphoning all the money from the bank account he shared with his wife Barbara into the brand-new accounts of Markham and Mildoon, rehearsing his 'drowning' on Miami beach, taking out five last-minute life insurance policies – without ever entertaining the idea that they could be proof of perfidy rather than insanity. Geoffrey Robertson, briefly engaged for his defence, was later to conclude: 'If it were madness, there was too much method in it ever to convince the jury.' But Julia is having none of it: 'With that kind of support, no wonder my father decided to defend himself.'

On hearing of her husband's arrest, Barbara flew to Australia, to be joined shortly afterwards by his pretty young secretary Sheila Buckley, with whom he had been conducting a secret affair for five years. When Barbara told him that if Sheila also flew out she would leave, Stonehouse grabbed her by the hair, flung her to the floor and banged her head up and down, shouting: 'What can't you understand?' Their son Mathew, aged fourteen, managed to pull him off, screaming: 'Stop it, Dad, stop it!' Mathew then told his mother to go into the kitchen and shut the door. When Barbara tried calling her husband's psychiatrist, Stonehouse snatched the phone, beat her head with it, then put his hands round her throat and hit her hard against the wall. Julia provides all this damning evidence, and then declares it to be further proof of his innocence. His personality had split in two. His behaviour was 'so out of character it was frightening'.

The jury refused to swallow it, and found him guilty. Mr Justice Eveleigh declared: 'It is clear to me that self-interest has been well to the fore. You aimed to get rich quickly. You falsely accused other people of cant, hypocrisy and humbug when you must have known all the time that your defence was an embodiment of all those three.'

Stonehouse was given seven years but, two heart attacks later, was out in three. He married Sheila and they had a baby. It was almost the life he might have enjoyed in Melbourne had he never been caught. I went to dinner with them in their small flat in Queen's Park. By then Stonehouse had followed Jeffrey Archer into writing thrillers, though without the financial rewards. Like Archer, he had a habit of looking you straight in the eye for perhaps a little too long, jutting out his chin to indicate resolution, trust and integrity.

'John's very serious about his novels,' explained Sheila, who sometimes got her words muddled up. 'He wants to write for prosperity.' They got on well. I asked them to my cottage in Suffolk. John said they'd prefer to wait until the end of summer: 'Sheila and I are keen blackberriers,' he explained. In its way, *Blackberrying with John Stonehouse* seems as incongruous an idea as *Making Cocoa for Kingsley Amis*, but he seemed at peace as he searched hither and thither among the hedgerows.

The last time I saw him was quite by chance. Working on the *Sunday Times* Atticus column one November, I chummed up with the poet Paul Muldoon at a launch party and he came with me to my next port of call, an event at Stringfellows, the saucy nightclub in Covent Garden. Who should be there but Stonehouse, sipping champagne with the mullet-haired Peter Stringfellow, the two of them sandwiched between a couple of vivacious hostesses who were certainly not dressed for the cold.

Years later he would be named as having been a spy, taking money from the Czechs for passing on secrets. Julia is adamant that this accusation is also false – the sloppy invention of a dodgy defector, Josef Frolík, 'a known liar'. She argues her case well; but whether or not it was true, Stonehouse was defenceless: 'A miasma of suspicion and contempt fell over my father and he was doomed.'

Who knows? Perhaps he had just been disappearing into other people, trying on more characters to see if they would fit. His final disappearance came after another heart attack in 1988, at the age of sixty-two. His last words were: 'Sheila, tell me you love me.'

Four Cambridge Spies

Kim Philby
Rarely wore a trilby
Though he'd hanker
After a ushanka.

Sir Anthony Blunt
Did not fish, shoot or hunt.
But if he spotted a hole
He'd make a noise like a mole.

Guy Burgess
Was possessed by urges
To yell from on high
'Coo-eee! I'm a spy!'

Donald Maclean
Made the same mistake over again:
He'd travel miles and miles
But forget his secret files.

Never Need a Reason, Never Need a Rhyme: Alan Clark

The audiotape of the *Alan Clark Diaries* – barely mentioned in this rather Dr Watson-ish, sensible shoe of a biography* – is well worth hearing. Alan Clark narrates it himself, in a wonderfully high-camp, pantomime manner, reminiscent of Kenneth Williams reading the *Just William* stories.

It's a rib-tickling comic turn, and adds a new dimension to the original book, an additional mirror reflecting on the first mirror at a jaunty angle. Clark's semi-parodic tone acts as a sort of wry critique on the diaries, which are themselves, of course, a wry critique on his life. Observing himself observing himself, Clark uses every inflection of his voice to bring out the humorous and the grotesque, the essential absurdity and self-delusion of Clark the anti-hero.

In the past few weeks, there have been grumbles from Alan Clark's old enemies, fed up with all the praise flying in his direction. 'Alan Clark was not wonderful,' wrote Dominic Lawson in the *Independent*. 'He was sleazy, vindictive, greedy, callous and cruel.' So he was, but then so, too, was Samuel Pepys; perhaps even more so. Unlike Clark, Pepys blacked his wife's eye, pulled her nose and called her a whore, as well as threatening to throw the family puppy out of the window when it peed on the carpet. Alas for Dominic Lawson, posterity forgives such bad behaviour, and even relishes it, just so long as its perpetrator keeps it going long enough and then makes his confession sufficiently lively.

How many robust, well-argued speeches in the House of Commons on matters of grave importance, delivered down the centuries by intel-

---

* *Alan Clark: The Biography* by Ion Trewin (2009).

ligent and passionate MPs, are now forgotten? Yet Alan Clark's tipsy ('We "tasted" first a bottle of '61 Palmer, then "for comparison" a bottle of 75 Palmer then, switching back to '61, a really delicious Pichon Longueville') rendering ('at 78 rpm instead of 33') of the Equal Opportunities Order in July 1983 will be long remembered, just as Gussie Fink-Nottle's speech to Market Snodsbury Grammar School is remembered, and for much the same reason. Unfair it may be, but, in the words of the song, when it comes to a diarist, 'It's not what you do, it's the way that you do it – that's what gets results.'

The first half of this biography, dealing with Clark's life before Westminster, is much the more interesting. In the second half, his biographer is obliged to go over ground already covered in the published diaries, often elbowing out their essential jokiness to make way for dogged paraphrase. He sometimes seems a little clod-hopping, a little slow on the uptake, so that the reader finds himself screaming 'Behind you!' For instance, Trewin writes of Clark's account of the fall of Margaret Thatcher, 'Not that those involved accept his every word as gospel – did he, they ask, allow his own bias to show through?' To which one simply wants to scream, 'Of course he did! Don't you realise? That's the whole bloody point!' And did Trewin really have to employ someone called Renata Propper, 'a graphologist who lives in the United States', to drop in regular 'A Doctor Writes' banalities concerning his handwriting over the years ('A man of some brilliant ideas, he was more of a thinker than a doer, although he had some enterprising spirit and motivating ambitions')?

Clark's *Diaries* tell their own story, so once they get going there's very little else to add. After all, they were hardly a cover-up job. Indeed, Clark loved spilling the beans all over himself, and took a Flashman-like delight in his own infidelities, mad fantasies, deceptions and skulduggeries. In criminal terms, he turned himself in, on a daily basis. So Trewin is denied the biographer's traditional role as copper's nark.

Those who continue to go goggle-eyed at the very idea of an Englishman actually enjoying sex will probably lap up all the details of Clark's affair, or near-affair, with his secretary. And there is a gossipy pleasure to be gained from reading the victim's unexpectedly prim remonstrances ('My future lies with someone else who has a surfeit, unlike your poverty, of principles. I am sad that you wore away some of my own, and lowered me in some respects to your level, but I, at least, am young enough to change my ways'). On the other hand, news of Alan Clark's extramarital affairs, like news of a postal strike or of the Queen Mother's joie de vivre, does lack a certain shock value.

Clark was forty-six when he became an MP ('at the age when most people start "slowing up" I suddenly gain a job'). At this point, his published diaries kick in and his biography loses its raison d'être. However, Trewin's account of Clark's prolonged youth is fresh and illuminating. His snobbery stood on shaky ground. Though he didn't have to buy all his own furniture, his great-grandfather, the founder of a cotton thread business in Paisley, certainly did; Alan's father, Lord Clark of *Civilisation*, only bought their stately home, Saltwood Castle, when Alan was twenty-four.

His parents were at the hub of arty-smarty society. As a child, Alan mixed with Edith Wharton, E. M. Forster, Henry Moore and Nancy Mitford. William Walton was in love with his mother. For four years he was an only child, but then twins came along and he 'had to stamp and yell if he wanted attention'. At lunch with, among others, Ivor Novello, Sibyl Colefax and Binkie Beaumont, his sister recalled the sixteen-year-old Alan showing off by trying to balance a glass: it fell and broke. This chronic attention-seeking lasted a lifetime, as did his other childhood fads for hypochondria (throughout his life he kept a thermometer and a sick bowl by the side of the bed 'just in case') and battles (as a schoolboy, he subscribed to *Jane's Fighting Ships*). The only teenage pursuit he seems to have abandoned in later life was stamp-collecting.

One contemporary recalls feeling sorry for the young Alan at Eton because his father 'was such a vulgar character': Kenneth Clark would, it seems, drive down to school in a yellow Rolls-Royce, puffing on a Havana cigar, like someone in an H. M. Bateman cartoon. Alan inherited his father's passion for flash cars, and greatly multiplied his natural inheritance of vulgarity. I barely knew him, but he once invited me to a summer party at the House of Commons. The guests were as naff as can be: most of them seemed to have stepped out of the pages of *TV Times*, and at least half of them had their own quiz shows.

'Why isn't Michael Winner here?' I asked him, having feasted on a glass too many of his champagne.

'Why do you ask?' he said, a little warily.

'Because every other awful person in London is', I replied.

Clark executed a half-smile. 'Well, to be honest, I did invite him, but he had to go to a premiere in the West End.'

But vulgarity is not to be sniffed at. Without it, he would never have been such a brilliant diarist, for what could be more vulgar than indiscretion? He once wrote a letter to his agent, Michael Sissons, in which he announced: 'All publishers have got one great prize to look forward to, and that is my witty, revealing, salacious and enlightening memoirs … I already know enough about the internal workings of the Conservative machine to write a really appalling book.' Remarkably, he wrote this back in 1973, before he had even entered Parliament.

On his first day there, he was hailed in the Strangers' Dining Room 'with incredible hurrahs' by his fellow Old Etonian, Jeremy Thorpe. It would make the perfect opening number in *Alan Clark: The Musical*, the pair of them executing a Dick Van Dyke dance ('never need a reason, never need a rhyme, kick yer knees up, step in time!') in their fancy waistcoats.

Over the years, the House of Commons was to provide him with the perfect platform on which to smash more glasses. He could then retire each night to describe, in tranquillity, the mess he had just created. Would he have got further in politics had he never had the need to fuel a diary? Was his diary his downfall? A diarist, particularly a knockabout diarist like Clark, feeds off calamity. Without enough calamity, he will have to generate more by saying or doing something appropriately inappropriate. High-flying politicians have a much stronger capacity for dullness.

But having created his bad-hat Captain Hook character (Hook was, incidentally, another OE), Clark was obliged to carry on playing it to the end. 'In writing it down, he detached himself from the self who acted out the scene,' wrote Claire Tomalin of Pepys. It was true also of Alan Clark. As he lay dying, he seems to have drawn solace from this dual perspective: it allowed him, in the most awful circumstances, to detach himself from his cancerous body, and to look down at himself and smile. His entry for 12 July 1999 reads: 'The stage hands are fiddling about with the curtains.' That's a very Alan Clark sentence: self-aware, poetic, funny and true. Less than two months later, he was dead.

The Greatest Oprah Winfrey Interviews of All Time: (2) Jaws

OPRAH: Thank you for inviting me to your lovely home in the sea.

JAWS: You're welcome. It's a pleasure.

OPRAH: You look great! And your smile! Those famous teeth! And, oh, my goodness – so this is the famous blue ocean off Amity Island! Tell me about your days as a baby shark. Did other fish, maybe the tuna or dolphins, ever call you names? Fish can be so cruel.

JAWS: Yeah [*looks downcast, lower jaw trembles*]. Now I'm getting all choked up.

OPRAH: Take your time.

JAWS: Yeah … in fact, it was they who first called me Jaws.

OPRAH: Mm-hmm. So what was your real name? What did your mom call you?

JAWS: Giles.

OPRAH: A beautiful name. Did it break your mom's heart when you told her the other fish were calling you Jaws?

JAWS: Uh-huh.

OPRAH: Take your time. So let's move on to 1975. It was a hot, hot summer, here on Amity Island. You were – what? Just enjoying basking in the warm water, taking it easy, like everybody else? Were you even inside your body at that time?

JAWS: No, I didn't have many people inside my body at that time. See, I was on the 5:2 diet. But then someone … made me cry, claiming I'd eaten an adult holidaymaker.

OPRAH: Wh-what? Let me get this right. They said … you'd eaten an adult holidaymaker?

JAWS: Right. When really the reverse happened.

OPRAH: Explain what you mean by that …

JAWS: She – the holidaymaker – tried to eat me. And that hurt my feelings. But I don't want to get into the detail. I just felt a little nibble, so I had to retaliate.

OPRAH: Mm-hmm. Like anyone would in that position.

JAWS: As you say, like anyone would. And that was when … Police Chief Brody started putting out nasty information against me.

OPRAH: Notices appeared all over town saying things like 'Don't go in the water, Jaws will eat you alive' and 'Danger: Jaws'.

JAWS: Yeah. I was just doing my job, swimming and smiling, showing my lovely white teeth. It was, like, character assassination.

OPRAH: You must have been hurting. What was going on with you, internally, at that time?

JAWS: You mean, digestion-wise? I found those Lycra swimsuits a problem.

OPRAH: No one wants to be accused of eating people alive. That's hurtful.

JAWS: Right. Then I heard they'd put a $3,000 bounty out on me.

OPRAH: Wh-what? Say that again! Whoah! I'm shocked!

JAWS: And I would sit up at night, thinking, like, how can this be happening? And my mom and my friends, they were calling me, crying, saying: 'Giles, this is doing nothing for your reputation as a shark. How can they let this happen?' At some point you're going to go: 'But, you guys, someone just tell the truth.'

OPRAH: You have your own truth. Not only that, but you have your own tooth. Am I right? And, as a shark, you have to learn to love yourself.

JAWS: Right. I was always there for the tourists and holidaymakers. I wanted to reach out to them. I loved them all to bits. To little bits.

OPRAH: So you must have hurt when you read those headlines in the *Amity Gazette*, saying 'Jaws Weighs Three Tons'.

JAWS: It was fat-shaming, pure and simple. And, like, I'm speaking as someone who's had issues with his body image. Over that summer I'd been working on my beach body, through swimming and exercise, and cutting down on tourists, just eating the little ones. So I'd got my weight down to 2.8, 2.7. I was so proud. So that's when they print these doctored photographs making me look like an XXL and claiming I'm, like, over 3 tons.

OPRAH: Hold up! No one should have to go through that!

JAWS: Then my friends told me Police Chief Brody had sent three men to chase after me in a boat armed with rifles and harpoons.

OPRAH: Wh-what?

JAWS: And whenever I appeared, he'd make sure that this horrible, threatening music was played – like, da-da-da-da-DUM-DUM! – to make people think I was some kind of threat.

OPRAH: Mm-hmm.

JAWS: When – hey! – I was just dropping by to say 'hello'. But no one thought to say: 'Thank you for all your hard work patrolling the ocean.' All I ever wanted – sob! – was to make them proud.

OPRAH: Thank you for trusting me to share your narrative.

Onion Scrubber

'Those whom the gods wish to destroy', runs the proverb, 'they first make mad.' But how to make them mad? How about setting them on the trail of Jack the Ripper?

There are five or six books a year published about Jack the Ripper. They have titles like *Case Closed* and *The Final Solution*. Each of them promises to reveal the Ripper's true identity, until the next book comes along. He was a policeman; he was a doctor; he was a clergyman, a barrister, a fish porter, a journalist. He was an American; he was a Freemason; he was a Jew. He was a she. He was King George V's brother, Sir Winston Churchill's father, Queen Victoria's physician.

One author argued that he was Dr Barnardo ('of that, there can be no doubt'). Another was convinced, just as fervently, that he was Lewis Carroll, and singled out phrases from *Alice's Adventures in Wonderland* which contain anagrams that point to a full confession. Fourteen years ago, the American crime novelist Patricia Cornwell published *Portrait of a Killer: Jack the Ripper – Case Closed*, pointing her finger at the versatile English painter Walter Sickert. She spent $2 million on research, buying thirty-two of his paintings and cutting one of them into pieces in the vain hope of finding a clue. When her theory was dismissed by British critics, she bought full-page advertisements in the *Independent* and the *Guardian* begging that her work be taken seriously, and arguing that the Ripper's victims 'deserve justice'.

And now comes the longest, and maybe the oddest, of them all.* Bruce Robinson, the author and director of the classic British comedy

---

* *They All Love Jack: Busting the Ripper* by Bruce Robinson (2015).

Withnail and I, has spent the past twelve years and £500,000 researching and writing the 800-page *They All Love Jack*, which is confidently subtitled *Busting the Ripper*. It is a strange, mind-boggling mixture of pedantry and craziness in which Robinson's attempts to set out his extraordinarily complex argument in sober, rational terms are continually undermined by sugar-rushes of sudden mad invective. 'So look out, Jack!' is the way in which he concludes his introduction. 'We're stepping off the kerb, and I'm going to bust your arse.'

Anyone coming blind to the book might think it a collaboration between Dr David Starkey and Johnny Rotten. Among the principal characters, we are told that Prince Albert Victor was 'this effete little useless pederast', the Chief Constable of Bradford a 'fucking idiot', the Commissioner of the Metropolitan Police 'a self-serving idiot', Lord Kitchener 'belonged to Satan', the Earl of Euston was 'a classic pile of shit' and the Home Secretary 'a rotten little whore'.

It could be argued that these frequent bouts of Tourette's add drive to what might otherwise have been an impenetrable maze of rumour, speculation and conspiracy. But they also undermine Robinson's credibility as a disinterested historian, and his ability to build up a convincing case, particularly as the story he tells is as far-fetched as can be. In brief, he contends that Jack the Ripper was a successful Victorian songwriter and man-about-town called Michael Maybrick, whose brother James has previously been named as Jack by other sleuths, or 'Ripperologists', as they term themselves. 'Not that I'm accusing devotees of James Maybrick of imbecility,' he adds, 'simply that they're up the right arsehole on the wrong elephant.'

As well as having been, in Robinson's considered judgement, a cold-blooded, psychopathic serial killer, Michael Maybrick was an eminent Freemason. So, 'the last thing anyone wanted was an arrest, God forbid. It would have put an entire (and clandestine) ruling elite in the dock … Justice? Forget it. Fuck who he killed so long as the bastard doesn't interfere with their divine right to rule. The Ripper must and would go free'. This entailed a cover-up of Olympian proportions, involving virtually anyone who was anyone in Victorian society. 'The more outrageous he was, the more the police must cover him up.'

Maybrick's motive remains a little misty, but it clearly had something to do with sex. Was he a homosexual? 'I don't actually know if Maybrick was homosexual, but predicated on that infallible adage, "If it walks like a duck, etc.", he was probably a bit of a ducky.' At the same time, Maybrick was after revenge, however broad-based. 'It's my view that he killed these women as surrogates, punishing them for the sexuality of another, and I believe one woman in particular was on his mind. She was a mother-angel who had proved herself lower than the filthiest whore.'

The woman in question was Florence, adulterous wife of his brother James, who might possibly have once spurned a sexual advance from Michael (assuming he was going through a heterosexual phase). After multiple killings – many more, argues Robinson, than have previously been acknowledged – 'Michael Maybrick framed his brother James as Jack, offed him with a hotshot of poison, then framed Florence for the murder.' Florence was then wrongly convicted, primarily because everyone involved, including her defence counsel, was in on the conspiracy.

'Let me just stop and interview myself here,' interjects Robinson, like TV's Chatty Man. 'Are you saying that Michael Maybrick set James Maybrick up as Jack the Ripper, murdering him with the state's acquiescence, and blaming Florence Maybrick for the deed?

How about 100 per cent?'

After the trial, Michael Maybrick, aka Jack the Ripper, retired to the Isle of Wight where, according to the author, he bowed to Establishment pressure and 'transformed himself from a celebrity into an anonymous recluse', staying in his study with his door locked for years on end. 'It was as if McCartney had vanished into wilful obscurity after "Yesterday" or "Hey Jude".'

All very well, but Robinson neglects to mention that, during this period, Michael Maybrick was five-times Mayor of Ryde, Chief Magistrate of the Isle of Wight, President of the Ryde Philharmonic Society and Chairman of the Isle of Wight Conservative Association, as well as representing the Isle of Wight at the coronations of both King Edward VII and King George V in Westminster Abbey. It only takes a click on Google to find his long and glowing obituary in the *Isle of Wight County Press*: 'Few could make a more acceptable after-dinner speech than he. All the sunshine of his nature, all his evident joy of life ... were poured forth in abundance, and he played on his audiences as he played the piano or organ, with the hand of a master.'

Has an 'anonymous recluse' ever been more celebrated, more gregarious? This is far from the only place in the book where, confronted by awkward facts, Robinson either organises his own cover-up or smudges the truth. For instance, it suits his purpose to suggest that Florence's defence counsel, Sir Charles Russell, was secretly acting on behalf of the prosecution in 'one of the most despicable got-up outrages ever to poison an English court'.

Yet Kate Colquhoun, who published an impartial account of the trial last year, saw no evidence for this, and even commended Russell's summing-up as 'a masterclass in legal oratory, tunnelling effectively under the prosecution's case, reminding them repeatedly of the uncertainty that existed'.

Other forthright statements by Robinson evaporate under even the most momentary inspection. Over and over again, Robinson succumbs to the traditional temptations of the conspiracy theorist: admitting only those pieces of evidence that tally with his conclusion; allowing conjecture to solidify, within a few sentences, into certainty; attributing lack of proof to evidence of a cover-up; detecting pseudo-meaningful patterns in random events; and dismissing contradictory expertise as necessarily bogus.

And here lies the path to madness. He reminds me of someone manically scrubbing onions in the hope of finding the real onion at its centre. For instance, though he admits 'I know nothing of graphology', he refuses to let his ignorance hold him back. 'Experts have been at work on this letter,' he writes of one of the Ripper's mad scrawls, 'and have determined that it was written by a "semi-literate person" with a particular pen; and from this I determine that they are experts at bugger-all.'

He can also be very slapdash. The very first sentence on page 1 of the book turns out to be made up: words he attributes to Margaret

Thatcher – 'We must return to Victorian values' – were in fact never said by her. Why didn't he check?

Eight hundred pages later, at the very end, Robinson copies Lewis Carroll conspiracists by uncovering an anagram and presenting it as the final proof. His evidence lies buried in a letter he argues was secretly written by Michael Maybrick but which is signed:

MOREAU MASINA BERTHRAD NEUBERG

Who is the mysterious Neuberg? Hey presto! He discovers that, if you jig the letters about, it turns into:

I BEGAN A BRUTE MASON MURDERER HA

But, on the other hand … there are twenty-six letters in the alphabet, offering infinite possibilities for anagrams, meaningful or otherwise. Take this one, for instance: if you jiggle about with:

BRUCE ROBINSON

it turns into:

ONION SCRUBBER

Spoo-keeey!

Winner Hand

One of the many oddities of the Thorpe/Scott affair was the number of characters who employed bogus names. Norman Scott was born Norman Josiffe, and briefly changed his name to The Hon. Norman Lianche-Josiffe. Staying with Jeremy Thorpe's mother, Thorpe persuaded him to tell her that his name was 'Peter Johnson'.

The three-day-event rider who gave Scott an early job styled himself The Hon. Brecht van der Vater but his real name was Norman Vater. When staying in Los Angeles, Thorpe's sidekick and fellow Liberal MP Peter Bessell styled himself 'Dr Paul Hoffman'. He later explained that this was for 'security reasons'. And the failed hitman Andrew 'Gino' Newton first introduced himself to his intended victim as 'Peter Keene'.

In 1994, when it was reported – wrongly, as it turned out – that Andrew 'Gino' Newton had fallen to his death while climbing the Eiger in Switzerland, he was said to have been living under the alias 'Hann Redwin'. At the time I thought that, of all the names to switch to, 'Hann Redwin' was singularly strange. Was it, I wondered, an anagram? I then got out my pen and paper and worked out that it was: juggle the letters in 'Hann Redwin', and up pops 'Winner Hand'. In my forty years as a journalist, this is the only scoop I have ever had. As exclusives go, it may not be Watergate, but it's better than nothing.

For a man who had just tumbled to his death, Newton's anagrammatic pseudonym struck me then as yet another example of his capacity for making duff choices. But it now appears that he went on to live undetected as Hann Redwin for a further twenty-four years, so I take it back. Perhaps he did, after all, play a Winner Hand, at least until 2018, when he was traced to Dorking, Surrey.

Oddly enough, Dorking is itself an anagram of 'Rink Dog'. Eeek! Rinka, I need hardly remind you, was the name of the Great Dane Newton shot dead in the pitch-dark on Bodmin Moor. Moreover, Bodmin Moor is an anagram of 'Morbid Moon'.

Winner Hand, Morbid Moon, Rink Dog: a conspiracy theorist might well conclude that Andrew 'Gino' Newton's destiny has been driven by anagrams. And what of the name 'Andrew "Gino" Newton'? It anagrams into the phrases 'Endanger to Winnow', 'Wrongdo Went Inane' and 'Denote Own Warning', all of which carry overtones of the event for which he became notorious.

In the Middle Ages, and well beyond, many believed that a person's character or fate could be discovered by finding the anagrams that lay buried in their names. Over the centuries, some have taken this belief to the extreme. When a seventeenth-century Frenchman called André Pujom worked out that his name anagrammed into 'pendu à Riom', or 'hanged at Riom', he deliberately committed a murder so that he would, indeed, be hanged at Riom, in the Auvergne.

In our own time, there are plenty of people whose names have anagrammed into their characters and destinies. Oliver Reed was an anagram of 'Erode Liver' and Gore Vidal of 'I Love Drag'. Marie Osmond has 'Mormon Ideas'. Meat Loaf was 'O Fat Male'. Melinda Messenger has 'Massed Men Leering'. Felicity Kendal is 'Fine Tickle Lady'. Equally, it's been said of Elle Macpherson that 'Her Men Collapse'.

Nigel Havers is 'Girls Heaven' and Woody Allen is 'A Lewd Loony', Alec Guinness was 'Genuine Class', the evangelist Billy Graham was a 'Big Rally Ham' and Chairman Mao could rightly claim 'I Am on a March'. Michael Grade is deft at the 'Mega Rich Deal', while Germaine Greer has a tendency to 'Emerge Angrier'. The ill-tempered Russell Crowe shows that 'Scowler Rules', while Ian Botham is proud to boast, 'Oh Man, I Bat!'

Both sides of the Brexit debate will have their prejudices confirmed by anagrams of Michael Heseltine – 'He Is the Ill Menace', and Norman Lamont – 'Not Normal Man'. On the other hand, it would surely be going too far to call Nigel Farage 'A Leering Fag'. And is Peter Mandelson really a 'Lamented Person'?

No one seems to be sure where Andrew 'Gino' Newton is now, but he will be glad to know there are others with names more fraught with peril than his own. After all, his late colleague Peter Bessell, whose testimony as chief prosecution witness the judge condemned as a 'tissue of lies', anagrams into 'Tells Beepers'.

Piers Morgan's Life Stories:
Kim Jong-Un

PIERS MORGAN: It's been the most amazing roller-coaster life.

KIM JONG-UN (on VT): There's been tremendous highs and
incredible lows. There's been a lot of laughs and a lot of tears. But –
hey, you know what? – I wouldn't have had it any other way!

PIERS MORGAN: Ten years I've been trying to get you to do this.
And finally you've succumbed to my advances! Why now?

KIM JONG-UN: You know what, Piers? I feel I owe it to my fans.
They've been with me through the good times and the bad. I'm so,
so grateful to them. And I believe in giving something back to the
community.

Applause

PIERS MORGAN: So, Kim Jong-Un, let's go back to where it all began. You were born the youngest son in what was, by any standards, a pretty amazing family! Your dad, Kim Jong-Il, was not only the Supreme Leader of North Korea but the Supreme Commander of the Korean People's Army and, by all accounts, the best-loved guy in the whole country.

KIM JONG-UN: No one ever said a word against him, Piers.

PIERS MORGAN: So living up to the high standards set by that incredible dad can't have been easy …

KIM JONG-UN: You know what, Piers? Before I came on tonight, I promised myself I wouldn't well up [*wipes away a tear*]. But, yeah, you're so right. It's been a struggle.

Applause

PIERS MORGAN: And through an extraordinary mixture of talent and sheer hard graft, you propelled yourself to become one of the greatest dictators on the planet, the JFK of the Far East – and a global superstar!

Applause

PIERS MORGAN: But along the way, you had to grapple with your demons.

KIM JONG-UN: No problem, Piers – I eradicate them!

PIERS MORGAN [*laughs*]: Actually, Jong-Un, I was thinking of your weight issues! Am I right in thinking you really do love your food?

KIM JONG-UN: No, Piers – I always try to maintain a balanced diet!

PIERS MORGAN: Oh, c'mon, admit it! Don't tell me you're never tempted by a lovely bar of chocolate, or a delicious slice of creamy cake? Tell the truth!

KIM JONG-UN: OK, hang it, I'll tell the truth! You're such a great interviewer, Piers! Yes – I do have quite a sweet tooth!

PIERS MORGAN: Tough question, this. But – forgive me – I'm going to ask it anyway. Tell the truth. Chocolate eclair or creamy meringue?

KIM JONG-UN: Oh, Piers! You really got me there! That's an IMPOSSIBLE choice!

PIERS MORGAN: Come on, Jong-Un, I'm not going to let you wriggle off the hook that easily! You can only have one of them – chocolate eclair or creamy meringue?

KIM JONG-UN: It's so hard, Piers … but I guess it would have to be CREAMY MERINGUE!

Laughter, applause

PIERS MORGAN: So, Kim Jong-Un, you're the straight-talking boy from North Korea who grew up to become a global superstar – and one of the biggest dictators on the planet. Let's hear what others say about you.

COLONEL-GENERAL OH HEK: He's always been 110 per cent authentic, and very down to earth!

SISTER KIM YO-JUNG: He was such an adorable baby, always smiling. He really puts his heart and soul into making North Korea the happiest, most prosperous nation in the whole wide world!

MAJOR-GENERAL GAW BLY-MI: All in all, I'd say he was The Decisive and Magnanimous Leader, Father of the Nation, Guardian of Justice and Bright Sun of the Twenty-First Century!

Applause

KIM JONG-UN [*wiping tears away*]**:** That's made me quite emotional that. I never knew they loved me so much! Love you, guys! [*sobs, makes heart sign with his hands*]

PIERS MORGAN: With your peachy complexion, cuddly physique and glamorous shock of jet-black hair, attracting the fairer sex was never going to be a problem for the young Kim Jong-Un. But life wasn't always easy, was it? My investigations tell me your older brother Kim Jong-Nam was a bit of a nightmare!

KIM JONG-UN: Too right, Piers! He was such a like total bitch!

Laughter, applause

PIERS MORGAN: But you soon put paid to that!! Is it true you had him bumped off with poison at Kuala Lumpur airport?

KIM JONG-UN: No way, Piers! [*chuckles*] Do I look that kind of guy?

PIERS MORGAN: Honestly?

KIM JONG-UN: Ye-e-es!

PIERS MORGAN: You don't seem too sure!

Laughter

KIM JONG-UN: OK, Piers – so I did it! But he shouldn't have said those nasty things about me! And, anyway, it was just a bit of fun!

Laughter, applause

PIERS MORGAN: Among some incredible highs, there have been dark times, too. How did you feel when the President of the United States, my old friend Donald Trump, first described you as 'Little Rocket Man'? That can't have been easy?

KIM JONG-UN: He got me at a very vulnerable time, Piers. I was literally shattered and like totally in pieces.

PIERS MORGAN: It must have been an incredibly difficult time in your life. You were hurting. Just talk me through what happened.

KIM JONG-UN: I was in a bad place. It came like a bombshell [*brings out handkerchief and dabs eyes*].

PIERS MORGAN: Take your time … It must have been hard?

KIM JONG-UN: Very, very hard, Piers. And so unfair! All I'd done was let off a few little bombs!

PIERS MORGAN: So how did you … get through it?

KIM JONG-UN: I just told myself I had to be strong. And carry on. For the sake of the kids. But inside, I was *hurting* [*sobs*].

PIERS MORGAN: You're very brave talking about this issue. I know it's very raw.

KIM JONG-UN: Yup. But I owe it to all my loyal supporters. They're literally the best ever.

PIERS MORGAN: So let's move on to happier times. Because, in the end, you and my good friend Donald went on an amazing journey together – and emerged the best of friends! Let's hear what US President Donald Trump says about you now:

TRUMP: 'I like him. We get along great. He's as sharp as you can be, and he's a real leader. He's a real personality and he's very smart.'

PIERS MORGAN: How did you feel when you heard him say that?

KIM JONG-UN: I was the happiest guy in the whole wide world.

PIERS MORGAN: And now you're the best of buddies?

KIM JONG-UN: Yup. You know what, Piers? Donald's a real inspiration. Now we can both start healing together. And bring all the great, great people on this planet into one beautiful brotherhood of man.

PIERS MORGAN: That's a lovely note to end on. Kim Jong-Un, thank you very much.

KIM JONG-UN: Thanks, so much Piers! You're the absolute best!

Applause

Sixteen Clerihews for the
Trump Administration

Steve Bannon
Was a loose cannon.
Once a big hitter
He's now banned from Twitter.

Rudy Giuliani
Says 'Well, I'll be darned'; he
Still wonders why
One should never say dye.

Mike Pence
Sits on the fence
He yearns to shout
But the words won't come out.

Sean Spicer
Couldn't be nicer;
But whatever you do,
Never say, 'Is that true?'

Mike Flynn
Was in
Then out:
For three weeks he had clout.

Reince Priebus
Said 'Finders keepers!
You gotta laugh
I'm Chief of Staff!'

Ivanka
Might've married a banker
But Daddy was pushin' her
To wed Jared Kushner.

Steve Mnuchin
Doesn't do spin;
'I think it's healthier
To make the wealthy wealthier.'

Jeff Sessions
Admits no transgressions
Though he becomes a blusher
If you mention Russia.

Sean Hannity
Has no vanity:
'Mr President, do you suppose
I may kiss your toes?'

Barron Trump
Is inclined to slump;
While others fawn
He stifles a yawn.

Kellyanne Conway
Saw the vote go the wrong way
And urged them to mount
A recount.

Sidney Powell
Threw in the towel
After being chucked off the team
For being a touch too extreme.

Kim Jong-Un
Scoffs, 'And they thought *I* was a wrong un!
Donald used to mock it
But I've still got my rocket.'

Pastor Paula White
Wants to do what's right:
In return for bungs
She'll talk in tongues.

Nancy Pelosi
Is far from cosy
Though Trump's fall from grace
Brought a smile to her face.

ROYALTY

Shooting Devilled Kidneys:
Inaccuracies in *The Crown*

Sir: I was left astonished by inaccuracies in the second episode of *The Crown*. I refer, of course, to the scene in which Princess Margaret was being savaged by a great white shark while on holiday in Mustique. As her body was being swallowed up, she could clearly be seen wearing the Poltimore Tiara.

This is utterly absurd. Her Royal Highness kept the Poltimore Tiara – which she purchased at auction for £5,500 in 1959 – under lock and key at Kensington Palace. She would never have dreamt of taking it to her holiday residence, still less on a swimming expedition.

Yours faithfully, Lady Ann Chovie

Sir: I share your previous correspondent's distress at the hideous inaccuracies in *The Crown*.

Imagine my horror when, in episode three, the Queen Mother pulled a gun on Princess Diana and screamed: 'I'll teach you manners, bitch!' All very well, but in the background Princess Anne can clearly be seen tucking into a plate of what look like devilled kidneys. Surely everyone knows the Royal Family never serve devilled kidneys for breakfast at Balmoral, only at Windsor Castle. This rule was established by Prince Albert in 1858, and all subsequent generations have adhered to it.

Rumour has it that, in a later episode, the screenwriter Peter Morgan plans to show the Royal Family shooting devilled kidneys as they fly through the air on a crisp autumn morning.

I pray to God this is not to be. Famously, one never shoots devilled kidneys unless there's a 'p' in the month.

Yours faithfully, R. Madillo (Hon.)

Sir: As a staunch royalist, I, too, am mortally offended by the untruths peddled in *The Crown*. I refer, of course, to the treatment of the Prince of Wales. In episode nine, as the Prince emerges from 10 Rillington Place bearing a corpse in a sack over his shoulders, his walking shoes are scuffed and dirty. The ignorant viewer would be left to labour under the misapprehension that the Prince of Wales takes little or no pride in his footwear. Nothing could be further from the truth. He is famously the three-times winner of the Most Highly Polished Shoes (International) Gold Cup, proudly sponsored by Everest Windows.

One further outrage. In episode four, Ruth, Lady Fermoy says 'Pardon me' before attempting to push Princess Diana off the White Cliffs of Dover. As a personal friend of Ruth, Lady Fermoy, and as someone who used to accompany her to those cliffs in similar circumstances, I shudder at the idea that she would ever have uttered such a common phrase. Instead, she would say 'My sincere apologies', or a simple 'sorry', before executing a discreet shove. When 'dealing with people' her manners were always impeccable.

Yours etc., Lady Nora Bone

A Special Affection for Magnolias

Faced with a box of chocolates, most people tend to find that one strawberry creme is quite tasty, two strawberry cremes is one too many, and three strawberry cremes make you feel a little bit sick.

Well, I have just eaten 1,000 strawberry cremes in a single sitting, and doctors are recommending a stomach pump. William Shawcross's official biography of the Queen Mother is over 1,000 pages long, and every page comes with its own soft centre.*

The young Elizabeth, we learn, enjoyed an 'idyllic' childhood in 'one of the most splendid buildings in Scotland'. She was 'a vivacious child who, from an early age, loved the company of adults as well as children'. Aged eighteen, 'she was joyous, vivacious and delightful company'. And – hip, hip, hooray! – 'From a charming, vivacious aristocratic but unsophisticated girl, she became a much-loved queen.'

But back to her youth. At house parties, 'she was the carefree and enchanting centre'. She managed to catch the eye of the King's second son and 'each time he saw Elizabeth, the Prince evidently fell more in love'. Eventually, she accepted his proposal of marriage, and the Prince took her to meet the King and Queen. 'Both immediately thought Elizabeth pretty and charming … Elizabeth enchanted them all.'

And they would have us believe that Barbara Cartland is dead! The book is full not only of carefree joy and enchanting vivacity but also of thrills. In 1924, the young couple plan to go on safari. 'The prospect was thrilling,' observes Shawcross. One morning they go in search of a lion. 'It was too thrilling,' Elizabeth writes to her mother. Her husband

---

* *Queen Elizabeth the Queen Mother: The Official Biography* by William Shawcross (2009).

shoots an elephant. 'The Duchess was thrilled,' observes Shawcross.

And there is plenty of delight, too. Indeed, if you shut the book too abruptly, you may well find delight oozing out of its sides. Returning from Australia, the young royals hear that the King is 'delighted with the enthusiastic reception' they have been given. For her birthday, the King and Queen give Elizabeth a Chinese screen. 'She was delighted,' enthuses Shawcross.

Off on another trip, she leaves the children with Queen Mary. 'The Queen was, as always delighted,' writes Shawcross. In time, Elizabeth and George are elevated to King and Queen. Her husband bestows the Order of the Garter upon her. 'She was delighted,' writes Shawcross. She meets President Roosevelt, whom 'she thought delightful'. She also found train drivers 'delightful people', and she 'delighted' in mimicry. After the coronation, she visits Balmoral. Can you guess what it was like? Right first time. 'It was delightful,' reports the new Queen.

Whenever a king or queen dies, the Royal Family authorises a writer – invariably well spoken, well connected, a 'safe pair of hands' – to write the official biography. The author then beavers away in the Royal Archives and ploughs his way through every last thank-you letter and press cutting. ('Her Majesty smiled her way into the hearts of the people … her kindly glances, the sweetness of her manner, her whole attitude of gracious charm have won for her a love which must last as long as those who have seen her shall live' – editorial, the *Kingston Daily Gleaner*, 1927.) After three or four years, the author emerges with a large, suitably reverential tome in which, with all due care and attention, any shortcomings of the deceased monarch have been swept beneath a thick red carpet of gracious charm and vivacious delight.

William Shawcross has, on these terms, performed a magnificent job. The book's place on the coffee table at Balmoral is assured. In fact, it is so heavy that, had it come with a pair of folding legs, it could have doubled as a coffee table.

Whatever task the Queen Mother undertakes, however simple, it is always a huge success, and the world loves her all the more for it. 'Once again Canadians had shown that they loved her and she had shown that she loved Canada' is a typical conclusion, variations cropping up after each trip embarked upon, each banquet attended, each garden fete opened.

Of course, some might say that this bubbling stream of warm gush is no less than the Queen Mother merits. Whatever it is that a queen is expected to do, she did it with aplomb, smiling and waving and asking soothing questions and generally keeping out of trouble for a century or more. She was, in theatrical terms, a star.

As a record of a star performance, this book is entirely in tune with its subject. Her devoted followers would not wish to hear that the Queen Mother had simply forked out for a new set of clothes. No: they want Shawcross to write that 'the new dresses were exquisite and their effect was mesmerising', and then to supply a full description of virtually each dress. And so he does.

'The Queen was elegant in a pale-grey dress of light wool, with long slit sleeves edged with fur and a hat with a becomingly unswept brim', he writes of a dress she wore in Canada back in 1939. (That it should come to this! Shawcross is the same man who was once called 'the foremost investigative journalist of his generation' and exposed, with surgical intensity, the USA's secret bombing of Cambodia.)

Nor would fans of the Queen Mum expect Shawcross to ignore the little things, like flowers. He dutifully records, in a suitably prim and proper style, that King George VI 'loved rhododendrons, about which he became knowledgeable, and planted many new varieties', whereas Elizabeth 'had a special affection for magnolias'. Furthermore, 'she was happy for the British Gladiolus Society to name a seedling after her but asked that it be called Queen Mother rather than Queen Mum'.

But anyone hoping for something more nutritious than strawberry cremes must look elsewhere. This is a description of the performance, not the performer. Here and there, one catches a glimpse of someone rather more ruthless and self-centred – for instance, on page 800 we learn that her house guests knew they had to let her win at Racing Demon – but then Shawcross, ever the watchful butler, swiftly draws shut the curtains, stopping the audience from spotting any more goings-on backstage.

Nevertheless, we are allowed to overhear one or two noises off. There is an interesting chapter on her late friendship with the Poet Laureate, Ted Hughes, who, when he wasn't hawkish, could sometimes be mawkish, and there is some new material on her politics (far to the right of Prince Philip). There is quite a bit, too, on her deeply frosty relationship with the Duke and Duchess of Windsor. Other books have touched on the way she tried to block the Duke's wartime appointment as Governor of the Bahamas, but Shawcross provides us with a memo (or at least some of it) in which she argued that the Duchess 'is looked upon as the lowest of the low'.

I suspect she was a tough old thing, who guarded her immense good fortune with a diamond-studded knuckleduster. Stephen Tennant, the ultra-camp brother of one of her early suitors, described the young Elizabeth to Hugo Vickers, her last biographer, as 'hard as nails', and the Duke of Windsor called her and his mother 'ice-veined bitches'. Both men were jaundiced, but might they have been on to something? Keeping all the strawberry cremes for yourself takes fierce elbows.

Just as owners grow to be like their dogs, do royal biographers grow to be like their subjects? Shawcross and the Queen Mother share an evasive quality, discarding anything upsetting. For instance, in his biography, Hugo Vickers revealed that when Sir Martin Gilliat, her private secretary of thirty-seven years, was on his deathbed, the Queen Mother donned her blinkers and refused to visit him, owing to her 'ingrained dislike of visiting dying friends'. Gilliat, says Vickers, 'railed against his employer, declaring that he had wasted the best years of his life in her service'. But Shawcross makes no mention of this, simply saying she felt his death 'keenly'.

And, as the book rolls on, Shawcross's opinions seem to meld with the Queen Mother's, his occasional state-of-the-nation overviews growing ever more reactionary. But Buckingham Palace will be delighted with his efforts. Arise, Sir William!

A Ray of Sunshine:
The Memoirs of Margaret Rhodes,
Former Woman of the Royal Bedchamber

Sometime in 1990, Queen Elizabeth the Queen Mother asked me to lunch at Clarence House. Ruth, Lady Fermoy, the exceedingly elegant grandmother of Princess Diana, was also there. As I entered the drawing room, Ruth, Lady Fermoy was already on her hind legs, begging for choccie drops.

It was an old Clarence House tradition, and, like so many of those old traditions, the most tremendous fun. The Queen Mother would have us all line up and beg for choccie drops. We, in turn, would raise our front paws to our chins and bark and whimper. I can remember only one occasion when proceedings got 'out of hand'. Ruth, Lady Fermoy was rather overdoing the whimpering, so the irrepressible Queen Mother smacked her smartly around the jaw, causing her to topple over!!

Needless to say, the rest of us hooted with laughter, as Ruth, Lady Fermoy lay there, nursing her wounds like a crybaby! But she learnt her lesson, and from then on we experienced no more stuff and nonsense from that particular quarter!

I had joined a household legendary for its hospitality, conviviality and wit, but underscored by an inexorable sense of duty.

The Queen Mother had the most tremendous regard for rich and poor alike, though she preferred the rich, as they were less trouble; 'sadly, many of the poor have been born with the most almighty chips on their shoulders,' she observed. Before employing new staff at Clarence House she would always ask them to remove their 'tops', ready for shoulder inspection. Anyone with a chip visible could expect short shrift!

* * *

I have never encountered a human being so selflessly dedicated to sheer hard work. It meant nothing to her to devote three minutes or more of her precious time to talking to a total stranger. 'They remember it for the rest of their little lives,' she once explained. 'For them, it's a ray of sunshine amidst the prevailing gloom of being so dreadfully ordinary.'

She loved ordinary folk, and they loved her. She would often sit and study them going about their daily business on favourite television programmes such *Upstairs, Downstairs*.

She and the Prince of Wales shared the most tremendous love of architecture. The pair of them would stay up to the early hours discussing the relative merits of various different buildings. They both preferred the large and the old to the small and the new. Looking at some of the more modest homes on the road out of Windsor, she would often wonder out loud where on earth they found space for their ballrooms.

A myth has grown up that the Queen Mother was over-fond of drink. It was, I suppose, an affectionate old canard, but nothing could have been further from the truth. All I can say is that the idea of her having a drinking habit was quite simply unimaginable. Her intake was strictly rationed and never varied. Before lunch, she would have a gin and Dubonnet with a slice of lemon and a lot of ice. Then, before she went in, she would have another couple of quick ones, without the ice or the lemon. Over her meal, she might just manage a bottle or two of wine, but largely for form's sake. After lunch she would relax with a brandy and, if it was a 'working day', possibly a large port too. In the evening she would have a dry Martini followed by champagne, then red wine and a Drambuie or Grand Marnier, rounded off with whisky, to remind her of her beloved Scotland. I am glad to have been able to put the record straight. There was certainly no question of excess.

She possessed a rare magic, and her engagements had the most wonderful sense of theatre. I remember Sir Martin Gilliat telling me: 'When she steps out of her car, it's like curtain-up. She puts her sausage roll back in her bag, snaps it shut, then gets going with all the grinning and the waving.' In her final decades, she had a battery-operated prosthetic arm fitted, to halve the bother.

Introduced to local dignitaries, she had the innate gift of making everyone believe they were the only person in the world she wanted to talk to. Of course, nothing could have been further from the truth. If ever anyone wouldn't stop talking, she had the most charming way of shutting them up. 'Shut up' she would murmur, before moving briskly on. She was no believer in stiff formality.

The Queen Mother had simple tastes. She took every opportunity to have lunch al fresco. She simply adored eating out of doors in the Scottish Highlands. If rain looked likely, she would simply get the staff to bring a suitable shelter up the hill, plus chairs, dining table, silver, and so forth. 'Such fun!' she would say, urging them on with a stick she had sharpened with her trusty penknife.

Her staff were all utterly devoted. They would have worked for nothing, but, being an angel, she insisted on paying them, largely in boiled sweets. Those who had served her for over fifty years would be given barley sugar, the rest Fox's glacier mints. At the turn of the century, many of them were well over ninety years old, but she never allowed them to retire, insisting it would make them bone-lazy. Every now and then, one old retainer or another would collapse and die in service, but she was always sympathetic, even if it had involved a spillage at table. 'These things happen!' she would smile, ringing a discreet bell attached to the table to summon the Comptroller of the Royal Coffins to make the necessary arrangements.

I was in my eightieth year when, carrying her piggy-back over a roaring Scottish burn, I stupidly slipped and fell. Luckily, the Queen Mother fell on top of me, and so didn't get wet. She stayed there without complaint until rescued by a kindly ghillie. I was underwater for a good minute or two, so wasn't able to offer my apologies until later. From that moment on, I always kept a pair of goggles and a snorkel 'about my person', just in case.

His Serene Highness Albert II, Prince of Monaco: Our Exclusive Landmarks

I am honored to be your guide to the glamorous international land-marks of the Principality of Monaco, where sunshine meets premium-quality sophistication, tradition meets modernity, and a very real concern for the underprivileged meets luxurious fast-tracked streamlining for the world's highest achievers.

Monaco is known throughout the global world as the go-to destina-tion for banking, luxury brands, yachting, elegant gambling opportunities and enlightened tax breaks. However, while we continue to welcome those of an advanced age, it is our desire to highlight the many high-end facilities we offer a new generation of wealthy young influencers.

Le Grand Théâtre Sir Philip Green

In Monaco, we pride ourselves on our age-old appreciation of prestige drama from around the world. Thanks to a generous donation from an anonymous sponsor, the freshly renamed Le Grand Théâtre Sir Philip Green continues to present a range of exclusive cutting-edge plays and operas. This year, after our hugely successful *Black and White Minstrel Show*, we look forward to a revival of *Jesus Christ Superstar*, with iconic Des O'Connor in the title role and international chanteuse Dame Joan Collins as his blessed mother, the Virgin Mary.

How to Get There: From Grand Plaza Hugo Boss, take a sharp right into Boulevard Benito Mussolini. After fifty yards, you will find it off the main square, in the Place Nicholas van Hoogstraten.

Galerie Tina Green

One of my all-time favorite art galleries, this fabulous mecca of world-beating modern and contemporary art occupies a very special place in the hearts of all true Monegasques, offering expertly curated artworks to those in need of both long- and short-term investment strategies.

Galerie Tina Green is currently proud to exhibit Tracey Emin's acclaimed series of installations 'Sometimes I Feel So Fucking Real It Like Hurts But Not Always Now I Come To Think Of It', with prices ranging from $81,000 to $3.2 million. Exclusive openings at Galerie Tina Green attract the cream of the international jet set. Among the VIPs attending last year's dazzling Jeff Koons opening sponsored by American Express were Peter Andre, Paris Hilton, Roman Abramovich, the Duchess of York, Robert Kilroy-Silk and The Hon. Tamara Pringle, iconic heir to the high-end Pringles crisp fortune.

How to Get There: Head for Avenue Kenneth Noye, then at the Savile Roundabout take the third exit, signed Boulevard Haw-Haw.

The Monte Carlo International Festival of Luxury Brands

Each year, hundreds of thousands flock to the Principality's International Festival of Luxury Brands, which has been running every year in an unbroken line since 2009.

Last year, I was delighted when my good friend Princess Camilla of Bourbon-Two Sicilies, glamorous heir to the Bourbon biscuit fortune, agreed to attend the official opening. The festival takes place every year at the Hôtel Grand Palais Weinstein, where luxury VIP penthouse suites start at $27,575 a night, inclusive of escort. With pavilions devoted to Hermès, Louis Vuitton, Bulgari and Rolex, all tastes are catered for. Incidentally, I myself always take care to wear my Patek Philippe Tourbillon Perpetual Calendar Platinum wristwatch when I perform my private charitable works in the local hospitals and children's homes. I find its superb Swiss craftsmanship brings a look of delight to the faces of those perhaps less fortunate than myself.

How to Get There: Traverse the HRH Prince Andrew Underpass, then take an immediate left on to Boulevard Silvio Berlusconi. Leaving the Prince Rainier Luxury Casino to your right, drive straight through to the Plaza Francisco Franco and you can't miss it.

The Monte Carlo Festival of International Statuary

There is a lot of excitement around this wonderful new project – destined to become a much-loved part of the Monaco calendar for years to come.

In August, history will take the front row as vintage statues collected from all over the world are exhibited in the verdant surroundings of Le Grand Jardin du Ecclestone Bernard. We premiere with an exclusive collection of ancient statues of some of history's most inspirational movers and shakers, from Bristol UK's premier philanthropreneur Edward Colston to Virginia USA's renowned statesman President Jefferson Davis. We are truly proud to announce that the exhibition will be opened by the celebrated multi-award-winning South African sportsman Oscar Pistorius, travel permitting.

How to Get There: Le Grand Jardin du Ecclestone Bernard is situated on Boulevard Al-Fayed, which can be accessed via Avenue Max Clifford.

Cinéma Historique de Monte Carlo

My late mother, Her Serene Highness Princess Grace, brought a touch of Hollywood glamor to the Principality when she married my father, His Serene Highness Prince Rainier, in a sparkling wedding attended by many leading members of the international jet set including Frank Sinatra, Sam Giancana, Carlo Gambino and Tony 'Big Tuna' Accardo.

In honor of her memory, the Cinéma Historique de Monte Carlo regularly runs seasons of the classiest movies of all time. This October, we are proud to present Winner: A Retrospective, featuring the highly acclaimed films of Michael Winner, including *Death Wish*, *Death Wish II*, *Death Wish III*, *Death Wish IV*, *Death Wish V* and the consistently underrated *Death Wish VI*.

All the films will be followed by discussion and Q & A sessions led by Stuart Hall.

How to Get There: Follow Avenue Richard Desmond until you arrive at Place de Karl Lagerfeld. Take the third turning on your right, to Rue de Joe Exotique, and the Cinéma Historique is straight ahead.

The Yacht Club de Monaco

A favorite port of call for owners and their superyachts (over 40 metres min.) and a convenient base for key designers and the major brokers, the Principality of Monaco has long been an exclusive destination. Uniting as it does the most prestigious private yachts in the world under its flag, the Yacht Club occupies prime position in the luxury yachting fraternity and is available exclusively for luxury-brand product launches and high-end liquidation auctions.

Visit the Yacht Club de Monaco to view the luxury yachts of the future, including the $600 million 181-metre *Désirée du Jour* megayacht, featuring a choice of luxury bedroom suites to accommodate up to three top-of-the-range silk-veneer helicopters, three ballrooms, a football stadium and a 8-foot-diameter Patek Philippe luxury solid-gold watch so large and heavy it demands to be worn by two men at a time.

How to Get There: Turn left down Rue Strauss-Kahn, along Boulevard Bernie Madoff and from there direct to the Trump Marina.

Little Sign of Slowing Down:
Alan Titchmarsh meets HRH Prince Philip,
Duke of Edinburgh

ALAN TITCHMARSH: As he approaches his ninetieth birthday, Prince Philip shows little sign of slowing down. The Queen's consort is, by anyone's standard, something of a phenomenon. His natural exuberance and energy would exhaust a man half his age. It is one of the great privileges not only of my life but of my children's lives that he has agreed to meet me on what is – remarkably – the eve of his ninetieth birthday, when, it must be said, he shows little sign of slowing down!

Sir, would I be right in thinking that, as you approach your ninetieth birthday, you show little sign of slowing down!!

PRINCE PHILIP: What a fatuous thing to say! You need your head examined. Why should I? I mean, if you've got nothing better to ask …?!

TITCHMARSH: Ho, ho, ho! Marvellous, sir! You certainly show little sign of slowing down! Now, might I take you back to your childhood, sir! By all accounts, it was, in royal terms, pretty unconventional!

PRINCE PHILIP: Depends what you mean by unconventional. Damn fool question. Is there much more of this?

TITCHMARSH: Am I right in thinking, sir, that, as a child, you were, by all accounts, something of a handful?

PRINCE PHILIP: Who ARE you? Who IS he? Are you the chauffeur? Get me away from here!

TITCHMARSH: Excellent! Now, you were born nearly ninety years ago, sir. That's a remarkable achievement, especially for someone of your advanced years. Does it really feel that long?

440

PRINCE PHILIP: Ghastly little man. Haven't the foggiest who he is.

TITCHMARSH: I am now hugely privileged to be in the gracious presence of Her Royal Highness Princess Anne the Princess Royal. Thank you kindly for having me, ma'am, and may I say at once –

PRINCESS ANNE: Is there much more of this?

TITCHMARSH: Your father is, if I may say so, ma'am, obviously a truly remarkable man, ninety years young! May I ask you, ma'am, what it felt like growing up with such a truly remarkable man as your father?

PRINCESS ANNE: If you must.

TITCHMARSH: What did it feel like, ma'am, growing up with such a truly remarkable man as your father?

PRINCESS ANNE: Perfectly stupid question. What do you THINK it felt like? I didn't have another father to compare him to, did I?

TITCHMARSH: An excellent answer, ma'am! Some say, ma'am, that your father is not the type to suffer fools gladly?

PRINCESS ANNE: Insufferable question.

TITCHMARSH: Might I now be so bold as to ask you, ma'am, whether having Prince Philip as a father meant that –

PRINCESS ANNE: Time up! I haven't got all day. Run along.

TITCHMARSH: Thank you most graciously, ma'am! It's been a huge privi –

PRINCESS ANNE: Next!

TITCHMARSH: You are now, sir, by my reckoning, the longest-serving consort in British history. What does that mean to you?

PRINCE PHILIP: What does what mean? Get on with it, man!

TITCHMARSH: The fact that you are now the longest-serving consort in British history, sir. What does that mean to you?

PRINCE PHILIP: What on earth do you think it means? How long is a piece of string? What's the square root of twenty-nine? How am I meant to know? Are you completely daft? Who do you think I am? What's the point? Where's the sense? Who are you? What the hell are you doing here? Who let him in?!

POSH OLD LADY: More tea? Back in those days, Philip was a young man, oh, very much so. He did the sort of things that were the sort of things we all did at the time. But of course, that was a good many years ago. As time went orn, he grew older, as we all did. Oh, very much so. In many ways, he's the same now as he was then. As we all are. Though in other ways, he is rather different. As we all are. Oh, very much so.

TITCHMARSH: Tell me about your naval career, sir.
PRINCE PHILIP: It was a career. It was naval. Nothing more to say.
TITCHMARSH: There must have been some amusing or exciting moments?
PRINCE PHILIP: Quite possibly.
TITCHMARSH: Do any spring to mind, sir?
PRINCE PHILIP: No.
TITCHMARSH: Marvellous! Then, in 1947, you married Her Royal Highness the Queen.
PRINCE PHILIP: What's it to do with you?

GYLES BRANDRETH: The Duke's sense of humour is truly second to none. In all the years I've known him, he's always been HUGELY amused by my repartee. It's one of his most appealing characteristics, and one for which, frankly, he's far too seldom given credit. I once saw him ROARING with laughter when an underling stepped on a corgi and fell over backward, breaking his neck!

TITCHMARSH: How important was fatherhood to you, sir?
PRINCE PHILIP: What do you mean?
TITCHMARSH: Fatherhood, sir. Was it important to you?
PRINCE PHILIP: In what way?
TITCHMARSH: I was wondering whether, to you, fatherhood was important, sir?
PRINCE PHILIP: Depends what you mean by important. Depends what you mean by fatherhood. Damn fool question. Next you'll

try telling me that two and two makes five. Are you ON
something? How much more of my time do you intend to waste?

TITCHMARSH: Wonderful! You show little sign of slowing down,
sir! Incidentally, sir, I have brought my tongue along with me, sir. I
wondered if you be so gracious as to allow me to take this
opportunity to lick your –

PRINCE PHILIP: Ghastly little man.

TITCHMARSH: Oh, but thank you kindly, most gracious sir!

Harry and Meghan in Four Acts

1

November 2017
Meghan: My New Dawn

Harry's family have all been so welcoming, reaching out to make me feel a very, very special part of their family. Three days ago, I met his Aunty Anne, and she was so intimate and cosy, full of real human warmth and understanding. 'Welcome aboard,' she said, before turning around to greet one of her mother's corgis.

Two brief words.

But a whole world of compassion.

Harry's Uncle Andrew is a beautiful person, too. He looked at me with those lovely wide eyes of his. I could tell he wanted to see the whole me, the real me, stripped of all the layers. And he reached out and made a connection. The human touch is so important. Then he used one of those quaint old English expressions I'd never heard before. 'You're a bit of all right,' he said. Harry later told me it signified a deep and enduring appreciation of who I am and where I come from.

And Harry's beloved gramps Pip is so sweet and natural and awesome: overflowing with the wisdom of years. I thought he seemed so old he must even, like, remember The Beatles. Had he ever met them? The way he told it, they were like fresh rain sent by the heavens to nurture our planet. 'Absolute shower,' he told me. Poetry flows through those elderly veins. We exchanged wisdom. I said that sending love and good vibes and positivity into our universe is, for me, the only thing in this life that truly matters. He told me that, for him, it was important to have a good, strong handshake, to speak up, and to look the other person fairly and squarely in the eye.

He seemed so vulnerable, almost – how shall I put this? – like a little kid who's lost his way. I so wanted to bring him out of his shell, to put him at his ease. 'All that matters is that you be YOU!' I said. 'That's the greatest contribution to humanity that any one of us can ever make. Follow this rule, and your footstep on this, our planet, will be profound. After all, it's the only one we have.'

He went silent. I knew he was lost in thought, imbibing the truth in my words. 'Shall we go through?' he said. Just four short words. But so deeply profound.

I can't believe how authentic the Queen is. No wonder her family nickname is 'Her Majesty'! Well deserved? You bet! Whatever she does, wherever she goes, she's just so refreshingly AUTHENTIC. There's no other word for it. Like the great Meryl Streep, who she's clearly learnt so much from, she puts so much time and energy into authenticity. And that's something I respect.

Another truly amazing thing about the Queen (my grandmom-in-law-to be!!) is that, even at her venerable age, she still wants to LEARN. Only last week, she was telling me about her 'Christmas message', where all the networks offer her ten minutes prime-time to talk freely about the things that are troubling her. So I thought, maybe she's, well, not envious exactly, because she's not that kind of person, but, like, maybe she's thinking it would be nicer in some ways to have the forty-four minutes a week we get to have on *Suits*, but I wanted to be totally positive, so I was, like, 'CONGRATULATIONS! I mean, ten minutes is literally AMAZING! You should be so PROUD! I mean, there's so much you can DO in ten minutes! It's a great platform!'

We made such a connection. Like me, she's really proud of who she is and where she comes from. And – also like me! – she's passionate about broadcasting, and yearns to focus her energies on just getting better and better. And at her age that's so inspiring.

'I so want you to tell me all about your Christmas show!' I said to her. She told me her method. She just looks to the camera and keeps talking! 'Wow! That's great!' I said. And she looked so happy.

Encouragement means so much to all of us. It was Mahatma Gandhi who said, 'Don't be the reason someone feels insecure. Be the reason someone feels seen, heard, and supported by the whole universe.' And that's always been my watchword. So I touched her gently on her beautiful old wrist and I said, 'You know what? You've developed such a totally AMAZING show. And there was me thinking *SUITS* was long-running! So who am I to offer advice!!!?!!!'

At that point she gave me a lovely, soft, gentle, almost beseeching look. It seemed to shout, 'Hey! All tips welcome, Meghan! Together, let's turn this show around!'

So I told her maybe it would be even more amazing if she didn't just launch straight into her monologue, awesome though it is, like maybe she should make it a teensy bit more inclusive by stretching her arms out wide and welcoming viewers 'to our beautiful home here in London, England'.

And you know what? She looked so hungry to learn. As an actress, I've made a lifelong study of my fellow human beings. I've developed a – I don't know – call it a 'sixth sense'. I don't know how, but I instantly identified that 'tell me more!' look in her eyes. And I was getting so excited, so I said, 'And – hey! – wouldn't it be great if we had Prince Philip throwing a log on the fire, and maybe wiping a little tear from his eye, straight to camera? And like Harry and I could put our heads out from behind your Christmas tree – SURPRISE! – and then Wills and Kate could appear, and we'd all go hand in hand, and – I'm thinking on my feet here! – we could get some really big, big stars like, say, Bill Murray and Meryl and Barbra with some schoolkids, singing "Rudolph the Red-Nosed Reindeer", and we could have fluffy snow falling from the Palace ceiling, with all your beautiful corgis wagging their cute little tails, and maybe some footmen all in scarlet and braid performing a couple of cartwheels or some such! But now I'm getting ahead of myself!'

'That sounds most interesting,' she replied. 'We'll certainly bear it in mind.' She's so sweet, the way she hides her feelings. But I could tell she was literally OVER THE MOON! Maybe not this year, maybe not even next year. But one day soon, she's going to make the Christmas broadcast she was born to deliver. And at long last Lilibet and her beautiful family will be on the map.

2

August 2020
Finding Freedom

Oddly enough, this* is not the first royal book to feature the word 'Finding' in its title. Back in 2011, the Duchess of York published *Finding Sarah: A Duchess's Journey to Find Herself*. Dedicated both to 'Oprah who pulled me out of the darkness' and to 'my dearest Andrew who holds on to the Real Sarah', *Finding Sarah* came sprinkled with words of 'Wisdom from the Duchess'.

Each chapter was prefaced with a breezy truism, generally based on the sky, or flying, or both. 'The clouds pass but the sky stays'; 'We have the power to choose where we fly, and how high'; 'The lighter you travel, the farther and higher you can go'. And so on.

Did Meghan Markle read *Finding Sarah*? I only ask because when she launched her own website, 'The Tig', two years later, she went in for the same sort of airy philosophising, sandwiched between plugs for moisturisers and scented candles: 'Travel often; getting lost will help you find yourself'; 'Being yourself is the prettiest thing a person can be'.

Finding Freedom: Harry and Meghan and the Making of a Modern Royal Family kicks off with a quote in the same vein, from Ralph Waldo Emerson: 'Do not go where the path may lead, go instead where

---

* *Finding Freedom: Harry and Meghan and the Making of a Modern Royal Family* by Omid Scobie and Carolyn Durand (2020).

there is no path and leave a trail.' Along with much else in the book, this choice of quote from the nineteenth-century guru of the self-trust, self-love movement has Meghan's fingerprints all over it. Though the authors deny taking dictation from Meghan, they keep dropping giant hints that this is indeed the case. 'As a rule, no member of the British Royal Family is officially allowed to authorise a biography,' reads their coy introduction. But why say 'as a rule' or 'officially' if you are not signalling an exception? Naturally, the next sentence begins, 'However …' Similarly, in their authors' note at the end, they boast of having spoken with 'close friends of Harry and Meghan … and, when appropriate, the couple themselves'.

That 'when appropriate' looks like a get-out clause to me. After all, if you are writing a biography of a couple, when would speaking to them be inappropriate? My guess is that whenever they ascribe a quote to 'a source close to Meghan', that source is Meghan herself. On the very last page, they tell us that 'Above all, the couple want to continue with what they have always set out to do: empowering others. "To accentuate, celebrate, and get people to recognise their place in both the world and in the communities around them," a source close to Meghan said.' As it happens, a source close to this reviewer says this is all gobbledegook.

Finding Freedom focuses largely on Meghan; Harry remains a shadowy figure, by turns malleable and prickly, and increasingly 'furious' at perceived snubs to Meghan. But no detail about Meghan is considered too irrelevant for inclusion. We hear, for instance, that she is 'the type of girl to grab a smoothie after a hot yoga or Pilates session' and that 'her morning ritual' starts 'with a cup of hot water and a slice of lemon, followed by her favourite breakfast of steel-cut oats (usually made with almond or soy milk) with bananas and agave syrup for sweetness'. Hold the front page!

Clothes and make-up are given due prominence, not least on the day of the wedding, when her make-up artist, Daniel, wants 'the right look: natural but effervescent, almost lit from within'.

Working with none other than 'Julia Roberts's long-time hairstylist, Serge Normant', Daniel 'gave Meghan a dewy glow with a mix of toner, moisturiser, a sunscreen primer, and just a spot treatment of foundation on her T-Zone', whatever that may be. He then 'finished up by smudging chestnut, cocoa and rust shadows on to her lids, lining her eyes, and applying lashes to the corners'.

In many ways, this is an old-fashioned royal book, chock-a-block with fluff and gush, in which nothing is so banal that it cannot be glorified by the royal touch. Gooey descriptions of dresses are followed by even gooier descriptions of food. At the wedding reception, Harry and Meghan and their guests tuck into 'exquisitely presented canapés of Scottish langoustines wrapped in smoked salmon with citrus crème fraiche, grilled English asparagus wrapped in Cumbrian ham, garden pea panna cotta with quail eggs and lemon verbena, and poached free-range chicken bound with a lightly spiced yogurt with roasted apricot'.

In their joint ITV interview on the announcement of their engagement, Meghan employed the touchy-feely language of Californian mindfulness. She spoke of 'a learning curve', 'investing time and energy to make it happen', 'nurturing our relationship' and 'focusing on who we are as a couple'.

The language Harry used was quite different. Still fresh from the army, he spoke of Meghan's entrance into the Royal Family as though it were a military manoeuvre; she would, he said, be a useful addition to the team. 'For me, it's an added member of the family. It's another team player as part of the bigger team, and you know for all of us, what we want to do is be able to carry out the right engagements, carry out our work and try and encourage others in the younger generation to be able to see the world in the correct sense.'

There is none of this old-fashioned, stiff-upper-lip, steady-as-she-goes stuff in *Finding Freedom*. Nowadays, Harry talks like Meghan. Unwittingly, the authors make it clear that Windsor has been colonised by California.

'The couple were both fans of self-help books, with Harry counting *Eight Steps to Happiness* as a favourite, while Meghan read *The Motivation Manifesto*.' Furthermore, 'Meghan expanded Harry's spiritual world, introducing him to yoga through her own practice and buying him a book on mindfulness that, like all her gifts, came with a handwritten note.'

Theirs is a world populated by celebrities, public relations maestros, skincare gurus, energy healers and 'brand ambassadors'. Incidentally, Meghan herself was once a 'brand ambassador' for Ralph Lauren. Idris Elba agrees to DJ at the wedding; the Clooneys fly the happy couple to Lake Como in their private jet; Serena Williams hosts 'a star-studded baby shower', at which 'approximately 20 of Meghan's closest friends', including 'NBC cable entertainment chief Bonnie Hammer' dine on a menu prepared by the 'Michelin-starred' chef Jean-Georges Vongerichten while an equally renowned harpist plays in the background. When Archie is born, 'Ellen DeGeneres and wife Portia de Rossi ... stopped by'. Inevitably, Fergie's old mentor Oprah Winfrey 'reaches out' to Meghan's mum. Would Oprah have 'reached out' to Doria Ragland if she wasn't Meghan's mum? It seems doubtful.

In this fluffy, fuzzy world, the boundaries are blurred between virtue and fame, between commerce and philanthropy, between friendship and networking, between the authentic and the artificial. We are informed that as a sexy young actress in the Toronto-based TV series *Suits*, Meghan entered 'an exciting, fizzy social scene' filled with high-profile charity events, the openings of new hotspots, fabulous restaurants and fancy friends like Michael Bublé. Developing her shopping-and-gushing lifestyle website Tig – 'a place to curate all her passions (food, fashion and travel as well as social issues such as gender equality)' filtered through an 'aspirational girl-next-door vibe' – she would 'reach out' to useful strangers, assisted by 'London-based PR firm Kruger Cowne'.

Meanwhile, 'she began commanding cash – upward of $10,000 an appearance – to turn up at red carpets'. In a speedy aside, the authors sheepishly admit that 'Meghan, before she met Harry, had occasionally set up a paparazzi photo here and there or let info slip out to the press'. In time, some of her sparkly new friends, acquired through social media, had to be let go.

In his largely adoring 2018 biography of Meghan, Andrew Morton revealed that after she had launched Tig in 2013, Meghan got in touch with Ivanka Trump, who was 'one of her female idols'. Meghan was, it seems, 'thrilled when she accepted her invitation to meet for drinks and dinner the next time Meghan was in New York'. And so began a bout of vigorous back-scratching. 'Don't get me started on her jewellery collection: the late-night "window shopping" I have done on my computer, snuggled up in bed with a glass of wine, staring longingly at her beautiful designs,' wrote Meghan of Ivanka. 'When we have drinks, I will make sure I order whatever she does – because this woman seems to have the formula for success and happiness down pat.'

But the authors of *Finding Freedom* conveniently airbrush Ivanka from the record, perhaps fearful that the Trump formula for success and happiness might jar against Harry and Meghan's new mission to 'build a humanitarian legacy that will make a profound difference in the world'.

The first two-thirds of *Finding Freedom* cover the Cinderella-ish tale of the home-town girl, remembered for 'her willingness to help others and her drive to excel'. Young Meghan rises to become one of twenty-six briefcase models in thirty-four episodes of the American version of *Deal or No Deal* before popping up in an episode of the TV series *90210*, in which 'her character, Wendy … was caught giving oral sex to playboy student Ethan Ward in a school parking lot'. Happily, Cinderella escapes this life of drudgery when she lands a starring role in *Suits*, her springboard into a world in which celebrities share their 'visions', more often than not a heavenly mix of social awareness and luxury goods.

On a self-promotional trip to London she tweets Piers Morgan, whom she has never met. 'I'm in London for a week of meetings and Wimbledon. Would love to say hi!' Later that evening, she meets Prince Harry for the first time, before returning to her hotel. Though 'she had been offered a heavily discounted stay at the five-star Dorchester Hotel', she plumps instead for a 'luxurious room' secured by her 'pal' Markus Anderson, Soho House's global membership director.

Harry and Meghan fall in love. 'She was smart, independent, adventurous, optimistic and beautiful. But perhaps most important to Harry,

Meghan came across as authentic.' But for Harry and Meghan, every silver lining has an authentic cloud. The last third of the book makes way for an ever-expanding series of disappointments. First, 'according to sources', William advises Harry: 'Don't feel you need to rush this. Take as much time as you need to get to know this girl.' Harry, thin-skinned at the best of times, is duly infuriated. 'In those last two words, "this girl", Harry heard the tone of snobbishness that was anathema to his approach to the world.' In the months that follow, the brothers barely speak, and Kate does 'little to bridge the divide'.

From then on, the world proves unequal to the high standards set for it by Harry and Meghan. Hooked on social media, they take rapid offence at any disapproving comment. When no offence is available, the authors of *Finding Freedom* duly invent it: for instance, they say Meghan was 'lambasted' by the press for wearing trousers to the Endeavour Fund Awards, when the records show she was applauded; equally, they say the couple were 'pummelled with criticism' on their first trip to Wales, when in fact they were praised. Yet Harry and Meghan got into a spiral of hurt and fury about even the tiniest of misunderstandings. 'One story had her demanding spray-bottle air fresheners for her wedding day to spritz around "musty" St George's Chapel ... The truth was that the discreet Baies scented air diffusers for the chapel provided by Diptyque ... had been okayed by all parties involved.' They then became even more hurt and furious when corrections were not issued, sensing a Palace conspiracy to downgrade them. To adapt Enoch Powell's old aphorism about politicians: 'For a royal to complain about the press is like a ship's captain complaining about the sea.'

Instead, as we all know, their solution was to stomp off to pursue their 'vision' abroad, full of fresh fury at having to relinquish their royal patronages. 'Harry didn't want to be in his brother's shadow,' argue the authors. But, like it or not, being in your brother's shadow is the job description for the second son born into a hereditary monarchy. And Harry's life is fated to become even more shadowy: having been born third in line to the throne, he is now sixth, behind little Prince Louis, and is likely to end up in the low twenties.

Will Harry and Meghan really Find Freedom in California? Or will they end up like the Duke and Duchess of Windsor, toytown royals, living in ghostly exile, dreaming of the way things might have been?

3

September 2020
Our Blueprint for the Future of Humanity

HARRY: It's not going to be easy, but, let's face it, guys, there should be no place in this world for things which really have no place in it. We've got to find a way to move on. Because unless we move on, there's no turning back. And that's what we're so proud to communicate in our amazing new project with Netflix. You see, we both understand the inspirational power of the human spirit, the need to listen all voices, great and –

MEGHAN: – and that's why I want to share something with those of you who are crying out for change in this world. It was five, six years ago. I had just grabbed a guava and agave smoothie and I was walking along the sidewalk when something in a shopfront caught my eye.

Call it happenstance. Call it synchronicity. Call it providence. But what I saw that day changed my life. It was a sign. And it said: 'TOMORROW IS THE FIRST DAY OF THE REST OF YOUR LIFE.' And that's what I want to talk to you about today. Tomorrow –

HARRY: – not yesterday, not today –

MEGHAN: Tomorrow is the first day. Of the rest. Of our lives.

HARRY: Not just our lives, but your lives too.

MEGHAN: Ten little words, but they mean so much. Because, you know what? Together, Harry and I have embarked on a journey to open a new chapter in the history of mankind.

HARRY: So, the way I see it. In the old days, when I went on night patrol with the totally brilliant guys in my regiment, we'd have this fantastic sense of being in this thing together, like it was us against the world, and, given the chance we'd just, like, blow the bloody enemy to smither –

MEGHAN: But this time, no one's 'against' anyone else. Together, we're poised to harness the values of a generation to rebuild our broken world and set a tone for a more inclusive and – yes – empathetic direction not only for all humanity, but for all humankind.

You know, a wise person once told me –

HARRY: And we so need wise people in these troubled times. If you're in need of wisdom, a wise person should be your first stop.

MEGHAN: So a wise person once told me that the most important part of the healing process is the conversation. Put it this way: you would never visit a doctor without having a conversation. Because without a conversation, nothing heals.

HARRY: And without heels, there are no shoes. And – yes – we desperately need shoes to walk with. Because, as I learnt from my time in the armed forces, without a decent pair of shoes –

MEGHAN: What I can't believe is that the Palace offered us absolutely no help with our shoes. Remember, I was totally new to this game. So when Kate saw me in my new pair of Louboutins, of which I was so proud, and she said nothing, anyone could see why I'd be hurt, very deeply hurt.

HARRY: And William didn't mention those shoes either, even though he knew how proud you were of them. I was furious. And when I mentioned this to Granny, she just changed the subject and asked how the building works were coming along. And that makes my blood boil – not just for the two of us, but for all of humanity.

MEGHAN: A word of praise costs nothing. Anyone who has the extraordinary courage to wear a pair of new shoes deserves encouragement, regardless of their race or gender. That's why there's no turning back. We must own this conversation. We need to show the world that from one little grain of salt, you can grow a forest.

HARRY: We have one planet. Just one. And that's like incredibly few. There's not another planet attached to this one, or if there is, we haven't discovered it yet. The nearest other planet is literally miles away, out in space. So let's treat our planet the way we would treat our best friend. Share some laughs with it, down a few, give it a high-five. Yes, put it there!

MEGHAN: Sometimes, I look at the moon and I worry it's sidelining me, or treating me, as a woman, with disrespect. I'm sorry, but Princess Anne's the same. She's never once complimented me on a single episode of *Suits*, even though it was such a landmark series and contains some of my finest work as a woman of colour.

HARRY: We continue to represent and support Her Majesty, albeit in a more limited capacity.

MEGHAN: I have such deep respect for Her Majesty. Despite her immense old age, she's still a great listener. So why has she never asked me for fashion tips, when she knows I used to manage my own hugely successful fashion and lifestyle website?

HARRY: So hurtful. I was furious.

MEGHAN: Well, it just makes me sad on her behalf. You see, I know she admires me, and the feeling is mutual. But do I detect a hint of, I don't know – envy? Envy at our friendships with George and Amal, with Oprah and Idris and David and Victoria? Envy at the way Harry and I have created a life of our own in the sunshine, putting all our energies into creating our own brand for truly helping mankind?

Last time I saw Her Majesty, I looked into those beautiful, blue, young-at-heart eyes of hers, and reached out to her with a pearl of wisdom to treasure forever.

'With fame comes opportunity – the chance to advocate and to share,' I told her. 'And if we girls are given the right tools to succeed, we can create incredible futures, not only for ourselves, but for all those around us. Elizabeth – you are a child of the universe. And you have a right to be here.'

In her position it must be so tempting to like focus on the clothes and the shoes and the glamour and applause, so easy to ignore those less fortunate. So I had privileged her with a glimpse into another reality. And you know what? Her gratitude shone through.

I'll never forget her reply. That truly great old lady looked me deep in the eyes, as if she could see into my very soul, its passions, its ideals, its heartaches. And she said: 'Have you come far?'

Four little words – but a universe of experience.

'Yes, I have come far,' I said. 'Do you have a problem with that?'

4

7 March–14 March 2021
The Week of Harry, Meghan and Oprah

In our ever-changing world, there is one fixed point. You can always rely on a vicar on Radio 4's *Thought for the Day* to say something daft. The rules are simple: you pick a topical issue, and then relate it, in any way possible, to your beliefs. It's the virtue-signallers' answer to *Just a Minute*. After waffling for a minute or two, every speaker concludes that whatever topic they have picked points to 'a deeper malaise in our society'. At the close of a particularly dizzying week, Wednesday's *Thought for the Day* once again came up trumps. The speaker was Jayne Manfredi, billed as 'an Anglican ordinand': 'Jesus of Nazareth was once dismissed as a liar by people who told him: "You are testifying on your own behalf, your testimony is not valid." To which he replied: "I know where I've come from and where I'm going."'

At this point, I thought that if I were writing a spoof of *Thought for the Day*, at this juncture I would have the Rev. Jayne compare Meghan Markle to Jesus. Hey presto! As if by magic, she did just that. 'This idea that our own truth isn't good enough on its own is something we've seen play out in the media over the last few days to devastating effect,' she said. 'Prince Harry and Meghan told their version of the truth and to some this is invalid testimony. What is truth and who has the right to tell it? These are important questions that are worth asking.'

No sooner had the Rev. Jayne posed the questions than she dealt out all the answers. She spoke of 'the harsh and deeply personal nature of the backlash' against Meghan and Harry, which – tarantara! – all pointed to 'a deeper malaise in our society'. She ended with a biblical tale from the Book of Jeremiah. God asks Jeremiah to bury his loin-cloth under a cleft of rock. 'Many days later, God asks him to dig it up again and when he does, Jeremiah discovers that the loincloth is now useless.'

From this, the Rev. Jayne interpreted God's message to mean that Harry and Meghan were right to talk to Oprah Winfrey. 'There is something to be said for washing our dirty loincloths in public. If you keep them buried forever, they quickly become good for nothing.' Not only that, but 'When we tell vulnerable truths, we testify to our humanity and confess to our helplessness as precious children of God.'

At the start of the week, there had indeed been something weirdly biblical about the way Harry and Meghan and a film crew chose to squeeze into a hen coop with the all-seeing, all-knowing figure of Oprah Winfrey.

'She's always wanted chickens,' explained Harry.

'Well, you know, I just love rescuing,' added Meghan. Harry looked sheepishly at the ground.

'What are you most excited about in the new life?' asked Oprah, adding, 'Here, chick-chick-chick-chick.'

'I think just being able to live authentically,' replied Meghan.

'Mm-hmm,' said Oprah.

'Right? Like this kind of stuff. It's so, it's so basic but it's really fulfill-ing. Just getting back down to basics,' added Meghan.

Being interviewed by Oprah Winfrey in a designer hen coop called 'Archie's Chick-Inn' is certainly an exciting new way of being authen-tic.

'Authentic' is one of Meghan and Harry's key words, along with 'trapped', 'lost', 'truth', 'share' and 'compassion'. Later, Harry said that, unlike other members of his family, he wanted to 'just, like, just be, just be yourself. Just be genuine. Just be authentic.' The pair of them employ these words in all sorts of unconventional ways. 'There's a lot that's been lost already,' Meghan told Oprah. 'I grieve a lot. I mean, I've lost my father. I lost a baby. I nearly lost my name. I mean, there's the loss of identity.' From this, an outsider might conclude that her father was dead. In fact, he is alive and kicking, and giving grouchy interviews, complaining that Meghan won't see him and that he can't see his grandson. In this context, what Meghan means by 'lost' can be loosely translated as 'sent to Coventry'.

Likewise, the word 'compassion', which Harry confuses with 'contempt'. Having revealed that his father had stopped taking his calls and that he and his elder brother were 'on different paths', and having hinted that one or other of them might be racist, he said: 'My father and my brother, they are trapped. They don't get to leave. And I have huge compassion for that.' Ah, bless!

The moment the interview finished screening – 'Well, thank you for sharing your love story,' cooed Oprah – the world was swamped by a torrent of opinions, strongly for or strongly against, and sometimes both at the same time, on Twitter and phone-ins and TV news programmes, from friends and former friends and wannabe friends, from sports personalities and disc jockeys and vicars and celebrities and former celebrities and professors and politicians and pop stars and people in the street and – surely the most forlorn of all categories – from an endless parade of 'royal experts'.

'Is this the beginning of the end for the royals?' asked the presenter Ian Collins on Talk Radio, inviting his listeners to phone in with their opinions. Martin from Tottenham said he was black and, 'I'm sat here wondering how I'm going to get to the end of this month.' He found it 'sickening that these idiots, multi-millionaires that go and sit down with a multi-billionaire and just effectively playing the race card, they don't live in the real world, these people'. Martin added that 'That's what these new royals are, they're not about stiff upper lip, they're not about being the best this country can be, they're about how much of a victim can I be and how much can I get paid for it?'

Erica from Eastbourne, a mixed-race woman of sixty-nine, was equally unimpressed. She said that when she was born everyone asked the colour of the baby. Her brother 'was actually born white and his skin tone changed after about three months'.

'All these questions are quite normal,' she insisted, adding, of Meghan, 'she's obviously got an agenda'.

Others were equally convinced that speculating about the colour of a baby's skin was beyond the pale. 'I thought it was the most extremely distasteful thing for somebody to say,' said the Labour MP Diane Abbott; 'to be worrying about quite how dark the child will be could only be described as racism.'

Once or twice a year, a fresh news story brings forth a host of half-remembered faces popping up to deliver a heated opinion before you have a chance to reach for the off button. It's the twilight celebrity version of whack-a-mole. Fast out of the trap was Princess Di's gooey former butler Paul Burrell, ready for a busy week ahead.

'I felt tremendous sadness,' he confided to Billy Bush on Extra TV in America. Oddly enough, he looked almost deliriously happy. At a time like this, TV cameras can be a great comfort. 'There's blood in the water and the sharks are circling,' he said with a smile. Never backward in coming forward, Burrell boasted that he had known Harry 'since he was a little bump in his mummy's tummy. He's a very good boy. He's Diana's son – how could he not be a good boy? But he's been mesmerised by Meghan ... I don't want to see his heart broken again.'

Burrell prides himself on relaying the inner thoughts of all the most prominent royals, even if he has not spoken to them for twenty years. 'Our poor Queen is worried sick about her husband ... is he lying in bed taking his last breath? We don't know.' It turns out he is convinced that Harry is hurting and that he himself is hurting because Harry is hurting. 'He's very uncomfortable with the way things are turning out, I'm sure he is ... I'm hurting because of that.'

The more solemn news programmes clearly see the race issue as a godsend, because it lets them talk about the whizzy topic of the Royal Family, but in suitably concerned tones. 'It was always likely to be bad – but in the end, it was worse,' fretted Emily Maitlis on *Newsnight*. On Zoom from America came Professor Wendy Osefo, 'star of *The Real Housewives of Potomac*'. Sadly, Professor Osefo had just got going on the fairy-tale wedding – 'we tuned in only to find out her fairy-tale was actually a nightmare' – when the screen froze. 'Wendy, we've lost you,' said Emily, swiftly turning to another academic, Emma Dabiri, who described as 'incendiary' Harry's vague recollection of someone-or-other asking something-or-other at sometime-or-another 'What will the kids look like?' Dabiri went on to demand nothing short of 'an honest and truthful reckoning with British history'.

It was a bumper week for the clergy, too, everyone eagerly awaiting their take on Meghan's claim that the Archbishop of Canterbury married the couple in private, three days before the real thing. The Rev. Green, doubtless sitting on the Cluedo board in the lounge with the lead piping, tweeted furiously from St Mary's, West Malling. 'You can't get married twice? If it was a marriage, what on earth are we doing "playing" at prayer/holy matrimony for cameras?'

By now, everyone was tweeting away. Spring is here! The mad March hares are leaping! Amanda Gorman, the knowing young poet who spoke at President Biden's inauguration, tweeted: 'Meghan isn't living a life without pain, but a life without a prison.' Eh? For the former *X Factor* winner Alexandra Burke, Meghan's experiences were 'heartbreaking and disappointing'. The tennis star Serena Williams upped the ante, and won the Hyperbole Open by tweeting that Meghan is 'my selfless friend ... She teaches me every day what it means to be truly noble.'

When no one famous is available, there are always people in the street to fall back on. *Channel 4 News* collared a desultory cross-section of pros and antis loitering within spitting distance of Windsor Castle. A woman in a white coat talked of wake-up calls and brushing things under the carpet. A woman in a black coat said it was a bit sad, really, and should have been done behind closed doors.

They also asked the former *Times* editor Simon Jenkins what he thought. Over the course of the week, he was one of the few souls honest enough to admit to both ignorance and indifference. 'I haven't seen the programme, and my inclination is to say it's nothing to do with me. I've seen two very unhappy young people and I feel very sorry for them.'

A secret law obliged all newscasters to say 'bombshell' every few seconds. 'Well, it officially qualifies as a bombshell interview ... the revelations just kept on coming,' said Tom Bradby on *News at Ten*. Another forgotten figure, Princess Diana's old stenographer Andrew

Morton, solemnly declared: 'Make no mistake, the fallout from this will shudder down the generations.'

It was one of those self-generating stories in which even the fallout has its own fallout, summoning forth yet more opinions. At the crack of dawn on Tuesday, Piers Morgan waddled off the *Good Morning Britain* set, having fallen out with the weatherman over the Meghan issue. 'You can trash me, mate, but not on my own show. See you later.' His later dismissal acted as a red rag to the tweeters – Gary Lineker and Sharon Osbourne were pro-Piers, while John Cleese and Jedward were anti. 'We've turned down multiple appearances on @ GMB cuz of that dope! And now the future is JEPIC!' tweeted Jedward, exultantly.

By the end of the week, it was hard to think of anyone, butcher, baker or candlestick-maker, who had not delivered a bullish opinion on matters royal. Everyone turned into their own caricature. Hillary Clinton said she found it 'heart-rending to watch'. Virginia Giuffre, Prince Andrew's accuser, said the royals 'should all hang their heads in shame'. Tucker Carlson from Fox News said: 'He's weak and unhappy, and she's a manipulative opportunist.' Jacob Rees-Mogg said: 'Her Majesty is held in enormous affection.' The acidic Samantha Markle said that her half-sister had a 'narcissistic personality disorder'. Beyoncé thanked Meghan 'for your courage and leadership. We are all strengthened and inspired by you.' The singer-songwriter Jamelia called for 'an overhaul of every single institution that the monarchy are the head of'. His Imperial Highness Karl von Habsburg, Archduke of Austria, called what the wayward royal couple said 'gossip and garbage'. The talk-show host Trisha Goddard described Meghan as 'a huge beam of light'. And on her YouTube channel, the odd-bod 'royal expert' Lady Colin Campbell broadcast a marathon one-hour-and-twenty-one-minute monologue consisting of thirty-eight points against Meghan, concluding: 'You are an ingrate and a bare-faced liar.'

In the long run, it might be quicker to list those who said nothing, or had nothing to say: as I write, Dilyn the Dog has kept his opinions to himself, and so have Bob Dylan, the Dalai Lama and Kim Jong-Un. Speaking on a personal level, I was binge-viewing all six seasons of the

New Jersey mafia series *The Sopranos* before I was diverted by *The Sussexes of California*. I now can't wait to get back to *The Sopranos*. I fancy a little peace and quiet.

SELF-HELP

The Art of Discarding

There are seven drawers in our kitchen, apart from the one with the knives and forks. This is a list of what I found when I opened one of them.

A mouth organ; a pair of scratched spectacles; a broken earring; three batteries, presumably used; six pencils, all but one of them broken; one plastic (curtain?) ring; five birthday cake candles; five identical passport photos of my son; two light bulbs, out of their boxes so therefore presumably used; one media pass to Conservative Party press conferences for the 1987 general election; a small camera; a bottle opener; a tiny plug; a comb; a mock-velvet scrunchy; a golf ball; six golf tees.

A tube of lipsalve from Boots; a pack of cards; a yellow crayon; five hairclips; two 1p stamps; a packet of nails; a DVD of a film called *Snake Dance*; an old Trivial Pursuit card (first question: 'Where are the famed Kew Gardens?' answer: 'London'); a receipt from Schott Music, Great Marlborough Street for £15, dated 18 December 2015.

A combination lock, unopened, with no sign of its combination; six needles; a 1977 Queen's Jubilee commemorative coin in a plastic envelope; six tickets for Count Arthur Strong at the London Palladium this coming May; two soluble Solpadeine tablets; the head of a screwdriver; a tiny yo-yo, perhaps from a Christmas cracker; a bottle opener; three corks; an old-fashioned film for a camera that no longer works; a Tate Gallery membership card, expiry date December 2014.

Are you still with me? It so happens that the book I am reviewing is called *The Art of Discarding*, which its publishers confidently describe as 'The book that inspired Marie Kondo's *The Life-Changing Magic of Tidying Up*'.* It has, they add, already sold two million copies in Japan.

'Throwing stuff out: it's a fundamental issue,' reads the very first sentence. Quite clearly, I am the target audience. The chapter titles give the gist of what is to follow: 1: Don't Keep it 'For Now'. 2: Avoid 'Temporary Storage' – Decide Now!'. 2: 'Sometime' Never Comes. 4: 'Really Convenient!' to Somebody Else – Irritating Junk to Me. 5: Nothing is Sacred. 6: If You've Got It, Use It.

And so forth. On page 7, the author squeezes the message of the entire book into a single sentence. 'It's very simple: keep things you use and discard those you don't.' The rest of *The Art of Discarding* is little more than a repetition of this basic message, over and over and over again. Even though it is an extremely short book – 168 pages with big type and a lot of blank space – it seems much too long. A recurrent phrase is 'As I've said already'. If only the author had followed her own strictures and discarded anything unnecessary, she could have boiled it down to a couple of paragraphs at most.

Like many self-help manuals with a message too brief to fill up the allotted pages (diet books, for instance, are all long-winded variations on two words: 'eat less'), *The Art of Discarding* includes a survey conducted by the author from her circle of acquaintances. 'The majority of responses were from the Tokyo area, but some were also from Osaka, Kyushu, Shikoku, Chubu and Hokuriku,' she adds, helpfully.

Asked, 'Are there any things in your everyday life you find difficult to store?' virtually everyone said 'Yes'. Men said books first and clothes second, while women said clothes first and books second. Nagisa Tatsumi then reveals herself as a leading figure in the IBO (Institute of the Bleeding Obvious) when she says that people find it hard to get rid of books because they have 'high information content', and clothes and bags 'because these are things that are worn or carried' and 'people tend to grow fond of them'.

She has also discovered – tarantara! – that people don't like to get rid of 'things with special emotional significance'. She concludes this

* *The Art of Discarding: How to Get Rid of Clutter and Find Joy* by Nagisa Tatsumi (2017).

section with the words, 'Letting stuff pile up will only cause trouble in the end. Be brave and get rid of it.'

Thank goodness she never rootled around in our kitchen drawers, or I'd never hear the end of it. And here we come to the nub of the matter. What sort of 'trouble' can this pile-up of stuff really cause? To take just one example, the miniature Christmas cracker yo-yo has probably been in our drawer for a good ten years, along with the broken earring, the Trivial Pursuit card, the mouth organ etc. etc., but it has never caused us the slightest bit of trouble. What sort of trouble does Nagisa Tatsumi expect a miniature yo-yo to give you? Does she think it will one day leap out of its drawer, Colditz-style, and yo-yo its way around our kitchen, creating havoc and discontent?

In fact, all the stuff in our drawers – crayons, golf tees, light bulbs – has always behaved in a very civilised manner, and with the utmost discretion: we don't hear a squeak out of it from one year to the next.

She reserves a particular scorn for those of us who keep things because 'they may come in useful'. 'Little girls dream that some day a prince will come along – but that day is never likely to arrive,' she says. Well, yes and no. I agree that I am unlikely to put a broken earring, a used light bulb or a 1987 media pass to good use, but who is to say that one day I won't be in need of a golf ball, a cork, a mouth organ or a miniature yo-yo?

'Think like this!' she keeps saying, in her bossy-boots way, before telling us what to do. 'The key is to know yourself. You're not someone else. You're you.' Words of wisdom, indeed! One thing is for sure: I'm certainly not her. 'If you keep this in mind,' she says, 'then you'll know that you don't want things that don't seem necessary.'

Aha! That's where she's wrong. You see, I DO want things that don't seem necessary – in fact, as unnecessary as possible, and the more of them the merrier. What I don't want is for my house to look like a science lab, with everything spick and span as though ready for a post-mortem. 'Don't you think our city is beautifully laid out, Mr Fields?' said the mayor of Christchurch in New Zealand when he was showing W. C. Fields around. 'Yes, indeed!' replied Fields. 'Tell me, when did it die?'

There is a particular sort of house, generally lived in by trendy architects or 'design gurus' and featured in colour supplements. Everything in it is immaculately 'cutting-edge' and uncluttered, with spotless surfaces and nothing human in sight. Staring at these photographs, I find myself yearning to sneak in a child of five and let him loose with a squeezy bottle of tomato ketchup and a pack of magic markers.

Perversely, for someone who has sold two million of them, Ms Tatsumi has a thing against books, and never stops coming up with reasons to get rid of them. In a chapter called 'Nothing Is Sacred', she declares that 'when you die, it will all be rubbish. If you were to die right now in a traffic accident, that album you've kept so carefully will be thrown away. Your books will be bought up as a job lot by a second-hand bookshop. Wouldn't it be better to clear things out instead and enjoy a clutter-free life while you can?' This is a curious argument, suggesting that human existence is just a dress rehearsal for death.

The book grows increasingly nutty as it goes on. Having exhausted her basic message – discard anything that isn't useful – by page 2, she turns her fire on everything else. 'Think like this!' she says. 'The moment you notice something is the moment to get rid of it. If you don't, it may stay there for a long time.'

She then urges parents to indoctrinate their children in the sacred art of binning. 'Every year, say on or around the child's birthday, get them to decide what to throw away.' And Happy Birthday to you, too! Has she ever met a child? Or do they do things differently in Japan? Under the heading 'Dolls, soft toys', she writes, 'Through my survey I was surprised to discover that many Japanese people find dolls and soft toys difficult to throw away because "they have eyes", or "they might curse you".'

Who knows? Perhaps something was lost in translation, such as sense. For the time being, I'm planning to stick with my strict non-binning policy, though for this book I might make an exception.

Playing the Game

Unfashionable though they may be, there is plenty to be said in favour of the Boy Scouts.

At my boarding school, I rose through the ranks to become the Patrol Leader of The Falcons in the 23rd Basingstoke Troop. To this day, it remains the only position of responsibility I have ever held, though at the time I must have thought it the first rung on a long ladder.

In our Scout Hut, a framed photograph of our founder, Robert Baden-Powell, moustachioed and wiry, looked disapprovingly down on us, and underneath it the Scout Motto, 'Be Prepared'. But Be Prepared for what? No one ever told us, and we never found out. I now think it is one of those gnomic statements – 'Only Connect' is another – that means both everything and nothing.

Baden-Powell was a veritable mine of advice, or, more accurately, a minefield. Whenever he opened his mouth, out poured the tips: by the end of his long, long life – born 1857, died 1941 – he had published nearly thirty books, among them *Life's Snags and How to Meet Them* (1927), *Lessons from the Varsity of Life* (1933) and *Paddle Your Own Canoe* (1939), as well as his classic *Scouting for Boys* (1908), which has been translated into thirty languages.

Playing the Game is a Baden-Powell anthology, published to coincide with the centenary of the Boy Scout movement.* It comes with a foreword by his grandson, the current Vice-President of The Scout Association, and presents a portrait of Baden-Powell as a jolly Mr

---

* *Playing the Game: A Baden-Powell Compendium* edited by Mario Sica (2007).

Chips figure, full of chummy advice and daredevil yarns about facing 70-foot-long snakes and Zulu warriors and surviving for months eating nothing but bananas ('never felt fitter in all my life').

It would be hard for even the most thoroughgoing liberal to pick a fight with the majority of the aphorisms reprinted here. There is, for instance, not much to choose between Baden-Powell's 'The really rich man is the man who has the fewest wants' and Kris Kristofferson's 'Freedom's just another word for nothing left to lose'. And which of us would argue with advice like 'Life without an appreciation of beauty is like a dull day without sunshine'?

B-P regularly stresses the need to think of other people. 'Before you go to camp, and the whole time you are away, say to yourself, "I am going to make this the most enjoyable camp there ever was for the other Cubs", he suggests – advice that might usefully be pinned up all over the Big Brother House in time for the next series.

Yet, even in a celebratory anthology such as this, which has been edited with a view to turning this old Edwardian general into an easy-going twenty-first-century Blair babe, there are glimpses of another, much loonier, Baden-Powell. The editor devotes much space to B-P's more politically correct beliefs – he doesn't approve of shooting elephants, for instance, and after witnessing the horrors of the First World War, he became a dedicated peace campaigner. But there are times when the certainty with which he states his opinions is matched only by their idiocy. Is it really true that 'you can tell a man's character from the way he wears his hat'? Or that, as his dogged research concluded, '46 per cent of women are liable to act on impulse'?

He was never one to pass up an opportunity to state the obvious. A keen amateur actor – he once performed in *The Pirates of Penzance* in Kandahar clutching a sword, because of the 'danger of the Ghazis rushing down on us at any moment with their nasty great knives, awfully unpleasant things' – he dishes out advice to budding young thespians. 'The great step to success is to play your part as naturally as you possibly can, just as if you were not in front of a lot of other people but actually doing the things that you are pretending to do.' Who would have thought it?

Often, B-P sounds like Harry Enfield's Mr You-Don't-Want-To-Do-It-Like-That, popping his head over the fence to offer unwanted words of wisdom. His unstoppable advice even extends to the best way to breathe. 'Scouts breathe through the nose, not through the mouth,' he states.

On the whole, women are obliged to take a back seat in his world, though this compendium does include advice he gave to a young man who sought his advice on marriage. 'Choosing a wife is a most delicate and difficult job, and fellows are too apt to fall in love with a pretty face and not to look too closely into the character behind it. It is the character which makes all the difference in after years.'

Oddly enough, B-P himself only took the plunge at the age of fifty-four. From the back, he noticed that a woman thirty-four years his junior – 'a total stranger to me and whose face I had not seen' – walked in a way that, in his estimation, showed her to be full of common sense. Two years later, on board a ship, 'I recognised the same gait in a fellow passenger.' Hey presto! – it was the same woman. 'So we married – and lived happily ever after.'

This book contains a number of fleeting glimpses of something decidedly peculiar at the heart of Baden-Powell. But the book's editor, Dr Mario Sica, a bigwig in the international Scouting movement, has dutifully removed most of his hero's warts before compiling this centenary portrait. For a more sustained study of B-P's less palatable side, you would have to look elsewhere.

You would, for instance, have to dig around in other works to find some of his more free-range observations on women or natives. 'Like a woman, a horse is subject to moods' is one of his little sayings not included in the present volume. Nor is 'An occasional lick from a whip is, to an unintelligent savage, but a small matter.' And nor is this, on the subject of Africans: 'They must, as a people, be ruled with a hand of iron in a velvet glove, and if they writhe under it, and don't understand the force of it, it is no use to add more padding – you must take off the glove for a moment and show them the hand. They will understand and obey.'

Baden-Powell was celebrated as the hero of the Siege of Mafeking, and the compendium includes some of his reminiscences about that time, including advice on the best way to eat a horse, and locusts too ('locusts are brutes and deserve no pity'). But Dr Sica is sadly circumspect when it comes to printing the more off-putting of B-P's recipes. For instance, it might have been bracing for readers to hear his memories of eating iguana. 'When he was boiled and put on the table he looked exactly like a headless baby with his arms and legs and little hands,' recalled Baden-Powell, adding 'He tasted like a baby too, sort of soft chicken flavour with violet powder.'

It's all a far cry from Delia. Of course, Baden-Powell was born 150 years ago, and it would be absurd to flap one's arms in self-righteous indignation at attitudes that were fairly commonplace at the time. But Dr Sica's sieving of the complete works for advice and anecdotes that will be palatable for the youth of today has, I think, been a little too assiduous.

It is all very well to be reminded of Baden-Powell's pacifist attitudes in the years after the First World War – at one point, he even quoted Buddha on love – but perhaps we might also have been reminded of his admiration of Mussolini ('a very charming, humorous and human man') and of his suggestion in 1937 that the British Scouts should do 'something to be friendly with the Hitler Youth'.

There is something sweet about Baden-Powell's sunniness, and even about his stress on outdoor activity as a means of warding off 'the sickly-minded sloppy slacker who talks dirt and has no backbone'. But for a final word on this extraordinary man, it is worth recalling P. G. Wodehouse. The great comic writer once included him in a novel as Major Brabazon-Plank, who 'had for years been horning in uninvited on the aborigines of Brazil, the Congo and elsewhere, and not one of them apparently had had the enterprise to get after him with a spear or to say it with poisoned darts from the family blowpipe'.

The Secret of Life:
Paulo Coelho

Live your dream, or your dream will live you.
    Achieve your dream, or your dream will achieve you.
    Chew your gum, or your gum will chew you.
    Before you go out in cold weather, be sure to wrap up well.

'Father,' said the child, 'why is the sky above us?'
    'Child,' said the father, 'the sky is above us because if it were below us, we would have nothing upon which to stand.'

The secret of life is to discover the secret of life.

If you dance around a cauliflower, then every now and then, from certain angles, and in the right light, it will look like the sun.
    But most of the time, it will look like a cauliflower.

To a piece of bread, another piece of bread is a thing of wonder. And when the first piece of bread sees that other piece of bread has butter on, he marvels, 'How smart he looks in his new suit!'
    But if every piece of bread in our universe had butter on it, every slice would dream of jam.

The wise man is he who is not daft. The daft man is not wise because if he was wise he would not be daft.
    For the same reason, the wise man is not daft because if he was daft then he would not be wise.

And that, my son, is why the daft man is daft, and the wise man is wise.

'Where can I find wisdom, father?' asks the child.

'Wisdom, my son,' replies the father, 'lies in knowing where wisdom is to be found.'

We are all travellers on a cosmic journey, stardust swirling and dancing in the eddies and whirlpools of infinity. Every moment is precious. Except for this one, which you have just wasted.

And this one too.

I do not live in my past or my future. I am interested only in my present.

Where is my present? My present is here, now. And my present is ready for unwrapping. 'What have you brought me this time?'

When I see it, I am filled with sadness. 'But I have already got one of those! You must take it back and change it. Or you are no friend to me.'

Even when the lawn is mown, the grass continues to grow. But the mower will never grow, no matter how hard it mows the lawn.

The boy had a verdant oak growing in his heart. Each day he watered this verdant oak, and it grew taller.

'Father,' he said, 'why is this verdant oak growing in my heart?'

'Because when you were a child, my son,' replied the father, 'I made you swallow an acorn.'

I look in the mirror and see myself looking back. But is this really me? Or only my reflection? Am I my own reflection? And is my reflection really me? When the wise man looks in the mirror he knows that what he sees is but a reflection of himself.

The man who paints his window black will never see out of it.

You cannot make a fruit salad with an apple alone. And you cannot make a fruit salad with a peach alone.

So the man with an apple says to the man with a peach, 'Let us combine my apple with your peach and we will have a fruit salad.'

And the man with a peach says to the man with an apple, 'That is a good idea. But first let us find a man with a banana.'

So the man with the apple replies, 'I see it clearly now. With my apple and your peach and the banana of the other man, we will make a fruit salad. But I enjoy grapes in my fruit salad too. And we have no grapes.'

And the man with the peach says, 'I have the solution, oh man with an apple. We will combine your apple and my peach and the banana of the other man, and then we will find a man with a bunch of grapes.'

'And what will we say to the man with a bunch of grapes when we find him?' asks the man with an apple.

'We will say to him, "Oh, man with a bunch of grapes, we are striving to make a fruit salad. We have a peach and we have an apple and we have a banana. But we have no grapes. If you let us, we will combine your grapes with our peach and our apple and our banana. And we will make that fruit salad of which we have dreamt for so long."'

And then the man with the apple suddenly remembers that he likes melon too, so he says to the man with the peach, 'We have a peach and we have an apple and we have a banana and we have our grapes. But we have no melon.'

And the man with the peach replies, 'We have spoken about this for too long. The night has now come. Darkness reigns in our universe. The man with the banana and the man with the grapes and the man with the melon have all gone home, and are asleep. Let us buy a ready-made fruit salad from the 24-hours supermarket.'

And the man with the apple replies, 'Why the fuck didn't you say that in the first place?'

The Soul of the Universe whispered in my ear, 'I have loved no man so much as I love you, Paulo.'

And to The Soul of the Universe I replied, 'Me neither.'

How to Win Friends and
Influence People

This is a true story about the power of words. In 1936, a failed actor called Dale Carnegie published a book called *How to Win Friends and Influence People*. He had earlier changed his name from Carnagey to Carnegie, perhaps to suggest that he came from one of America's wealthiest families.

His book became an overnight bestseller. It continues to sell 300,000 copies a year, although the publishers have removed one of the origi-nal chapters, 'Making Your Home Life Happier', as it contained pieces

of advice that now seem out of date, such as telling wives to 'give your husband complete freedom in his business affairs'.

The main thrust of *How to Win Friends and Influence People* is that the best way to manipulate other people is to persuade them you agree with them. If you want other people to do something, says Carnegie, you must first implant an idea into their heads, and then you must convince them they had that idea first.

Over the years, Dale Carnegie's influence spread far and wide. One of those who studied his book was a young convict imprisoned in Terminal Island Penitentiary in Los Angeles for car theft. In 1957, he passed an IQ test with flying colours, so the enlightened prison authorities fast-tracked him on to a special Dale Carnegie course, to help him forge a better life on his release.

He was considered an outstanding pupil, having absorbed all Carnegie's key lessons, such as 'Everything you or I do springs from two motives: the sex urge and the desire to be great.' He had been particularly struck by Carnegie's advice on how to influence people: 'The only way on Earth to influence the other fellow is to talk about what he wants and show him how to get it ... Let the other fellow feel that the idea is his.'

That same year, on the other side of America, an eleven-year-old boy was also studying *How to Win Friends and Influence People*. The boy's father, a successful New York property developer, had taken the Dale Carnegie course in order to overcome shyness. He was determined that his children should follow suit.

Who were these two young self-help addicts, the small-time criminal and the ambitious young heir to a property fortune?

The heir was Donald J. Trump, who was elected President of the USA in 2016. Trump continues to adhere to the lessons he learnt from *How to Win Friends*. It is thought that he reread it in his late sixties: over the course of a year, he repeated some of Carnegie's key maxims in a series of tweets. At 5.53 a.m. on 27 November 2012, Trump tweeted: '"Take a chance! All life is a chance. The man who goes farthest is generally the one who is willing to do and dare" – Dale Carnegie.'

This was followed by: 'Feeling sorry for yourself is not only a waste of energy but the worst habit you could possibly have' (17 July 2013); 'If you want to conquer fear, don't sit at home and think about it. Go out and get busy' (19 July 2013); and 'Success is getting what you want. Happiness is wanting what you get' (17 September 2013).

The car thief was Charles Manson. On his release from prison in 1967, he headed straight for San Francisco, where he dutifully followed Carnegie's advice. 'That was Charlie's big trick,' a prison friend told Manson's biographer Jeff Guinn. 'He'd decide what he wanted to do, and then talk about it so the girl or whoever would think that she thought of it and it was her idea. I saw him do it all the time. I mean, it was a constant.'

The friends he won over – his so-called 'family' – were drawn from the lost and damaged souls of the hippy movement; he influenced them into multiple murders.

And so two of the most famous men in America used the same advice from the same book to rather different ends. One ended up dying in a high-security prison, serving a life sentence on multiple counts of murder; the other ended up in the White House. Such is the power of words. Should Dale Carnegie take credit for one, but not the other? Or can we blame him for both?

Simon Heffer's Correct Englsih

Access is a noun, not a verb. 'Can I access your website?' is thus doubly wrong, since there is no such thing as a 'website'. A web is the gossamer structure produced by a spider. A site is the location used for a town or building. So were it to exist at all, which it does not, a 'website' would refer only to that location chosen by a spider within which to weave its sticky gossamer structure. By this I do not mean that the proposed gossamer structure is to be composed of sticks. I am employing the adjective 'sticky' in its primary sense of 'tending or intended to stick or adhere'.

Andes is the range of mountains which forms the western fringe of South America. 'Today I am climbing the Andes. My lady wife has kindly agreed to carry the hamper.' **Andes** must on no account be confused with

And he's, which is the sloppy manner in which the poorly house-trained breed of American youth, invariably armed with a repeat-action shotgun and chewing on a 'hot dog', prefers to pronounce the three words 'And he is'.

In the unfortunate circumstance of a visit to America, it is important to remember that over there a 'hot dog' is a sausage-based comestible rather than a perspiring canine. Poor unfortunates in the later stages of Americanisation might also be prone to terming a four-legged animal, to which they may or may not be sexually attracted, a 'hot' dog, though this is to be avoided by civilised persons. **And he's** must never be confused with

Andy's, which means belonging to a gentleman called Andrew whose perfectly acceptable Christian name has become hopelessly corrupted by vulgar and over-familiar colleagues. A notable victim of this linguistic slide is the egregious romper-suited former stage and television 'personality' Mr Andrew Pandy.

'And he's due to be executed tomorrow' is never to be used as a substitute for 'Andy's due to be executed tomorrow', unless the villain in question also happens to be called Andy.

Aunt: Without presuming to insult the intelligence of my readers, I have nonetheless made certain depressing assumptions, perhaps erroneous.

One is that many of you will not have been taught the difference between **Aunt**, meaning the sister of one's mother or of one's father (or, in certain circumstances, the wife of the brother or the sister of one's mother or one's father) and **Aren't**, the abbreviated term for **are not**.

Further confusion may arise with **ant**, an eight-legged insect identified by its elbowed antennae and the distinctive node-like structure that forms a slender waist.

The vulgar expression **ain't** should be avoided at all costs.

Bottom: This word refers to the lowermost part of an object or geographic feature. Journalists working for tabloid newspapers have been known to employ it to refer to a particular area of the human body. If this area must be mentioned at all, and there is no comprehensible reason why it should, then it is more seemly to call it the **behind**. However, the expression 'I am behind with my work' should not be taken to indicate that the user is in the practice of employing his behind on a professional, or even a semi-professional, basis.

Cat: The noun **cat** should never be used to mean **dog**. It cannot be stressed too often that they are different animals. When one writes 'The cat sat on the mat', one is not referring to a dog; even a dog such as a Pekingese or Chihuahua which may, from certain angles, be said to resemble a cat. A **mat** is a generic term for a piece of fabric or flat material, generally placed on a floor or other flat surface, and serving a range of purposes both decorative and functional.

Don't: Don't is incorrect: **do not** is correct. Both should be distinguished from **donut**, a type of fried dough comestible popular in many countries but rarely found in establishments of sophistication or refinement.

Eskimo: An inhabitant of Eskdale in the Lake District of Great Britain should never be referred to, either wittingly or unwittingly, as an **Eskimo**. An **Eskimo** is a foreigner who lives in an igloo, preferably abroad, eats raw fish and grins far too much for the simple reason that he does not know any better.

Fan: A **fan** is an implement waved by a member of the female gender for the purposes of ventilation. The word **fan** should on no account be employed to denote an obsessive follower of a popular singer or group. The correct term for such a person is **lout**.

Gaga, Lady: A daughter of Lady Gaga should be styled The Honourable Felicity (assuming Felicity to be her Christian name) Gaga. A son of Lady Gaga should be styled The Honourable Freddie Gaga (assuming Freddie to be his Christian name) up to that time when his father dies, at which point he should be styled Lord Gaga, if his father was an hereditary peer, or the Earl of Gaga, if his grandfather was a duke. This is not, as some suggest, a matter of snobbery; simply good manners.

Hang: 'shoplifters should be hung' is wrong; '**shoplifters should be hanged**' is correct. To hang shoplifters thus serves a twin purpose: justice is done, and correct grammar is maintained.

Incorrect English: It was my recent misfortune to read the opening sentence of a book that the publishers, in their infinite wisdom, sought to deem a 'classic work of literature'. Nothing could have prepared me for the horror. It read as follows: 'You don't know about me, without you have read a book by the name of *The Adventures of Tom Sawyer*, but that ain't no matter.'

How does one begin to list the infelicities contained therein? Clearly, the author does not possess even the most shaky grasp of the English language, and would thus never merit employment as a columnist on the *Daily Telegraph*.

Jam: **Traffic jam** denotes a build-up of motor vehicles. **Strawberry jam** is that which one consumes on bread or toast for one's afternoon tea. The two should not be confused.

K: Enoch Powell, a superb stylist of Orwellian abilities, insisted that the word **'knicker'** should never be employed in the plural, other than in instances in which one was wearing two examples of the aforesaid garment at once. For Powell, **'a pair of knickers'** meant two separate garments, so that when, as an undergraduate, he was instructed to wear **'a pair of knickers'**, for the next three years he wore two. As his biographer, I fell under his spell and so together we would walk around wearing two knickers each, or four in all. Over luncheon (sometimes incorrectly termed 'dinner' by the ill-educated) we would often take the opportunity to compare knickers. The great man also taught me that it is incorrect to award the noun **pant** (plural: **pants**) an apostrophe, as in **pant's**, or **pants'** other than in the exceptional circumstance of the undergarment in question being in possession of that to which is being referred.

Powell also taught me that excrement placed by imaginary negroes through the letterboxes of anonymous old ladies should properly be termed **excreta**, as it is invariably delivered in the plural. Incidentally, *Daily Telegraph* readers go to the **lavatory**, never the **toilet**. If no lavatory is available, they should go in their **underpants**, never **pants**.

Lay: Lay is a transitive verb. Lie is an intransitive verb. The two should not be confused. She **lies** in bed, longing for one to remove one's knicker. Later, she will **lay** the table before one partakes of luncheon.

Man: For the sake of clear English, women are most usefully to be classed as men.

Nosh: Food, or an approximation thereof, consumed by the ignorant underclass.

Obvious, stating of the: One lesson, not only of good journalism but indeed of persuasive writing in any form, is to do more than state the obvious. This is not to suggest that the obvious may not be stated, nor that the statement of the obvious is not in itself to be commended. However, the statement of the obvious is rarely sufficient to stimulate the mind of the intelligent reader. Other than that which is of itself most obviously stated, the (*continued on the page numbered 94*).

Robinson Accrueso

Sylvain Tesson enjoys a reputation as France's foremost travel writer.

In 2010, he planned to spend six months by himself in a tiny log cabin on the shores of Lake Baikal in Siberia, a six-day walk from the nearest village. Baikal is 435 miles long, 50 miles wide and nearly a mile deep. In winter, it is covered with ice more than a yard thick, allowing it to be crossed in a heavy truck.

This, Tesson's book about his life as a hermit in Siberia, won the prestigious Prix Médicis in 2011.* 'From February to July 2010, he lived in silence, solitude and cold,' promises the book's blurb.

In his introduction, Tesson states: 'I'd promised myself that before I was forty I would live as a hermit deep in the woods,' adding that 'I took along books, cigars and vodka. The rest – space, silence and solitude – was already there.'

But after four pages, he admits he took along rather more. A two-and-a-half-page inventory of fifty-eight items reads like a particularly exhaustive version of the family car game I Packed My Bag. It includes a kayak, sleeping bags, ten boxes of pills 'for vodka hangovers', a carpet, kitchen utensils, a lamp, Russian icons, a few backpacks and even a GPS.

Towards the end, Tesson sneaks in some catch-all headings such as 'provisions', 'electronic appliances' and – ahem – 'solar panels, cables and rechargeable batteries'. Is his life as a hermit going to be quite so spartan as he would have us believe?

He arrives at the cabin with his truckful of bric-a-brac on 12 February. Fortunately, it has already been heated up for him by a forest

---

* *Consolations of the Forest* by Sylvain Tesson (2013).

ranger, and Tesson has brought along two friends to help him with the unpacking. Sadly, he finds the cabin's interior decoration not to his taste. 'In Russia, Formica reigns supreme,' he sniffs. 'Bad taste is the common denominator of humanity.'

Over the next two days, he and his friend Arnaud strip away the linoleum, the oilcloth and the plastic wallpaper until it looks much more tasteful. 'We have brought two yellow pine double-paned windows from Irkutsk to replace the cabin windows, which shed a dreary light,' he adds. Oddly enough, he forgot to mention these two yellow pine double-paned windows in his original inventory.

As time goes by, a number of other home comforts pop up out of the blue. A week into his life as a hermit, he writes: 'I've equipped my home with solar panels, which run a small computer ... I listen to Schubert while watching the snow.' At this stage, it dawns on the reader that Tesson is not so much Robinson Crusoe as Laurence Llewelyn-Bowen.

His journal favours the self-consciously French Poetic style, combined with a touch of Walt Disney. This means he turns everything in Nature – the sun, the moon, the fish – into a cutesy human being. 'A timid moon is looking out for a kindred spirit,' he observes at one stage, and at another, 'One day, the sun will reveal to us where it finds the strength to get up at dawn.'

Four days after waving goodbye to his friends, he grabs a couple of hours to gaze into space. 'I am learning the art of contemplation,' he writes. He is never short of self-approval. Two hours later, his contemplation is disrupted by the arrival of eight four-by-fours, radios blaring, full of Russian tourists. They cut a hole in the ice and take turns plunging into the water with great yells and whoops. Tesson is not amused. 'What I came here to escape has descended on my island: noise, ugliness, testosterone-fuelled herd behaviour,' he harrumphs.

Once the tourists have left, he retreats into his sauna.

His what?

Oh, yes, he forgot to mention that his hermit's cabin comes complete with a spacious new sauna, 16 feet by 16. Even a premier chalet at Birmingham's own Crossroads Motel never boasted such a luxury.

Three days after the departure of the Russian tourists, he observes: 'When I awaken, my days line up, eager virgins, offered in blank pages.' But not for long: two days later – after just ten days in the cabin – he decides to pay a visit to his gamekeeper neighbour, Volodya, nine miles away. Volodya is entertaining a group of opinionated fishermen, and they enjoy a raucous dinner together. Tesson stays the night, then goes home. The next day, his social whirl continues with a visit from a meteorologist called Yura and an unnamed Australian woman. Once they have left, he snatches a day alone to describe his life as a hermit. It turns out the solitary life makes him feel very, very special indeed. 'As the nature of objects reveals itself, I seem to pierce the mysteries of their essence. I love you, bottle; I love you, little jack-knife, and you, wooden pencil, and you, my cup, and you, teapot steaming away like a ship in distress.' And you, too, little sick-bowl, you might want to add.

But he is not easily deflected from his mission. 'The hermit gains in poetry what is lost in agility,' he observes. It might be worth remembering that, so far, he has been a hermit for just a fortnight, and in that time he has seen Yura and the Australian woman plus Volodya and his fishermen friends, not to mention eight cars full of Russian tourists. He is the Pippa Middleton of Lake Baikal, the Nicky Haslam of hermits. Later the same day, he gets a call on his satellite phone telling him his sister has had a baby. Ah yes, the satellite phone! Something else he forgot to mention!

March sees no let-up in this hermit's hectic social whirl: on the 2nd two fishermen drop by, on the 6th he stays again with Volodya, on the 8th he stays with two more friends, Anatoli and Lena, on the 9th he stays with someone called Sergei, and from the 10th to the 12th with someone else called Yura. On the 13th he sees the first Yura again, on the 14th he enjoys a bottle of cognac with a couple called Mika and Natalia, and on the 15th he is finally driven home in a Mercedes by a businessman from Irkutsk.

Back in his cabin, he takes a breather to fill us in on life as a hermit. 'I am the ambassador of the human race in a forest devoid of men,' he says, never backward in coming forward. Five days later, four fishermen pop in for vodka and sausages. Over the next few days Volodya drops by, plus four people working on the hydroelectric plant nearby.

'A hermit does not threaten society, of which he is at most the living critique,' writes Tesson – he is a great one for theories – and next day Sergei calls by and offers to drive him to Pokoyniki, where they enjoy a shindig with the new director of the nature reserve and his colleagues, along with Sergei's wife Natasha.

By now, we are well into April. On the 20th, he takes a break from his journal because – whoops! – he has to nip off to the city for eight days in order to renew his visa. On his return, it's still all Hermit-a-go-go, with an endless procession of friends and strangers. It's a wonder he finds the time to jot down his solitary thoughts, but he does so in the purplest of ink, e.g.: 'A russet moon rose tonight, its reflection in the shattered lake ice like a blood-red Host on a wounded altar.'

By my calculations, the longest he spends without seeing anyone else during his entire stay is just a month, from 9 May to 8 June, and by then the ice has melted, the sun is shining, and who would ever say no to a little me-time in a cabin?

The rest of June and the first half of July involve yet more heavy socialising, with two French painter friends staying for five days, and two journalist friends for a week. They leave on 15 July, which gives him just a day to write about his life of solitude. 'Cabin life is like sandpaper. It scours the soul, lays bare one's being, ensavages the mind, and reclaims the body for the wild, but deep in the heart it unfolds the most sensitive nerve endings.'

Next day, a couple come for supper; two days later Volodya arrives to help him pack up. Then it's back to Paris, to grab a little peace and quiet in order to polish up his account of his days as a hermit.

'The loneliness', insists his publisher, 'was crippling.'

Cupboards Are Ideal for Putting Things In: Mary Berry's Household Tips

If you tend to feel the cold, why not invest in an extra blanket?

When the time comes for choosing a new sofa, remember that a very large sofa may not fit into a very small room. On the other hand, a very small sofa will almost certainly fit into a very large room, but it's all a matter of personal taste.

Keys. Hang your front door keys inside the door, not outside, or burglars may use them to gain entry.

Personally, I always prefer a nice soft sofa to a rock-hard one, but that's just a matter of taste. Sofas stuffed with feathers tend to be softer than those stuffed with something harder, such as iron, rocks or household implements.

Cupboards are ideal for putting things in. They generally come with a door, or even two doors, so they can be shut when not 'in use'. For instructions on how to shut your own particular cupboard, refer to the manufacturer's guidelines.

The marvellous thing about a mirror is that it enables you to see your own face in it, looking back at you.

Adding mushrooms to stock lends it a lovely mushroomy flavour.

A garlic press is excellent if you want to press garlic, but I find it not quite so good for wiping sticky surfaces.

The best way to follow a recipe is from start to finish. If you start at the end, you may find yourself taking all your ingredients out of the oven before you have mixed them together or cooked them.

Flowers always brighten a room. Try placing them on a table rather than on the floor, where they might be knocked over. I always think they look at their best with their polythene wrapping removed, though this is a matter of personal taste.

Before giving a dinner party, consider how many people you want to invite. Too few can be not quite enough, and too many can be rather too many. Sitting twenty or more guests around a table designed for four may prove a bit of a squeeze.

Shopping is quite an art in itself! Butchers are wonderful places for finding meat, while vegetables are readily available at most green-grocers.

Caring for shoes. If it's raining and muddy, then it's best to wear something waterproof, such as wellingtons. Wellington boots are generally considered unsuitable for smart dinner parties or society balls, but, if you must wear them on these occasions, do give them a good wipe first.

When eating a boiled egg, be careful to remove the shell first, or it can be a little crunchy.

Things that shouldn't go in the dishwasher: cutlery with bone handles, china with gold or silver detailing, velvet cushions, fresh flowers, household pets, large items of furniture.

Leftover gravy can be very useful for getting rid of red wine stains. Just spread two or three gallons of leftover gravy evenly across your carpet, and the wine stain will disappear beneath the rough brown hue. And the smell will get those tastebuds going!

Never take anything piping-hot out of the oven with your bare hands, or you may suffer serious burns. I swear by 'oven gloves', and like to place one over each hand. Placing both hands in the same glove can sometimes make things tricky to handle. So I place my left hand in the left glove and my right hand in the right glove, but it's very much a matter of personal taste!

Bookshelves are perfect for storing books. I place mine on the shelf with the spine facing outwards. This lets me see what the book is without having to pull it out.

Most books are numbered at the bottom of each page, so you can tell at a glance what page you are on. To keep the flow going, books are best read in the order of the numbers at the bottom of the page.

Fireplaces. Before making a fire in your living room, first make sure you have a fireplace. A roaring fire lit any-old-where in your living room may damage your carpets and furniture.

The hallway is an excellent place for storing umbrellas. I always put my umbrellas 'down' before storing them, as it leaves more space. But this is very much a matter of taste.

Packing your suitcase. If you are going somewhere hot, it's unwise to pack too many woolly jumpers or anoraks. On the other hand, if you're going somewhere cold and wet, you don't want to be caught with only a T-shirt or skimpy top! I always look and see where I am going before setting off, and then pick my clothes accordingly.

Whenever I wash dishes in my bedroom, I find that the sheets and blankets get awfully wet. The kitchen is a much better place for doing the washing-up. But avoid pouring hot soapy water on to your cooker, especially if it's electric!

If you are having elderly or infirm people to stay, it's best to keep a defibrillator in every room, and possibly one extra on the landing, just in case.

In all hurly-burly of modern life, it's so easy to forget things. Why not keep a Memo Board with handy notes to yourself about what you're meant to be doing on this day or that? Of course, it's all too easy to forget where you put your Memo Board. Not to worry! A series of sticky-backed 'Post-it' notes with arrows, scattered all around the home, should do the trick!

If the telephone goes while you are ironing, it can lead to a terrible muddle. A medicine box in the corner of the room can prove an absolute lifesaver for those with severe burns around the ears.

These days, it's quite usual to shop in a 'supermarket'. They can be awfully muddling, but if you approach one of the ladies by the tills and give her your list, she'll be delighted to 'fetch and carry' for you.

There's nothing more infuriating than a jam jar without a label, or with a label facing the wrong way. If ever I find one, I smash it into little bits with a hammer and/or a rolling-pin, before placing it in the bin, which I always mark 'Bin'.

MEMORY LANE

Michael Caine Remembers

I tell you this for a fact. Ours was the first generation to thumb its nose at convention. Back in the 1950s, if a working-class bloke like me had tried going into the West End without a jacket and tie, he'd've been horsewhipped. But my generation changed all that. Forever. By the end of the 1960s, you could wear whatever you fancied – and, believe me, some of the birds preferred to walk around in the all-together, at least in my pad, bless 'em! You'd walk into somewhere like Flowers, a great little trattoria just off the King's Road, and you'd bump into everyone. Twiggy. Vidal Sassoon. Herman's Hermits. Che Guevara. Christine Keeler. Bill and Ben. Little Weed. And they'd all be wearing what the hell they liked. We were inventing a whole new world as we went along. And at last we felt free to do what we wanted, not what the toffee-nosed bigwigs told us we should want. And it felt like freedom. But now what's happened? I'll tell you for a fact. You go into a restaurant these days, people just don't care. The trouble is, they can't be bothered to make the effort. They just lounge around looking like they just got out of bed. Not a suit in sight, and they've probably never seen a tie in their life. It's as though they're all scared bloody stiff of looking halfway presentable. So now, in my restaurants, I insist on a decent dress code. Nothing too formal and posh, mind, but at very least a jacket and tie. It's all about respect. And if they can't muster up the respect, well, we show them the door, son, and quite right too.

In the 1960s, everybody you knew became famous. Suddenly, all the doors were thrown open. I had this friend, Billingsgate lad like me called Jeff Bird, loved his fishing did Jeff. So I was a struggling actor, and so was Jeff. And, over a pint one night in 1960, 1961, I'll never forget this, Jeff says to me, 'Tell you what, Maurice' – 'cos that was my name back then – 'Tell you what, Maurice, I plan to give up this acting lark. Instead, I'm going to grow myself a beard, put on a little hat, create my own frozen-fish empire and make a bloody fortune!' Of course, I laughed in his face. 'Oh, yeah?' I say. 'Pull the other one.' Then he says, 'But I'll market them frozen fish under my real name, and with my proper naval ranking.' So I say, 'What's your real name and ranking then, Jeff?' And you know what he replies? I'll never forget it. 'Captain Birdseye.' And the rest, as they say, is history.

By the late 1960s, my old pal Cap'n Birdseye was a regular at the Ad Lib Club down Leicester Square. You'd always see him on the dance floor in his trendy naval uniform with its shiny gold buttons and his peaked hat and his beard, chatting up all the dolly birds – Samantha Eggar, Mary Quant, Marianne Faithfull and that Aussie bird with the opinions – that's the one, Germaine Greer, bless her. Of course, they was crazy for the Cap'n's produce because, like me, they'd all been through the war and the rationing, and suddenly there's this bloke offering them this beautiful ready-battered frozen cod. And you know what it felt like? It felt like freedom. Everyone went to the Ad Lib Club in them days. It was the centre of things. On a regular Tuesday night, you'd see Eric Burdon of The Animals chatting up the young Barbara Cartland in her psychedelic miniskirt, you'd see Julie Christie on the dancefloor with Cliff Michelmore, and strike me down with a feather, who's that over in the snug in the corner? Why, if it isn't Sandie Shaw discussing the French new wave with Simone de Beauvoir and Freddy 'Parrot Face' Davies!

We were driven by this urge to break out of the iniquitous British class system. Working-class kids like me and Twiggs had been told we couldn't do what we wanted to do and that made us all the more determined to do it, whatever it was. And, what's more, whatever it was we wanted to do was what we did, so we could do what we wanted to do whenever we wanted to do it, whatever it was. Back in them days, it was only posh people like Noël Coward and Charlie Chaplin and Tommy Steele and Little Arthur Askey who were allowed into show-business. There was so much snobbery back then, but between us we brought the barriers down forever. Nothing would ever be the same again. And now, to cap it all, this working-class lad from Elephant and Castle has been made a knight of the realm – and addresses five Crowned Heads of Europe and a dozen Peers of the Realm as 'mate'.

I mentioned this to my good mate HRH the Prince of Wales at a private luncheon the other day, and he couldn't have agreed more. You see, like me, he got his big break in the 1960s, what with the Investiture and that. And this is what many young people today refuse to under-stand. It only takes a bit of hard graft and you can get wherever you want to be, and don't tell me you can't. I tell you what. Around that same table was Camilla Parker Bowles. The whole point of the 1960s was that you had to take people as they were, and so I always take Camilla as she is, which is a very dignified and gracious Duchess, as well as being, to my mind, a lovely lady in her own right. If memory serves, I first bumped into Camilla when she was scrubbing the toilets at the Flamingo on Wardour Street in '61, '62 and I was auditioning for *Alfie* – a movie that was set to destroy our outdated class system once and for all. And now look where Camilla is – waited on hand and foot in her very own palace, and no need to nip down the eel-and-pie shop ever again! So don't go telling me the world hasn't changed for the better. Yes, in the 1960s, we created a social revolution that was going to change the world forever. But mention that to the young today, they just don't understand. Ask me why, and I'll tell you in one word. Yobbos.

Who Is the 'You' in 'You're So Vain'?

JULIAN FELLOWES: I may or may not have dallied with Miss Carly Simon in my youth. That must remain between myself and Miss Simon. But let me make something perfectly clear. One should never ever EVER walk into a party wearing a hat, unless, of course, one is attending an open-air gathering, e.g. Royal Ascot, at which hats are obligatory – though, even then, it is dreadfully common to dip one's hat 'below one eye'. Furthermore, I would ask Miss Simon to withdraw her allegation that 'your scarf, it was apricot'. As we both know, white scarves are permissible at the opera, and scarves of sober colouring may be worn at shooting parties (though then only *en plein air*). The very idea that one would have worn an apricot scarf AND a hat to Miss Simon's party is really too ghastly. One hates to say this about any woman of 'a certain age', but I'm sorry to say that Miss Simon lacks breeding.

GERMAINE GREER: For Chrissake, everybody who was around at the time was agreed that Carly Simon was the poor plug-ugly fat-lipped tub of lard who no one in their right mind wanted to talk to, let alone go to bed with. Guys like Mick and Warren would see her coming and run a mile rather than go through the intensely tedious and frankly soul-destroying process of having to snog her. So it frankly makes me hopping mad when I hear her trying to make out that they had it off with her. Cut it out, Carly! I was there at that party, and for what it's worth Mick and Warren and Kris and Jack Nicholson were all gathered around me, and let's face it, when YOU walked into the party you were so grotesquely unattractive that all the guys rushed out the back door with me, and that's a fact.

KENNETH ROSE: I walked into the party as though I were walking on to a yacht. My hat was strategically dipped below one eye; my scarf, it was apricot. I had barely gone a few yards when I saw Carly Simon coming towards me. I believe her grandfather used to shoot with the Earl of Westmorland on occasion. Miss Simon was wearing what I believe is known as a 'sweat-shirt', with her *embonpoint* vulgarly prominent. Luckily, at that moment I spotted Quintin Hailsham at the other end of the room, so I made a beeline for him, and the peril was thus swiftly averted.

WILL SELF: She had me several years ago when I was still naive. Ten-year-old Will hadn't removed himself from his faeces-enclogged shorts before the nauseating Ms Simon with rhinoceros mouth and barrage-balloon breasts began to smother me with scuttlebutt rumours of our smuttily sexual dithyrambs. Vain, indeed, of the oleaginous Carly, if that was her name, to imagine that Will would give a fig for her memories, real or otherwise.

DONALD J. TRUMP @realDonaldTrump: Of course that song is about me! Anyone who says it isn't is a totally dishonest stupid lowlife scum loser! That girl went totally nuts over me! My approval rate from Carly is 99 per cent – highest on record!

RACHEL CUSK: Why does she say I'm so vain? What right has she? We've never even met, but the hatred in her song screams out at me. It makes me want to scream back, 'Why me? Why are you telling everyone I'm so vain? Why do you want me dead? I am blameless!'

It's my former husband who has put her up to it, of that I am certain. I can't take this any more. I pick up her record and hurl it across the room. It hits a priceless vase and smashes it into a thousand little pieces. The shards stare back at me, bent on a revenge I don't deserve.

MARY BEARD: When I had Carly Simon on my show, I put the question to her that has been on everybody's mind these past forty-six years.

'So, Carly,' I said, 'wonderful to have you "on the show", as it were, and great that I should now have what I might call the "golden" opportunity to "put to you" the question that has been at the root of "public discourse", if I might call it that, for what is getting on for half a century now, and that question, if one can call it a question, which, on reflection, I think one can, is this, and this alone: to what extent is the "true identity" of the person you are addressing in "You're So Vain", which is, I might add, a song that is a personal favourite of mine, to what extent is the "true identity" of that person – though obviously we'll have to examine in some detail, whether any one of us can ever really have what can be called a "true identity" – so, as I say, to what extent is the "true" or "real" identity of the person in question a valid subject for speculation, given the confines of what one might call the "popular song", and, if it is a valid subject for speculation – that is to say, if the question may be asked in any remotely legitimate or "proper" way, then I would very much like to ask it of you, notwithstanding any objections, personal or otherwise, you may have to my so doing? But, very sadly, we're out of time, so let's move "swiftly on" to the fascinating exhibition of Spode Tableware we've all been to see at the Anstruther Gallery in Bath ...'

Paul Johnson:
Ten People Who Met Me

ALBERT EINSTEIN (1879–1955) knew nothing worth knowing about physics. But he did know a lot about cooking.

He was a master at cauliflower cheese. But I have never liked cauliflower cheese. Too cauliflowery, too cheesey.

I prefer roast beef. But Albert was no good at roast beef. He overcooked it.

He was always asking me for advice on relativity. I told him it was a complicated and foolish business, not worth the fuss. But he persisted because he always loved the media attention.

It did for him in the end. Today, Albert is barely remembered outside the pages of the specialist magazines.

MARILYN MONROE (1926–62) had no sex appeal. But she was desperate to get on. Sometimes I would find myself sitting next to her at the Beefsteak Club. No one else would touch her with a barge pole. She was dowdy in the worst sense of the word.

She was always grateful for my beauty advice. But it was an uphill struggle. She was a bad listener.

'Men never like a woman who shows too much cleavage and pouts,' I explained. 'If I were you, I'd wear a long skirt in brown or beige. Stop colouring your hair. And stop speaking in that silly way.'

I once introduced her to Noël Coward, a well-known womaniser. He showed no interest in her.

No one remembers Marilyn any more. Her films, such as they were, are never watched.

NELSON MANDELA (1918–2013) was a funny little man with nothing to say for himself. He wore colourful shirts and went around grinning. How did he become so famous? I put it all down to ruthless ambition. He couldn't sing. He couldn't dance. But he knew what the public wanted. In the latter part of the twentieth century, grins and colourful shirts could take you a very long way.

SHERLOCK HOLMES (1865–1928) was not nearly so clever as his brother Mycroft, whom I knew well. Sherlock considered himself a big cheese but he never solved a case worth mentioning. Men who smoke pipes make poor detectives. Their attention is always on the pipe, never on the case.

WINSTON CHURCHILL (1874–1965) was always pestering me for advice, even though I was only eleven when war broke out. He was desperately unsure of himself.

I had been the first to alert him about Adolf Hitler. Winston took him for a charmer, but I told him he was up to no good. 'Never trust a man with a side-parting,' I warned, 'he'll always try to put one over you.'

And so it proved. But Winston got the better of Adolf in the end. On VE Day, he collared me in the Savoy. 'Ay oop lad. You were right about Hitler,' he conceded in his broad Lancashire accent.

During the latter months of the war, Hitler proved a perfect pest. Not a day would go by without him telephoning me from his bunker, begging for advice on how to extract himself from this pickle.

'Sorry Adolf. No can do,' I told him. But it never put him off asking. Finally, I was brutally honest. I told him he hadn't a hope. The next day he shot himself.

PRINCESS DIANA (1961–97) had a stubborn streak. She would never take no for an answer, even when I insisted I was married. She was the most intelligent woman I ever met, fascinated by everything I said. She died in a car crash in Rome. They say she was holding a copy of one of my books, I forget which.

MAHATMA GANDHI (1869–1948) was much fatter than he looked. He used to wear a baggy loincloth, size XL, to cover up his great big belly. He was the fattest man I ever knew.

He was notoriously pugnacious. A quick jab from Mahatma and you'd be on the floor, begging for mercy. He disapproved of boxing-gloves, saying they were for sissies. What made him so aggressive? I put it down to all that meat he ate. 'You should eat more fruit and veg, Mahatma,' I told him.

He wore funny little spectacles. They did nothing for his image. I told him to buy something more manly, with proper horn rims. He failed to do so and he was assassinated.

He came from India, but knew nothing of its people or traditions.

BUGS BUNNY (1938–63) cut a ludicrous figure. He had big ears and protuberant teeth and generally went around with nothing on. He often had a carrot in his hand. He affected a lisp. I used to meet him at Kingsley Martin's flat and later at J. B. Priestley's.

He once sought my advice. 'There are three rules for a great rabbit,' I said. 'Never show off. Don't act the giddy-goat. And if you must go into the movies, make sure you only go after the serious roles.'

MUHAMMAD ALI (1942–2016) made a name for himself as a boxer. We met briefly. He was well built. I found him receptive to good advice. I taught him how to improve his game. 'Stop dancing around. Concentrate. Act like a man. And remember to punch.' It did the trick.

He had dark skin, which led some to mistake him for a negro.

REGINALD KRAY (1933–2000) had the finest manners of any person I ever knew. A typical Balliol man. He would always stand up when a woman entered the room, unless she was ugly or had fat ankles. A lot of gossip has been spread about his involvement in crime. Stuff and nonsense. He was the finest Christian I ever knew, apart from Pope John Paul II, who wasn't English. Reggie always remembered to say his prayers, particularly when there was a dead body in the room.

The Art of Irritation:
Kingsley Amis

Irritation is generally considered a minor emotion, less noble than anger, less operatic than rage. Over the centuries, it has inspired no great poem, speech or drama, though it must have prevented quite a few from seeing the light of day.

But in Kingsley Amis's *Ending Up*, irritation is raised to the level of art. Just as his old friend Philip Larkin thought that 'deprivation is for me what daffodils were to Wordsworth', so Amis's daffodils were irritation. He was both irritable and irritating, equally adept at both feeling intense irritation and dishing it out.

His first wife, Hilly, noticed Kingsley's remarkable dual capacity in this area soon after they first met in Oxford in 1946, when he was just twenty-three years old. From the start, she was aware of his 'endless complaints about what seemed to me harmless things like apparently ordinary, nice people going through the swing-door at Elliston's restaurant. He'd start muttering, "Look at those fools, look at that idiot of a man," and so on. If doors got stuck, or he was held up by some elderly person getting off a bus, or the wind blew his hair all over the place, he would snarl and grimace in the most irritating fashion.'

As a young novelist, he knew how to channel this curse into prose. Throughout his oeuvre, irritation plays on the Amis landscape like sun on sea. His first novel, *Lucky Jim* (1954), bristles with it. Its anti-hero, Jim Dixon, lacks any sort of capacity to brush things off. 'He wished this set of dances would end; he was hot, his socks seemed to have been sprayed with fine adhesive sand, and his arms ached like those of a boxer keeping his guard up after fourteen rounds.' Figures in authority, notably his professor, are particularly annoying. 'Welch's driving seemed to have improved slightly; at any rate, the only death Dixon felt himself threatened by was death from exposure to boredom.'

Subsequent Amis novels extend the boundaries of irritation to form something approaching empire. 'It was no wonder that people were so horrible when they started life as children,' observes the protagonist in *One Fat Englishman* (1963). More often than not, Amis's characters are drawn into a spiral of irritation at themselves. 'Feeling a tremendous rakehell, and not liking myself for it, and feeling rather a good chap for not liking myself much for it, and not liking myself at all for feeling rather a good chap,' observes the narrator of *That Uncertain Feeling* (1955).

But it was not until he was well into middle age that Kingsley Amis decided to pluck irritation from the chorus line and place it centre stage. For some time, he had been living in the countryside outside London with a slightly ragtag group of people: his second wife, the novelist Elizabeth Jane Howard, her brother Colin, known as Monkey, and Monkey's artist friend Sargy Mann. For three years they had been joined by Jane's mother, Katherine 'Kit' Howard, 'an unhappy woman with a sharp tongue, not an easy presence in the household for anyone', in the words of Amis's biographer.

One day, Elizabeth Jane had wondered aloud what would happen 'if we all went on living together and grew old together'. With these words she planted the seed for *Ending Up*. Interviewed by Clive James after the novel was published in 1974, Kingsley Amis said that the idea had come from his own experience of 'relations and people living in ... what would this sort of arrangement be like if one had a pack of characters who were all about twenty years older?'. He had imagined 'a situation where everybody was old, everybody had got to the end of their lives, and everybody had been there for a good long time so that all knew how boring one another was, and exactly the areas where one another was most vulnerable'.

Before he embarked on writing *Ending Up*, on 29 January 1973 Amis compiled eight pages of notes, kicking off with a list of forty-five 'ways of being annoying', each of which pops up in the novel. Alongside each way he then added one of five letters, indicating the character who would best personify it: A for Perverse shag (Adela), B for Egotist (Marigold), X for Shit (Bernard), Y for Fool (Shorty) and Z for Bore (George). Thus:

X – Being deaf – the which? – contemptuous when told
Z – Talking quietly, then v. loudly
Y – Repeating the wrong bit
A – Telling people to do what they'll do anyway & what they know
A – Wrong end of stick through eye of needle
X – Anger at simple questions
B – Whining – I'm old, on scrap-heap
Y – Punning – dud spoonerisms
Y – Polysyllabic facetiousness
B – Lying about what's happened, whose side was on in argt.

And so forth. He then wrote suitably merciless short biographies for each of the five characters, such as:

'A <Adela> (72). X's sister. Never married (too ugly, but really too boring or annoying). Ex-matron. Runs house ...'

and:

'B <Marigold> (74). A's oldest friend. Widow. Ex-actress. Has children. Hates X & Y. Laxative (for Y). Rt wing. Hates homos, lefties, n******, EEC ... Makes convenience of A, enjoys showing herself superior to her. Upper class. Amnesia just starting.'

Beside X for Bernard (76), who was to become the pivotal character, Amis wrote: 'Old queer but has child. Deaf. Malicious. Amnesiac. Hates everyone. Telephone wire for B. Heated wine for Y. Funny. "Bad leg." Dying & knows it. Waterpistols cats. India (for laxative). Can't drink. Small pension. Reads. Not enough to do.'

Amis's method seems to have been to gather forty-five ways of being from the inhabitants of his own home and then to redistribute them, in roughly equal proportions, among his fictional characters. For instance, he told his official biographer, Eric Jacobs, that Elizabeth Jane Howard's most annoying characteristic was primarily conversational. 'Amis would ask Jane a question and instead of answering she would ask why he'd asked it, as if nothing could be straightforward, not even a simple question.'

This tic reappears in the conversation of Marigold. Unlike Marigold, Elizabeth Jane was never an actress, but Amis once mentioned to Jacobs that she had complained that the publisher Victor Gollancz could never remember who she was and always mistook her for an actress, a mistake with which Amis later sympathised, given that she was, he said, so 'affected'.

Cruel, perhaps, but he was crueller still in his characterisation of Bernard, who appears to be an exaggerated and accelerated version of Amis himself. John Cleese once remarked that every young comic plays the character he dreads becoming. At the age of fifty Amis was far from young, but his portrait of Bernard is surely a projection of all his most objectionable tendencies, enlarged by old age. The only joy Bernard is able to extract from life is in making it worse for others: 'his only relief, and that a mild, transient one, had turned out to lie in malicious schemes, acts and remarks'.

In 1971, Amis said, 'If you can't annoy somebody with what you write, I think there's little point in writing.' His most thorough biographer, Zachary Leader, suggests that 'the desire to irritate and annoy animated Amis all his life'; *Ending Up* represents the most extravagant, unbridled and, it must be added, hilarious animation of this perverse desire.

What do they think has happened, the old fools,
To make them like this? Do they somehow suppose
It's more grown-up when your mouth hangs open and drools,
And you keep on pissing yourself, and can't remember
Who called this morning?

Philip Larkin finished his poem 'The Old Fools' a little over a fortnight before Kingsley Amis began writing *Ending Up*. The two works share an almost rapturous sense of disgust at the various afflictions of old age – fear, panic, incontinence, amnesia, paralysis.

'One thing the book isn't going to be is a serious, in-depth etc, study of old age,' Amis wrote to an interviewer when he was roughly halfway through. 'It's about five particular people who wouldn't be behaving as they do if they weren't old.'

The finished product is short and brutal, a series of cackling vignettes of man's cruelty to man, all conveyed in Amis's crisp, beady prose. It is also very funny, and grows funnier with each fresh misery, mishap and atrocity. The blurb on my Penguin edition draws attention to its 'humanity', but it might more appropriately have highlighted its inhumanity: few novels have ever been quite this bleak, quite this nasty. Even the pets at Tuppeny-hapenny Cottage become embroiled in the general unpleasantness, in a manner that mirrors their masters: 'Mr Pastry and Pusscat were locked in their peculiar form of combat, one that started as a mixture of fight and game in about equal proportions, with an escalating trend in favour of the fight element.'

Amis's well-loved misanthropy had never been so extreme. When an interviewer from the *Paris Review* suggested it was 'very bleak', he replied: 'Yes, well, no book is the author's last word on any subject, or expresses what he feels all the time. So if I were to walk under a bus this afternoon, then *Ending Up* would be my last novel, and people might say, "Well, he ended in a fit of pessimism and gloom." This wouldn't really be so. Each novel can only represent a single mood, a single way of looking at the world, and one feels bleak from time to time, and takes a fairly pessimistic view of one's own future and chances. But there are other times when one doesn't, and out of that other books emerge.'

Yet it is also, to my mind, one of the funniest of his novels, its pessimism refined and polished so that it shines with glee. It is also one of his most irresistibly inventive, as he employs the verbal tics of each different character to create a succession of conversational cartwheels, most notably with poor old George, who, following a stroke, suffers from nominal aphasia and is always groping for the right word. 'Did you watch, you know, the thing on the switching it on last night?' he says, meaning television.

On its publication in the USA, *Ending Up* was reviewed glowingly in the *New York Review of Books* by Matthew Hodgart, who suggested that its author had derived its structure from a baroque suite or a classical work in sonata form, possibly Mozart's String Quintet No. 4 in G minor K. 516. Amis's response was characteristically dismissive. 'Is he mad?' he asked an American friend, adding: 'as far as I know I've never even heard that Mozart quintet. Still, the review certainly won't lose any sales.'

Amis despised artists who gave themselves airs and made sure he never did it himself, much preferring to play the role of the anti-intellectual philistine. While writing *Ending Up*, he took issue with an article Frank Kermode had written in the *Daily Telegraph* in celebration of Ezra Pound. 'Few would deny he had genius,' proclaimed Kermode. Amis retorted in a letter to the editor: 'No indeed; only it was a genius not for poetry (he had not even any particular talent in that direction) but for behaving sufficiently like a great poet to gull the gullible.' Ten days later, Pablo Picasso happened to die, and Amis's reaction was similar: 'My dear Philip,' he wrote to Larkin on 9 April 1973, 'so Pablo the piss-poor paint-pusher has fallen off the hooks at last, eh? Ho ho ho. Beckett next?'

Yet, despite its author's fierce denial, there remains something musical about *Ending Up*. It is an elaborate dance of death, the five protagonists following the manic, fateful steps preordained by their characters, right up to that moment when the music stops and they all collapse. But Amis's mischievous delight in language and the extreme brevity of his chapters also give the work a jaunty feel, so that the great sombre themes of old age and death are transformed into the prose equivalent of a jig.

In one way in particular, *Ending Up* was eerily prophetic. Ten years later, Kingsley Amis had, by all accounts, turned into an only slightly paler version of Bernard Bastable – grumpy, cussed, dedicated to causing offence. His sixtieth birthday, in 1982, was marked by the *Observer* with a dinner in his honour at the Garrick Club, attended by no fewer than four editors and five columnists. At the end of dinner, the editor delivered a fulsome toast. In reply Amis stood up and said, 'I just want to make a few remarks. The first thing I've got to say to you is the *Observer* is a bloody awful paper.'

Julian Barnes had long been a friend and admirer of Kingsley, but, as the years went by, he came to find that 'The price you had to pay for his company got higher. Every meeting would involve at least one remark, aside, riff at which you thought, well, I'm just not going to rise to that. It would be n******, it would be Jews, it would be women, it would be Irish, it would be gays. You would think, we'll let that pass, but increasingly … it seemed that the price to pay was swallowing what you believed about things.'

Another example of life following art, of a prophecy fulfilled, came in his last days, when this most articulate of men lay in hospital, the power of language having all but deserted him, now more George Zeyer than Kingsley Amis.

'I feel a bit … you know.'

'What, Dad?'

'You know.'

'Anxious? Uneasy?'

'Not really. Just a bit … You know.'

His son Martin writes movingly about it in his memoir, *Experience*. At one point he asks Kingsley, 'Do you remember the book you wrote called *Ending Up*?' and goes on to regale him with the wit and brilliance he applied to George's nominal aphasia.

"'All this, Dad, in the book *you wrote*."

He is contemplating me with delighted admiration.

"Do you remember?"

No, he said.'

Memory Lay:
Mick and Keith Remember

KEITH: It was like, totaw madness.

MICK: Yeah. Totaw maaaadness. What we talkin' about?

KEITH: Y'know. The totaw madness.

MICK: Righ! Yeah! Totaw maaaadness. But TOTAL!

KEITH: Totaw wha'?

MICK: Maaadness. Totaw fuckin' maaadness!

KEITH: Yeah, totaw madness.

MICK: Yeah. It was like, totaw maaaadness.

MICK: First chick I ever shagged? Yeah, righ. Wooh! Righ! You gomme there!

KEITH: Grace.

MICK: Wha? Grace Slick? You never shagged her!

KEITH: Nah. Gracie Fields. Round the back of the wodgermicallit.

MICK: Camper van?

KEITH: Thassit. Camper van. While you was inside with Ruth?

MICK: Ruth? Ruth? Nah! Remind me?

KEITH: Ruth, Lady Fermoy. Jeez! Talk about Lady in Waiting! Not much waiting when she was around, hur, hur!

MICK: Totaw madness!

MICK: Keith and me, we firs met somewhere – where was it, Keith?

KEITH: In the stree. We met in the stree. You member!

MICK: Yeah, in the stree! Dr Livingstone, I presume! Righ!!!

KEITH: Nah, I don't member Dr Livingstone? Who the fuck's Dr Livingstone when he's at home?

509

MICK: He wasn' at home. That's the whole fuckin' point of Dr Livingstone, he wasn' at home. He was abraw. Anyway, so Keith and me, first time we met, it was in the stree.

KEITH: Or it may of bin indoors.

MICK: Thassit. Indoors! It was indoors! Keith and me, first time we met, it was indoors! Classig!

KEITH: Not OUTdoors, but INdoors! There's a fuck of a difference, Mick. Outdoors is out, an' indoors is in.

MICK: Well, it was either outdoors or indoors. Or, to put it another way, indoors or outdoors. The main thing was we met.

KEITH: Thas if we DID ever meet. I can't member.

MICK: Course we fuckin' met, Keith! If we hadn' met, we wouldn't be, like, here today –

KEITH: We're talkin' bow years ago. Litree years and years ago.

MICK: Fifty years ago!

KEITH: You're kiddin'.

MICK: Thas the whole fuckin' poin', Keith! Thas wha' we're celebraaaatin'!

KEITH: Fifty years. Fifty fuckin' years!

MICK: Fifty fuckin' years of like totaw fuckin' maaaadness! Bring it on, maaan!

MICK: Alta-wodever.

KEITH: Altamont.

MICK: Yeah, righ. Altamont. Totaw fuckin' maaaadness.

KEITH: Totaw fuckin' maaadness as you say.

MICK: Asasay, totaw fuckin' maaaadness. So when was it, then?

KEITH: When was wha'?

MICK: Altamon? When was Altamon?

KEITH: Altamon? Sixties, man. Or Seventies. Maybe the Eighties or wodever. Definitely not this year, though, or I'd've membered it.

MICK: Was a totaw nighmare. All these freaks havin' a really bad trip, and this geezer killed with like a ping-pong bat or sumthin'.

KEITH: Billiard cue.

MICK: Wodever. Something not nice. Highly regrettabaw, blah blah blah.

KEITH: Yeah, heavy shit. But at least we got it on film.

MICK: Yeah, at least we got it on film. Awesome.

MICK: We've always bin anti-establishmen'.

KEITH: Yeah, we've always really hated the anti-establishmen'.

MICK: Nah, Keith – we're *anti*-establishmen'. That means we don' hate the *anti*-establishmen', we hate the *establishmen'*.

KEITH: Swotter sed. Hey, man, I'm coo.

KEITH: Firs time we were on Tobbaverpobz. When was the firs time we were on Tobbaverpobz? Was it wiv the chick in the tartan skirt. Wossername? You know, she sang 'You'll take the fuckin' high road and I'll take the fuckin' wodever road, and we'll be somewhere like cool in the morning.'

MICK: Andy Stewart? He wasn't a chick, he was a bloke, Keith, a Scottish bloke in a kilt.

KEITH: Who gives a fuck, maaan? Helluva naughty little lady, bless her heart. Made an old man very happy, hur hur hur.

MICK: So, history-wise, there was Brian –

KEITH: Wodever happened to him?

MICK: Dead.

KEITH: Shame. Rest in wodever.

MICK: Then there was Mick –

KEITH: Thought you was Mick.

MICK: Yeah, I'm Mick but there was another Mick too.

KEITH: Two Micks. Faaaar out. Two Micks. That really does me head in. Wappened tim then? 'E die too?

MICK: Nah, jus left.

KEITH: Same difference, hur hur hur.

MICK: Then came Ronnie.

KEITH: Ronnie? Who the fuck? Remind me.

MICK: Y'know – Woody.

KEITH: Thought you said 'e was called Ronnie.

MICK: Ronnie Woody. Spiky hair. Guitar.

KEITH: Always wondered who 'e was. 'Bout time someone told me. Had some good times together, man.

MICK: Yeah, memriz!

KEITH: Yeah, righ. But wha' memriz? Remind me.

Joan Collins:
The Men in My Life

I'll always regret the day I married Mr Pastry.

In those days, there wasn't a girl in the world who didn't want to be Mrs Pastry.

To a young woman in her twenties, he seemed impossibly glamorous, with his signature walrus moustache and dashing bowler hat.

Au contraire.

He was incapable of doing even the simplest things. He was always walking into unopened doors and falling headlong into jelly trifles.

On our honeymoon, I lay in bed waiting for Mr Pastry clad in the most ravishing lingerie specially designed for me by the legendary DuPont of Paris.

But as he was about to leap into bed, he tripped over a ladder, a bucket fell on top of his head, then he lost all sense of direction and careered straight out of the window.

Sadly, this incident caused me to lose a great deal of respect for him. Our marriage ended there and then.

As luck would have it, the very next day at the Gare du Nord I met Struwwelpeter, who was to become my fourth husband.

I was attracted by his magnificent shock of hair and his hellraiser reputation. The moment the divorce from Mr Pastry came through, he rushed me to the altar.

But Struwwelpeter refused to cut his fingernails so he lacked the tender touch. *Au contraire.* I can still feel those scratches. Consequently our wedding night was a disaster and I was obliged to divorce him soon after.

As an incurable romantic, I refused to give up my search for love. The next day, I felt inexorably drawn to Struwwelpeter's friend Little Johnny Suck-a-Thumb.

Our whistle-stop courtship ended in marriage. I was blind to his failings.

It was on a sunny day in June that I became the first Mrs Suck-a-Thumb. Sadly, I was soon to discover his dreadful secret. Behind closed doors, and even in public, my new husband simply would not stop sucking his thumb. I suppose the clue was in the name. But why had no one warned me? *Au contraire.*

People are so inconsiderate.

To a young lady straight out of acting school, there's no one more glamorous than a doctor.

With his discreet spectacles and his svelte moustache, I felt myself inexorably drawn towards the gentle, soft-spoken Dr Crippen. But he let me down.

It was a tough lesson, but now I know never to fall for a married doctor who has recently cut up his wife's torso and buried it in the cellar of their three-bedroom home in North London.

At least I learnt my lesson. What a stark contrast to today's young-sters. These days, far too many young women rush headlong into bed with married doctors. These young sluts couldn't care less that these doctors haven't made the slightest effort to dispose of their wretched wives.

Sadly, the age of chivalry is dead.

Today's little darlings could learn a lesson from generations past.

Ours was a more innocent generation. At fifteen, I was still playing with dolls.

Two years later, I was appearing in my first feature film, *Lady Godiva Rides Again*.

In retrospect, I may have appeared nude in it, but I did not know it at the time. *Au contraire*.

I simply took my clothes off while they were filming. Which only goes to show how innocent we all were.

When today's so-called 'actresses' like Kate Winslet and Gwyneth Paltrow appear naked on screen, they do so without a second's hesitation.

What a stark contrast to my own generation. You would never have seen HM the Queen Mother, who graciously led us through two world wars against Adolf Hitler, appearing topless in public without a very good reason.

It is time to rebuild our society. We need leaders like the Queen Mother.

She took a fierce pride in her appearance. You would never see her out in public in jeans or slacks and a grubby sweatshirt.

As she rode graciously down The Mall in her horse-drawn carriage, she did not spend her time 'texting' or shouting the 'C' word at her devoted subjects.

But society today is in meltdown. Shoplifters are let off with a slap on the wrists rather than being summarily executed after a fair trial.

Today, my daughters can't even walk down the street without the possibility of something unpleasant happening. *Au contraire*. The other day, one of them boarded a London bus but its driver – foreign-born, of course – refused in no uncertain terms to take her to her cottage in the countryside.

It wasn't like that in the 1950s. *Au contraire*. Life may not have been perfect. Yes, there may have been one or two murderers. But they only murdered the ugly and the overweight.

Whatever happened to good manners? Yesterday, I told a passer-by to carry my bags for me, and he flatly refused.

No doubt he spent the rest of the day ram-raiding corner shops with his trousers hanging below his buttocks, his shoelaces undone and his headphones going full-blast.

Yes, our liberal society has much to answer for.

Today's youngsters simply refuse to listen to advice.

I was once briefly married to Basil Brush, the well-spoken TV personality.

To the outside world, he was a genial TV personality with an infectious laugh.

It was only after marrying him that I discovered he was just a useless glove puppet, entirely under the control of an unseen hand.

At least I have had the sense to learn from my mistakes. The same cannot be said of the young today.

Au contraire.

There are many things today's young do not possess, the chief of which is wisdom.

Downturn Abbey
Act Three: The World as We Know It

LORD GRANTHAM: It matters less how a man handles his fork, Carson, than how he handles his women folk.

CARSON: Yes, milord.

LORD GRANTHAM: After all, Carson, a fork is just a fork. But a woman is a human being. [*glances at watch*] I fear it cannot be long now before the First World War breaks out, and the world as we know it is changed forever.

CARSON: Might I have a word, milord?

LORD GRANTHAM: Can't it wait, Carson? I am up to my neck in cufflinks, and my iPod is on the blink, dash it!

CARSON: I do apologise, milord. But I wish to tender my resignation.

LORD GRANTHAM: Your resignation, Carson!? What, pray, is your reason?

CARSON: I would rather not say, milord.

LORD GRANTHAM: Look here, Carson. You at least owe me that.

CARSON: It's about that chocolate cake, milord.

LORD GRANTHAM: Ah yes. The chocolate cake.

CARSON: One of the under-maids served it to Her Ladyship without providing the requisite spoon and fork. Consequently, the chocolate smeared itself all over Her Ladyship's face.

LORD GRANTHAM: The poor darling resembled a member of the redoubtable Black and White Minstrel Troupe! Had the Slave Trade not been abolished by my good friend Lord Palmerston some fifty years thither, she might have found herself chained to the oar of a slave ship bound for the West Indies, Carson!

CARSON: I shall never forgive myself, milord. And for that reason, I wish to tender my resignation.

LORD GRANTHAM [*tenderly*]: I won't hear of it, Carson. We must let bygones be bygones. Far better that I should dock you six months' pay and forget all about it!

CARSON [*discreetly wiping away tears of joy*]: I promise you, milord, you shall never regret your decision!

LORD GRANTHAM: It behoves the well-born to overlook the minor misdemeanours of those less intelligent than themselves, Carson. [*glances at watch*] And, with poor Archduke Franz Ferdinand shortly to be shot, and the First World War looming, who knows what the future may hold?

CARSON: Yes, milord. Might I have a word, milord?

LORD GRANTHAM: Can't it wait, Carson?

CARSON: I'm sorry to bother you, milord, but it's just gone noon, and it appears that the First World War has come to an end.

LORD GRANTHAM: That's marvellous news, Carson. War is a tiresome business, particularly when leading to bloodshed.

CARSON: Indeed so, milord [*prepares to exit*].

LORD GRANTHAM: One moment, Carson. You mentioned The FIRST World War. Did you mean to imply that ANOTHER may be on its way?

CARSON: Indeed so, milord. I regret to say that Mr Churchill has just this minute announced the commencement of the Second World War.

LORD GRANTHAM: That's terrible news, Carson, particularly for our boys on the front. A human life is a precious thing, Carson.

DOWAGER DUCHESS: One had barely grown acclimatised to The First World War – and now they tell us that a Second is on its way! The inconvenience!

CARSON: Might I have a word, milady?

LADY CORA: Can't it wait, Carson?

CARSON: This telegram has just arrived, milady.

LADY CORA [*opening telegram*]: The good news is that the Second World War is at last drawing to a close. Mr Churchill himself has just been good enough to send us this telegram. He says that Mr Hitler has committed suicide in a bunker.

DOWAGER DUCHESS: A BUNKER? What sort of fellow commits suicide in a BUNKER, I ask you! He was clearly no gentleman! And that simply DREADFUL moustache!

CARSON: Might I have a word, milady?

LADY CORA [*sighs*]: Can't it wait, Carson?

CARSON: The news has just reached us, milady, that the England football team, under the sterling captaincy of Mr Robert Moore, has been victorious in its effort to win the 1966 World Cup.

DOWAGER DUCHESS: A solitary cup? And not a saucer in sight?! It's the last straw!

LORD GRANTHAM: That's marvellous news, Carson. And a welcome boost to our beleaguered nation as we struggle to come to terms with our loss of Empire.

THOMAS [*under his breath*]: I wanted the Germans to win.

O'BRIEN: Me too!

CARSON: Might I have a word, milord?

LORD GRANTHAM: Can't it wait, Carson?

CARSON: This telegram has just arrived, milord.

LORD GRANTHAM [*opens telegram*]: Bad news, everyone. I don't know how to put this b-b-but … The Beatles have decided to go their separate ways.

DAISY: You mean they've split up?!

MRS PATMORE: Daisy! Mind your language!

DAISY: Sorry, Mrs Patmore! It's the shock!

MRS PATMORE: There, there, Daisy. Dry those eyes!

LORD GRANTHAM: It is never pleasant when a popular singing combination decides to part company. We must all pray that these four doughty Liverpudlians meet with success in the separate careers upon which they are preparing to embark.

THOMAS [*under his breath*]: Not me. It's Yoko I like.

O'BRIEN: Me too!

DOWAGER DUCHESS: Such catchy tunes! 'She Admires You Yes Yes Yes', 'You Make Me Dizzy Miss Elizabeth', 'Why Don't We D-Do It in the –'

CARSON: Might I have a word, milord?

LORD GRANTHAM: Can't it wait, Carson?

CARSON: The news has just arrived, milord, that the Prime Minister, Mr Edward Heath, has this instant placed the country on a three-day week.

THOMAS [*under his breath*]: Good, I love a double-dip recession!

O'BRIEN: Me too!

DAISY: Does that mean we're going down the plughole?

MRS PATMORE: Daisy! Mind your language!

DAISY: Sorry Mrs Patmore!

MRS PATMORE: There, there, Daisy. Dry those eyes!

CARSON: Might I have a word, milord?

LORD GRANTHAM: Can't it wait, Carson?

CARSON: Word has just come through, milord, that the British forces have recaptured the Falkland Islands. I thought you should be the first to know, milord.

LORD GRANTHAM: Excellent news, Carson. In the fullness of time, it should do much to restore national morale.

THOMAS [*under his breath*]: Not for me it won't. It's General Galtieri I like.

O'BRIEN: Me too!

Dibble Knows What Pitstop Likes:
Jonathan Meades's A–Z of Children's Television

ANDY PANDY: The incremental yet covertly unsustainable suscepti-bility of Andrew Pandy to the obtrusive valedictory remark is overtly exemplified in his obstinately tiresome refrain, 'Time to go home, Time to go home, Andy is waving goodbye'. Yet on the day immedi-ately following the preceding day he inevitably reappears, ready to weary us again with his quasi-fascistic salutes, the only excuse for which is his role as an exemplar of incompetent puppetry, the indis-putably shoddy mechanisms of his strings made visible by the over-wattaged glare.

BEAR, PADDINGTON: The sight of this Peruvian dwarf inexpertly masquerading as a nondescript caniform bearing a suitcase or *valise* neither betokens credibility nor denies credulity.

CAT, TOP: Feline delinquent biped, sparsely whiskered and boastfully inarticulate yet insistently demanding.

DAWG, DEPUTY: Slovenly law-enforcer who never rises beyond his avowedly secondary ranking despite relentlessly wholehearted court-ing of sordid popularity: his near-nudity and resentful gawkiness represent the death gurgle of a civilisation.

DIBBLE, OFFICER: Uniformed sub-McCarthyite disciplinarian, inexpert, obese, ill-educated.

DOO, SCOOBY: Execrably drawn canine mouthpiece for the universally preached, seldom practised, utterly trite and entirely unrealistic doctrine of infantilistic spiritualism.

DO, YABBA DABBA: Quasi-Dadaist outcry of antediluvian cross-dresser Fred Flintstone.

DOUGAL: Hirsute monosyllabic draught-excluder from Magic Roundabout (*Le Manège Enchanté*).

DUMPTY, HUMPTY: Triumphalist ovoid wall-dweller tellingly transmogrified into offbeat omelette.

ERMINTRUDE: The history of Ermintrude, the doggedly unrealistic *vache* on *Le Manège Enchanté* (*see DOUGAL*), Serge Danot's peculiarly obtuse and quasi-imbecilic experiment in sub-utopian neo-fascism also represents a parallel history of bovine languorosity.

FLOWER POT MEN: It is emblematic of the deep conservatism of the British countryside that these two feeble artisans, aka William and Benjamin, should opt to remain domiciled *à deux* in a terracotta receptacle *du jardin*.

GRANGE HILL: The point about Grange Hill is that the education it provides, if education it can be said to be, is not conditional on authoritarianism; rather, it is the product of an essentially Rousseau-esque belief in the primacy of the untutored.

HONG KONG PHOOEY: My ignorance of this nevertheless paltry aberration of a canine detective remains conditional on my refusal to manipulate the knobular control on my television towards the requisite channel.

IVOR THE ENGINE: Characteristically massive in scale, self-consciously futuristic in form, decidedly rediffusionite in outlook, and determinedly unfit for travel, Ivor the Engine remains an unashamed misnomer, having been constructed wholly from cardboard.

JACKANORY: Tiresomely trite narratives unsuited to all but the most ignorant viewers.

JASON: An ostentatiously argonautical name forced upon the first *Blue Peter* cat by the Führer Noakes.

JERRY, TOM AND: Anti-authoritarian rodentalist propaganda.

KNOCKOUT, IT'S A: It is undeniable that to dress as an unrealistic courgette and leapfrog over cushions is to transport oneself to a Dante-esque world beyond redemption.

LOO, LOOBY: Unfeasible quasi-rural female who resides in *le panier pique-nique* with two male co-basketeers, Andrew Pandy and Teddy.

MAGPIE: *One* for a cause or occasion for grief or regret, *two* for a mental state of happiness or well-being, *three* for a pre-adolescent female homo sapiens: the theme tune of this bi-weekly series was, like VD or TB, considered *catchy*.

MUTLEY: Few races were less wacky, more tediously circular nor more unforgivably inconclusive than those in which Mutley and Dick Dastardly were forced to compete.

NOAKES, JOHN: 'Down Shep!' Risibly demanding, boorishly monosyllabic and quasi-fascistic, this was the inane yell of society's Little Man, that most disreputable and megalomaniacal of nature's nondescripts.

NOG, NOGGIN THE: Pontificating arch-bore of indeterminate parentage.

OKE: Popular ignorance of the way in which Diane Louise Jordan's summer expedition to Japan in 1991 resulted in the naming of the *Blue Peter* cat 'Oke' is of such magnitude that one can only suppose that state education remains a duo-terminological contradiction.

PITSTOP, PENELOPE: Pitstop's sluttishness, combined with her psychopathic, Clarksonian lust for speed, demands comparison with the more refined and coquettish appeal of her namesake Lady Penelope, who, with her neo-Lawrentian chauffeur Parker, remains unchallenged in her primacy.

PLAY SCHOOL: It is one of the great fallacies of twenty-first-century civilisation that these two antonyms should be forcibly adjuncted. 'Here's a house, here's a door. Windows, 1,2,3,4.' Four windows for an entire house is indicative of architectural neglect.

PURVES, PETER: The biological and intellectual superior of Noakes, Purves exercised the minoritarian will towards programmatic dominance, but can be seen to have succeeded only in the relatively abstruse area of overnight intercourse with Singleton.

QUICK DRAW MCGRAW: Anthropomorphism reached its upper level of experiential absurdity in the quotidian notion that a horse not only wears a hat and kerchief but also enforces law in the Wild West by effortlessly brandishing a loaded pistol in each frontal-based hoof.

RUBBLE, BARNEY: Flintstone's deuteragonist lickspittle.

SMURFS: *De Smurfen* parade their truncated Netherlandishness in a vivid mortuary blue.

TANK ENGINE, THOMAS THE: The popular obeisance of the rampant dehumanising of industrial transport is encapsulated in Thomas, whose wide-eyed pusillanimity prompts anything from vague resignation to muted indifference.

WEED, LITTLE: Her place in the flowerpot is unconditional on her silence.

YOGI BEAR: Sub-normal counter-jumping sidekick of the resolutely bourgeois Boo Boo.

ZEBEDEE: Spring-posteriorated, unforgivably moustachioed, gaudily repetitive, the malodorous Zebedee remained, predictably, an enthusiastic collaborator in Vichy France.

Four Soap Stars

Annie Walker
Was a most refined talker
Treating everyone as inferior
While insisting, 'I HATE to sound SUPERIOR ...'

Amy Turtle
Refused to hurtle,
Extracting poetry from prose –
'He's cut off his face', she said, 'to spite his nose.'

J. R. Ewing
Had them all queuing
To shoot him; in the end, he was peppered
By his mistress, Kristin Shepard.

Dirty Den
Was the gentlest of men
If looks could kill
He'd be murdered by Dot, Mo, Charlie, Pat
And the Mitchell Bros: Grant and Phil.

The *Garbblach* Has Come Home to *Karst*:
The Ancient Journey of Robert Macfarlane

I wake, or *waakken*, as it is in Old Norse, or *Njorss*. The frost lies prone on the ground, gnarled like a dragon's breath on the back of an earth-like lizard. With both eyes, I peer outside my bedroom window, relishing the unknowability of it, our universe. Rarely have I felt so sensitive to the vibrations of place, or *Plass*.

I feel the call of nature, demanding to be answered. Trickle turns to torrent and back again to trickle. I experience an intense feeling of oneness with what the Inuit call the *splasshe* that surprises me with its force.

Placing my right hand on the banister, I steel myself to take the journey down, down, down to the *kvitchun* belowwe. 'When I die, I would like to be reborn as a banister,' I think, 'so that I might help travellers traverse the stairs that confront them.'

Fear squeezes my heart. Just fourteen steps, so simple for others. But, as a writer, I am compelled to take them in alphabetical order – eight, eleven, five, four, fourteen, nine, one, seven, six, ten, thirteen, three, twelve, two. This makes my downward progress, leap on giant leap, doubly hazardous: one slip and I could be pitched headlong into a limbless future.

Arriving safely at the *kvitchun*, my chest is gripped by a nameless terror. A polar bear can smell another living animal up to twenty miles away. Is one lying in wait, ready to tear me apart? My larder, home to breakfast cereals I prefer to call by their ancient Gallic names – *Vadabigz, Ry Shkrizhpiz, Svairdiz* – would certainly be large enough to hide a polar bear, if it didn't mind squeezing up, hunching its shoulders and crossing its legs. Might an errant iceberg, bewildered by an ecosystem in distress, have borne this lonesome polar bear to the centre of Cambridge, so many thousands of miles from its natural habitat? With an effort of will, I dismiss this crippling fear from my brain. Before I have poured the first *flakks* of cereal into my bowl, handmade by our local potter, Bob – a man gentle of manner and kindly – my head begins to tingle and my back and my chest start to shake, and I find myself crying, sobs shuddering my body. It is as if the realisation that I might have been savaged by a ravenous polar bear, here, here in my Cambridge *kvitchun*, has only just caught up with me, rendering me as vulnerable as a leaf blown hither and thither on the *windyskar hotspeers* of an ancient Saxon settlement high in the Cairngorms.

Early morn, late spring: milk from the cow, skimmed semily, poured plangently o'er puffs of sugar; coffee roasted over fire of the ancient gods, in the manner of the Hokikoki tribe of South-Eastern Indonesia, as sharp as a long-handed scythe; across the airwaves, like a Laugavallalaug geyser in Iceland, music from *Kajagoogoo* hand-selected by Ken Bruce, venerable *jokki-ov-diskken*.

I place some marmalade, organically grown by Ted – a warm, friendly man with a lovely smile, who was in the Royal Navy for some years before venturing into the marmalade and jam trades, and remains a remarkable poet – on my toast, and, while doing so, realise with a jolt that I am unconsciously echoing the manner in which in the fourth century BC a woman's corpse was prepared for burial in Thessaly by placing a coin on her lips, there to pay the ferryman who would carry her towards the realm of death. Marmalade: a coin: lips. Each one of us is his own ferryman.

I take time to reflect on the nature of marmalade, and death. We spread marmalade on toast with a frequency that is, by its very nature, disarming; but is it not high time we reversed the procedure, or *prokkedorr* – and spread toast on marmalade? It is only by changing our habits, and shooting our bronze arrows of hope at all such barnacled traditions, that mankind can ever hope to reverse our drive – *driv* – towards planetary extinction and, by doing so, find some form of salvation, however sticky to the touch.

Outside, a dragonfly rustles past, so discreetly that I neither see nor hear it. To the west, a jackdaw trimmers on the spandickle. High up above, glued against the sky like a piece of card cut with a pair of safety-scissors by a wonder-filled child, hovers a blackbird, black as black in his blacky blackness. He has arrived from a distant place with story and metaphor caught in his feathers, ready for me to pick them out, give them life, and let them dance upon my page.

I would not have expected that soaring blackbird to have read my books, well regarded though they are; or at least not all of them, for a bird is a busy *thynge*, his avian calendar a relentless circle of foraging, nesting, flying, perching, foraging, nesting, flying, perching. Yet, in some curious way, it seems to me, as the two of us exchange glances, that he is as excited by my presence as I am intrigued by his; perhaps more so, for his own sensitivity to the relationship between immortal landscape and mortal animal has, sadly, yet to achieve fulfilment in prose, an inadequacy transformed into awe by the sight of the *Aukthor* below.

On the track ahead, a banana skin, a denuded starfish of pulpily nutritious fruit, catches me unawares. Has this discarded skin been awaiting me, perhaps in the hope of hastening my personal voyage towards closer contact with that deep, dark, muddy earth?

My foot slips on the banana skin, causing the rest of my body to cartwheel head over heels into a muddy ditch (from the Gaelic *di-tch*, meaning literally 'bath of the gods'). One second, I am Icarus to the banana's Sun; the next, I am its Prometheus, spreadeagled in the splutter and blubber of the dirtiest of dirts. I have arrived at an intimacy with the ditch. I surface, gasping. In that instant, I have been baptised in mud. I am born again in my muddiness, no longer just another rambler with a notebook but a soul who has bathed himself in the dark sticky broth of the land. I emerge from my 'bath of the gods' as a wizard or wise man, emulsified from head to toe in its gloopy vestment of priestly slime.

I wander in this sacred garment through the wild places of the countryside, tacking *bach* and forth, moving through its myriad covert worlds: its dense and almost lightless thickets, its corridors and passageways, its sudden glades and clearings. The banana skin has, albeit unwittingly, acted as a magic carpet, transporting me through time to a special place, a place beyond human history.

I thereby beseek myself refuge in an ancient hostelry, known to craggy local *croits* as The Wetherspoons. As I chockstone myself into its *fedspare guaalainn*, the simple rustic folk reel to the walls, their faces scarred in horror, their gnarled fingers clutching at their misshapen noses. In some peculiarly sensitive, profoundly mystical way, it is as though they have somehow sniffed the arrival of a Fellow of Emmanuel College, Cambridge, and their sense of wonder is palpable. The *garbblach* has come home to *karst*.

A Paranoid Is Someone Who Knows
All the Facts: Simon Gray's Diaries

All but the last volume of Simon Gray's diaries were published while he was still alive. As they came out, I wrote about them. These are my reviews – appreciations might be a better word – of three of the final four: The Smoking Diaries *(April 2004),* The Last Cigarette *(April 2008) and* Coda *(November 2008).*

1

Most published diaries – by politicians, authors, diplomats, socialites and other grandees – exist as daily hymns of self-praise, their central message being 'How infinitely agreeable it is to be me'. Simon Gray's are the opposite. Has ever a man written such sustained and hilarious diatribes against himself?

'So here I am, two hours into my sixty-sixth year' is the way *The Smoking Diaries* begin. He then lists 'the things I've been doing more and more frequently recently, but have struggled to keep under wraps – belching, farting, dribbling, wheezing'. Before the book is over, he will have confessed to adultery, theft, alcoholism, paranoia, extreme irritability and at least two dozen varieties of neurosis.

Simon Gray attributes his wheezing and dribbling to his habit of smoking sixty-five cigarettes a day, 'so people are likely to continue with their inevitable, "Well, if you insist on getting through three packets, etc.", to which I will reply, as always – actually, I can't remember what I always reply, and how could I, when I don't believe anyone, even my doctors, ever says anything like, "Well, if you will insist, etc." In fact, I'm merely reporting a conversation I have with myself, quite often, when I find myself wheezing my way not only up but down the stairs, and when I recover from dizzy spells after pulling on my socks, tying up my shoelaces, two very distinct acts.'

Simon Gray is not one to blow his own trumpet. A paranoid, he once said, is someone who knows all the facts. His latest volume of diaries is a ramble – mad, maudlin, cross, nostalgic, despairing and very, very funny – through these facts. 'I caught sight of my naked self in the mirror,' he reports one day. 'Great stomach drooping, like a kangaroo's pouch, though without the opening at the top, thank God.'

That last aside, with its twist of humour – 'without the opening at the top, thank God' – is very characteristic. Though most of his reflections are melancholic, they always employ comedy to leapfrog self-pity. There is terrible sadness running through this book, but you feel that Gray is able to venture ever deeper into the darkness because he has such sure footholds in humour.

Early on in *The Smoking Diaries*, one of his oldest friends, the poet and biographer Ian Hamilton, dies of cancer. After the funeral, Gray observes that 'He was quite a tall man, as tall as me, and the coffin looked too small – but then that's often the way with coffins, miracles of packaging.' There are one or two other diarists – his playwright contemporary the late Joe Orton, for instance – who might have applied the adman's phrase 'miracles of packaging' to coffins, but in Orton the phrase would have been purely satirical, whereas with Gray it emerges from real grief, like a fist shaken at fate.

Only once does Gray's depth of sorrow go beyond words. Having finished a passage about his younger brother Piers, who 'from frustration and anger and then despair' drank himself to death, and whose grave in Kensal Green cemetery Gray visits every month, he begins the next chapter: 'I've just raked my pen across my yellow page, and jabbed it down and down and ripped it across. An attempt to write a primal scream.'

Reading a posthumously published book by Ian Hamilton, Gray is enthusiastic, but wonders why Hamilton gave away so little of himself in his writing: 'We got Ian's intellectual virtues without actually ever quite getting Ian.' The same could never be said of Gray. *The Smoking*

Diaries attempts to strip away the mask of writing – the careful polish, the urbane distance – that so often obscures the writer beneath. Like its predecessor, *Enter a Fox*, it is written in what is known as 'real time', incorporating the author's second-thoughts, hesitations, lost threads and arguments with himself. At one point, he confesses to having just rewritten a passage in order to refine it, and vows never to do the same again. 'Feckless, thoughtless, cruel and stupid, it doesn't matter, because in this case you are only what you write, never what you rewrite.'

This is, of course, the opposite of the discipline required to write plays, in which the individual voice of the playwright must always be submerged beneath the voices of his characters. Perhaps only someone who has spent a lifetime following this discipline could manage to keep a stream-of-consciousness narrative so wonderfully taut, and so wholly un-mawkish, at one and the same time so truthful, yet so conscious of its effect on any future audience.

Memories of his childhood and schooldays are intertwined with day-to-day life, but all the while he is preoccupied with the business of ageing, and how his sixty-six-year-old self relates to himself as a bright-eyed boy of seven. If the diaries have a common theme, it is the drift from innocence to experience, the dreadful immutability of the past. 'Oh, how I long to travel back/and tread again that ancient track!' wrote the poet Henry Vaughan. It is a sentiment very close to Simon Gray, who was, he maintains, 'an exceptionally pretty child, quite gorgeous, in fact, if early photographs are anything to go by (and remained so until my early teens, when my nose put on a spurt)'. Writing about his father, he maintains a very stern English emotional distance until right up to the end, when he disobeys a nurse and brings his dying father a last cigarette: 'He gave me such a smile, a smile of such gratitude, that I felt I'd become a son to him, and a bit of a father too.'

He looks obsessively back across the arc of his life towards his youth. At one point, alone in a cinema in Bayswater, he recalls himself as a student at Cambridge, and wonders what that young man would think of himself now. 'I would try to imagine his life, the hopelessness and uselessness of it, the squalor and pathos, etc.'

Everywhere, everyone is growing older, even those screen idols who were meant to stay forever young. Writing his diaries with the television on in the corner of the room, he spies the old film *Meet Me in St Louis* and notices for the first time that 'one of the sisters, the oldest, looks much older than the last time I saw the film, perhaps she was always a bit elderly for the part and I've only just spotted it – I hope so, I'd hate to think that she's ageing away on her own, and that one day I'll find her on the screen looking like her Grandpa's wife'.

If all this seems a bit gloomy, I should stress that *The Smoking Diaries* is filled with a completely natural humour, a humour that seems to spring organically from each sentence, as one thought leads to another. Writing about brotherhood and fatherhood, for instance, he suddenly finds himself waylaid by how 'hood' got tagged on to the end of such words, and from there he drifts to the story of Little Red Riding Hood ('it can't be that Hood is her surname, Red and Riding her Christian names').

Gray is the Nijinsky of irritation, dancing gracefully to its tune. Among his targets are sports commentators who keep saying 'to be fair', speeding police cars, an unnamed theatre critic, the Scots (though 'I'm half-Scot myself, or half-Scottish or half-Scottie, whichever is the most offensive'), a couple on holiday who make away with his deck-chair even though he has placed his lighter on it and, in one beautiful rant, the sentimental view of the old (he tries in vain to recall ever meeting a wise old man), the poems and personality of W. H. Auden, and the new fashion of men greeting other men with a kiss: 'I don't really like it, really rather hate it, especially when they have beards … they're rough on my skin, and probably full of food and insects, and they're smelly, but I see no way of repelling them unless I take to dribbling into them or blowing my nose over them, and word gets round that I'm to be avoided.'

2

In this latest volume, *The Last Cigarette*, which covers 2005–7, the playwright turns seventy. He is feeling his age. He now has false teeth. Years of dedicated smoking have left him wheezing so much that 'anyone who wanted to murder me would simply have to say three funny things in a row'.

One of his brothers, his beloved Piers, is already dead; the other, Nigel, dies in 2006, 'and I am suddenly all at sea, a brotherless man'. Much of Gray's time is spent looking back across the decades at everything he has done wrong, and trying to deal with the ensuing guilt. He recalls his mother on her deathbed and tries 'to block out the memory of her skeletal hand clinging to mine, and I determined not to look at my watch until I did, a swift, casual glance down at my wrist'.

She asked him to stay a little while longer, but he told her he had to pick up his son from nursery school, which wasn't quite true. 'I had enough time, more than enough time, to get to the nursery school, so I walked along Putney towpath, and thought about the kind of son I was, who would deprive his dying mother of a few more minutes, that's all she claimed, a few more minutes ... I am now nearly ten years older than she was when she died, I've had all these years more than she had, and I hadn't given her a few minutes of those years.'

Such painful thoughts, so honestly recounted, should make for equally painful reading. But for some reason they don't. I think this is because one always feels a sense of liberation when reading the truth, no matter how dark. Perhaps this is because the freeing of a single secret from the dungeon of remorse allows for the possibility of the liberation of all our other secrets, too.

At times, Gray wonders at the sharp difference between experiencing events and recounting them. He notices, for example, that he can enjoy the memory of a party without having enjoyed the party itself; in the same way he finds that writing down a worry is 'a completely unworrying experience ... Yes, I had fun writing down all my worries.' And, of course, Simon Gray's diaries are very, very funny. Written in a beautifully exact stream of consciousness – the prose equivalent of a clown speed-riding a unicycle across a high wire – they whizz back and forth between whimsy and terror, hilarity and gloom, with no pause for breath in between.

At the beginning of one page, he is fretting over the rewriting of an old play, worried that the surgery he is performing on it may be life-threatening. From there, he goes on to worry at his inability to let go of the past, and compares it to the neurosis an axe murderer might suffer, 'The swing of the axe being the desperate but deeply satisfying last step in letting go.' His mention of an axe murder then causes him to admit that, mired in the middle of writing a play, he has often felt like murdering himself, 'and violently, but I don't see how one could do it with an axe, how to get the leverage and balance required to swing the heavy blade in on oneself – except for the crotch, that would be the only easy target area – no, I've just tried it, stood with my legs apart and head down like a golfer, then swung a phantom axe upwards, and it turns out that the easiest slice would be right between the buttocks, and how would one guarantee that it would be fatal, and how attempt to explain it if one survived it? …'

It is this sense of writing in what one might call the extreme present tense – allowing the writer to stop halfway through a sentence in order to try out an axe-swing on himself, and then to report the results in the second half of the sentence – that makes Simon Gray's diaries so thrillingly alive. For over half a century, his old friend and fellow playwright Harold Pinter has had an adjective – Pinteresque – named after him. Grayesque doesn't sound quite right, and nor do Grayite or Grayist or Graysian, but it is surely time someone turned Gray's name into an adjective to describe this breathtakingly fresh, freewheeling, look-no-hands way of writing.

His up-to-the-minute style also gives Gray's endless trips back into his early memories an extraordinary immediacy, so that past and present become virtually indivisible. His youthful disappointments are as vivid as ever; his hurts still hurt, unshielded by the barnacles of time. Like him, we are all of us time travellers in our own minds. 'So we beat on, boats against the current, borne back ceaselessly into the past,' as Scott Fitzgerald put it.

There is something very moving about his recounting of a youthful affair and his reliving of his own jealous rage. 'It seems, in fact, that affairs are never over, or I wouldn't be writing about my affair with Donna, which was in its hopeless prime more than 45 years ago, two marriages ago, two children and four grandchildren ago, and yet here it is, long after her death, vexing me again this mid-October midnight.' As a diarist, Gray is so reliably and consistently funny that it is easy to overlook the stark beauty of sentences such as that one, and their underlying melancholy too.

Many of his day-to-day grumbles – against the sloppy overuse of the word 'racist', against hospitals 'where people die of illnesses they didn't bring in with them', against the notion of Europe, against mobile phones, against 'young men in ghastly sawn-off trousers, the tops of their knickers showing, tufts of hair on their faces, swilling from cans and bottles', against flies ('they defecate, urinate, salivate, vomit and probably masturbate over any bit of food they alight on') – may be shared by most people of his generation, but he expresses them in wonderfully energetic, young man's prose.

He gives irritability a good name, constantly pioneering new and wonderful things to be irritated by. The actress Demi Moore, for instance: 'What kind of name is Demi, anyway? It's a size, surely, half of semi, as in demi-tasse, but what would a demi-attached house be like, or a semimondaine, on the other hand, or a semi-Moore, would that be twice as much Moore as Demi, who though small and tightly built would never move you to call her petite?' On a flight to Greece, he finds himself sitting next to a woman with a bad cold. Like a malevolent sports commentator, he describes each fresh wipe and sniffle, blow, as it were, by blow.

For the rest of us, this would be pure hell, but Gray is an alchemist who can turn someone else's mucus into gold: 'she is now blowing her nose on little shreds of Kleenex about twice a minute, long, thick, wet blows, then she screws up the Kleenex and places it in a paper cup, already bulging, in the back of the seat in front of her. There is an already full paper cup beside the one she has now nearly filled. She is frankly a very disgusting person to find yourself sitting next to on a flight.'

Cigarettes, and trying to give them up, form the theatrical backdrop for this new volume, though he is far from messianic about it. At one stage he tots up how much all those Silk Cuts cost him each year, arrives at a grand total of £6,000 and concludes: 'Wow! Is that all? All those headaches, phlegm-driven coughing fits and rancid stomachs for only £6,000. And just think of all the things you can't get for £6,000!' He also points out that 'bad situations can be transformed into good ones if, while they're going on, you can take your cigarettes and lighter out of your pocket and enjoy a good smoke under pressure'. In this way, his diarist's pen is a bit like a cigarette, transforming misery into comedy, so that those witchlike things that nag away at us all in the middle of the night – mortality, grief, guilt, anxiety, etc. etc. – are miraculously made more bearable.

3

When Simon Gray asked his doctor 'How long?', he didn't mean how long did he have left to live, but how long it would be between his forthcoming operation and a prognosis. But the doctor misunderstood him, and told him what he didn't want to know: 'About a year.'

He records his reaction in *Coda*, his final volume of diaries. 'I wanted to say, "But I didn't ask that question, so kindly withdraw your answer." I also wanted to swear at him, "You stupid f***ing awful f***moron" sort of stuff ... I wanted to kill him, I wanted to kill him and say just as I pulled the trigger, thrust the dagger, whatever, "That's a year longer than you have, matey." The thing I think I understood immediately, before I'd even thought about it, was that a doctor who tells you that you have a year to live has taken the year away from you – from the moment the sentence was delivered – the sentence that delivered the sentence – the knowledge would never be cleared from my consciousness, the last thought at night, the first in the morning, for the rest of my life.'

That passage has all the characteristics of Simon Gray: a caustic honesty, a disarming kind of wide-eyed world-weariness, fury tempered by comedy (and vice versa). And also – perhaps above everything else – the unfakeable quality of lovability: reading Simon Gray's diaries is such a companionable experience that somehow he makes you feel as though you are inside his mind, and he is inside yours.

At one point he talks of the sympathy to be found in great literature. He identifies it as 'the recognition of other people's feelings through the awareness of those feelings, or the possibility of them, in myself'. And this is true of his own work, too: by writing with such skill and truth about his own condition, by describing exactly what it feels like to be a seventy-two-year-old playwright dying of cancer, he illuminates our own lives, and, as importantly, our own deaths.

Coda is Simon Gray's eighth volume of diaries. He wrote it knowing it would be his last: a coda is, among other things, the concluding section of a dance. On the very first page he describes it as 'the beginning of my dying', and then, typically, butting in on himself, teasing out anything affected or inauthentic, he wonders 'now, is that merely a perverse way of writing the end of my living – the ending of my life?'.

It is a book about facing one's own extinction, about how you think and how you feel when you know you have a year left to live. Few books can ever have been more rooted in the present tense. While reading it, there were times I found myself putting it down, anxious about reading on, lest by doing so I might somehow hasten the author's death.

As always, he shies away from self-pity, but sometimes the realisation of the inevitable bursts forth on to the page. Recalling last summer – which will turn out to be his last summer of all – he writes, 'One night I sat for a long time at my desk in my study without doing anything at all until I suddenly began to beat myself about the head, I think in an attempt to make myself cry. I know I quite often wanted to cry, as if crying would bring release, but release from what? … Knowledge, perhaps. Yes, it must have been knowledge that I wanted to be released from.'

At another point, he remembers going into the room of a friend who had recently died and seeing that 'over the chair in his bedroom was draped a pair of trousers, looking as if they were waiting for him to get into them'. He then finds himself imagining his own wife Victoria (the book is touchingly dedicated to 'Victoria – without whom, nothing') walking into his study after he's died. 'And when I get there, have got there, am gone, what will it be like for her? Going into my study, for instance. Well, I should think it'll be quite – quite – I can't imagine it. I suppose I mean that I don't want to imagine it –'. The entry dwindles into nothingness.

Yet amid such morbidity, there is also a good deal of simple joy, perhaps more so than in any of the other volumes. In better days, he might have thought it good manners to the reader to offer up a banana skin or two whenever he spoke of happiness. But now he takes the ultimate banana skin as read, and gets on with feeling cheerful. Near the end of the book he attends a posh christening, which, in normal circumstances, might have been a perfect source of comical irritations. But now it is different. Gray is one of the little baby's godparents. 'He gurgled with pleasure and it was a joy when it was my turn to dab his forehead and have him gurgle at me ... very little in these last few years has given me so much pleasure and made me so proud.'

But he also remains gloriously unsaintly, his observations as sharp and funny as ever. There are jokes galore. Of having spent a lifetime struggling to read the novels of Walter Scott, he writes, 'It's no good, as soon as I pick up a volume with one hand, the other hand snatches it away and puts it back on the shelf.'

On holiday in Crete, he sits in a swanky restaurant with tables around a swimming pool listening to a young female with 'a lousy voice that sets your teeth on edge. She likes to sway and screech on the edge of the pool, and so interferes with your meal as you keep watching her in the hope that she'll fall in.' Of his local Tesco, he complains that 'there is never anything I want in Tesco's. If occasionally they introduce a line that actually appeals to me they withdraw it the moment they know I've begun buying it.'

And there is, as you might expect from this master of the tragicomic, plenty of laughter in the dark, the valley of death offering the perfect arena for his morose comic vision. One of his little chapters, headed 'A Disgusting New Habit', is about his new interest in newspaper obituaries. 'How long did they live, these painters, politicians, actors, sailors, soldiers, civil servants, headmasters, criminals, television presenters? How many years did they manage? If they died at seventy or under, I feel a little surge of uplift, joy really, as if I'd beaten them in some tournament.'

He then confesses to envying anyone who dies above his own age and 'bitterness at the unfairness of it', particularly against those who were 'still climbing mountains at eighty-three, conducting symphonies at ninety-one, full of mirth at 106'. Finally, 'I'm glad to note that I am distressed when I read of anyone cut down unduly young, I manage not to compare their term with mine, and feel that I have a kinship with them, especially if they knew that they were dying, and I feel sad and angry for their families.' He then adds: 'Quite a pleasant feeling, in a way, that's the awful thing.'

As a diarist, Gray always charted his own inappropriate responses to the world with all the rigour of an intrepid explorer attempting to trace the source of the Nile. In *Coda*, he uses the same precision to chart his feelings about his forthcoming death. 'Well, what should I be writing?' he asks himself at one stage. 'Wisdom? But I have none. Consolation? But I am inconsolable.'

I think he was wrong on both counts. He was wise, and his consolation came from writing. Simon Gray died in August. His consolation – this book – is now our consolation too.

David Bailey's Swinging Sixties

AMIN, GENERAL IDI: You hear a lot of rubbish about him killing innocent people but it was just business. Fair's fair. He mainly killed people who got on the wrong side of him. When I took his photograph in the Sixties he couldn't have been more helpful. I got along great with him. One of the nicest men I ever met.

BARDOT, BRIGITTE: No great beauty. I hate a bird who pouts. I'd go, 'Stop poutin'!' But she couldn't stop, it was like a nervous twitch.

CHAPLIN, CHARLIE: Always toddling around the East End when I was a kid, with his little hat and his cane, fucking boring attention-seeker.

DIXON OF DOCK GREEN: I knew PC George Dixon in the Sixties. Used to hang out on street corners looking like the cat's whiskers. Everyone said he was this lovable bobby. But he wasn't. He was a cunt.

ELIZABETH II, HM QUEEN: I told her to stand still for her photo, but she wouldn't stop waving. But a bit short – 5 foot 4, max – and a bit on the fat side for me. I said to her one day, what you need is a national anthem. Then next day, they're all singing 'God Save the Queen' at the top of their voices. Not a word of thanks. Nice bird though, good jugs.

FIELDS, GRACIE: Always going on about how she had the biggest aspidistra in the world. As if I gave a fuck. I told her to shut the fuck up about it. That took the smile off her face.

GANDALF: I used to hang out with Gandalf at the Indigo. Michael Caine, Terence Stamp, Andy Warhol, me and Gandalf. He was going out with Catherine Deneuve at the time. Wizard this, wizard that. Very full of himself. But he wasn't as wise as he liked to think because all I had to do was wait till he went out to the toilet and then I asked Catherine if she wanted to fuck. We married a week later. Big mistake. Turned out she was French.

HAILE SELASSIE: We were down the Troubadour one night, and I said to him, you know, what you should do is become an emperor. That way, you could become a global icon. Next thing I know, he's tartin' around in his robes and his crown, all Jack the Lad, and worshipped as a God. All my idea. But did he ever thank me for it? Did he fuck.

IRON, ANY OLD: Any old iron? Any old iron? Any, any, any old iron? They'd always be dancing up to you and clickin' their heels and asking you that question when I was a kid. Why would I want any old iron? So I'd say, just fuck the fuck off.

JEFFREYS, JUDGE: One of the nicest men I ever met.

McCARTNEY, PAUL: Whenever I took his photograph, he'd keep badgering me for new song titles. Finally, I lost it. 'This is from me to you,' I said, 'it's getting better, but it's so yesterday, you've either got to get back or let it be.' I should have guessed what was happenin' when he took out his notebook. Never paid me a penny, fuckin' skinflint.

QUEEN MOTHER: Met her at Cecil Beaton's gaff in '61, '62. Rudolf Nureyev was there and Dirk Bogarde and Max Bygraves. She said, 'And what do you do?' I could tell she was tryin' to get off with me, so I said, 'Do you want a fuck?' But she just pretended not to hear, snooty cow.

ROLLING STONES: We'd often hang out in the Ad Lib Club in Leicester Square. One time, Mick comes up and says to me, how you doin', and I say, you know what, Mick, I can't get no satisfaction with these honky tonk women but, then again, you can't always get what you want. Typical Mick, I give him three hits, straight off, and he never pays me a fuckin' penny.

SAVILE, SIR JIMMY: One of the nicest men I ever met.

SHRIMPTON, JEAN: We all used to call her the Shrimp, fuck knows why. How the fuck should I know? Can't remember where I first made love to the Shrimp. Maybe in the countryside in Buckinghamshire or in Italy or under Brighton Pier, or it might of been Wimbledon Common. Nah – Wimbledon Common was someone else, I know that because it's where I used to hang out with my mates the Wombles when they were famous. It wouldn't have been Orinoco 'cos I'm not fuckin' queer. Probably Madame Cholet, not bad lookin' I suppose, as Wombles go, but I prefer a bird without a thick mane of hair all over her body, so we kissed but we didn't do it.

THERESA, MOTHER: She didn't like dancing at the Ad Lib. She just wasn't any good at it. Not that I ever asked her. You could tell she had rotten legs. Why else wear those long robes? I took her photograph once. Wasted my time. Asked her to show some cleavage and she just said no, she had her reputation to consider. Nasty woman: all me, me, me.

VICTORIA, QUEEN: One my first commissions was to photograph her at Windsor. When I suggested she slip out of her heavy clothes and pose in a bathtub with her hair all wild and her legs stretched out, she wouldn't fucking play ball, even when I said, OK, you can keep your undies on. Snooty, stuck-up bitch.

WEST, FRED: One of the nicest men I ever met.

ZEBEDEE: I was mates with most of the stars of the Magic Roundabout. We'd hang out most nights in the Flamingo, Dougal and Mr Rusty and Ermintrude and me. But Zebedee got on my tits. My golden rule is never to make friends with a bloke on a spring. He'd come back from the bar with the drinks sloshed all over the floor. What's with all that bouncing? I'd say. Then I'd tell him to fuck the fuck off. He still alive?

ACKNOWLEDGEMENTS

The pieces in *Haywire* first appeared in *Private Eye*, *The Daily Mail*, *The New York Review of Books*, the *TLS*, *The Mail on Sunday*, *The Oldie*, *The Spectator*, the *Guardian* and *The New Statesman*. 'Nothing Is Real: The Slippery Art of Biography' was the 2021 Baillie Gifford Prize for Non-Fiction Lecture at the Edinburgh International Festival. 'The Fragile Life of Brian Epstein' was the introduction to his autobiography *A Cellarful of Noise* (Souvenir Press). 'The Art of Irritation' was the introduction to *Ending Up by Kingsley Amis* (NYRB). I am grateful to all these publications for their permission to reprint the pieces here, and to all at 4th Estate for their customary encouragement and diligence. I am especially grateful to Linden Lawson for her eagle-eyed copy-editing, to Katy Archer for shepherding the book into print, to Jo Thomson for the lovely cover and to Nicole Jashapara for all her help. Thanks, too, to Cecily Engle for her expertise with contracts. Above all, I want to thank my good friend Nicholas Pearson, who has published my last four books with his usual combination of enthusiasm, tact, bravado and intelligence.

This might also be a good time to thank my friends and editors Ian Jack, David Robson, Shirley Lowe, Ann Barr, Frank Johnson, Ivan Barnes, Mark Boxer and John Gross for getting my career going, and Helen Hawkins, Sarah Sands, Charles Moore, Neil Armstrong, Keeba Critchlow, Susie Dowdall, Sandra Parsons, Ferdy Mount, Ian Hislop, Harry Mount and Susanna Gross for keeping it going. Finally, thanks to my wife, Frances, without whom nothing is possible.